Coalition Air Warfare in the Korean War 1950–1953

Proceedings

Air Force Historical Foundation Symposium
Andrews AFB, Maryland
May 7–8, 2002

Edited by
Jacob Neufeld
and
George M. Watson, Jr.

U.S. Air Force History and Museums Program
Washington, D.C.
2005

Library of Congress Cataloging-in-Publication Data

Air Force Historical Foundation. Symposium (2002 : Andrews AFB, Md.)
Coalition air warfare in the Korean War, 1950-1953 : proceedings, Air Force Historical Foundation Symposium, Andrews AFB, Maryland, May 7-8, 2002 / edited by Jacob Neufeld and George M. Watson, Jr.
p. cm.
Includes bibliographical references and index.
1. Korean War, 1950-1953—Aerial operations—Congresses. 2. Korean War, 1950-1953—Aerial operations, American—Congresses. I. Neufeld, Jacob. II. Watson, George M. III. Title.

DS920.2.A2A35 2002
951.904'248—dc22 2005029622

For sale by the U.S. Government Printing Office

Coalition Air Warfare in the Korean War 1950–1953

May 7–8, 2002
Andrews AFB, Maryland
Officers Open Mess

Presented by the
Air Force Historical Foundation
and the
U.S. Air Force History Office
in conjunction with the
Historical Foundations and History Offices of the
U.S. Army, U.S. Navy, and U.S. Marine Corps

Foreword

In commemoration of the fiftieth anniversary of the Korean War, the official history offices of the U.S. Army, Navy, Marine Corps, and Air Force and their respective historical associations collaborated to sponsor as comprehensive a symposium as possible, including as participants some of the coalition partners who contributed forces and weapons to the war.

The intent of this symposium, titled *Coalition Air Warfare during the Korean War, 1950 -1953*, was to focus not only on the contributions made by the armed forces of the United States, but also on those of America's allies. The diverse group of panelists and speakers included not only scholars with subject matter expertise, but also veteran soldiers, sailors, and airmen who had served in that conflict. It was hoped that the melding of these diverse perspectives would provide interesting, if sometimes conflicting, views about the Korean War.

The symposium organizers designated an agenda of six specific panels for investigation, including Planning and Operations; Air Superiority, Air Support of Ground Forces; Air Interdiction and Bombardment, Air Reconnaissance and Intelligence, and Logistical Support of Air Operations. Each session began with commentary by the panel chairman, which was followed by formal papers, and in some instances included a lively question and answer session.

The papers and most of the proceedings found their way into print and are recorded here in an effort to permanently capture the activities, challenges, contributions, and heroics of the coalition air forces and the airmen who fought during the Korean conflict.

About the Editors

Jacob "Jack" Neufeld is the Director of the Air Force Historical Studies Office. He previously served as Senior Historian and was the Director of the Center for Air Force History. Mr. Neufeld is also the editor of *Air Power History*, the quarterly journal of the Air Force Historical Foundation. He earned B.A. and M.A. degrees in history at the New York University and did doctoral studies at the University of Massachusetts, Amherst. Commissioned in the U.S. Army, he served with the Corps of Engineers at Ft. Campbell, Ky. and Ft. Belvoir, Va. from 1964-1966. He has written and edited numerous works in military history, and the history of technology, including the *Development of Ballistic Missiles in the United States Air Force, 1945-1960.* He taught history at the University of Maryland, Montgomery College, and American Military University. Currently, he is writing a biography of General Bernard A. Schriever.

Dr. George M. Watson, Jr. has had a long and productive career with the Air Force History and Museums Program. He is a 1966 graduate of the University of Maine, earned an M.A. from Niagara University in 1968 and attained a Ph.D. in Modern European History from The Catholic University of America in 1974. He is a veteran of the Vietnam War having served with the 101st Airborne Division in that country from 1969 to 1970. He has worked as a staff historian at the former Air Force Systems Command, Chief Historian of the Office of the Air Force Surgeon General, and Chief of the Air Staff Division history office in the Pentagon. He is presently the Chief of the Special Projects Branch at the Air Force Historical Studies Office. Dr. Watson has contributed to a number of edited volumes and journals and has interviewed numerous key Air Force personages, both military and civilian. He is the author of *The Office of the Secretary of the Air Force, 1947-1965* and co-author of *With Courage: The Army Air Forces in World War II.* He was a contributing author and editor of the two-volume history of the United States Air Force: *Winged Shield, Winged Sword.* His personal memoir of his Vietnam experience, entitled *Voices from the Rear: Vietnam 1969-1970*, was published in December 2001. His latest book, *Secretaries and Chiefs of Staff of the United States Air Force*, was published in 2002.

Contents

Session III
Air Support of Ground Forces

Session IV
Air Interdiction and Bombardment

Session V
Air Reconnaissance and Intelligence

Session VI
Logistical Support of Air Operations

Reprise

Welcoming Address

Gen. W. Y. Smith, USAF (Ret.)

Welcome to the eighth biennial symposium cosponsored by the U.S. Air Force History Office and the Air Force Historical Foundation. Our subject this year deals with coalition air operations during the Korean War, the first war fought under United Nations auspices. We are going to examine the assumptions and effects of American and allied air power in all environments—ground, sea, and air combat. And we will consider the roles played by intelligence and air mobility operations.

We are particularly proud that this symposium is a joint endeavor, involving sponsors and participants from all of the military departments and services, from the Army, Navy, Air Force, and Marine Corps. Moreover, we have the support of the various historical offices and foundations, and all of the United States military departments have participated in selecting the topics and speakers you will hear from today. We hope you will find the program stimulating and provocative.

Opening Remarks

Lt. Gen. Abbott Greenleaf, USAF (Ret.)

Working with our counterparts in the Army, Navy, and Marine Corps, we of the Air Force believe we have organized an exciting program. We expect this to be an informative, interesting, and enjoyable day and a half of recalling the Korean War and drawing some lessons from it. The Korean War is most often referred to these days as the "Forgotten War." A number of reasons might explain that, the principal one being that the Korean War was pushed to the background as the Cold War between the United States and its allies and the Soviet Union and the Warsaw Pact heated up in the subsequent years.

In terms of history, however, the Korean War is associated with a number of "firsts" that make it more important than is generally appreciated. It was the first war in the atomic/nuclear world to follow World War II, and nuclear weapons were not employed. Korea was the first "shooting war" in which the world's two major superpowers—the Soviet Union and the United States—chose sides. Twenty-two countries worldwide contributed forces to the first war conducted under United Nations command. It was the first war in which jet aircraft dominated air and ground combat operations, and Korea was the first war in which the airmen of the United States Air Force fought as an independent military service.

These are all important developments in the history of warfare. In our discussions today and tomorrow, we plan to investigate a variety of ways in which air power meshed with the other elements of military operations to create a fighting force that demonstrated that it was up to the tasks it was assigned. You will hear perspectives from all the military services of the United States and from some of our Coalition partners, which should give you a comprehensive look at how we fought this war.

Again, welcome. Let's now begin our discussions.

Planning and Operations

Remarks on Planning and Operations in the Korean War

Wayne Thompson

Twenty years ago, I wrote a chapter on the Korean War for an official history of the U.S. Air Force. On the basis of that rather slight connection with the Korean War, I was chosen to chair this opening panel. Not wanting to be utterly outclassed by my fellow panelists, I have chosen panelists who may not know much more than I do about the Korean War. To my knowledge, this is the first time a panel has been deliberately composed of people who know relatively little about the subject under discussion.

Now, you may well ask, how did I sell this novel concept to the symposium organizers? I argued that fresh thinking sometimes comes from people who are new to a subject. I pointed to my participation ten years ago in the *Gulf War Air Power Survey* (*GWAPS*), when accomplished students of air power were brought together to study that war under the sponsorship of the Secretary of the Air Force. It was exciting to be part of a pioneering study while the subject was still new, and I wondered whether it would be possible to recapture at least a little of that excitement by turning some of the same people loose on the Korean War. So here we are. By modeling our panel's approach to the Korean War on our approach to the Gulf War ten years ago, we hope to stimulate some fresh thinking. Like any experiment, this one may fail, but it seems worth a try.

GWAPS was organized into ten task forces, each of which wrote a book-length report. Our panel this morning represents four of those task forces. We have Dr. Mark Mandeles from the Command and Control Task Force, Col. Rich Blanchfield, USMC (Ret.), from the Weapons, Tactics, and Training Task Force, and Dr./Col. Tom Keaney, USAF (Ret.), from the Effects and Effectiveness Task Force. Tom was also the principal author of the survey's summary report. As the survey's historical advisor, I assisted several task forces. This morning, I represent the Planning Task Force.

Planning

If I were going to undertake a study of air planning in the Korean War, I would divide the subject into chronological slices. I would begin with the situation before the war, then move to the planning scramble in the first couple months, then address the reaction to the Chinese offensive, and finally look at some of the attempts made to rejuvenate air planning during the stalemate, including especially the interdiction campaigns and the air pressure campaign.

Over the years, I have discovered that many of my fellow citizens wrongly assume our military planners keep an array of plans available on the shelf for every conceivable contingency. In the case of the Gulf War, American military planners had at least begun to plan how to combat an Iraqi invasion of Kuwait and Saudi Arabia months before the actual Iraqi invasion. When North Korea invaded South Korea, on the other hand, no plans had been made to combat such a contingency. That is all the more puzzling because it was widely expected in the American government that North Korea would invade South Korea. The U.S. government may have been surprised by the timing of the invasion, but the government was even more surprised by its own reaction. When faced with the reality of the invasion, an American government that had expected to leave the defense of South Korea to South Korea decided very quickly to prosecute a war for South Korea. This was not a case of failing to understand the enemy. It was, instead, a case of failing to understand ourselves.

However much contingency planning has been done, when an enemy confronts us with war, our military planners have to scramble to develop a workable strategy. The main reason the United States had not planned to defend South Korea was the inadequacy of our military forces vis-à-vis the country that was deemed our principal enemy: the USSR. Having emerged recently from a global war, the United States was thinking in terms of a global war against international communism, led by the USSR. The American military judged that it had barely the forces necessary to defend Japan, let alone South Korea.

It was, after all, the Korean War that provided much of the framework for thinking about limited war within the Cold War. The Truman administration set limits on its conduct of the war in Korea in the hope that Soviet involvement would remain even more limited. No nuclear weapons could be used, and bombing would be restricted to Korea.

U.S. air planners in the Korean War did not have the luxury enjoyed by their counterparts in the Gulf War: six months without combat in which to plan an air campaign, and then six weeks to execute an air campaign before the ground campaign began. In Korea, our air forces had to immediately help stem an invasion.

As usual at the outset of war, air planning was occurring in many places, and the influence of the various planning groups was enmeshed in larger command-and-control issues, about which Mark Mandeles will talk. Suffice it to say now that because Gen. Douglas MacArthur lacked a truly joint staff in Far East Command, efforts to plan bombing at the joint level were less than successful. Ultimately, a committee with strong Far East Air Forces (FEAF) and Navy representation approved target selection. The Strategic Air Command under Gen. Curtis LeMay also prepared target lists for the Boeing B–29 Superfortress of FEAF Bomber Command, but in the summer of 1950, the Truman administration vetoed LeMay's request to use incendiaries against North Korean cities.

This rejection of the use of incendiaries did not change until the Chinese intervention of late 1950, which also raised the possibility of striking targets in China, and even of using nuclear weapons. General MacArthur, as usual, was more aggressive than the administration, but President Truman held firm, and permission to use incendiaries was the only major change in the limits already established. So began the long ground stalemate along the 38th parallel, attended by its companion stalemate in the air farther north along the Yalu River.

As in Italy during World War II, it was tempting to suppose that, given the geographical confinement of a peninsula, it might be possible to interdict enemy supply lines. As in Italy, though, this attempt did not prove very successful during a stalemate, when the enemy was not forced to expend munitions and other supplies faster than his supply lines permitted, however much they were bombed. In Korea, the attempt to interdict truck traffic between the rail heads and the front lines began in a relatively promising fashion because the United Nations counteroffensive northward toward the 38th parallel was still in progress, and the enemy was still expending his resources at a high rate. Once stalemate took hold, the interdiction effort clearly failed, and the shift to rail targets did not save the situation.

Most of the planning for these failed interdiction efforts was done at Fifth Air Force headquarters, but the Air Force as a whole got a black eye from the results. That was due not only to the failure of interdiction, but also to the unfortunate label "Operation Strangle"—the same overblown moniker that had been used in Italy. The Air Force argument that it made more sense to attempt interdiction rather than to bomb just frontline forces once they were dug in had merit, but the attempt to sell that argument with such hyperbole proved to be a mistake. Later today, Conrad Crane will discuss what happened to air planning after the failure of interdiction.

Command and Control of Air Forces during the Korean and Persian Gulf Wars

Mark D. Mandeles

War creates such a strain that all the pettiness, jealousy, ambition, greed, and selfishness begin to leak out the seams of the average character. On top of this are the problems created by the enemy.

—General Dwight D. Eisenhower[1]

Introduction

Military organizations are "political." They exhibit the same behaviors of more overtly political organizations, such as legislatures or executive-level departments. In all, different groups and cliques compete for influence; ruling coalitions are formed; conflict sometimes attends transfer and succession of power; changes by the ruling coalition are validated by reorganizations; decision rules reflect existing internal alliances; a new goal or change of goal signals a change in status and power relations; and disagreements over roles and missions are settled by negotiation and bargaining, not by the application of management techniques or contractual obligations.

In this essay I argue that, by viewing command and control as occurring in a political system, three common features of command and control are revealed at the highest levels of combat organization during both the Korean War and Persian Gulf War. First, command and control was not managed primarily in terms of military outcomes. Second, senior air officers were more concerned with political problems, including centralization of authority, assignment of roles, and apportionment of missions among the military services. And third, ad hoc relationships and organizations replaced and superseded preconflict doctrine and concepts of how command and control would operate.

Korea

The events in northeast Asia leading to the start of the Korean War are well known,[2] but for our purposes of examining command and control, they are less important than the political fight leading to passage of the National Security Act of 1947. The National Security Act established the position of Secretary of Defense, created the Central Intelligence Agency and the National Security Council, and, in President Eisenhower's terms, contrived an overall organization that is "little more than a weak confederation of sovereign military units."[3] In the aftermath of this legislation, U.S. Army and Air Force leaders remained suspicious and distrustful of their Navy and Marine Corps counterparts, and the converse applied as well. As combat on the Korean peninsula began, senior officers harbored doubts about each other's intentions and reacted cautiously to plans and proposals related to the command and control of operations involving more than one service. In a September 9, 1950, Eyes Only letter that Lt. Gen. George E. Stratemeyer asked be destroyed after being read, he observed:

> The Air Force is again being harassed by our sister services and although we have a war on in Korea, we have another one on the defense [of] our position reference tactical air from sniping attacks from both the other services.
>
> The Navy, having been whipped on B–36 skullduggery, has its very best PIO [public information officer] people here in the Tokyo area and throughout the Far East Command following the pre-designed, laid-out plan of advancing carrier based aviation as against land based tactical air.
>
> At the same time, General Mark Clark, Commanding General of the Army Field Forces, is putting on an undercover campaign to lay the groundwork to secure tactical aviation as part of the Army, and, from my observations, has influenced a number of the army's senior generals.[4]

One is tempted, after reading such a note, to call out, "let the games begin."

Military Outcomes and Command and Control

North Korean forces invaded the Republic of Korea on June 25, 1950, and the tactical situation deteriorated fairly quickly. Almost immediately, General Stratemeyer, Commander, Far East Air Forces (FEAF), and his counterpart Vice Adm. Charles Turner Joy, Commander, U.S. Naval Forces Far East (COMNAVFE), disagreed about priorities and processes to set targets and tasks. Shortly after June 29, 1950, when Commander-in-Chief Far East (CINCFE) Gen. Douglas MacArthur authorized attacks north of the 38th parallel, Stratemeyer argued with Joy over the issue of control of air units. A FEAF attack against a particular target was canceled because the Navy had scheduled an attack against the same target, and no effort had been made to coordinate the selection process.[5] A few days later, on July 11, Stratemeyer met Joy to form the unified command that he had recommended to MacArthur. Maj. Gen. Edward M. Almond, MacArthur's chief of staff, offered a compromise on operational control to Joy and Stratemeyer. (Almond was a student at the Air Corps Tactical School in 1938–1939, and, as historian Tom Y'Blood has observed, "he believed he knew more about close air support than any Air Force officer."[6]) However, the compromise did not clarify organizational authority. Joy and Stratemeyer pledged their staffs to "coordination control," but each commander interpreted the phrase differently.[7]

To be sure, the employment of incompatible communications equipment fed different interpretations of whether and how to effect interservice coordination. Navy leaders insisted on operations independent from the Air Force because the communications equipment they used differed from what the Air Force used, and even their service's philosophies guiding communication differed from the Air Force's. Because Navy communications tended to be short and based on briefed orders, its equipment was smaller and less capable.[8] Air Force communications were longer and overloaded the Navy's radio circuits, causing delays or mission cancellations. The Air Force and Navy would revisit this problem over the next forty years. During the Gulf War, air tasking orders (ATOs) had to be printed out and flown daily to the carriers because the Navy had not installed terminals for the Air Force's computer-assisted force management system (CAFMS). The reason for this lapse was simple: the Air Force had developed two different CAFMS software systems, one was for the Pacific, and the other was for the European theater. Because Navy carriers had to operate anywhere, and in several theaters in succession, instead of installing two sets of CAFMS terminals, it chose not to install any.[9]

In Korea, the number of targets, the number of forces in contact with enemy troops, and the number of air assets created many opportunities for disagreement between Navy and Air Force leaders over targeting priorities and assignment of assets.[10] These disagreements continued because MacArthur didn't devote attention to resolving them. When Stratemeyer discussed the issue with MacArthur, he believed MacArthur agreed to support the Air Force position. MacArthur's verbal support, however, often did not translate into directions and orders to naval and marine forces.[11]

Senior Officers' Concerns with Political Issues

Senior officers battled colleagues within their own services over command and control. For example, Admiral Joy reported to General MacArthur. The Commander-in-Chief of Pacific forces (CINCPAC) Adm. Arthur Radford ordered Commander-in-Chief of the Seventh Fleet, Vice Adm. Arthur D. Struble to report to Admiral Joy, giving Joy operational control (OPCON) of the Seventh Fleet. Struble, however, was senior to Joy, and they did not like one another. Because their commands were separate, their personal feelings for each other were irrelevant to the conduct of each's duties, that is, before hostilities broke out in Korea. Operations in Korea, in political scientist Donald W. Chisholm's words, "placed them in a close working relationship, which gave Struble [the supporting commander] considerable heartburn." Within a week of MacArthur's decision to conduct an amphibious landing, the primary site for the landing changed several times, and other disagreements emerged over command and control of naval air operations supporting the landing. Joy disagreed with Struble's recommendation regarding air strikes to cover the landing, but Struble wouldn't accept Joy's OPCON over the operation. Much as Army advocates of close air support for forces in contact with the enemy disputed the Air Force's position of the need to first establish air superiority, fast-carrier admirals did not want to tie down their forces to amphibious commanders. Fast-carrier admirals had their own understanding of how to use aviation to best effect. The Chief of Naval Operations (CNO), Adm. Forrest P. Sherman, sided with Struble, and told CINCPAC Admiral Radford to decide the issue in favor of Struble.[12] Such disagreements would continue. Resolution of conflict was temporary and necessitated the mediation and intervention of officers at the highest levels.

Political disputes also plagued the command of ground forces, even as preparations went forward for the Inchon landing. MacArthur did not like Eighth Army commander Lt. Gen. Walton Walker, nor was MacArthur satisfied with Walker's performance against the Democratic People's Republic of Korea. Walker did not like either MacArthur or his chief of staff, General Almond. MacArthur decided to create a separate command, X Corps, that would report directly to him. MacArthur chose Almond to command X Corps, and General Walker would also report directly to MacArthur. Almond had little experience as a combat commander and no experience in commanding amphibious landings. In choosing Almond, MacArthur rejected USMC Lt. Gen. Lemuel C. Shepherd, Jr., commanding general of the Fleet Marine Force Pacific. MacArthur's choice of Almond as the commander for X Corps was not received well by marines. Conflict between Almond and Maj. Gen. Oliver P. Smith, commander of the 1st Marine Division, began quickly. Consequently, Almond bypassed Smith in the chain of command several times, speaking directly and issuing orders to regimental units.[13]

Ad Hoc Organizations and Relationships

The formation of ad hoc command relationships is partly a result of the way politics permeates the American way of war.[14] Procedures for appointing commanders and establishing relationships among them during the Korean War were viewed as temporary expedients by the senior officers involved. Historian Frank Futrell has pointed out that, by the final year of the Korean War, FEAF and NAVFE worked well together, but the mutual accommodations made by NAVFE and FEAF resulted from the "fortunate personalities of the commanders concerned rather than from more stable dictates of command authority and organization."[15] Written exchanges between Stratemeyer and Joy were quite cordial.[16]

Senior officers maneuvered and bargained within the theater. For instance,

Navy and Air Force leaders disagreed about the command of air operations for the Inchon landing. On July 8, 1950, Stratemeyer wrote to MacArthur and appealed for "coordination control" of aviation for the planned Inchon landing.[17] A directive issued a week later included Stratemeyer's understanding of how command and control was to be assigned. On September 2, an air annex was released that differed significantly from Stratemeyer's understanding of the July 8 air coordination directive. On September 4, Stratemeyer wrote to MacArthur, seeking clarification. Stratemeyer did not receive a timely reply to this letter. On September 10, Stratemeyer and MacArthur met to discuss the situation, in which MacArthur appeared to endorse the FEAF position.[18] This disagreement was resolved through negotiation, but only for the Inchon landing.[19] Army leaders persisted in trying to control tactical air operations,[20] and the leaders of FEAF never received theater-wide control of assets.[21]

Some ad hoc organizational relationships were established to fulfill the need felt by senior military leaders based in the United States to acquire information, from a trusted source, about combat planning and operations. In late August 1950, CNO Admiral Sherman, a friend of Struble's, decided to augment Joy's staff, partly because of doubts about the proposed Inchon landing but also because of concern that Joy's World War II experience may be inappropriate to the current operations. Sherman assigned Capt. Arleigh Burke to COMNAVFE as deputy chief of staff and to take charge of the headquarters' wartime responsibilities. Burke had additional clandestine duties. Sherman gave Burke a cipher machine with instructions to send Sherman a daily personal message about the Inchon planning process.[22] Similar ad hoc relationships arose during the Persian Gulf War, often due to political considerations and the individuals' needs for independent sources of information.

Persian Gulf War

In some important respects, the Persian Gulf War differed significantly from the Korean War. The Persian Gulf War was shorter and fought under the provisions of legislation—the 1986 Goldwater-Nichols Reorganization Act—that did not generate the intense hard feelings among the services that the 1947 legislation had. The offensive air campaign was planned largely by Air Force officers, and the large numbers of Air Force assets in theater eliminated the need to fight over allocation of forces among missions. Nevertheless, political considerations guided and molded what and how events occurred.

Military Outcomes and Command and Control

The story of the offensive planning cell during Desert Storm—variously known as the Black Hole and the Guidance, Apportionment, and Targeting cell, or GAT—presents several compelling contrasts. First, building and executing an ATO proved very different in a static peacetime environment, where the decision problem was clear and well-structured, in contrast to a dynamic wartime environment where the decision problem was ill-structured and less manageable. Second, there was a difference between what senior leaders and planners believed they could manage and what was the reality of the war. The evidence shows that formal, mission-related, error-correcting feedback was often inadequate or nonexistent, and communications between the GAT and the wings were often confusing.[23] The costs to the United States associated with these contrasts were low only because we had a redundancy of aircraft and munitions, had air supremacy so that attacks could be applied at will, and had superbly trained and skilled pilots, air crews, and maintenance crews.

Gulf War air campaign disputes over command and control were thus partially masked by the predominance of Air Force assets in theater, including an abundance of aircraft. Lt. Gen. Charles A. Horner, the Joint Force Air Component commander (JFACC), allowed Navy and Marine Corps leaders to attack targets of their choosing rather than forcing an open contest for authority as the JFACC. For instance, USMC Maj. Gen. Royal Moore and Horner traded Air Force and marine sorties over the course of the air campaign,[24] and Horner did not have to tell Lt. Gen. Walter E. Boomer (commander of Central Command's Marine Corps component, MARCENT) to divert aircraft to carry out theater-level objectives. Boomer concentrated his aircraft on supporting marines in the Kuwaiti theater of operations (KTO),[25] while Horner made similar accommodations for the other air forces serving in the coalition.[26]

Command-and-control theorists try to design information strategies to resolve decision makers' uncertainties about future states of the world. Actual information-processing for command and control in Saudi Arabia does not fit this characterization. For instance, some GAT planners expressed surprise after the war at the range of planning conducted behind unmarked doors down the hall and by Central Command (CENTCOM) officers working in the Saudi Ministry of Defense building a mile away. In addition, a good deal of information was compartmentalized and kept only among people having the appropriate clearances and the crucial need to know. In other words, intelligence information was gathered and processed in various rooms of the Royal Saudi Air Force building with little regard for its relevance to the overall campaign. Significant gaps occurred in the GAT officers' knowledge of the range of activities occurring elsewhere in the building or in the tents set up outdoors in the parking lot. Even when they did have access to knowledge, GAT planners, guided by their own conception of strategic air warfare, discarded or ignored information that was inconsistent with their views.[27]

Senior Officers' Concerns with Political Issues

The organization fighting the war in Saudi Arabia was a political system in that a variety of goals and preferences that were ancillary to winning the war nevertheless found their way into the decision process, and these goals affected the way the war was run. Decisions about the JFACC and about command and control were influenced by the tacit recognition that battles over the budget, roles, and missions would be fought after the war. The JFACC concept was seen as the solution for long-standing political problems dating to the 1930s regarding the centralization of authority, assignment of roles, apportionment of missions among the military services, and the mediation of disputes between airmen and soldiers. Proponents of the JFACC concept seized the Gulf War as an opportunity to solve those long-standing political problems.[28]

Air Force officers cared about outcome—defeating the Iraqis—but they also cared about the symbolic meaning of the victory and the means by which the victory was obtained. Although it was evident very early that the allied coalition would defeat Iraq, it became vitally important to Air Force campaign planning officers that the victory show the decisiveness of air power and the indispensability of the JFACC in managing air power.[29]

Navy officers believed that postwar concerns defined Air Force decisions about command and control. In December 1990, Navy liaison officers in the tactical air control center in Riyadh observed that "the USAF [is] committed fully to the forward deployment and utilization of every possible facet of their force structure. This positioning was only thinly veiled...as positioning and preparation for the upcoming 'battles with Congress.' The Navy's leadership feared that the Air Force would be spared the resource cuts the Navy would be forced to take."[30] As my *Gulf War Air Power Survey* (*GWAPS*) colleagues and I noted, the observation of the Navy liaison officers also applied to their own service inasmuch as the Navy did its best to show the importance of its systems. Yet, the Air Force role was overwhelming, and senior Air Force and civilian leaders were in a better position to use the Gulf War to persuade Congress to spare them the kinds of cuts that planners in the services and in the Office of the Secretary of Defense could see coming as the response to the end of the Cold War.

Political imperatives also were in play one organizational level below the JFACC. The December 1990 reorganization of the CENTAF planning staff affected command and control by causing confusion in the execution of the ATO. The reorganization placed the former Black Hole staff firmly in charge of the air campaign planning effort. Air Force Brig. Gen. Buster C. Glosson was named chief of campaign plans, which complemented his authority as commander of the 14th Air Division (Provisional) (14th AD[P]). General Glosson, both as chief of campaign plans and as 14th AD(P) commander, was subordinate to General Horner. As chief of campaign plans, Glosson also worked for the CENTAF director of operations, Maj. Gen. John A. Corder. As the chief planner, Glosson was a staff officer and had no command authority over the execution of the ATO; however, as an air division commander, he had command authority over assets assigned to him, and he was responsible to the JFACC for executing the tasks given to his units through the ATO.[31]

The leader of the most critical element of the GAT, the so-called Iraqi Cell, was Lt. Col. David A. Deptula, who had contributed to the offensive plan since

August 1990. Lt. Col. Samuel Baptiste led the GAT KTO cell. Baptiste had access to the offensive plan early in Desert Shield, but he was so involved in the daily training and D-Day ATOs that he had little time to plan for the strategic air campaign. With the December reorganization, there would be no more duplicate ATOs, no more separate ground and air campaigns, and no question of planning and execution authority. The driving force of the Black Hole—the strategic air campaign against Iraq—became the focus of the CENTAF staff as a whole.

Participants in the planning process ascribed great importance to the reorganization. Deptula said that the centralization of authority in Glosson's hands was a key to the overall success of the air campaign because it reduced misunderstandings and upheld the intent of the plan in its execution. However, the integration of planning and execution authority under Glosson had consequences beyond promises of reducing misunderstandings between planners and operators. Unit-level representatives cited in the *Tactical Analysis Bulletin* argued that Glosson's proclivity to order mission changes after the ATO had been distributed to the F–117A, F–15E, and F–111F units created confusion. The centralization of planning and execution authority in Glosson allowed him to provide verbal guidance directly to the combat wings. Another cost to command and control resulting from the December reorganization was the willingness of GAT officers during Desert Shield and Desert Storm to make decisions based on little or poorly understood data and information. Theater intelligence officers believed that information received through informal channels to the Black Hole (and GAT) from the air staff was "nonvalidated."

Ad Hoc Organizations and Relationships

Once the air campaign planning staff got into the actual planning and execution of Desert Storm, they abandoned the prewar understanding of how the command-and-control organization would operate. The intelligence suborganization, whose staff identified and analyzed targets and attacks, was ignored in favor of ad hoc relationships at several organizational levels that, sustained by modern communications technology, allowed discussions over great distances about classified topics. When Iraq invaded Kuwait, Colonel Deptula was working on the staff of Secretary of the Air Force Donald B. Rice. General Horner chose Deptula to join the Black Hole staff. Using a STU-III secure telephone, Deptula was the "eyes and ears" for Secretary Rice for deliberations on planning and the conduct of combat operations.[32]

To direct attacks against mobile targets, senior planners bypassed the formal organization designed to transmit guidance for daily attacks to the flying squadrons. As a result, pilots who were redirected often flew without the necessary preparation or supporting aircraft. In each case, the formal hierarchy provided neither the means to make appropriate choices, comparisons, and evaluations, nor the communications channels capable of operating with the required short time lags. Because the formal organization for the 1999 Kosovo air campaign also was unable to provide timely tasking and target guidance, intelligence, and feedback about the effects of attacks, once again, an ad hoc organization had to be constructed to meet the demands for guidance while aircraft were flying combat missions.[33]

A serious issue not addressed by GAT planners in establishing their organization for exercising command and control was the existence, location, and purpose of designed feedback procedures to ensure that critical Iraqi targets were identified, attacked, and destroyed. A manager uses such feedback to provide staff with an error signal to denote the difference between the current situation and the desired goal. The GAT used very few official, formal feedback loops. The overall performance of the Tactical Air Control Center, of which the GAT was a component, was saved by the many ad hoc and informal communication links and organizations that functioned as short-term, error-correcting feedback loops, and by the skill of pilots and unit-level planners who flew their missions despite short planning periods, last-minute target and timing changes, and imperfect information about the effects of previous attacks, and regardless of the normal snafus that plague combat operations. Believing the planning system would cope, General Glosson ordered ATO changes regardless of how they would cascade through the system and affect, for example, operations such as the suppression of enemy air defenses or aerial refueling.[34] It is an open question whether Glosson made the system overreactive, that is, whether his behavior induced oscillation away from understanding the effectiveness of attacks against Iraqi positions, a condition that had to be resolved by the actions of officers working at night in Glosson's absence.[35]

Most of the information used to plan the Desert Storm air campaign was furnished by informal communications links that arose to supply battle damage assessment (BDA) and other critical and time-sensitive information to the GAT during the Gulf War. A diagram of these links would not show a clear and streamlined structure. Instead, information ties were redundant, overlapping, and linked across service lines that were unaccustomed to coordinating such activities in peacetime.

A very complicated ad hoc organizational architecture was built to control the large number of air sorties in Desert Storm. This architecture combined technology, compartmentalized information, numerous agencies, and many people having myriad occupational specialties and perspectives and sometimes conflicting organizational responsibilities. These elements had so many linkages and pathways that even naming all the connections, let alone tracing them, may be impossible. As such human-organization-machine systems become more integrated and complex, and more interdependent and interlocked, the probability of Tactical Air Control Center failures increases. At some point, the system may become so complicated that Gulf War–type organizational ad hoc solutions or fixes will prove inadequate.

At several levels of Central Command, air component key officers believed they were managing the chaos of war through planning. Yet, when the activities of the many significant participants are pieced together, the reality is that neither GAT planners nor General Horner, the JFACC, knew the details of what was happening in the air campaign or how well the campaign itself was going.[36] Planners sacrificed formal decision rationality to act on a timely basis. That is, they analyzed fewer alternatives, and they considered only potential positive results of decisions made. Critical elements of the plan—target sets chosen and simultaneous attack on those targets—might have been wrong (as evidenced by the fact that the Iraqi military collapse was incomplete), but these elements were not questioned. During the Gulf War, the wide use of STU-III secure telephones provided the GAT with an unplanned means to direct the attacks conducted by the units centrally and on short timelines.[37] The STU-IIIs also made possible the development of many ad hoc organizations and informal communications channels, which compensated for the failures of the formal organization. Properly understood and employed in conjunction with other nonmilitary technologies, STU-IIIs offer informal channels to exchange information and thus conduct very rapid analysis and evaluation of the effectiveness of combined arms warfare.

Conclusion

Thinking about military organizations in terms of choices made by senior leaders introduces systematic bias into interpretations of how people in organizations behave. The fundamental presumption of virtually all models and theories of decision making is that decision processes are organized around the act of making decisions and are understandable in terms of decision outcomes.[38] In this ideal vision of decision making, information clarifies decision options.[39]

Combat commands engaged in military operations are large, highly specialized, and complex. Military command-and-control relationships are predicated on achieving certainty concerning factors that affect the application of force. Yet the size, specialization, and complexity of military organizations inhibit attaining that certainty. The ideal decision-making vision assumes coherent decision processes for command and control that were nonexistent during either the Korean or the Gulf War air campaign. Organizational decision making involves many participants, each having individual preferences (and potentially different rank orderings of those preferences). These preferences have to be smoothed over somehow, much as politicians settle differences. Sometimes, political issues merely fester and continue for long periods. In Korea and Saudi Arabia, the explicit intentions of senior military leaders and the coherence of their command-and-control choices were often lost in the interaction among organizational components and the movement of people, problems, and solutions within the headquarters' organization.

The exercise of leadership and the management of command and control in combat remains one of the most difficult known organizational tasks. The requisites of leadership are also remarkably stable, despite changes in the technology of war. The variety of military technologies applied in modern combat increases the number, range, and interaction of factors that must be considered. Technology, however, does not obviate the role of "politics" in decision making at all levels of military organization. If the Korean War and Gulf War experiences presage problems facing future combat leaders, it is that politics—conflict of interest—affects the organization and exercise of command and control. Combat leaders should not expect that coordination agreements within and among services engaged in joint operations become set in stone once they are articulated. Only Moses on Mount Sinai could be assured of a timeless agreement.

Notes

1. Ltr, Gen Dwight D. Eisenhower to his wife, Mamie, Dec 16, 1942, quoted in *Letters to Mamie* (1978). Cited in Jay M. Shafritz, *Words on War* (New York: Prentice Hall, 1990), p 450.
2. T. R. Fehrenbach, *This Kind of War: A Study in Unpreparedness* (New York: Pocket Books, Inc., 1964).
3. U.S. Congress, Sen, Cmte on Amd Svcs, *Defense Organization: The Need for Change*, cmte print, Sen rprt 99-86, 99th Cong., 1st sess, 1985, p 51.
4. William T. Y'Blood, ed, *The Three Wars of Lt. Gen. George E. Stratemeyer* (Washington, D.C.: Air Force History and Museums Program, 1999), p 179.
5. William T. Y'Blood, "Command and Control of Air Operations: A Chimera of the Korean War," in Rebecca H. Cameron, ed., *Golden Legacy, Boundless Future: Essays on the United States Air Force and the Rise of Aerospace Power* (Washington, D.C.: Air Force History and Museums Program, 2000), pp 259–67.
6. *Ibid.*, p 260.
7. Robert F. Futrell, *The United States Air Force in Korea, 1950–1953* (Washington, D.C.: Office of Air Force History, 1983), pp 50, 151–52.
8. Y'Blood, "Command and Control of Air Operations," p 266.
9. Mark D. Mandeles, Thomas C. Hone, and Sanford S. Terry, *Managing "Command and Control" in the Persian Gulf War* (Westport, Conn.: Praeger, 1996), pp 130–31.
10. Futrell, *Korea*, p 50.
11. Y'Blood, "Command and Control of Air Operations," p 265.
12. Donald W. Chisholm, "Negotiated Joint Command Relationships: Korean War Amphibious Operations, 1950," *Naval War College Review* 53 (spring 2000): 70–76.
13. *Ibid.*, pp 81–85.
14. The lack of perfect anticipation of enemy plans, actions, and reactions to U.S. movements does not permit the formation of fully articulated combat organizations and functional relationships.

15. Futrell, *Korea*, p 493.
16. See, for example, Stratemeyer's diary entry for Sep 8, 1950, which includes a letter from Joy. *The Three Wars of Lieutenant General George E. Stratemeyer*, pp 176–77.
17. *Ibid.*, pp 165–68.
18. Futrell, *Korea*, pp 151–52; and *The Three Wars of Lieutenant General George E. Stratemeyer*, pp 179–81.
19. Chisholm, "Negotiated Joint Command Relationships," p 102.
20. Futrell, *Korea*, pp 45, 48.
21. Thomas C. Hone, "Korea," in Benjamin Franklin Cooling, ed, *Case Studies in the Achievement of Air Superiority* (Washington, D.C.: Center for Air Force History, 1994), p 461.
22. Chisholm, "Negotiated Joint Command Relationships," pp 89–90.
23. Mandeles, Hone, and Terry, *Managing "Command and Control,"* ch 2–4.
24. *Ibid.*, p 132.
25. W. E. Boomer, "Special Trust and Confidence Among the Trail-Breakers," *Proceedings of the U.S. Naval Institute* (Nov 1991): 50; and Royal P. Moore, Jr., "Marine Air: There When Needed," *Proceedings of the U.S. Naval Institute* (Nov 1991), pp 63–64.
26. Mandeles, Hone, and Terry, *Managing "Command and Control,"* ch 3.
27. *Ibid.*
28. Charles A. Horner, "The Air Campaign," *Military Review* (Sep 1991): 20–21. For a historical view of these problems, see Jeffery S. Underwood, *The Wings of Democracy: The Influence of Air Power on the Roosevelt Administration, 1933–1941* (College Station: Texas A&M University Press, 1991), ch 4.
29. Mandeles, Hone, and Terry, *Managing "Command and Control,"* ch 3 and 5.
30. *Ibid.*, p 130.
31. *Ibid.*, ch 2.
32. *Ibid.*, p 36.
33. Michael Ignatieff, "The Virtual Commander," *The New Yorker* (Aug 2, 1999), p 33.
34. The frequency and tempo of changes ordered by GAT officers early in the air campaign may have induced a cycle of other changes over several days. Because the planning and execution of the ATO cycle involved overlapping activities, the ATO planning process was unable to attain some sort of steady state. This issue regarding the implications of constant changes made in a process is similar to one described by W. Edwards Deming in "On Some Statistical Aids Toward Economic Production," *Interfaces* 15 (Aug 1975); see Mandeles, Hone, and Terry, *Managing "Command and Control,"* ch 3.
35. Informal efforts were made to prevent Glosson from overloading the TACC with changes. Maj. Mark "Buck" Rogers was designated the "BOC," the

Buster Control Officer. In addition, Glosson did not run the system twenty-four hours a day; his attendance at meetings away from the Black Hole limited his attention.

36. Mandeles, Hone, and Terry, *Managing "Command and Control,"* ch 2–3.
37. The cellular telephone may offer a civilian analogue for the use of STU-IIIs as a means for authorities to acquire information quickly from dispersed locations. In the Washington, D.C., metropolitan area, drivers (owning cellular phones) are making faster and safer commuting possible by calling police and traffic reporters with instant information about accidents and other delays. S. C. Fehr, "For Many Commuters, A Second Calling," *The Washington Post* (Feb 22, 1993): A1, A6.
38. Martin Landau and Paul Schulman, "Political Science and Public Policy," paper prepared for delivery at the 1984 annual meetings of the American Political Science Association, Washington, D.C.
39. James G. March, *Decisions and Organizations* (New York: Basil Blackwell, Inc., 1989); Michael D. Cohen, James G. March, and Johan P. Olsen, "A Garbage Can Model of Organizational Choice," *Administrative Science Quarterly* 17 (1972): 1–17; James G. March and Johan P. Olsen, "Garbage Can Models of Decision Making in Organizations," in March and Weissinger-Baylon, eds, *Ambiguity and Command*; Karl E. Weick, "Educational Organizations as Loosely Coupled Systems," *Administrative Science Quarterly* 21 (1976): 1–19; John W. Kingdon, *Agendas, Alternatives, and Public Policies* (Boston: Little, Brown, 1984); and March, *Decisions and Organizations*, pp 13, 390–91.

Weapons, Tactics, and Training

Richard J. Blanchfield

As you know, this august group was chosen because of our connection to similar aspects of the Gulf War and the *Gulf War Air Power Survey* (*GWAPS*). How work on the *GWAPS* makes one an expert on similar operations in the Korean War is still a mystery to me. In any case, I began my research for this essay by consulting the nearly 500-page, Volume IV of the survey. Due to obvious time constraints, I will not be able to cover as many topics nor provide the level of detail contained in that volume, a hallmark of the *GWAPS.* In this presentation, I shall take a very quick look at three crucial determinants of an armed force's overall capability. The first one is weapons—the tools used by the soldier, sailor, airman, and marine. The next is tactics—the way in which the tools are used to produce the desired effects. The final one is training—how the soldier, sailor, airman, and marine acquire the skills required to combine weapons and tactics into the operational art of warfare.

We should note that the Korean War was somewhat unique, in that it began with a bang and ended with a whimper. There can be little debate that the first six months were the most interesting and exciting period of the war: from the retreat and the defense of the Pusan perimeter, to the breakout, the Inchon landing and the race to the Yalu River, and then the reversal back to the area of the 38th Parallel. Like many others, I have concentrated on these early months of the war.

Enemy Weapons, Tactics, and Training

To frame later discussions and to establish a basis for comparison, I will begin with a short overview of the weapons, tactics, and training of the enemy forces. United Nations (U.N.) forces, including U.N. air forces, were confronted by an enemy not only from North Korea but also from the Soviet Union and the People's Republic of China (communist China).

In June 1950, the North Korean Army was composed of approximately 130,000 combat troops, many of whom were veterans of World War II when they fought in China with Chinese communist forces against the Japanese. In that conflict, the North Koreans had 500 tanks and artillery pieces, including some as large as 122 millimeters.

The North Korean Air Force consisted of approximately 132 combat aircraft and 30 transports and trainers. These were World War II hand-me-downs from the Soviet Union. In the Korean War, the old and rather small North Korean Air Force was relatively quickly destroyed as U.N. air superiority was established.

By December 1950, when the U.N. forces closed in on the Yalu River, the Chinese Air Force was believed to possess 650 combat aircraft, courtesy of the Soviet Union. These included 250 conventional and jet fighters, 175 ground-attack aircraft, 150 conventional twin-engine bombers, and 75 transports. By early 1951, Chinese jet fighter strength had increased to 1,000 aircraft, thanks again to the generosity of the Soviet Union.

The Soviet Air Force also had between 400 and 500 aircraft readily available for use in Korea. The most famous and effective of these was the MiG–15, flown by Chinese and Soviet pilots. During the first months of the war, U.N. airmen enjoyed virtually complete air superiority, but the appearance of the Soviet-built MiG–15 on November 1, 1950, changed everything. It made every American plane in the Far East obsolete. It easily outclassed the F–51 Mustang, which had no hope of surviving in an air battle except to keep turning inside a MiG, hit the deck, hope for the best, and run like hell for home. In level flight, the MiG was fully 100 miles an hour faster than the first-generation U.S. jet, the F–80, and it could climb away from the Shooting Star as if the F–80 were anchored in the sky. As for the Navy's new F9F Panther jet, the MiG was faster and could outclimb, outdive, and turn inside the Panthers. The wings of the MiG–15 were swept back, and the original models were powered by a 5,000-pound-thrust British Rolls-Royce engine. The aircraft had spectacular maneuverability and a level speed of approximately 660 miles per hour. The MiG–15 provided the principal threat to U.N. air operations throughout the war. Fortunately, the MiG–15, like U.N. jets, had very short legs—that is, it had a fairly short combat radius. (We should note that, as early as December 1947, MiG–15s were rolling off Soviet assembly lines at a rate of 200 per month. Today, we are lucky to get a total buy of 200 aircraft, and even that would be spread over ten to twelve years.)

The Chinese and Soviet MiG–15 pilots developed a tactic that took advantage of the sanctuary they enjoyed north of the Yalu River. They would climb to superior altitudes on their side of the river, cross the border at more than 30,000 feet, dive in firing passes against the Americans, and then scamper back to safety on their side of the river, only to renew the attack cycle if they so desired. They would also try to catch U.N. pilots who were ending their patrols with aircraft too low on fuel to fight. The level of competence of the communist pilots varied widely. The general consensus is that U.S. pilots must credit much of their initial aerial success to superior training, but this situation changed somewhat as more, better trained, and experienced Soviet pilots entered the war.

U.N. Aircraft and Weapons

Just as the *GWAPS* did not confine itself to only the U.S. Air Force contributions to the air effort, this essay will also include contributions made by the other services and even mention other U.N. air forces.

At the beginning of the war, the South Korean army consisted of 100,000 lightly armed soldiers. The army lacked both tanks and heavy artillery. The Republic of Korea (ROK) Air Force was that in name only. Although opinion differs somewhat concerning the exact number of aircraft the ROK had at the beginning of the war, the consensus is that it was fewer than twenty. The best estimate is sixteen aircraft, thirteen liaison and three trainers. One of my primary sources, *The United States Air Force in Korea,* by Robert F. Futrell, lists seventy-nine different friendly and enemy aircraft in the index. The U.S. Marines alone flew some fifteen different types of aircraft in Korea. Needless to say, I have neither the time nor the inclination to discuss all of these different types of aircraft. The criteria I used for choosing an aircraft for discussion were its importance to the war effort, interesting anecdotes, and the availability of research information.

The war began on June 25, 1950, when North Korea attacked South Korea. On the very next day, the Far East Air Forces (FEAF) was flying cover for noncombatant evacuation operations. By June 27, FEAF had begun to conduct air superiority missions over the Korean peninsula. Within a week, on July 3, 1950, carrier-based aircraft had arrived and had begun combat missions, and by early August 1950 the first marine aviation units to deploy from the United States had arrived with the 1st Marine Provisional Brigade. Within a little more than one month, lead elements of the U.S. air units—Air Force, Navy, and Marine Corps—that would fight the war were in place.

U.S. Air Force Aircraft

As of May 31, 1950, one month before the war began, the U.S. FEAF had 35,122 personnel and 1,172 aircraft: 504 F–80s, 47 F–51s, 42 F–82s, 73 B–26s, 27 B–29s, 179 transports, 48 reconnaissance aircraft, and 252 miscellaneous types. Of these aircraft, only 657 were available for combat in Korea, but not all were ready for combat. Those remaining were in storage or were being withheld for other Thirteenth and Twentieth Air Force missions, such as the defense of Japan.

Included in this initial group of Air Force aircraft was the F–80 Shooting Star, initially used as an air superiority aircraft and for bomber escort duty. The F–80 was no match for the MiG–15, and it was reduced to a secondary role after the F–86 Sabre appeared. However, an F–80 flown by 1st Lt. Russell Brown, USAF, shot down a MiG–15 on November 8, 1950, during the first all-jet dogfight.

The F–80s provided early cover for the retreating U.S. and ROK ground forces. Very short-legged, the F–80s were unable to provide much close air support after the loss of airfields in South Korea. One tactic to compensate for the aircraft's lack of range was to use external fuel tanks. Early in the war, the F–80s that flew from Japan were fitted with locally manufactured, jettisonable fuel tanks to extend their range. Later, the F–86s also used jettisonable fuel tanks when patrolling in MiG Alley. Another tactic to increase range was to fly patrols with no ordnance except .50-cal. machine guns. If no targets appeared, the Sabres would attack any ground target of convenience. Again, similar tactics were used forty years later, during the Gulf War.

The propeller-driven F–51 Mustangs were comparatively slow, World War II aircraft. Powered by a liquid-cooled piston engine, the Mustang was vulnerable to ground fire during strafing missions. However, and very importantly early in the war, Mustangs were available and could operate from the short, unpaved runways present in southern South Korea. Also, the Mustangs performed air-to-air and air-to-ground missions. Several of our allies flew the Mustang, including the Australians and the South Africans. The U.S. Air Force also transferred some of these aircraft to the ROK.

The F–82 Twin Mustangs were invaluable because they covered the evacuation from South Korea and were credited with scoring the first aerial victory of the war. As its name implies, the F–82 Twin Mustang had the rather bizarre appearance of two F–51 Mustang fuselages fused to a single wing. Its two pilots sat apart in separate cockpits, one in each fuselage. The secondary pilot served as a relief pilot or could assist with navigation.

The B–26 Invader was a light bomber used for both interdiction and close air support. The B–29 Superfortress bomber was used for both tactical and strategic air operations, including close air support, especially during the defense of the Pusan perimeter. The Air Force did not like using the big B–29s against tactical targets. During the siege of the Pusan perimeter, ninety-eight B–29s dropped 960 tons of high explosives over an area of twenty-seven square miles in the vicinity of the Naktong bridgehead. Additional examples can be found of the use of B–29 in a close air support role.

During the next three years of the war, several other U.S.Air Force aircraft arrived, chief among them, the F–86 Sabre. In terms of speed and maneuverability, the Sabre could outperform the F–51s and the F–80s. The Sabre's principal claim to fame was its ability to counter the Soviet-built MiG–15. During the war, Sabre pilots maintained a 10-to-1 margin of victory over MiGs. The MiG–15 could climb faster, but the Sabre could outrun it in a dive, and the Sabre was more responsive. Also, the Sabre's bubble canopy afforded better visibility. Both aircraft, however, had armament problems. The Sabre carried six M–3 .50-cal. machine guns, but the machine guns did not inflict enough damage. One of the Sabre's chief limitations was its short range. Carrying two 120-gallon wing tanks in addition to its internal fuel supply, the Sabre's combat range was only 490 miles. Challenges presented by this short range had a profound effect on the tactics of both enemy and friendly forces.

Over the course of the war, the Sabre received modifications that increased its performance. Wing slats were replaced with a fixed leading edge that reduced drag. Hydraulic controls were installed to improve maneuverability. A flying tail—a horizontal stabilizer that moved—was also installed to improve maneuverability. A more powerful engine replaced the 5,200-pound-thrust J47–GE–13 engine, and a radar gunsight replaced the K–18 gyroscopic computing gunsight.

The F–84 Thunderjet was a fighter-bomber used for counterair applications and bomber escort, especially when the F–86 was not available. The T–6 Mosquito trainer, a slow, unarmed aircraft, was used by tactical airborne coordinators who controlled close air support missions.

U.S. Navy and Marine Corps Aircraft

The carrier USS *Valley Forge,* with its air group of eighty-six aircraft, arrived off Korea on July 3, 1950, and launched the first carrier strikes of the war. By August 2, five carriers were in theater, including HMS *Triumph,* and a total of 250 U.S. Navy and U.S. Marine Corps aircraft. Some of the carriers were the small escort carriers of World War II.

The F4U Corsairs first gained fame with the marines in the Pacific during World War II. A number of different types and models were among the 12,571 Corsairs produced. Marine Corps and Navy carrier-based Corsairs provided close air support for U.S. and ROK forces near Pusan. Corsairs armed with rockets and napalm were an effective combination during the early days of the war. Because the short-legged F–80 jets had little loiter time and in-country airfields were not yet available, most of the support for the Pusan perimeter came from Navy and Marine Corps carrier-based aircraft. Corsairs from VMF–214, the famous Black Sheep squadron, conducted the first marine air strike of the war. Launched from the USS *Sicily,* the squadron was led by its executive officer, then-Maj. Robert P. Keller.

The AD–4, later the Douglas A–1 Skyraider, was flown by the Marine Corps, the Navy, and the Air Force. Its incredible longevity made it unique among the world's combat aircraft. Designed during the closing days of World War II, the Skyraider flew some of the first attack missions of the Korean War from the deck of the USS *Valley Forge.* (I served on the *Valley Forge* during her last deployment off Vietnam, when she was designated as an LPH, a helicopter carrier.) The Skyraider served with the Navy through the early years of the Vietnam War and with the Air Force until the early 1970s. This attack plane was one of the most versatile aircraft then in existence. It was used on electronic countermeasure, night fighter, and attack missions. The characteristic that the troops liked most about the AD Skyraider was that it could carry more than 5,000 pounds of ordnance, and its equipment included two wing-mounted 20-mm cannon.

The Grumman F7F Tigercat was a night fighter that provided important close air support. The graceful, well-proportioned two-seater was a twin-engine aircraft boasting a top speed of more than 400 miles per hour. It was considered too hot to operate from aircraft carriers, so the Navy decided to give the entire production run to the marines to fly from land bases. The F7F–3N incorporated a nose-mounted radar and a taller vertical tail. The F7F–3 was a single-seat model used primarily as a fast ground-attack aircraft. Night attack missions were usually under the control of Air Force forward air controllers (FACs). Tigercats were particularly valuable during the Wonsan-Chosin operation.

The R4Q–1 was the Navy and Marine Corps version of the Air Force Fairchild C–119 Flying Boxcar. This twin-boomed, twin-engine transport was essential to the Army's and Marine Corps's breakout from the Chosin Reservoir.

Marines of VMO–6, along with Air Force pilots, flew a number of different types of helicopters including the Sikorsky HO3S–1, HO5S–1, HRS–1, and S–55, and the Bell HTL–4. The helicopter was the one truly new vehicle to emerge in Korea. Helicopters were used to rescue downed pilots, conduct medical evacuation, and carry marines into battle. The OY Grasshopper was an unarmed artillery-spotting, airborne FAC aircraft.

U.N. Aircraft

The allies flew many of the same aircraft that the Americans did. Two British aircraft were the Fairey Firefly, a two-seat, single-engine, propeller-driven fighter, and the Supermarine Seafire, a shipboard version of the Spitfire.

Aircraft carriers made their most important contribution to the war effort when no airfields were nearby, which occurred primarily during the early months of the war, during the defense of the Pusan perimeter. Carriers also provided critical support during the landings at Inchon and in the winter retreat from the Yalu. Some would argue that the Korean War saved carrier aviation. As stated the British carrier HMS *Triumph* joined U.S. Navy carriers early in the war.

Five-inch rockets were a favorite close air support and interdiction weapon, especially for use against vehicles. U.N. forces used a variety of 100- to 1,000-pound bombs. A favorite technique involved dropping parademolition bombs with delayed fuzes. These bombs descended slowly by parachute to obtain maximum destruction; because they did not rebound or carom off the target, they were particularly effective against bridges.

Another favorite weapon for close air support used against troop concentrations and even tanks was napalm. Hand grenades carried by some of the Marine Corps observation pilots were tossed out over small groups of enemy troops who had fired upon them. Finally, the atom bomb was a weapon always under active consideration, but never used. Its threatened use may have ended the war.

U.N. Tactics

Not unexpectedly, tactics developed during peacetime did not always survive the first days of combat. Tactics had to be revised to accommodate the local situation, such as the introduction of new equipment by friendly forces or the enemy, the changing tactical situation, political restrictions, and equipment shortcomings.

Planning and Operations

Many of the tactics developed during the Korean War resulted from political decisions, the principal one being the sanctuary given to China and the Soviet Union. Not being permitted to cross the border in hot pursuit or to bomb targets in China or the Soviet Union—or even violate Chinese or Soviet airspace when attempting to destroy bridges over the Yalu River—necessitated some interesting new tactics. In one respect, we were fortunate that the Air Force was restricted from conducting bombing raids into China. Had the Air Force been allowed to fly over Chinese territory, the soldiers and marines would not have received any close air support.

Early in the war, B–29s could fly higher and faster than any of North Korea's Soviet-provided, World War II, reciprocating-engine aircraft. The introduction of the MiG–15 in November 1950 necessitated that B–29s be accompanied by escorts, normally F–86s. B–29 tactics changed again after MiGs slipped past patrolling F–86s and downed five B–29s in a single week. The Chinese air force became such a menace that U.N. forces were compelled to suspend daylight bombing raids over North Korea. After this, the B–29s began attacking exclusively at night. This change in tactics enhanced safety but decreased bombing accuracy. The big bombers then turned to the short-range navigation (SHORAN) electronic beam system, a network of ground-based radar beacons to aid navigation. SHORAN facilitated bombing at night and in bad weather. In response, the enemy used radar-controlled searchlights in conjunction with antiaircraft batteries. The B–29s, in turn, painted the underside of the wings and fuselage with black paint as camouflage and relied on chaff and jamming to frustrate radar operators.

Many in the Air Force envisioned a strategic bombing campaign against North Korea that would be modeled after similar operations during World War II. The United States organized and flew a number of large bombing raids. After the breakout, the focus shifted from the close air support that had been provided during the fight for the Pusan perimeter to the interdiction of North Korean supply lines. As in World War II, huge saturation raids by heavy bombers were not unusual, with literally hundreds of aircraft participating in a single strike. Examples included an attack on May 9, 1951, when a multiservice strike of 300 aircraft attacked North Korean airfields. In June 1952, some 500 aircraft—bombers with escorts—were directed at the Suiho hydroelectric dam and power plant, a vital target on the Yalu River. They also attacked oil refineries, transport centers, and industrial installations.

The main tactical air operations included air superiority, close air support, and interdiction in the vicinity of the battlefield. The main strategic air operations were establish control of the airspace over friendly territory, establish control over enemy airspace, and conduct strategic bombing of such targets as oil refineries, manufacturing complexes, and communications centers. Typically, the first aircraft would drop a napalm tank and the second would set the weapon afire with machine-gun fire.

Variety of Air Power

Enemy antiaircraft artillery, plus the requirement to follow the course of the river to avoid violating Chinese airspace, made it very difficult to destroy bridges across the river. Aircrew had to track radio-controlled bombs of World War II vintage all the way to their targets, ignoring antiaircraft fire and MiGs. And hitting a bridge across its short axis was much more difficult than bombing it along its long axis.

MiG Alley imposed new tactics for jet combat. In place of the fighter sweeps of the big World War II offensives, the Air Force substituted rather small defensive patrols. The initiative was with the Chinese. The Americans were in the reaction mode in that they had to establish barrier patrols. The short range of the F–86 (500 miles with jettisonable fuel tanks and no capability for in-flight refueling) meant that time was of the essence. Initially, patrols consisted of four F–86s arriving in MiG Alley at five-minute intervals and remaining for about twenty minutes. Their normal cruise speed would be a fuel-conserving 0.62 Mach. This relatively slow speed made the Sabres vulnerable to attack because of the time lag required to achieve fighting speed. After a near tragedy, they changed their tactics and increased their speed to at least 0.85 Mach. The strength of a patrol was standardized at sixteen aircraft, four flights of four arriving at five-minute intervals at differing altitudes. The optimum composition was the fluid four, four Sabres spaced generally in fingertip formation. The two element leaders carried the firepower while the wingmen covered the rear. (This was similar to the tactic used during the Gulf War to provide cover for the ground forces.) During night attacks, the Navy would assist by providing flares, another tactic that would find application in future wars.

U.N. Air Forces Training

Budget cuts after World War II reduced training time for everyone, especially for pilots. F–80 pilots based in Japan had little practice supporting troops in combat. This deficiency resulted from Air Force emphasis on strategic bombing—the merger of tactical and air defense missions—and lack of space that limited large-scale air-ground training exercises in Japan. Close air support had a lower priority in the Air Force than it did in the Marine Corps; consequently, marine pilots were better trained, more experienced, and therefore tended to support ground forces better than their Air Force counterparts did.

Generally, American pilots were superior to their communist adversaries. Many U.S. pilots were veterans of World War II. They may suffered from some lack of training and funds due to military cutbacks, but superiority is a relative concept, and the Americans were clearly better trained than the enemy was.

Conclusion

The conflict in Korea was a transnational from the standpoint of weapons, tactics, and training. It was characterized by a greater emphasis on change than on continuity. Although it was the first jet war, we would have been in serious trouble without our reciprocating-engine fighters in the critical early days. Carrier aviation looms large in that regard, and I do not think it would be an exaggeration to say that the Korean War saved carrier aviation. The greater effectiveness of carrier-based Corsairs in close air support in defending the Pusan perimeter was the key event. P–80s based in Japan were not as accurate, could not stay on target for as long, and were severely limited on bombload, assuming they could even find the targets. One of the big tactical lessons that the Air Force nearly forgot about was the effectiveness of airborne FACs. The Marine Corps did a bit better with that. The marines also pioneered the use of helicopters. Another major tactical lesson to emerge from the war was the importance of superior training in air-to-air operations. It was the combat over MiG Alley that inspired Col. John R. Boyd, USAF, to formulate his classic OODA Loop, the methodology of *o*bservation, *o*rientation, *d*ecision, and *a*ction. Key technologies, specifically the radar-ranging gunsight and the all-flying horizontal stabilizer with good hydraulically boosted controls, properly supported Boyd's theory. Also regarding technology, Korea saw the first engagements between second-generation jet fighters. (The first generation involved piston-engine airframes, aerodynamics mated to jet propulsion.) The United States also realized the inadequacy of .50-cal. armament, though it seemed adequate when compared to the Soviet weapons. This was due mainly to the fact that the MiG–15 lacked an all-flying tail and was a poor gun platform; it exhibited directional snaking at the high end of its speed range. Although it is debatable whether any targets were worth their use, B–29s demonstrated that they were viable high-performance bomb-haulers. On the other hand, they exhibited extreme vulnerability to MiGs.

A Gulf War Perspective on the Effectiveness of Air Power

Thomas A. Keaney

It is an honor to be among this group of scholars and veterans of the Korean War and be asked to speak on the use of air power in that war. Let me emphasize that I speak not as an expert on any aspect of the Korean War, but as an analyst of the performance of air power of a war forty years later against Iraq. My topic is how experiences in that later war might help in our Korean War perspective. The forty years that separated these wars represent a significant segment of air power history, and, not surprisingly, vast differences emerge when comparing their conduct. Subsequent panels will look at each aspect of air power in the Korean War, close air support, strategic bombing, reconnaissance, and so forth. I will remain at a more general level in this presentation, attempting to set the stage for those subjects by looking at the different circumstances and capabilities, of the conditions at that time, and of what had changed forty years later.

At least one similarity in these wars emerges: both were conducted by a United Nations (U.N.) coalition. The Korean War was the first to be so conducted; the Gulf War was the second, and so far the latest. U.N. coalitions in both wars, formed as much to display broad international political support as for the combined military power they produced, operated under the overall leadership of the United States. The conditions under which leadership was conducted within these coalitions are complex and describing them would take us well beyond the limits of this conference, but it is important to note the particular conditions of coalition air operations, because that is the symposium's title. Simply stated, just as in the Gulf War, coalition air power was under the near total control of the United States. Many countries sent ground forces; far fewer contributed aircraft. Countries that did provide aircraft provided some fighter and transport aircraft, but they were too few and not of a sufficient quality to be considered essential to the fighting force nor to permit their donors to have a significant voice in the conduct of the air operations. As a result, the story of coalition air power is the story of U.S. air power.

In Korea, the more interesting coalition aspects of air operations to consider concern the coalition of the four U.S. military services engaged. The Gulf War saw service clashes over issues such as targeting priorities and the authority of the joint force air component commander, but disputes were not nearly so fundamental as those in evidence in the Korean War. Recall that, when the Korean War began, the change to a Department of Defense was just getting underway, and the Air Force, not quite three years old, had already engaged in heated controversies with the other services. In the bruising debates of the late 1940s over service roles, the Marine Corps had fought for its life; the Navy, for control of its aviation; and the Army and Air Force, over procedures for air targeting and the priority given to close air support. Following the initial agreements on roles and missions of the services came the very public disputes involving the Air Force and Navy after the cancellation of the aircraft carrier USS *United States* and the subsequent debate over the value of the B–36 bomber. Consequently, in 1950 and throughout the war, not only was there no agreement on the overall control of U.S. air power, there was also no joint headquarters with any capability to deal with securing a cooperative effort among the services. In sum, although interservice disputes on various issues persisted into the Gulf War and beyond, the disputes were not of the depth that were encountered in Korea, where Navy, Marine Corps, and Air Force air operations coexisted, but were far from being joint.

Conditions within the 1950 Air Force itself further hampered both interservice cooperation and the Air Force's readiness for the Korean War. To confront the growing Soviet threat, the Air Force had its attention focused on building an atomic striking force of strategic bombers. In 1950, Strategic Air Command (SAC) and its mission were ascendant within the Air Force, and that command received top priority for resources. With its focus on the Soviet Union, SAC saw the Korean War as a distraction to its primary mission, and it therefore sent its least capable, less-well-manned B–29 units to the theater. The command's attention remained on manning its growing force B–36s and B–47s.[1] The emphasis on SAC prompted a consequent deemphasis within the Air Force on tactical aviation. When the Korean War began, Tactical Air Command (TAC), in fact, was not a major command but only a planning headquarters within Continental Air Command. All these conditions served to complicate not only the Air Force's readiness for this conflict but also its ability to deal effectively in coordinating with the Army on matters such as close air support.

These conditions stand in stark contrast to the Air Force's posture and readiness for the Gulf War in 1990. At the time of the Gulf War, Strategic Air Command had lost most of its Cold War importance and would be disestablished soon thereafter. The tactical air forces had supplanted SAC in both influence and importance. With the waning of the Cold War, SAC had adjusted by developing considerable expertise in conventional bombing and was prepared to undertake immediate operations. Whereas in 1950 strategic bombing had been left to the

World War II vintage B–29s, in the Gulf War the newest emerging systems—the F–117s and the Navy and Air Force cruise missiles (TLAM and ALCM, respectively)—were available for this role. Further, the tactical training centers of all the services—the Air Force Tactical Fighter Weapons Center and the Navy Strike Warfare Center, for example—had provided crews with realistic operational experience. And, whereas the North Korean attack came with no warning, aircrews in 1991 had nearly six months to prepare for combat in Desert Storm.

So much for organizational factors. As I look at the actual conduct of air operations in the Korean War, I am most struck by the factors that characterized air operations in the Gulf War, noting that these items were almost entirely missing forty years earlier. The *Gulf War Air Power Survey*, in its overall analysis of that war, selected five capabilities and technologies that best characterized the air campaign. They were stealth/low observability, laser-guided bombs, aerial refueling, the high-speed antiradiation missile (HARM), and the STU-III, a secure telephone.[2] Let us look at each of these capabilities in the Korean War context.

Curiously, two of these capabilities, stealth and the HARM, would have had little effect on the conduct of the war in Korea. These technologies were designed to counter or neutralize a system that had not yet appeared by the time of the Korean War—surface-to-air missiles and their supporting radars. The Chinese and North Koreans did employ some radars for searchlight operations and gun-laying, but those systems were limited to defending areas in the far north along the Yalu River; radars were often located across the border in China.[3] Missing, of course, were the generations of systems that came into existence between the Korean War and the Gulf War in which electronic combat featured so prominently. Considering the war in Vietnam, the F–117 and HARM, if available, would have become important factors. In the Korean War, however, they were systems whose time had not yet come.

Laser-guided bombs (a guided bomb version did make a brief appearance in Korea) would have had importance, but probably not in any dramatic way. Precision strike always brings advantages, but at least in the Gulf War it was used only against single-point targets. Korean War targets in this category consisted of leadership headquarters, electric power facilities, factories, and aircraft and their shelters. Early in the war, U.N. air forces destroyed most of those targets, and those that remained were located off the Korean peninsula, off-limits for political reasons.

Instead, the circumstances of the fighting in Korea would have favored the use of area weapons against large formations of Chinese and North Korean troops. Perhaps useful against troop formations would have been B–52s loaded with fifty to one hundred gravity bombs, such as were used in Vietnam and the Gulf War. In fact, such capabilities did exist with the B–29s used in Korea, but the Superfortress saw only emergency service in a ground support role. In instances in which B–29s used area bombing techniques against troops, Air Force leaders saw the practice as largely ineffective and a misuse of the bombers.[4] Much of that ineffectiveness could no doubt be attributed to poor communication with ground elements on the location of targets, issues that could have been solved with better coordination between air and ground elements. But SAC was preoccupied with its mission of strategic bombing and had little interest in using its aircraft as flying artillery. Just as in Vietnam and the Gulf War, although little specific damage had been reported, the Army commander on the ground gave his support to the air strikes because of the great psychological lift it had given his own troops, and the opposite effect it had on the enemy forces.[5]

The STU-III secure telephone presents the interesting picture of a non–air power asset with tremendous effects on air power employment in the Gulf War, but Korean War conditions tend to negate its potential impact. The secure telephone gained prominence in the Gulf War because it allowed planners at all levels in the theater and in Washington to share information and coordinate planning. That such information was available for sharing reflects the fact that other information technologies were in place to allow planners at all levels access to intelligence and operational information on which they could base their assessments. In the absence of broad access to targeting information, bomb damage assessments, and a host of data on aircraft capabilities, little relevant information would have been available to talk about had there been either secure or insecure lines. Secure telephones enhanced the operations of organizations already made flatter by access to extensive information systems. These circumstance simply did not apply to the U.S. military of the 1950s.

For the top leadership, access to a secure telephone might have had interesting applications. One can only speculate on the effect of President Harry Truman and Gen. Douglas MacArthur being able to talk on a daily basis. And who would not like to have had access to candid conversations on secure telephones between individuals such as Truman or MacArthur, George Marshall, Omar Bradley, or Louis Johnson? Their biographers, of course, would have found such records priceless.

Of the five special capabilities of the Gulf War, the most low-tech of these—aerial refueling—would have brought the most dramatic effects, had it been available. Perhaps at no other time in the history of U.S. air power, save in the early days of World War II, had the nation faced such a scarcity of aircraft and qualified crews, and having the ability to stretch those resources through the use of tanker aircraft would have had a great impact. In many situations, fighters on flights from Japan had to operate at their maximum range and thus could remain only briefly in the target area. Particularly for close air support missions, having air refueling for the attack aircraft would have greatly improved the response time and persistence in this mission. In fact, air refueling was becoming an Air Force capability at the time of the Korean War, specifically in SAC, and it has become integral to American air power ever since. Although many technologies, from space assets to stealth, still lay far in the future in 1950, air refueling just missed being available.

The comparison of technologies, although at times informative, does not define a war or the conduct of operations, either in Korea or the Gulf. For those tasks, one must look closer at how combatants dealt with the circumstances and used the weapons available. Looking at these operations, one can see great continuity between the Korean War and the Gulf War. As I noted earlier, similar problems arose concerning issues such as the command and control of the air forces; the relative effectiveness of strategic bombing, interdiction, and close air support; and tactics for air-to-air combat.

Notes

1. Richard H. Kohn and Joseph P. Harahan, eds, *Strategic Air Warfare: An Interview with Generals Curtis E. LeMay, Leon W. Johnson, David A. Burchinal, and Jack J. Catton* (Washington, D.C.: Office of Air Force History, 1988), p 87.
2. Thomas A. Keaney and Eliot A. Cohen, *Gulf War Air Power Survey Summary Report* (Washington, D.C.: U.S. Government Printing Office, 1993), p 223. The idea for this list came from the example of Dwight Eisenhower, who identified what he and his staff thought to be the five most important pieces of equipment contributing to success in Africa and Europe in World War II. They were the "duck," an amphibious vehicle; the bulldozer; the jeep; the 2½-ton truck; and the C–47 aircraft. See Dwight D. Eisenhower, *Crusade in Europe* (New York: Doubleday and Company, 1948), pp 163–64.
3. See Alfred Price, *The History of U.S. Electronic Warfare, vol II* (The Association of Old Crows, 1989), pp 93–112.
4. Robert F. Futrell, *The United States Air Force in Korea, 1950–1953* (Washington, D.C.: U.S. Government Printing Office, 1983), pp 138–39.
5. *Ibid.*, pp 139–40.

Air Superiority

The Contribution of the U.S. Marine Corps Night Fighter Squadrons

Ronald W. Harbison

As the situation became desperate in the Pusan perimeter, Gen. Douglas MacArthur requested marines to help in the defense. The 1st Provisional Marine Brigade was formed of marines from every base in the United States and from the reserves. The brigade's air arm consisted of two squadrons: VMF(N)–542, flying F7F–3Ns from its base at Cherry Point, North Carolina; and VMF(N)–513, flying F4U–5Ns out of El Toro, California. VMF–323 and VMF(N)–513 were loaded aboard the USS *Sitkoh Bay* and sailed on August 24, 1950. VMF–212 and VMF(N)–542 embarked on the USS *Cape Esperance* on August 27. The brigade's air arm arrived in Japan on July 31. VMF–214 and VMF–323 checked out at Itami Air Base and then flew to the escort carriers, USS *Sicily* and USS *Badoeng Strait*. The night-fighter squadrons flew from Itazuke Air Base (AB) on the west coast of Japan. VMF(N)–513 flew day and night strikes in support of the marine brigade, and it also flew for Army units. VMF(N)–542 had security and strip alert at Itazuke AB.

From September 3 to 14, VMF(N)–513 flew seventy-nine day and night close air support (CAS) missions in support in the Pusan perimeter. As the defense stabilized around Pusan, MacArthur was planning the invasion of Inchon. The 1st Provisional Marine Brigade was pulled out of Pusan and embarked to join the 1st Marine Division for the landing at Inchon on September 15. As the marines advanced, they captured the airfield at Kimpo and, on September 19, VMF(N)–542 moved with their F7F–3Ns from Itazuke AB to Kimpo, near Seoul, and began operations. The squadron had only twenty trained night-fighter pilots. The rest were reservists with good experience and a desire to become night fighters. The squadron claimed the distinction of flying the first marine combat mission from Kimpo at 0735 on September 20 when four F7F–3N aircraft destroyed two enemy locomotives after expending 3,000 rounds of 20-mm ammunition. The 5th Marines exercised extreme care to minimize damage to the location because they knew that planes flying from that field would help them in the near future.

Used as a night fighter during the early years of the war, the two-seat, twin-engine Grumman F7F–3N Tigercat, with its distinctive nose-mounted radar and taller vertical tail, repeatedly proved its capabilities. (Marine Corps Historical Center Photo Collection)

During this time, VMF(N)–513, flying their F4U–5Ns out of Itazuke, supported General Walker's breakout from the Pusan perimeter. Between September 17 and 19, the squadron flew fifteen daylight CAS missions for U.S. Army units. As the planes ranged over the entire extent of the Pusan perimeter, they attacked enemy troops, tanks, vehicles, and artillery. Meanwhile, VMF(N)–542 was flying support missions for the 1st Marine Division as it attacked northward. When Wonson AB was captured, VMF(N)–513 flew from Itazuke. Night operations did not begin until late October, when runway runway lights became available. They flew daytime missions with VMF–312 under the control of tactical air control parties (TACPs). Both night-fighter squadrons continued to support the marines as they advanced northward. As all air units continued to harass supply lines, the North Koreans began to move more supplies at night, the time when the night fighters were most effective. During the Chosin Reservoir campaign, VMF(N)–513 and VMF–542 flew day and night in support of the marines. On December 31, the two night-fighter squadrons flew twenty CAS missions. On December 7, 1950, 1st Lt. Truman Clark of VMF(N)–513, flying a torpedo bomber, the TBM Avenger, helped evacuate 103 casualties from Koto-ri. Capt. Malcolm G. Moncrief, Jr., of VMF–312, a qualified landing signal officer, directed the torpedo bombers into Koto-ri with paddles. After the evacuation at Hungnam, the two night-fighter squadrons were flying into Itazuke, patrolling the skies between Japan and Korea.

In January 1951, VMF(N)–542 assumed the duties of VMF(N)–513, which deployed to K–9 at Pusan. Beginning on January 27, the squadron flew armed

The twin-engine Douglas F3D Sky Knight jet night fighter gained the respect of many "former" members of the Chinese Air Force. With its state-of-the-art avionics, the big jet was soon tasked with escorting Air Force B–29s, which had been assaulted by enemy MiGs. (W. T. Larkins Collections, Naval Aviation History Office)

reconnaissance missions and an occasional deep support mission for the Eighth Army. As the allies pushed northward, VMF(N)–542 received orders to conduct long flights from Itazuke to as far as Seoul, Korea, and to maintain continuous patrols to report enemy attempts to cross the frozen Han River. They shot up camp areas, convoys, and other lucrative targets. In addition to all of the various duties they were assigned, they also served as spotters to direct naval gunfire. Late January saw the first successful instance of marine air-to-ground cooperation since the Chosin Reservoir campaign. In February, VMF(N)–513 moved from Itami, Japan, to K–3 Pohang on the east coast of Korea. VMF(N)–542 transferred from Itami and Itazuke to K–1 Pusan. In March, VMF(N)–542 was sent home to El Toro, California, for conversion and training in the F3D Sky Knight all-weather jet fighters. The squadron's F7F–3Ns were left with VMF(N)–513, now a composite squadron, attacking from K–1 during the day with its F4U–5Ns and during the night with its F7F–3Ns. During May, the planes of VMF(N)–513 killed hundreds of Chinese soldiers.

In late May, marine R4D transports were outfitted to drop flares. They worked together with the F7Fs and F4Us to illuminate targets at night. On June 12, the Navy provided the 1st Marine Aircraft Wing with PB4Y–2 Privateers for the night-illumination missions. The planes would fly in the general area, and when one would find a likely target, they would join up. The flare plane would drop flares and the night fighters would fly beneath them and attack targets of opportunity. This was extremely hazardous because the enemy would know they were being targeted. The operation was almost always conducted along known supply routes in deep valleys among the mountains, and the enemy was known to stretch cables between the mountains over the routes. These missions were eventually terminated due to the high cost of men and planes. Afterward, the planes patrolled on their own, searching for targets. Mostly, they were looking for truck convoys driving with their lights on. The attrition rates dropped because the enemy was no longer forewarned by the flares.

In June, VMF(N)–513 moved to K–18 at Kangnung on the east coast of Korea. The 4,400-foot-long runway was reinforced with pierced steel planking. This field was only forty miles behind the 1st Marine Division, a proximity that allowed the aircraft much more time over the target. During this period, the enemy was flying light planes over the main line of resistance (MLR), even over the Seoul area. One such plane was the Po–2, a biplane made mostly of wood and fabric which made it difficult to pick up or track by radar. The Po–2s would drop mortar shells and other types of ordnance that proved more of a hindrance and bother than anything else; they acquired the nickname, Bedcheck Charlie. The Po–2 could fly at 60 mph, whereas the lowest speed that an F7F, with wheels and flaps down, could safely maintain was 110 mph, a speed that did not allow it to make any turns. The F4Us were not much better. In June, July, and September, two F7F–3Ns and one F4U–5N each shot down a Po–2 by using radar intercept. In June 1952, an F4U–5N shot down a Yak–9. As hard as it was to intercept and shoot down these Bedcheck Charlies, the effort to do so at least had the effect of chasing them away.

Another mission of VMF(N)–513 was nightly patrols to protect Cho-do, an island ten miles off of the west coast of North Korea and north of the Haeju peninsula. Cho-do had a radar installation and an air-sea rescue service, and the dusk-to-dawn mission was to protect it from being bombed at night. Loitering on station for the night was a monotonous, though necessary, duty, but planes returning over the Haeju peninsula were free to attack any targets of opportunity that presented themselves.

Another tasking that allowed closer air support on the MLR at night was the MPQ radar missions flown by the F7F–3Ns. At the beginning, a pilot would fly the plane while maintaining a prescribed altitude and speed. He would arm the plane according to instructions from a radar plotter on the ground. The plotter would give directional requests and tell the pilot when to release ordnance, which could be one bomb at a time or all ordnance at once. Bombs carried on these missions ranged from 250 to 2,000 pounds. After dropping any ordnance, the pilot would always watch for secondary explosions. The planes were eventually adapted so that the pilot had only to maintain altitude and speed. The ground operator would still request the ordnance he wanted dropped on each run, and the pilot would fly the plane to the target and attack. This became very accurate and effective. The pilots were called in by forward observers, and damage reports would sometimes be given before the planes left the area.

The F7F–3Ns also escorted Air Force B–26 Invaders on nightly interdiction missions. These missions were hard on the B–26 radar operator because some missions lasted for as long as six hours and the radar operator was jammed into a small space originally designed to hold an eighty-gallon gas tank. Largely unable to move during a mission, the operator was exposed to freezing temperatures that were difficult to endure.

On March 30, 1952, VMF(N)–513 moved from K–18 to K–8, from Kangnung in the east to Kunsan on the west coast, 105 miles south of Seoul. Of note is that this move was accomplished without losing even one day of operations. K–8 was an Air Force base, and the squadron was reinforced because it was the only marine squadron on the base. At that time, VMF(N)–513 was flying both the F7F–3N and F4U–5N. Now the night interdiction missions were becoming extremely hazardous because the MLR was stagnant. The enemy was able to concentrate very heavy antiaircraft artillery along their main lines of supply. Planes sat on strip alert nightly and would scramble whenever enemy planes were spotted south of the MLR.

Another mission for the F7Fs added at this time was night close air support (NCAS) on the MLR for the 1st Marine Division. The plane would be loaded with eight new types of firebombs which did not explode in one big fireball like napalm, but would travel above the ground and spread fire in all directions. The bombing run would commence at 5,000 feet, and the pilot would release the bombs on the pull-up at 1,000 feet. Accuracy was improved by two searchlights that crossed their beams on a mountaintop several miles back. The F7F would arrive on station and report to a spotter plane, which would use crossed searchlight beams as a reference to provide directions for the first drop. After the first drop, the spotter would give the direction from there to drop the other bombs. After eight of these drops, it would seem as if the whole mountain were on fire. The effectiveness of these firebombing mission was enhanced with a slight—but unofficial—change in tactics. The pilot of the first plane would delay his takeoff for a short period, and the next pilot would hurry up and leave a little early, so that they arrived at the target area at approximately the same time. As the first plane began its bombing run, the second plane would start strafing behind it. When the first plane finished its runs, the second would bomb while the first strafed behind it. This was neither sanctioned nor known officially, but it proved very effective. Pilots received very little ground fire because the enemy troops knew they would get personal attention. Just imagine three planes in the same area at night without running lights. These were very successful missions and broke the back of many enemy attacks.

During the late summer of 1952, VMF(N)–513 received twelve F3D Sky Knight night fighters. With this acquisition, the 513th became the only squadron with three types of planes actively flying combat missions at the same time during the Korean War. After some modifications, F3Ds began assisting on the night combat air patrol (NCAP) missions for Cho-do. About this time, the F4Us were phased out and the F3Ds were training to escort the nightly B–29 raids. These raids would require as many as eight F3Ds at one time. Due to the limited time an F3D could be airborne compared to the time the B–29 would be in flight, escort for the bombing run from the MLR to the target and back required several planes. One plane would pick up the B–29s at the MLR and escort them to the initial point. Another plane would then escort them to the target. One plane would perform combat air patrol over the target area, and the other F3Ds would escort the B–29s out across the MLR. This system proved so effective that B–29s losses ceased. At times, two targets being struck simultaneously would increase the workload on the escort planes and crew.

As the F7Fs were being phased out during the first few days of May 1952, the crews transitioned to the new F3Ds. The radar officers (ROs) learned the new radar and navigation equipment while still flying F7F missions. The pilots were also switching to the F3Ds.

By June, VMF(N)–513 had moved to K–6 Pyontaek, about fifty miles south of Seoul. Its mission was now mainly escorting the B–29s and performing NCAPs over Cho-do. The F3D had a fantastic radar at that time. It had long-range mapping, and its range reception was very good. It had a target lock-on system that virtually ensured a hit if the target was within range, and it was able to shoot down enemy planes without its pilot ever seeing them. Until the cease-fire, F3Ds continued escorting B–29s and patrolling over Cho-do. After the cease-fire, the F3Ds patrolled south of the 38th parallel until they redeployed to Japan.

The F4U was well known as a CAS plane from World War II. In the postwar period, it was equipped with radar and made into a night fighter, but with a single pilot, it was difficult to fly because he had to operate the radar simultaneously. The F7F began flying at the end of World War II and did not see any combat in that conflict, but it too was later configured as a night fighter and patrolled in China after World War II. With the addition of a radio observer (RO) doing the navigation, part of the radio work, and directing the pilot on intercepts, it was an easier life for the pilot. The F7F may have been the toughest fighter plane ever built. It often came home on one engine, many times dragging wires or parts of trees, and with cables wrapped around it. The F3D was a new plane with state-of-the-art equipment. With a crew of two and the bulky radar equipment, it was not as fast as other jets of the era, but its interception equipment and tail-warning radar made it one of the best planes.

There was a significant difference between the pilot's and RO's jobs in the two planes. The F7F was noisy and cold, whereas the F3D was quiet and warm. In the F7F, the RO sat with his feet four inches below his rear, and he could not stretch out. The cockpit was so narrow that he was unable to put both arms down beside his body. The canopy was so close to the seat that, if he was taller than five feet eight inches, he had to ride with his head bent forward. The plane was equipped with South Wind gasoline heaters that never seemed to work. Riding in this cramped, cold position for as long as six hours and unable to move was difficult and uncomfortable. Also, sitting between the two engines made it hard to hear anything. The ROs flew in any clothing they could find to try to keep warm on missions. However, after a crewman was lost due to exposure, we got rubber exposure suits. We were issued "Mickey Mouse" thermal boots which helped, but because a man could not move his feet for the entire flight, his feet still got extremely cold. Bailing out of the F7F was a problem for the RO. The pilot would go out between the cockpit and the engine in front of the wing. However, the RO, sitting lower than the top of the wing, had to roll out onto the wing after he released his canopy. If he went out too high, he would be blown onto the elevator. If he went out too low, the airflow would hold him on the wing. He had to rise up just enough to be blown off low.

Transitioning from the F7F to the F3D was like riding a motorcycle in the winter and then getting into a limousine. In the F3D, you sat side by side in a cockpit that was pressurized and heated or cooled, as the situation demanded. You entered the plane through a forty-inch square hatch on top of the cockpit. To bail out, the crew had to use a tunnel between the seats that exited from the bottom of the plane. The main thing to remember was to not go out head first. For its time, it was a wonderful plane and a pleasure to fly. Marine night fighters were introduced during the island battles of World War II and later improved into what was used in Korea. That was the end of combat flying for night fighters because all planes since then were used as both day and night fighters, and the squadrons were designated as attack squadrons.

None of the aforementioned accomplishments would have been possible without the dedication and sacrifice of all of the support people in the squadron. The planes were maintained in excellent condition, and the entire squadron was well taken care of, in spite of some primitive conditions. Missions were never missed or curtailed due to lack of maintenance. When the squadron moved to new bases, flying operations were never missed. Pilots took off from the old base, flew their missions, and simply landed at the new base. This put an unbelievable strain on support personnel, but they never failed to complete their mission.

Note

This essay is based on my logbook and memory. I also consulted "U.S. Marine Operations in Korea, 1950–1953," the official, five-volume history of the United States Marine Corps published by the Historical Branch, G–3, Headquarters, U.S. Marine Corps, and the "U.S. Marines in the Korean War Commemorative Series," a collection of seven pamphlets published by the History and Museums Division, Headquarters, U.S. Marine Corps and available from the Superintendent of Documents, United States Government Printing Office.

A Wingman in Korea

Brig. Gen. Michael E. De Armond, USAF (Ret.)

This presentation will briefly address the role of an F–86 wingman in air-to-air combat against the MiG–15 during the Korean War. It will identify the attributes required of a good wingman, his duties in combat, those most likely to be assigned as wingmen, and their attrition rates. I will also briefly compare the combat capabilities of the F–86 against those of the MiG–15.

The Wingman

As a second lieutenant, I flew as a wingman with the 335th Indian Head Fighter Squadron, 4th Fighter Group, stationed at Kimpo Air Base, South Korea (K–14), from December 1951 to April 1952, when I was shot down in a dogfight over the Yalu River. I spent the remainder of the war as a POW.

Pilots assigned to the 4th as wingmen were normally junior rank, less experienced F–86 pilots. The probability was high they would remain wingmen for most of their combat tour of one hundred missions because duty with the 4th was a highly coveted assignment, sought by many higher ranking and experienced fighter pilots.

A wingman's job was to fly either number two or number four in a four-ship flight, which was then the standard air combat patrol formation. Each two-ship element cleared for the other, with each wingman clearing for his lead. The flight did not fly in close formation; it flew in a loose, or spread, formation that provided for better attack and defensive maneuvering. It also provided better clearing opportunities for the wingman. A tucked-in wingman, in close formation, can see nothing but his lead. Normally, the flight would break into separate elements in the confusion of a dogfight.

The main attributes of a good wingman are good eyes and the ability to hang with his lead through often violent maneuvers. All pilots have good eyes, but some pilots just see better and must have swivel necks and squinty eyes. Most attacks will come on them from the six o'clock position and out of the sun, if the enemy knows his business. And this is where the wingman should spend most of his time looking, while still holding position on a rapidly maneuvering lead.

This requires skills including the ability to hold formation while near stall speeds at 44,000 feet, split S-ing for an attack, hanging in on square loops and rapid rolls, while still clearing six for the lead.

It would be interesting to study the attrition rate for wingmen compared to that of flight leads . Suffice it to say that the wingman, in combat, is more open and vulnerable to attack than is the flight lead for three reasons. First, he is usually trailing his lead by several hundred yards, purposely, to allow maneuvering room for the lead. As such, the wingman is the closest aircraft to an enemy attacking from the six o'clock position, so he's normally the first aircraft to be fired upon. The second problem is clearance provided by the lead, particularly during a dogfight. If attacking, the lead is normally fixated on the enemy aircraft he is attacking and, unless he is really good, he is not clearing for his wingman. Often a wingman's first indication that his flight is under attack is when a burst of enemy fire goes past his canopy. The third reason is flight lead competence. There are good leads and bad leads, and bad leads lose more wingmen than the good ones do. For example, the day I was shot down, I was the fourth wingman lost by my lead. Good wingmen know potential leads and prefer assignments with the good ones. On occasion, a wingman will be assigned to a "MiG-hungry" lead who has little regard for a wingman or who will use his wingman as bait, if things are slow. In this case, the lead would direct his wingman to hold altitude while he climbed high and positioned himself behind his wingman, hoping a MiG would initiate an attack on the solo wingman, and he, in turn, could attack the attacker.

In summary, a good wingman is one who never loses a lead and one with sufficient discipline not to abandon his lead in order to attack a target of opportunity. This is tough. Wingmen are fighter pilots who, in combat, want to shoot, but they seldom get the chance until their lead runs out of ammunition. A fat target is a terrible temptation.

MiG–15 Versus F–86 Capabilities

A major attribute of the MiG–15 was its excellent engine, an illegal copy of the Rolls-Royce Nene turbojet. This permitted the MiG–15 to climb faster and higher than the F–86, which gave it the tactical advantage of initiating the attack from above the F–86 or, if its pilot did not like the odds, of choosing not to engage. The MiG–15's turning radius was also tighter than the F–86's. This advantage was mitigated, however, by the fact that Russian pilots flying MiGs in Korea had no g-suits, which compromised their ability to hold sustained g's while they were in a dogfight.

A significant advantage that the MiG–15 had over the F–86 was its heavier firepower: two 23-mm guns and one 37-mm cannon. A hit by these weapons caused significant damage. The F–86 with its six .50-cal. machine guns had to get significantly closer and score more hits to do equivalent damage. It frustrated many an F–86 pilot to score hits on a MiG only to watch it climb away.

The F–86 could outdive the MiG–15, and it possessed a radar-ranging gunsight. The F–86 outperformed its adversary in the regime from 40,000 feet down to the deck. It did not carry missiles, but, as in World War II, the F–86 could get close to an enemy, aim the aircraft, and fire lead bullets. Most air-to-air combat broke down to individual two-ship elements. All in all, the MiG–15 and F–86 were equivalent performers below 25,000 feet, with the greater kill ratio of the F–86 due to superior training and tactics.

The Korean Air War

AVM W. "Paddy" Harbison

As a member of the 4th Fighter Group based at K–14, Kimpo, in Korea, I was one among many other British citizens who were significantly involved in the Korean War from the outset. The Army and the Royal Navy (RN) were the main players. The role of the Royal Air Force (RAF) was limited, by comparison. The British Army contingent was central in the Commonwealth Division, and the RN was involved from the very beginning of hostilities.

The RN operated and maintained light fleet aircraft carriers on a rotational basis in Korean waters, in addition to supporting surface units. The carrier's aircraft complement were piston-engine Sea Furies and Fulmars. A Sea Fury destroyed a MiG–15 in one engagement.

The RAF rotated three Sunderland flying-boat squadrons through Iwakani from Singapore, and these did valuable service in the maritime role. The RAF Transport Command, in conjunction with the Canadians and Australians, provided logistical support to the Commonwealth forces. The RAF provided air support and medical evacuation back to the United Kingdom via Hong Kong and Singapore, a lengthy trip by any measure.

Two RAF air observation flights operated with the British Army to provide gun spotting, reconnaissance information, and liaison flights. Because the U.S. Air Force had a critical shortage of photo interpreters, the RAF supplied personnel and the requisite facilities in the theater.

Like the USAF, indeed like all participants, the RAF had suffered a considerable drawdown after World War II. United Kingdom forces, in particular the RAF, was at full strength in Malaya due to the communist confrontation and the need to defend the Hong Kong base. Too, the United Kingdom considered it paramount to increase Cold War vigilance in Europe, and the United States endorsed its position.

Korea was the first jet-versus-jet air war, and RAF interest was intense. The fighter fraternity deplored the lack of RAF combat involvement. Events were to confirm that our then frontline fighter, the Meteor, would have been outmatched and outperformed by the MiG–15.

Coalition Air Warfare

I was on the staff of the Central Fighter Establishment (CFE) at RAF West Raynham in 1951, having gone there on return from an exchange tour with the USAF 1st Fighter Group based at March Air Force Base (AFB), California. The 1st Group had introduced the F–86 into the U.S. air operational inventory, and I had the privilege and indeed good luck to fly it from February 1949 on. The CFE was the center of RAF fighter expertise and was involved in the development of tactics and equipment. It was a mini Nellis AFB, and the RAF Day Fighter Leaders course was an equivalent to the U.S. Top Gun course. Members of the Tactics Branch at CFE were anxious to get first-hand information on Korean air operations, and after the RAF chief of the air staff approached him, Gen. Hoyt S. Vandenberg, the USAF chief of staff, agreed to to send four CFE pilots to observe and report on Korean air operations. Wing Commander John Baldwin, a World War II ace and noted tactician, was the senior pilot, I was a squadron leader, and Flight Lieutenants. Brian Sprague and Rex Knight were the other two pilots.

Conversion to the F–86 involved three flights with the 81st Tactical Fighter Wing at Bentwaters. I was given two flights because I was already experienced on the aircraft. Flying hours at Bentwaters at that time were in short supply.

Preparation before departure for Korea is a story in itself. Outfitted with the latest RAF flying gear, we set off via Singapore. After checking in with the USAF authorities in Tokyo, we were taken by air transport to K–13 at Suwon where we were split up and assigned to four different squadrons. Flight Lieutenant Sprague and I went to the 4th Fighter Group at Kimpo. Baldwin and Knight went to the 51st Fighter Group at Suwon. I was assigned to the 335th Tactical Fighter Squadron and, because of my previous F–86 background, quickly completed the very useful Clobber College, the short course used to acquaint personnel new to Korea on tactics and survival training.

As a point of interest, although I was by any standard experienced on the F–86, I soon found out that, here, the F–86 was flown to its limits and much closer to the edge of the envelope than I had experienced. When I completed Clobber College, I found myself in the cockpit of an F–86, flying missions and observing the air war along the Yalu River, arguably the best seat in the house.

In addition, my previous exchange tour at March AFB proved invaluable because I not only knew the system, I met at least thirty people whom I had known previously, mostly former pilots of the 1st Group. On quickly graduating to element leader status, I was fortunate indeed to have Mike De Armond fly my wing. He was a handsome young second lieutenant and, like many of his colleagues, fearless. You have heard him speak and mention his ordeal as a prisoner of war.

Wing Commander Baldwin went missing on a weather reconnaissance on March 13, and to my horror it fell to me to produce the required report. Quite apart from the loss of a fine RAF officer, I was now in the hot seat with more to do than enjoy the missions. The air operations at Kimpo and Suwon were aimed at gaining and holding air superiority to enable the fighter-bombers to operate unopposed. It was a very personal conflict, with the enemy operating from the Antung clutch of airfields just across the Yalu versus the five F–86 squadrons, three at Kimpo and two at Suwon.

Time does not permit a long discussion on tactics; however, tactics evolved to counter those of the MiG pilots. It was suspected, but not 100 percent confirmed at the time, that the MiGs were in the main flown by Russian pilots. Their operations were cyclical. They would start simply and become more aggressive as they gained experience. I refer here to the time frame of early 1952, from February on.

The F–86 and the MiG–15 were closely matched in terms of performance. The MiG could reach a higher altitude than could the F–86, thereby dictating when its pilot wished to engage. Communist and U.N. pilots both enjoyed advantages. The MiGs were operating over their own territory and enjoyed relative sanctuary across the Yalu in Manchuria. They were under close radar control. The F–86 pilots, on the other hand, had no discreet radar control, and the Mark I eyeball, plus intelligence, was the only warning we had on the MiG formations. The F–86 pilots were also at maximum distance from their bases in South Korea.

The United Nations had control of the seas around the battle area and stood a good chance of rescuing downed airmen if the coast could be reached. The MiGs did not normally operate beyond the coast. The rationale was for their pilots to avoid capture and not be picked up by U.N. forces, and thus not reveal their identities. This has since been confirmed by published Russian reports on their operations in the Korean War. Some MiG pilots were very capable, but, in general, the F–86 pilots performed much better. The main difficulty was to get scheduled for a mission, such was the competition to fly.

Despite the limited runway capacity at Kimpo, missions were flown that under peacetime flight safety rules would have limited the numbers considerably. Dead-stick landings by F–86s with no remaining fuel were accommodated. The g-suit and the URC4 radio were invaluable; pilots who were shot down could talk to their rescue forces while still in their parachute and on the ground. Some forty-two RAF pilots flew with the USAF, and thirty-two flew with Number 77 Royal Australian Air Force (RAAF) Squadron. No. 77 was equipped with Meteors and operated in the ground-attack role from Kimpo. The RAF lost ten pilots, four with the USAF and six with No. 77 Squadron. The Royal Navy lost thirty-four. The Sunderland flying-boat squadrons lost eighteen in weather-related accidents. (These figures are approximate.) The CFE report on the F–86 versus the MiG–15 became available under the thirty-year rule and, given that it was produced some fifty years ago, has proved to be remarkably accurate. My conclusion was that, given the numerical advantage and the superior altitude performance of the MiG–15, the answer to the 8-

to-1 or 10-to-1 ratio that was claimed was inescapable: better training and more aggressive pilots. The difference was the human element. Had the MiGs been more aggressive, the results could well have been different.

Aces and –86s: The Fight for Air Superiority during the Korean War

Kenneth P. Werrell

U.S. airmen won air superiority during World War II against two competent foes. Although both had numerical, technical, and pilot advantages early in the conflict, the Army Air Forces (AAF) and the Navy overcame these, seized air superiority, and permitted air power to play a major role in winning the war. Five years later, initial U.S. air operations in Korea were relatively easy as American fighters, mostly piston-powered, quickly cleared North Korean aircraft from the skies.

The air war dramatically changed in November 1950, however, when the communists introduced the jet-powered MiG–15, which outclassed USAF aircraft. These Soviet jets rendered obsolete both the best bomber (the Boeing B–29 Superfortress) and arguably the best fighter (the North American P–51 Mustang) of World War II, as well as the first USAF operational jet-powered fighter, the Lockheed F–80 Shooting Star.[1] The Korean air war is probably best remembered as the first in which jet aircraft squared off against each other. On November 1, 1950, six communist jets attacked American aircraft but caused no damage. A week later, about four miles south of the Yalu River, eight MiG–15s attacked four American F–80s. The USAF claimed one communist fighter destroyed, the first victory of one jet over another.[2]

In fact, the first kill may actually have come later. Communist records indicate no losses during the day of the first USAF MiG claim; according to their records, the first MiG loss came on November 10, shot down by a U.S. Navy Grumman F9F Panther.[3] In any case, neither the F9F nor the F–80 was to become the chief MiG killer; that distinction fell to the North American F–86 Sabre.

In May 1945, the AAF accepted a North American Aviation aircraft design for a straight-wing, jet-powered fighter. Meanwhile, the company's engineers found American and German research that indicated the possibility for attaining higher speed by sweeping back the wing's leading edge. In November, the AAF approved the manufacturer's proposal to sweep the wings back 35 degrees, a change that added 70 mph to the aircraft's top speed, although it probably delayed the aircraft's operational debut by a year. The fighter made its first flight in October 1947, set a world speed record of 669 mph in September 1948, and went into squadron service in May 1949.[4]

The Soviets were making comparable progress. They also benefited from German research, but even more so from the British government which sold them their best jet engine, allowing them to overcome a major technical deficiency. Answering Joseph Stalin's call for a high-performance interceptor to counter American strategic bombers, the Mikoyan–Guryevich bureau (named after designers Artrem Mikoyan and Mikhail Gurevich) got the MiG–15 airborne for the first time in December 1947, only a few months after the maiden flight of an F–86. By March 1948, Stalin ordered the MiG–15 into production.[5]

The Sabre and the MiG had a similar appearance with nose-engine intakes and swept-back wings and tails. The MiG was 25 percent lighter and about 10 percent smaller than the F–86. The MiG was powered by an engine of equal thrust and held the advantage in climb, acceleration, and ceiling compared to the American fighter. Simple, rugged, and reliable, the Soviet jet mounted one 37-mm and two 23-mm guns consistent with its antibomber mission. In contrast, the Sabre mounted the AAF's World War II standard armament of six .50-cal. machine guns that spewed out smaller bullets but at a much faster rate. Compared to the Soviet fighter, the American aircraft was a bit faster at altitude, could fly farther, dive faster, and had better pilot visibility. Some disagreement exists over which of the two could turn tighter, but the Sabre was an easier plane to fly and control, and it could transit more quickly from one maneuver to another. In contrast, the Soviet machine proved to be heavy on the controls, demonstrated directional instability at high speeds, and was prone to unintentional spins at high altitudes. The MiG–15 also had a slower roll rate than did the F–86, and its canopy defrosting was inadequate as well, both considerable disadvantages in air-to-air combat. In summary, the MiG–15 had a definite edge over the Sabre (–86As and –86Es) above 35,000 feet, enjoyed a marginal advantage from that altitude to 25,000 feet, and was about equal in performance below 20,000 feet. American pilots rated the MiG–15 a tricky aircraft for mediocre pilots to fly, but an effective one for experts.[6] An American general who flew the MiG after the war called it a "beautiful flying machine."[7] Perhaps the most authoritative opinion on the Soviet fighter was that of test pilot Chuck Yeager who tested early F–86s and got to fly a MiG–15 shortly after the end of the war. In his memoirs, he details its faults, chiefly that it was not "an honest aircraft," meaning that it got into dangerous maneuvers without warning. The MiG–15, he noted, was a "quirky aircraft that killed a lot of its pilots."[8]

American pilots described the F–86 as a forgiving, hot aircraft, with some calling it the finest U.S. fighter ever made. The Sabre was a stable gun platform with a superior gunsight. It was also a pretty aircraft, in the tradition of the P–51

Mustang, and pilots put great stock in an aircraft's looks.[9] One pilot, credited with destroying nine MiGs, said, "there never was an airplane so beautiful, dependable, maneuverable, and deadly when in the right hands."[10] No one speaks ill of the Sabre.

When the MiG–15 first appeared, no F–86s were in the theater. Within days of the first MiG engagement, however, the USAF ordered one wing of Sabres to deploy to Korea. The 4th Fighter Interceptor Wing flew its first mission over North Korea on December 15. Two days later an F–86 downed a MiG–15, the first kill of many. F–86 pilots were almost always outnumbered in the air-to-air battles. Allied intelligence estimated that the communists had hundreds of MiGs in the area, many times the number of F–86s.[11] Sabre–MiG duels occurred generally in northwestern North Korea, which became known as MiG Alley.

This air battle proved to be different from World War II fighter combat in several ways. First, jet combat was fought at higher speeds and altitudes than had been customary in the previous war. Second, air-to-air combat was briefer and missions were shorter due to higher air speeds and fuel consumption. Third, politics played a significant role in Korea, unlike conditions in World War II. American airmen decried the fact that decision makers ordered American pilots to fly only on the Korean side of the border and forbade hot pursuit of communist aircraft. The fact that the communist air forces were based just across the river, and U.S. pilots could observe their takeoffs and landings, only added to American frustrations. Unlike in World War II, when the airmen won air superiority by bombing enemy aircraft factories, destroying aircraft on the ground, and engaging in air-to-air combat, only air-to-air combat was used in Korea because of geography and politics.

On the other hand, several continuities in fighter combat can be noted between the Korean War and World War II. Fighter-to-fighter engagements were again quick-maneuvering battles fought at close range. Surprise, initiative, training, and aggressiveness continued to be major factors in successful air-to-air combat. As in World War II, a few pilots downed a disproportionate number of enemy aircraft. In the end, pilot skill proved more important than technological advantage.

During World War II, the AAF, with its greater number of superior piston-powered aircraft and better-trained pilots, defeated the Luftwaffe.[12] In the Korean conflict, the USAF may have been at a disadvantage with respect to its aircraft inventory, but it had a greater advantage with respect to its pilot training. We know little about the Soviet pilots except that a number had World War II experience and some were aces. In general, however, both they and their Chinese and North Korean comrades exhibited mediocre flying and tactics in air-to-air combat. The Soviet policy of rotating entire units in and out of combat proved inferior to the American method of rotating individuals within the units.

Overall, U.S. pilots were more skilled than their foes. A number of the American pilots had seen action in World War II. Eleven of the 38 USAF aces in

Korea had claimed victories in World War II, and 48 of the 424 pilots who posted kills in Korea had also scored in World War II.[13] Just more than 25 percent of the pilots who flew with the 4th Fighter Group had earned their wings during World War II.[14] When the 4th arrived in Korea, it had a high proportion of combat veterans—eleven were World War II aces—but this gradually declined as pilots completed their hundred-mission tours and rotated home. As early as December 1951, unit commanders complained that a significant number of replacement pilots had no F–86 experience. This was exacerbated in May 1952 when twenty-one pilots from the 18th Fighter Bomber Group transferred to the 4th and none had much, if any, experience flying jets. In September 1952, approximately 95 percent of the pilot replacements were recent graduates with perhaps 350 total flying hours and 100 to 140 hours in jets. In April 1953, the 4th Fighter Group commander noted that most of the new pilots assigned to the unit had fewer than 500 hours total flying time. One change that moderated this lack of flying time was better training at the newly formed Combat Crew Training Course at Nellis AFB, Nevada. There, Korean veterans gave the new pilots better preparation for combat than had been the case previously.[15]

For all its stellar features and overall record, the Sabre did encounter some problems. At first the landing gear, especially the nose gear, gave everyone fits. The engine and fuel system also proved troublesome.[16] Another recurring problem was the radar-ranging computer gunsight that quickly replaced the World War II computer gunsight on the first F–86As arriving in Korea. It promised greater results because one of the most common pilot gunnery errors was to open fire at too great a distance, a practice that resulted in poor accuracy and wasted ammunition, and even warned the prey of impending attack. Unfortunately, the device proved troublesome as maintenance problems surfaced in mid-1951 and continued for about a year despite a priority effort to fix them. Frustrated pilots tended to doubt the equipment, leading some to cage (disable) the radar and gyro inputs, which reduced the device to a fixed sight. Some pilots used tracer ammunition for sighting, a crude and useful technique but also one that could warn the intended target of an attack if the enemy pilot spotted tracers passing by. As late as February 1952, the Fifth Air Force director of operations complained that the sight was too complicated to be maintained properly.[17]

Both the manufacturer and the Air Force sent teams to work out the problems, which eventually were resolved. Better training for the pilots also helped, but the process was not easy. In summer 1952, fourteen Korean War aces met with Gen. Hoyt S. Vandenberg, Air Force chief of staff, and recommended removing the radar-ranging feature and returning to a manual sight. The primary complaint was that the sight's unreliability rendered it nothing more than 200 pounds of surplus weight. The older pilots were more critical of the gunsight than were the recent graduates of flying school. Col. Francis Gabreski, credited with 6.5 kills in Korea and 28 in World War II, remarked "I just stick a piece of chewing gun on my windscreen and use that as a sight."[18]

This meeting in September 1952 prompted General Vandenberg to direct both the Fifth Air Force and the Air Proving Ground Command to investigate the problem. The latter used six Korean War aces and two of its own pilots to test radar-ranging and manual-ranging sights. From these trials, the command concluded that the radar sights had twice the kill probability of nonradar sights. It recommended that the reliability of the sighting systems, particularly the radar, be improved. Fifth Air Force brought together its current aces in September 1952 to discuss the gunsight problem. They wanted to keep the computing sight, reasoning that most of the MiG kills were from short range and minimum deflection due to the limited range of its .50-cal. guns, whereas future armament would allow combat at longer ranges and greater deflection. They also noted that, although experienced pilots could do well with manual sights, as Gabreski's comment and record made clear, this was not true of younger pilots. The theater command, Far East Air Forces, stuck with the more advanced gunsight.[19]

Malfunctioning gunsights continued to present a problem. When the F–86F came into service in August 1952, it had a new gunsight as well as the same old problems of poor reliability, parts shortages, and high maintenance. It took the system about four months to adjust to the new equipment; nevertheless, during the last five months of the war, the gunsight malfunctioned on 13 percent of the F–86 sorties.

Another problem was that the sights had been designed to engage slow and nonmaneuvering bombers, not fast and vigorously maneuvering fighters at close range. Thus, the sights tended to be oversensitive in dogfights. The Air Proving Ground developed the Jenkins Limiter to reduce the sensitivity of the sight at long range and give the pilot a visual indication when the target was within a preselected maximum firing range. A postwar report stated that the computing sight evinced only a small advantage; at best "it is difficult to contend that these data show superiority for the computing sight as used in F–86 vs. MiG–15."[20]

Whereas difficulties with the new and sophisticated gunsight might have been anticipated, Air Force problems with an older and far simpler technology, that of drop tanks, is less understandable. The Air Force encountered several difficulties with the external tanks, the most frequent and serious being failure to release properly. The tanks created drag, costing 25–50 mph in airspeed, depending on altitude. Consequently, it became policy to abort the mission if both tanks did not release prior to combat. In December 1950, for example, approximately 7 percent of the tanks failed to release. This is remarkable because drop tanks are a simple technology and had been used extensively in World War II. The problem was due partly to poor field conditions, such as storage and service in the open which allowed moisture to enter the shackles and subsequently freeze at altitude. By July 1951, the USAF solved this problem by adjusting the shackles and using a compound to prevent moisture from entering the device.[21]

Another part of the problem resulted from the poor supply of drop tanks in early 1952, forcing fighters to fly with only one drop tank. (The USAF contributed to this problem by converting a second unit, the 51st Fighter Interceptor Wing, to F–86s in late 1951.) The need for more tanks, as soon as possible, compelled the USAF to use a number of manufacturers who produced nonstandardized, reduced-quality tanks. The positive aspects were that the numbers of drop tanks increased, and the unit price per tank each fell.[22]

Additionally, after being jettisoned, sometimes the tanks flew back into the aircraft's wing, damaging the aircraft. This problem was solved in the field by riveting a small piece of sheet metal on the top of the tank so that, when it dropped, aerodynamic forces pushed it down, away from the aircraft.

The USAF also had to overcome parts and maintenance problems that, in January 1952, accounted for the grounding of 45 percent of the F–86s. By March, through extraordinary means (going out of channels), the airmen largely solved these problems. Hoarding of parts was another problem until strong leadership came to bear.[23]

The airmen took several measures to enhance the Sabre's performance. They increased its climb performance by installing small pieces of steel inside the tailpipe which increased exhaust temperatures and, along with disabled throttle stops, permitted overboosting the engine. Although this made tailpipe temperatures and engine rpm more critical and decreased engine life, these modifications allowed the pilot to have 100 percent power to 45,000 feet, which was otherwise impossible.[24]

The USAF investigated other measures to allow full-thrust operations at higher altitudes. One method adjusted the tailpipe nozzle area and changed the fuel spray pattern, producing 15 percent more thrust at 35,000 feet. However, the wear on the engine was judged too great to be practical for operations in Korea because of marginal logistical support. The USAF considered water-alcohol injection at high altitudes, a method already used to boost power on takeoff. The airmen rejected the scheme because of a half-ton weight penalty.[25]

The USAF tested another engine-boost program in combat in mid-1952 with five or six F–86Fs. The Air Force fitted each fighter with three rocket boosters that produced additional power for brief periods to increase speed in a climbing turn by 20 knots. Airmen dropped the scheme by the end of the year because the booster weight of 600 pounds before use and 450 pounds afterward made the fighter tail-heavy and induced a porpoising oscillation at 35,000 feet.[26]

From January through May 1953, another project, Gun-Val, tested heavier armament on the F–86. The Sabre's .50-cal. machine guns were generally ineffective beyond 1,000 feet, and the angle of a tail attack rendered only 6 percent to 10 percent of the bullets capable of destroying a MiG. The MiGs, and jets in general, were less vulnerable to gunfire than were piston-powered fighters with their large propellers and complicated engines. Further, combat at high altitude nullified the .50-cal. armor-piercing incendiary projectiles that had proved so effective during World War II. In addition, jet fuel (kerosene) was less volatile than high-octane gasoline. The project replaced the standard armament of eight F–86Fs, swapping the six .50-cal. guns for four 20-mm guns.[27]

Although the range and impact of the 20-mm gun was greater than that of the .50 cal. weapon, installation of the 20-mm guns brought a number of disadvantages. First, the limited load of 20-mm ammunition gave the pilot only 4.6 seconds of firepower, compared with 15 seconds with the .50s. Second, the 20-mm installation weighed 230 pounds more than the .50-cal. arrangement. The most serious problem was that, during the tests in Korea, gases from the 20-mm guns caused twenty engine compressor stalls and the loss of two Sabres. One source states that the solution was to weld shut the gun doors and drill four holes to relieve the pressure. An Air Force source writes that the USAF installed a selector switch to allow the pilot to fire two guns until they were out of ammunition and then fire the other two, thus reducing the volume of gun gases and doubling the duration of fire.

How well did the 20-mm guns perform? The Air Force credited Gun-Val aircraft with the destruction of six MiGs during 284 air-to-air missions.[28] To some degree, Gun-Val was not a fair comparison with the standard F–86s because its pilots had more than the average experience, and included several aces.[29] These pilots were also given more latitude than that given other pilots: they were allowed to fly at their own pace and pick the days and times that gave them a better than average chance of engaging MiGs. As a result, they spotted MiGs on half their sorties, compared to the overall average of one-third. The evaluators concluded that the 20-mm rounds were 2.8 times as lethal as the .50-cal. rounds but that the system was not "strikingly more effective than the .50s." The pilots, however, disliked both the limited time of fire and the compressor stall problem.[30] The USAF planned to mount 20-mm guns on the F–86F, but this was not accomplished until later in the series, on the –86H that did see service in the war.[31]

The USAF used three F–86 models in the Korean War: –86As, –86Es, and –86Fs. The –86E was essentially the same as the –86A except it was 565 pounds heavier and had a power-operated, movable, horizontal tail. The controls were fully powered, giving the pilot much better control, which especially improved handling at high speeds (above Mach 0.9). Because the USAF had so few F–86s, General Vandenberg was reluctant to commit more to the war, but the grave situation forced his hand. In October 1951, he ordered the Air Defense Command to send seventy-five F–86Es to Korea, and they entered combat on December 1.[32]

The USAF deployed the F–86F to Korea in mid-1952. It was the ultimate air superiority model. Heavier by 700 pounds than the –86E, its engine produced 15 percent more thrust, more than compensating for the extra weight. The –86F also mounted 200-gallon drop tanks instead of the previously used 120-gallon ones.[33] The most important innovation in the F–86F, however, was its modified wing. The original F–86 had leading-edge slats that extended at low airspeeds to increase the wing area and camber of the wing. The increased area improved lift and, consequently, lowered takeoff, approach, and landing speeds, thus making takeoffs and landings easier and safer. The tradeoff was that the slats increased drag and reduced performance at high speeds. North American suggested modifying the leading edge to a solid one. A further change extended the leading edge of the wing six inches at the fuselage and three inches at the wing tip. The 6-3 wing, as it was called, increased wing area from 288 square feet to 302 square feet. These wing modifications increased the aircraft's speed at sea level by 7 mph; extended its range; increased the ceiling by 4,000 feet, which permitted flight at 52,000 feet; allowed dives up to Mach 1.05; and boosted its rate of climb by almost 300 feet per minute. The Air Force retrofitted these wing changes into the F–86E. Fifty of these conversions were in action by the end of 1952, and the entire F–86 fleet in Korea was converted by the end of the war.[34]

The wing modification, however, had one a disadvantage. The new wing reduced performance at lower altitudes and speeds. More critically, the modification increased the stall speed by about 10 knots and made low-speed stalls more severe, necessitating higher takeoff, approach, and landing speeds. Overall, however, the change was beneficial, for, as one pilot correctly noted, "the air war is not won in the traffic pattern."[35] The bottom line was that the F–86F with the 6-3 wing and boosted engine thrust achieved equivalent performance with the MiG in all categories except acceleration and climb.[36]

By the end of 1952, the USAF had replaced the F–86As with –86Es and –86Fs. This upgrade helps explain how the USAF increased its combat advantage over the MiGs as the war progressed. The withdrawal of Soviet units was clearly another factor. During the last three months of the war, the USAF claimed 164 victories in air-to-air combat at a cost of only four of its own—an amazing 41-to-1 ratio. In these three months of action (10 percent of jet combat), the USAF scored 20 percent of its victories and suffered 5 percent of its air-to-air losses.[37] The overall Air Force MiG claim in air-to-air combat for the war was approximately 792 MiG–15s downed by the F–86s at a cost of 79 Sabres.[38] This was quite a record, but these numbers are based entirely on U.S. documentation.

Although examination of communist records promises to clarify the Korean air-to-air war, these records thus far only confound the researcher. The Soviets claim between 594 and 650 F–86s destroyed in battle, and the Chinese and North Koreans another 211 to 330, a total somewhere between 805 and 980.[39] The USAF initially admitted to losing as few as 58 F–86s in air-to-air combat, but they later boosted this to 79. In addition the Air Force lists between 26 and 38 as lost to unknown causes. Surely some of these, if not most, were lost to MiGs. Another USAF source lists 175 F–86s lost to enemy action, which would include ground fire. Therefore, Sabre air-to-air losses were probably in the range of 100 to 150, a far cry from the 600-plus the Russians claim killed and the 300 or so claimed by the Chinese and North Koreans.[40] An example of Soviet overclaims is that, in December 1950, the first month of F–86 operations over Korea, the

Soviets claim eleven to fourteen Sabres destroyed. That month the USAF lost but one F–86 in aerial combat.[41]

On their part, the American airmen claimed 841 MiGs destroyed in the air, with 792 claimed by the F–86s.[42] The Soviets admit losing 335 to 345 aircraft and from 120 to more than 200 pilots, and the Chinese acknowledge 224 to 271 MiGs.[43] Although U.S. records make distinctions of their losses to various causes (MiGs, antiaircraft artillery, accidents), thus far we have no similar breakdowns from the communists. Certainly there are definition problems, such as how does one credit an aircraft that runs out of fuel after engaging in combat? Until historians can carefully examine and analyze communist records, we are forced to conclude that the communists clearly and grossly overclaimed their kills, just as Sabre pilots likely overclaimed MiG kills as well, although perhaps to a lesser extent.

Another issue that Soviet records raise is that of numbers. It was widely believed, then and now, that the communists had a vast numerical superiority in the air-to-air battle. Again, part of the problem lies in definitions. Certainly they had more fighters in the theater: more than 500 against 75 until late 1951, and more than 700 versus 150 for the remainder of the war. It also appears that more MiGs took to the air than did Sabres. But the numbers of fighters that actually engaged in combat is another matter. A 1970 USAF study (that used figures from July 1951 through the end of the war) shows a USAF numerical advantage of almost two to one, presumably of aircraft engaged in combat. The USAF credits the F–86 with a total of just over 87,000 sorties in the war, most of which were in the air superiority role. In another enumeration, the USAF lists 74,000 sorties flown in the counterair role, 68,000 by the F–86. Communist records indicate about 63,000 Soviet sorties and 22,000 Chinese and North Korean sorties. Until we get accurate daily communist sortie information—and a clear distinction between sorties flown, observed, and engaged—we will be left in confusion over this issue.[44]

Another controversy involving MiG Alley is the matter of U.S. pilots who violated Chinese and Russian territory. At the appearance of MiGs in November 1950, U.S. decision makers considered the concept of hot pursuit. The Joint Chiefs of Staff, Secretaries of Defense and State, and the President all favored granting such permission, but American allies strongly opposed such a policy, fearing an expansion of the war. In deference to the allies, official U.S. policy was to respect the borders of both communist countries.[45] Nevertheless, a number of F–86 pilots believed a hot-pursuit policy did in fact exist, and they certainly acted as if there were such a policy. Sabre commanders such as Francis Gabreski, George Jones, Walker Mahurin, and Harrison Thyng permitted and encouraged crossing the Yalu River, and they did it often themselves. It also appears that top commanders knew of these violations but winked at the practice. The best example of this attitude is that of Gen. Frank Everest, who commanded the Fifth Air Force between May 1951 and June 1952. After admonishing two group commanders for violations of the border, he left the room, and then reentered and stated that, if the pilots were going to violate the order, they should at least turn off their identification, friend or foe devices to make it less obvious.[46]

Sabre pilots crossed the Yalu, engaged MiGs over China, buzzed communist airfields, and downed enemy fighters. Russian sources note that the Americans were constantly crossing the river and destroying MiGs over their own airfields. One report to the Soviet dictator Joseph Stalin in 1952 stated that, during one three-month period, the Soviets lost forty-eight aircraft, twenty-three over their own airfields.[47] The F–86 pilots made a fine distinction in these cross-border flights: they would engage MiGs in the landing pattern, but they would not attack communist aircraft on the ground. To cover these forays, Air Force officers destroyed gun-camera film that indicated action over China, and they also falsified locations of engagements and shootdowns.[48]

From their own testimony and that of others, at least half of the U.S. aces from the Korean War crossed the Yalu River. Three of the top eleven aces (those with ten or more credits) admit crossing the river, and we have testimony that two others did the same. At this point, we have no indication about five of the top aces, but we have secondary evidence that only one (Royal Baker) of the eleven did not cross the Yalu.[49] One F–86 pilot later commented that the high-scorers crossed the Yalu, whereas those with fewer or no kills likely never crossed it. In his words, "There were a lot of airplanes shot down in Korea by guys who took it in their own hands to not necessarily play by the rules."[50]

Apparently only two F–86 pilots were disciplined for violating the border. Joseph McConnell, who ended the war as the top U.S. ace, was grounded for two weeks for crossing the river. Dolph Overton, however, did not fare as well. During a visit to an American radar site located off the coast of North Korea and behind communist lines, he learned where the MiGs gathered to descend for landing. Using this information, he downed five MiGs in four days, all of them across the Yalu River. It was the quickest rise to ace in the war. Unfortunately for him, Swiss diplomats traveling through communist territory saw one of these dogfights and complained. When Overton was asked, the West Pointer admitted he had flown across the border. He was grounded, sent home, temporarily stripped of his medals, threatened with a court martial, given a bad officer's effectiveness report, and even threatened that the five kill credits would be taken away.[51]

Such aggressiveness, however, helps explain how the USAF overwhelmingly defeated the MiG–15 despite inferior numbers, difficult geography, inadequate radar control, and aircraft that were equivalently matched at best. The final FEAF report summarized, "it is believed the ten to one victory ratio of the F–86 over the MiG–15 was gained by superior tactics, well-trained, experienced and aggressive pilots, and a superior armament and fire-control system."[52] Conspicuously absent was any mention of aircraft design and improvement.[53]

The F–86, however, most certainly did not have an advantage in engine, airframe, or armament over the MiG–15, but the Air Force did decrease, if not close, the gap between the two aircraft with its modified F–86F. The airmen had some technological advantages in fielding superior auxiliary equipment, specifically antigravity suits (g-suits) and radar-ranging gunsights. Better cockpit visibility and defrosters, along with a superior control system, also became important advantages.

These facts emphasize that the most significant reason for the lopsided victory-to-loss ratio was not technical; instead, it was the ability, experience, training, and aggressiveness of American fighter pilots. The air war demonstrated the need for a variety of technologies, such as better radar coverage, armament, aircraft, identification, and night-fighting capabilities. Yet, the civilian and military decision makers believed that the Korean War was an anomaly and that the next conflict would be different. Some held that the dogfight, quick maneuvering, and close-in aerial combat were relics of the past. With this in mind, the USAF never equipped its next generation of fighters with guns, instead opting for a full complement of air-to-air missiles. In the 1950s, the USAF also built an impressive number of bombers and fighters designed for nuclear war. But in its next war, in Vietnam, the USAF fought another limited conflict and faced a different combat challenge that made these efforts ineffective, if not counterproductive.

Notes

1. Materials found at the Air University and USAF Historical Research Agency, Maxwell Air Force Base, Ala., are abbreviated AUL and HRA, respectively. Robert Futrell, *The United States Air Force in Korea, 1950–1953* (New York: Duell, Sloan, & Pearce, 1961), pp 51, 64, 66, 83.
2. Warren Thompson, "Fighter Combat over Korea," *Wings of Fame*, vol 1 (1995): 26–27; and Futrell, *USAF in Korea*, pp 207, 211.
3. Ralph Wetterhahn, "The Russians of MiG Alley," *Retired Officer* (Aug 2000): 70–71.
4. John Anderson, *A History of Aerodynamics and Its Impact on Flying Machines* (Cambridge, UK: Cambridge University, 1997), pp 425–28; Marcelle Knaack, *Encyclopedia of U.S. Air Force Aircraft and Missile Systems*, vol.1, *Post–World War II Fighters, 1945–1973* (Washington, D.C.: Office of Air Force History, 1978), pp 53–54; and Stewart Wilson, *Sabre, MiG–15 & Hunter* (Fyswick, Australia: Aerospace, 1995), p 25.
5. Bill Sweetman, "MiGs," in Bernard Fitzsimons, et al., eds, *The Great Book of Modern Warplanes* (New York: Crown, 1987), pp 401–03.
6. United States Air Force Operations in the Korean Conflict, 1 Jul 1952–27 Jul 1953, Historical Study no 127, Jul 1956, 51-52 AUL MU27218-127.
7. USAF oral history interview, Gen Earle Partridge by Thomas A Sturm and Hugh N. Ahmann, Apr 1974, 639 HRA K239.0512–729; USAF oral histo-

ry interview, Col John R. Boyd by Lt Col John N. Dick, Jr., Jan 1977, 141-42 HRA K239.0512–1066; and Robert Dorr, Jon Lake, and Warren Thompson, *Korean War Aces* (London: Osprey, 1975), pp 21–22.

8. Chuck Yeager and Leo Janos, *Yeager: An Autobiography* (Toronto: Bantam, 1985), p 205. The United States captured significant pieces of MiGs during the war as well as briefly examined two Polish MiGs in 1953. AFMC, "Foreign Materiel Exploitation (FME) of MiG–15."
9. A note for nonflyers: there is an old saying among aviators "if it doesn't look good, it can't fly good." A sleek airframe will have cleaner aerodynamic lines and less drag than a more cluttered airframe, and thus better performance. See, for example, Donald Lopez, *Fighter Pilot's Heaven: Flight Testing the Early Jets* (Washington, D.C.: Smithsonian, 1995), p 8.
10. Cecil Foster, "F–86 Sabre," in Robin Higham and Abigail Siddall, eds, *Flying Combat Aircraft of the USAAF–USAF* (Ames: Iowa State University, 1975), p 77. Other pilot comments are from USAF oral history interview, Brig Gen Robinson Risner by Capt Mark C. Cleary, Mar 1983, 12–13 HRA K239.0512–1370; USAF oral history interview, Lt Gen Joseph H. Moore by Capt Mark C. Cleary, Sep 1984, 126–27 HRA K239.0512–1611; and USAF oral history interview, Lt Gen Dale S. Sweat by Capt Mark C. Cleary, Feb 1984, 34 HRA K239.0512–1572. Futrell, *USAF in Korea*, pp 231, 236; P. E. Shanahan, Report on Pilot Interrogations Concerning Fighter Operations in Korea, Nov 1954, 15 AUL M34822-17; Ray Wagner, "MiG–15," *Aerospace Historian* (spring 1988): 46, 48, 51; and Wilson, *Sabre, MiG–15 & Hunter*, pp 89, 93–94, 137–38.
11. Futrell, *USAF in Korea*, pp 232–33, 235, 372; United States Air Force Operations in the Korean Conflict 1 Nov 1950–30 Jun 1952, Historical Study no 72, Jul 1955, 107 AUL MU27218-72; USAF Historical Study no 127, pp 49–50; and Mike Spick, *Jet Fighter Performance, Korea to Vietnam* (London: Ian Allan, 1986), p 154.
12. From 1939 through September 1942, German pilots averaged approximately 245 total flying hours and 80 in combat aircraft; in the period July 1943 through June 1944 this fell to 175 and 25 hours, respectively. During the first period, AAF pilots averaged 200 and just over 50 hours, but 320 and 120 hours during the second. *The United States Strategic Bombing Survey, Over-all Report (European War)*, Sep 1945, p 21.
13. One Navy pilot got five credits at night in a prop-powered fighter. John Bolt, a Marine Corps ace of the war (flying F–86s with the USAF), had downed six Japanese aircraft in Pappy Boyington's famous Black Sheep squadron in World War II. "Two Aces in Korean Air War," *Naval Aviation News* (Sep 1953): 16; and *USAF Credits for the Destruction of Enemy Aircraft Korean War*, Historical Study no 81, 1975.
14. Two units flew mainly air superiority missions, the 4th and later the 51st Fighter Group. Dennis Strawbridge and Nannette Kahn, "Fighter Pilot Per-

formance in Korea," Nov 1955, p 9, 30 AUL M34822-18 1955-10.

15. USAF oral history interview, Col William J. Hovde by Lt Col Gordon F. Nelson, Lt Col John N. Dick, Jr., and Maj Jesse Green, Jan 1977, p 24, 57 HRA K239.0512–1062; Col Royal Baker, "Report on F–86 Operations in Korea," 1 Apr 1953, pp 2–3, HRA K-GP4-Su-Op; 4th Fighter Interceptor Group History, Apr 1952, May 1952, Dec 1952 HRA K-GP4-Hi; 4th Fighter Interceptor Wing History, Mar 1952, p 34, Jul–Dec 1952, 59 HRA K-GP4-Hi; 334 Fighter Squadron History, Dec 1951; and 336 Fighter Squadron History, both in 4th Fighter Interceptor Wing History.
16. The USAF suffered 643 major F–86 accidents through Aug 1, 1953, of which 290 were attributed to material or maintenance failure. Of these, 90 were associated with the engine, 30 with the fuel system, and 60 with the landing gear. The nose wheel did not operate properly on the Sabre's first flight, and half of the first ten accidents involved the landing gear.
17. USAF Historical Study no 72, p 119.
18. History Air Research and Development Command, Jan–Dec 1953, vol 1, 494 HRA K243.01; USAF Historical Study no 72, pp 119–20.
19. USAF Historical Study no 72, p 120.
20. John Wester, "Effectiveness of the Gunsight," pp 68, 67, in University of Chicago, Institute for Air Weapons Research, "F–86 vs. MiG–15: A Digest of the Briefing on the Analysis of the Korean Air War," May 1954 AUL 34822-14a; Baker, "Report on F–86 Operations in Korea," p 6; FEAF Report on the Korean War, vol 1, pp 11–12 HRA 168.7104-52; USAF Historical Study no 72, p 119; and USAF Historical Study no 127, pp 64–66.
21. Two 120-gallon tanks on the F–86A. Air Proving Ground, "Letter Report on Relative Aerial Combat of the F–84E versus the F–86A Capability, " Jan 1951 DTIC AD-B971840; and USAF Historical Study no 72, p 123.
22. The tanks were originally designed for ferry missions and cost $750 each. By the end of the war, the Japanese were building the tanks for $185 each. FEAF Korean War Report, p 15; and USAF oral history interview, Maj Gen John Giraudo by Hugh N. Ahmann, Jan 1985, pp 92–93, HRA K239.0512–1630.
23. Larry Davis, *MiG Alley* (Carrollton, Tex.: Squadron/Signal, 1978), p 25; and USAF oral history interview, Gen Frank Everest by Lt Col John N. Dick, Jr., Aug 1977, pp 192–93 HRA K239.0512–957.
24. Giraudo interview, pp 92–93; and Historical Study no 127, p 67. See "F–86 Correspondence" documents, no 203, 238, 239, 366, and 256. HRA K202.1-57.
25. USAF Historical Study no 127, p 67.
26. Dorr, *Korean War Aces*, pp 64–66; USAF Historical Study no 72, p 121; and USAF Historical Study no 127, 67–68.
27. USAF Historical Study no 127, pp 63–64.
28. This sortie-to-kill ratio of 47:1 is almost twice that of the overall F–86 ratio

of 86:1.

29. Vermont Garrison—7.5 in World War II and 10 MiGs; George Jones—6.5 MiGs; and Lonnie Moore—10 MiGs.
30. The report concluded that improved 20-mm fuzes and greater high-explosive content (215 grams vs the existing 110 grams) would further increase the advantage of the 20-mm gun. Davis, *MiG Alley*, p 55; Clayton Thomas, "The Searching and Positioning Phase," p 25; and George Morgenthaler, "Comparison of Two Fighter Armaments Used in Korea," pp 57–66, both in Institute for Air Weapons Research, "F–86 vs. MiG–15 Digest"; FEAF Report on Korean War, vol 2, pp 173–74; USAF Historical Study no 127, p 64.
31. Directorate, Procurement and Industrial Planning: Jan–Jun 1951, Aircraft Section AFMC R1-645.1a.
32. Ray Wagner, *American Combat Planes* (Garden City, NY: Doubleday, 1982), p 417; hqs 4th Fighter Interceptor Group: F–86E Combat Evaluation, 1 Nov 1951 HRA K-Wg-4-Hi (Oct 51); 1953 ARDC History, 496; and USAF Historical Study no 72, pp 88–89.
33. Dorr, *Korean War* Aces, p 61; Knaack, *Post–World War II Fighters*, p 61; and Far Eastern Air Forces (FEAF), Report on Korea, draft, vol 2, sec 1, 14 HRA K720.041.
34. Knaack, *Post–World War II Fighters*, pp 59, 62; Davis, *MiG Alley*, p 60; Futrell, *USAF in Korea*, p 476; Baker, "Report on F–86 Operations," pp 5, 14; USAF Historical Study no 127, p 68; and Ray Wagner, *The North American Sabre* (Garden City, NY: Doubleday, 1963), pp 57–58.
35. USAF Historical Study no 72, 121–22; and USAF Historical Study no 127, p 68.
36. USAF Historical Study no 127, p 68.
37. FEAF Report on Korean War, vol 2, p 5; and Knaack, *Post–World War II Fighters*, p 55.
38. USAF Historical Study no 81, pp 46–47; Korean Air War Summary: 25 Jun 1950-27 Jul 1953, 12,15 HRA K720.04D-1; FEAF Report on Korean War, vol 2, p 5; USAF Statistical Digest, FY 1953, 53 HRA K134.11-6; and USAF Historical Study no 72.
39. Soviet claims are from Stephen Sewell, "Russian Claims from the Korean War 1950–53: The 1059 Document," Internet, available at www.koreanwar.com/sovietunion.html; Hans Seidl, *Stalin's Eagles* (Atglen, Pa.: Schiffer, 1998), p 245; Vladimir Babycia, "MiG's in Local Conflicts," Internet, available at www.aeronautics.ru. Chinese claims are from William Y'Blood, *MiG Alley: The Fight for Air Superiority* (Washington, D.C.: Air Force History and Museums Program, 2000), p 44; Seidl, *Stalin's Eagles,* p 245; Sergey Uskov, "On Guard For Peace and Labor," *Mir Aviatsii*; Duncan Curtis, *North American F–86 Sabre* (Ramsbury, UK: Crowood, 2000), p 80; and Jon Halliday, "Air Operations in Korea: The Soviet Side of the Story,"

in William Williams, ed, *A Revolutionary War: Korea and the Transformation of the Postwar World* (Chicago: Imprint, 1993), pp 167–49.

40. Futrell, *USAF in Korea*, p 649; USAF Statistical Digest FY 1951, p 199; USAF Statistical Digest FY 1952, p 186; and USAF Statistical Digest FY 1953, p 218. Overall, the USAF lost 218–246 Sabres to all causes (MiGs, AAA, operational, and nonoperational causes) in the Korean War. Analysis of unit records and Department of Defense, Defense Prisoner of War/Missing Personnel Office, Korean War Resources, and KORWALD Reports database (Internet: www.dtic.mil/dpmo/pmkor/korwald afct.htm). F–86 casualty figures support an estimate of USAF F–86 air-to-air losses of about 100. The most recent figures list a total of 54 pilots dead, 26 returned prisoners, and 40 rescued. Of these 120 pilots, 22 were lost to antiaircraft artillery or operational causes. KORWALD Reports and 4th Fighter Group and 51st Fighter Group unit histories. Another set of data indicates that 175 F–86s were lost to "enemy action" during the Korean War. This includes losses to antiaircraft artillery as well as aircraft that made it home but were written off as "beyond economic repair." "USAF Aircraft Losses by Cause," USAF Statistical Digest, FY 1951, p 199; FY 1952, p 186; and FY 1953, p 218.
41. Sewell, "Russian Claims"; Mark O'Neil, "The Other Side of the Yalu: Soviet Pilots in the Korean War. Phase One: 1 November 1950–12 April 1951" (Ph.D. dissertation, Florida State University, 1996), pp 144–52; and 4th Fighter Group History.
42. Historical Study no 81, p 47. Earlier sources use slightly lower figures for the Sabres: USAF Statistical Digest, FY 1953, p 20; Futrell, *USAF in Korea;* and FEAF, Report on the Korean War, vol 1, p 12.
43. If the Soviets had the same ratio of aircraft losses to pilot casualties as did the USAF, about 2:1, then these figures are relatively consistent. Halliday, "Air Operations in Korea," pp 150, 167–49; *On Guard*; Seidl, *Stalin's Eagles*, p 245.
44. USAF Statistical Digest, FY 1953, pp 20, 26; USAF Assistant Chief of Staff, Studies and Analysis, "The Relationship between Sortie Ratios and Loss Rates for Air-to-Air Battle Engagements During World War II and Korea: Saber Measures (Charlie)," Sep 1970, 4 AUL MU 42210-75; FEAF, Korean Air War Summary, pp 21, 47; and Wetterhahn, "Russians of MiG Alley," p 72.
45. 82d Congress, 1st sess, Hearings on the Military Situation in the Far East, part 1, pp 399–400, 507, 597; Report of Certain Members of the Joint Armed Services and Foreign Relations Committee of the United States Senate, Apr 1951, 3583 ibid; Gen Jarred Crabb Journal (Nov 2, 1950), frame 0430 USAFA.
46. Dorr, *Korean War Aces*, p 41. The Everest story is from Walker Mahurin, interview with author, May 23, 2000, and his book, *Honest John* (NY: Put-

nam, 1962), pp 88–89.

47. "Report by the Military Ministry of USSR to J. V. Stalin," No. 48321, 28 May 1952 in "Participation by the USSR in the Korean War" (New Documents), Voprosi Istorii 12/94, pp 30–45; and Halliday, "Air Operations in Korea," pp 154–55; and Wetterhahn, "Russians in MiG Alley," p 75.
48. Larry Davis, *The 4th Fighter Wing in the Korean War* (Atglen, Pa.: Schiffer, 2001), p 149; Jack Hayes, *Cavalry Trooper to Fighter Pilot and Three Wars* (Manhattan, Kans.: Sunflower, 1997), p 136; and Mahurin, *Honest John*, pp 72, 83.
49. Author interview with Lt Gen Charles Cleveland, Mar 2000; USAF oral history interview, Gen John A. Roberts by Lt Col Gordon F. Nelson, Lt Col John N. Dick, Jr., and Maj Jesse Green, Feb 10, 1977, 35 HRA K239.512-1076; Capt Joseph McConnell, Internet, available at www.acepilots.com; Giraudo interview, p 98; USAF oral history interview, Col Vermont Garrison by Frederick D. Claypool, Sep 1982, 13 HRA K239.512-1556; Harold Fischer, "Captured," in Eric Hammel, *Aces in Combat: The American Aces Speak*, vol 5 (Pacifica, CA: Pacifica, 1998) p 241; Frederick Blesse, "Check Six" (New York: Ivy, 1987), pp 79, 88; and Joe Foss and Matthew Brennan, *Top Guns* (New York: Pocket, 1991), p 239.
50. Roberts interview, p 28.
51. In short order, Overton resigned from the service. Giraudo interview, p 98; Cleveland 2000 interview; and Dolph Overton, "The Air Force."
52. FEAF Report on Korean War, vol 2, p 16.
53. Two earlier drafts make the same major points; one added, however, that these advantages were "combined with a high quality aircraft of superior aerodynamic qualities, better construction, and a vastly superior fire control system." FEAF Report on Korean War, draft, Feb 1954, 139 HRA 720.04D; and "Evaluation of the Effectiveness of the USAF in Korea," draft, nd, 146 AUL M38486.

Luncheon Address

A Half Century's Retrospective of the Korean War

Adm. James L. Holloway III, U.S. Navy (Ret.)

Korea was a war that America did not expect to fight and, indeed, had no plans for fighting. Nevertheless, it was a war that America had to fight. In the years since, it was known as the forgotten war because, for many, its memories were so bitter. Today, half a century later, viewed from the broader perspective of two generations of Americans, Korea has evolved as one of this nation's more important wars in terms of its long-term effect on American history.

The Korean conflict came at the beginning of a much larger and more desperate struggle that lasted for four decades: the Cold War. Nikita Khrushchev, the leader of our adversary, the Soviet Union, famously pledged "we will bury you."

The USSR possessed an enormous army, numbering two hundred active divisions against twelve of the United States. Clearly, the Soviets had the capability to overwhelm Western Europe. With their nuclear arsenal roughly equivalent to ours, they had the capacity to inflict eighty million casualties on our population and literally destroy our industrial economy.

The communist plan was to take what they wanted in Europe and Asia while daring us to use our nuclear weapons to defend our allies. The Soviet strategy was to use its surrogate armies to fight the war and posture their own forces to threaten an escalation to general war.

As mentioned, the United States was woefully unprepared for the war in Korea, and our choices were few and difficult. The first choice was to do nothing, to abandon our allies and our integrity, and await our inevitable defeat. The second was to react with nuclear weapons, spark a nuclear holocaust, and participate in the mutual destruction of the civilized world. The third was to fight the Soviet's surrogates with our own conventional forces and depend upon our citizen armies to defeat the communist aggressions wherever they might erupt.

Of course, the United States chose this third strategy of conventional warfare. It was the only honorable recourse. In Korea, in July 1950, America drew the line in the sand and fought.

The first year of the war reflected America's lack of preparedness as well as the resiliency of its people and its institutions. The nation experienced a period of disheartening losses and hard-fought recoveries. In the initial months of the war, all of America's tactical airfields in South Korea were overrun at least once, but all were retaken. Seoul, the capital of South Korea, was lost—twice—and twice recaptured. Twice, the commander of the U.S. forces in Korea proposed to the Joint Chiefs of Staff that all U.S. troops be evacuated from Korea to avoid being pushed into the sea. Twice, the President said to stay and fight.

Korea was the first time in the Cold War that the United States committed American troops to combat in its armed confrontation with the communists. Had the United States elected not to fight in Korea and the war had not been concluded successfully, it would have been to the grave disadvantage to the United States.

Korea was admittedly not the place where the United States wanted to stage this first showdown with communism. In 1950, Korea was the wrong enemy at the wrong time and in the wrong place. Secretary of State Dean Acheson put it well, "If the best minds in the world had set out to find us the worst possible place to fight a war, the unanimous choice would have to be Korea."

But the United States and its allies were not offered a choice in the selection of the initial arena for this long-term struggle for the survival of the free world. The communists had seized the initiative with their sudden, overpowering assault across the 38th parallel. The United States and its allies would collide with the surrogates of the Soviet Union—China and North Korea—while the whole world watched. Were the democracies willing to go to war for their principles? Would they fight? Could they hold their own against the tough, battle-tested communist troops who were indoctrinated to sacrifice themselves for a sacred cause? At stake were no less than the prestige of the United States and the survival of free nations.

In 1950, Americans were enjoying the rewards of a welcome peace earned by a hard-fought victory in World War II. That war had been an all-out mobilization that affected nearly every citizen. After the war, with no military threat on the horizon, the victorious United States dismantled its massive armies and fleets. Armament production was halted, materiel and supplies were abandoned overseas, military equipment was scrapped, ships and aircraft were mothballed, and citizen soldiers returned to their jobs, families, and schools. By 1950, force levels of ships, aircraft, and divisions had fallen well below prewar totals. Of special significance was the exodus of veterans from the active-duty ranks. We were tired of war.

The U.S. Navy, which in World War II operated more than a hundred aircraft carriers, was programmed to reduce its active inventory of fleet carriers—those capable of supporting jet fighters—to just five.

The U.S. Army troops in the Pacific theater were untrained for combat. Recruited largely on the promise that they would learn a trade, the young and inexperienced soldiers were enjoying duty in Japan, which in 1950 remained an occupied country under the command of Gen. Douglas MacArthur. The troops were equipped with obsolescent weapons with which they were only marginally proficient. Neither the soldiers nor American leadership ever expected they would be exposed to real battle.

But the war in Korea was a bitter struggle. It lasted three years and claimed some fifty-five thousand American lives. But we ended the war on our terms, restoring the borders between North and South Korea close to their original lines, and establishing a cease-fire that has endured for five decades and permitted our ally, South Korea, to flourish as a modern industrial democracy.

In the course of the war, the United States and its allies essentially destroyed the North Korean army. When Chinese communists invaded across the border to drive the Americans off the Korean peninsula, our troops drove them back and held them near the original line of demarcation, the 38th parallel.

Although the United States eventually prevailed in Korea, it was not a clear-cut victory, such as had been achieved in World War II with the unconditional surrender of Germany and Japan. Nevertheless, peace was attained on conditions that were still acceptable. Geographically, the Korean War ended as it began, along the general lines of the 38th parallel. The entire war, in which more than four million men, women, and children were killed on both sides, involved twenty-two nations. It was fought entirely on the Korean peninsula, a piece of land configured approximately like Florida and only 25 percent larger.

For each of the combatants, the outcome of these three years of intense warfare was different. For North Korea, it was clear defeat. Its objective of annexing South Korea was not achieved, its army was destroyed, its capital city of Pyongyang was leveled, and its casualties numbered more than three hundred thousand soldiers killed or missing in action.

The end position for communist China can be considered a draw. Flexing their muscles in a show to the world of their new military might, the Chinese entered the war to rescue North Korea and to demonstrate that China would not tolerate any military threat near its borders. The result was that the Chinese communists suffered losses of more than 420,000 soldiers killed and missing, and they were unable to defeat the American-led United Nations forces. In the end, China was forced to accept an armistice that simply reflected the status quo. Especially demoralizing to the Chinese was the failure of 120,000 Chinese regular troops to defeat the 25,000 Marines of the 1st Marine Division, even though they had completely surrounded the marines at the Chosin Reservoir.

For the United States, it was perhaps a limited victory; but then, it was a limited war. The Americans accomplished their goal: prevent the communists from seizing and annexing South Korea by force.

From the prospect of the United Nations, the war in Korea was a success of historic proportions. For the first time, the United Nations had organized a multinational military force, exercised its command, and successfully reversed territorial incursions of an aggressor state. Furthermore, the results were lasting. South Korea has not been attacked or invaded since.

Historically, the Korean War has become a unique chapter in the annals of modern warfare, setting precedents and providing lessons that guided U.S. foreign policy and national strategy throughout the Cold War.

Lesson One

Korea defined limited warfare in the military lexicon. Henceforth, limited wars were conflicts to be fought by a unique set of rules: for example, the United States could not fight to win unconditionally. To do so, it was said, would engulf the United States in a general war with China on the Asian mainland.

Also, the United States could not abandon the war because our honor, prestige, and leadership of the free world were at stake. The war was also limited to fighting the Asian communists. Throughout the conflict, NATO forces facing the Soviet communists in Europe and the North Atlantic maintained a readiness posture to deter a Soviet invasion of Western Europe.

Korea also introduced the concept of sanctuaries in limited wars. Neutrals and nonbelligerents had always been a feature of major wars and had proved useful to both sides mainly as a diplomatic conduit for negotiating with the enemy. In Korea, and later in the Vietnam War, the enemy used bases in neutral countries to stage military attacks on friendly forces. Airfields at Antung, just north of the Yalu River, hosted as many as two hundred MiGs (many flown by Soviet pilots) at one time.

In Korea, F–86s patrolled MiG Alley, the corridor just south of the Yalu River that blocked Antung from the allied forces. When Sabres would run low on fuel and head for their bases near Seoul, the MiGs would swarm across from China to pick off any trailing fighters, and then contine south to shoot up other Air Force, Navy, and Marine Corps aircraft conducting interdiction and close air support of our ground forces along the main line of resistance. However, allied aircraft were prohibited from crossing the Yalu into China because allied leadership believed that to do so could bring China and possibly the USSR fully into the war.

Lesson Two

Korea was the first conflict in which the United States had an operational inventory of nuclear weapons. All of America and, indeed, the world were waiting to see how U.S. policy regarding the use of these weapons of mass destruction would evolve. By the time of the Korean War, tactical nuclear weapons had attained yields greater than the yield of the bomb dropped on Hiroshima. The USSR was also in the nuclear arms race by then. The chance of escalation to nuclear warfare and the resulting mutual destruction had become the overriding concern in our national security policy. Although the inventory of nuclear weapons continued to grow in number and in effectiveness, the requirement that the President release them made it clear that their use would be restricted for extreme situations in which national survival was at stake.

In another sense, during the Korean War, nuclear weapons played a key role in our national survival. With America engaged in a full-scale war in Korea, the USSR could see this preoccupation as an invitation to launch an attack on Western Europe. The persuasion of America's readiness for strategic warfare, constantly displayed by ongoing SAC operations, served as the compelling deterrent to a Soviet invasion across the East German plains.

Lesson Three

As the war in Korea crystallized our tactical nuclear weapons policy, it suggested that future U.S. national defense planning must be as much concerned with conventional warfare as with nuclear deterrence. Nuclear weapons had not deterred the war in Korea, nor could they have been used tactically. American national security policy would in the future have to be prepared to fight and win conflicts by conventional arms, reserving the nuclear arsenal to deter Soviet military forces from becoming involved and thus escalating the limited war. It was an essential lesson for our new Department of Defense: advancing technology would not necessarily make obsolete the proven fundamentals of conventional warfare.

As an example, in 1949 the chairman of the Joint Chiefs of Staff, Gen. Omar Bradley, had stated in congressional testimony that amphibious landings were a thing of the past. He predicted that it would not be feasible to assemble and concentrate the shipping required for such an operation because a naval force of the requisite size would provide too inviting a target for atom bombs. Bradley implied that the entire U.S. Marine Corps was no longer needed as part of the defense establishment. However, on September 15, 1950, at the Korean west coast port of Inchon, just fifteen miles southwest of Seoul, the U.S. Navy launched an amphibious operation conducted under the most difficult conditions of terrain and tide imaginable. Some fifty thousand troops were put ashore, and they then drove eastward to link with the Eighth Army, breaking out of the Pusan perimeter to complete a massive encirclement of the North Korean army that led to its utter rout.

Also to be remembered was that the Korean War was the first conflict to occur after the creation of the U.S. Air Force by the National Security Act of 1947. As would be expected, the American public took great interest in how the changes effected by the reorganization evolved, especially in the realm of air combat and cooperation among the armed forces.

From the start of the war, Air Force commanders from Pentagon-level officers to those serving in operational positions showed a clear understanding and commitment to their joint service role. They accelerated doctrinal changes and made equipment available for forces committed to the air-to-ground task, for instance, changing back to propeller aircraft, when the P–51 replaced a number of F–80 squadrons for the air-to-ground mission.

Although historians generally agree that the Korean War could not have been won by air power alone, consensus holds that without tactical aviation as a component of the combined arms support for the ground forces, the enemy could not have been stopped. The consensus also holds that without the total air superiority, largely provided by the F–86Es and their supremacy in air combat with the MiG–15, the United Nations would have lost the war to the Chinese.

The Korean War also marked a turning point in the evolution of the roles and missions within the U.S. Navy, specifically the reaffirmation of the preeminence of the aircraft carrier and naval aviation in the U.S. fleet. With the advent of the new Air Force in 1947, air power advocates had pushed to have the new service absorb virtually all airborne missions, including those in the maritime environment, which the U.S. Navy hoped to retain and exploit.

These issues transfixed the Congress in the 1948 hearings regarding the B–36 Peacemaker bomber. Congress debated the relative capabilities and merits of the aircraft carrier versus land-based heavy bombers and whether naval aviation should have a future role in carrying nuclear weapons. An outcome of these hearings was the cancellation of the Navy's first postwar carrier, the USS *United States.* The debate also produced the "Revolt of the Admirals" which culminated in 1949 with the Chief of Naval Operations, Adm. Louis E. Denfeld, resigning in protest.

Although some patching up was done, by 1950 the Navy was facing a reduction in its 1951 force levels to just five fleet carriers, that is, those that could operate first-line jet aircraft. Then, with remobilization after the start of the Korean War and the pressing need for tactical aviation, nineteen Essex-class carriers were taken out of mothballs, put back into commission, equipped with air groups, and deployed to the operating fleets. Ultimately, twenty-one carriers of all types served in the conflict, and carrier aircraft flew more than 30 percent of all combat sorties during the Korean War.

The Korean experience demonstrated the utility of the carrier task group, which became the primary mobile striking force for conventional warfare on a worldwide basis in our Cold War strategy. Carrier force levels remained at about twenty-five large carriers until the drawdown after the Vietnam War. This resurgence of the World War II aircraft carrier would not have occurred unless it had been possible to modernize these ships to handle the new technology, jet aircraft, that transformed military aviation. When the first jet squadrons were deployed aboard the fleet carriers in the early postwar years, the results were not impressive. But naval aviation worked hard to overcome seemingly insurmountable technical and operational difficulties. By July 1950, when the USS *Valley Forge* launched the first carrier strikes into Korea, each fleet carrier had been equipped with two squadrons of jet fighters. The first jets were the Grumman F9F–2 Panthers, soon to be followed by the McDonnell F2H–2 Banshee. Neither of these planes could be considered MiG killers, and the only plane in the entire free-world inventory that could be called that was the Air Force's North American F–86E Sabre.

By the time the Essex-class carriers were deploying regularly to Korea in the late summer of 1950, all of the embarked aircraft—Panthers, Banshees, and Corsairs—proved capable for their missions, and the Douglas AD–2 Skyraider had no equal anywhere for the support of ground forces.

The U.S. Navy was able to build on these foundations to achieve remarkable results in the future. The McDonnell Douglas F–4 Phantom II, initially a Navy carrier fighter, became the standard tactical fighter for virtually all of the free-world air forces. Today, eleven nuclear-powered carriers are operating with the fleet or are under construction.

Fifty years of subsequent history has put Korea into its proper perspective. Korea was a victory, though perhaps a limited one, and it exerted a profound influence on the eventual outcome of the Cold War. The war in Korea was fought on the other side of the world, as far away from the Pentagon as it is possible to be and yet remain on the surface of Earth. And the Chinese were fighting only two hundred miles from their own national borders.

This demonstration of America's willingness and capability to fight in the remote reaches of the world such as Korea, and then to win, was not lost on the USSR. Later, it could only compare its abysmal experience in Afghanistan where first-line Russian troops were losing to irregular forces in a war only one hundred miles from the Soviet Union.

Korea was the first of a series of limited wars, which in the aggregate constituted the Cold War. The United States won the Cold War with the collapse of the Soviet Union in 1991. Korea was instrumental in our success in that larger conflict. The commitment of American citizens to risk their lives in far-off Asia in support of our promises and principles gave critical substance to American foreign policy credibility.

It was this credibility that held the Soviets in check. Because of Korea, our threat to go to war to support our allies was believed. Similarly, the Kremlin carefully weighed our willingness to resort to nuclear weapons, if necessary, to protect our most vital national interests. This credibility, established by Korea, prevented a Soviet miscalculation of our intentions, an action that threatened to take the United States and the USSR over the brink into a nuclear Armageddon. This fact perhaps represents the ultimate contribution of the Korean War to our present national security.

Air Support of Ground Forces

Air Support of Ground Forces

Charles D. Melson

This panel's members represent the perspectives of the Army, Air Force, and Marine Corps on the use of air forces to aid ground troops on the battlefield. The four presentations cover the spectrum of service views about the value of air power ranging from close to direct air support during the Korean War. The panelists reflect on differing philosophies, and in some cases equipment, that were in play during the Korean War. The need to fully integrate different arms of service is a long-standing and frustrating challenge which remains so even today. As one panelist concluded, "Today's doctrine recognizes the uniqueness of each of the air services and protects their sovereignty."

Fred H. Allison, of the Marine Corps Historical Center, follows a single Marine Corps fighter squadron (VMF–214) to show its transformation from an air-to-air focus to concentrating on the specialty of close air support, employing a somewhat unique system. This modification gave control to the ground forces, using the pilots themselves on the battlefield to ensure that the method worked. An oral historian, Allison's research is part of a dissertation in progress.

William "Tom" Y'Blood, of the U.S. Air Force History Support Office, looks at the issue from the perspective of conflict between certain ground commanders, notably Maj. Gen. Edward M. Almond, USA, and the Far East Air Force commanders, Lt. Gen. George E. Stratemeyer and Maj. Gen. Otto P. Weyland, over who should command air units in the close air support role.

Donald W. Boose, Jr., addresses the Army's close air support doctrine at the start of the Korean War; the experiences and perspectives of Army commanders and soldiers regarding the effectiveness of close air support during the war, and the consequences of these perceptions on postwar doctrine and structure. A retired colonel, he is an instructor and adjunct professor at the U.S. Army War College.

Keith F. Kopets's presentation compares and contrasts the Navy–Marine Corps method of close air support with that of the U.S. Army and Air Force during the first year of the Korean War. A captain at U.S. Marine Corps University, he also explores the dichotomy in air power philosophies that ultimately proved to be the cause of the interservice entanglement regarding close air support.

Black Sheep in Korea: A Reflection of Mission Transformation

Fred H. Allison

Aboard the escort carrier USS *Sicily*, underway off the coast of South Korea on August 3, 1950, a correspondent for the *New York Herald-Tribune* reported that "specially trained" Marine Corps aviation units had "made aviation history today." The aircraft were catapulted from the "decks of the mobile high speed air bases" and conducted a surprise attack on targets west of Pusan.[1] This "specially trained" unit was not a bombing squadron: it was Marine Fighter Squadron 214 (VMF–214), otherwise known as the Black Sheep squadron of World War II and Gregory "Pappy" Boyington fame.

Led by the squadron's executive officer, Maj. Robert P. Keller, this strike of eight F4U Corsairs marked the first blow delivered by any Marine Corps unit in the Korean War. The Black Sheep remained in Korea for fifteen months, when they flew more than 8,000 combat sorties, mostly in support of marine and U.S. Army infantry units. None of the missions flown in Korea, however, involved air-to-air combat, which was the source of the squadron's long-lasting fame in World War II.[2]

In its four World War II combat tours, the Black Sheep squadron accrued a distinguished record, downing 127 aircraft in aerial combat and earning a Presidential Unit Citation for its role in the attacks on Rabaul during the Solomons campaign. Boyington won the Medal of Honor for shooting down twenty-eight enemy aircraft.[3] Although the squadron flew over islands where ground combat raged, only one of its World War II missions was in direct support of friendly ground units.[4] The contrast in missions flown in these two wars reveal that, although the squadron flew the same aircraft in both wars, a shift in mission priority had occurred.

At first glance, one could explain the contrasting missions by the time, place, and vagaries of the war being fought. After all, many Navy and Air Force squadrons also employed World War II air superiority fighters in Korea, now flown by World War II veterans in a ground-attack role.[5] But there was a differ-

Joe Murphy (left) of VMF–214 and Bill Magin of VMF–311 sit in front of VMF–214's tent number 6, July 28, 1951.

ence. As one correspondent noted, VMF–214 had been specially trained for this mission. He was right: special training had prepared the Black Sheep pilots for providing close air support, a unique and demanding skill. The VMF–214 pilots were not unique in this skill, however, because all marine fighter pilots had been similarly trained and had obtained similar results.

The use of aircraft in support of ground units has been the heart of marine aviation since its inception in 1912.[6] Effective close air support had been hampered by limits in communication, aircraft, ordnance, and command and control. In World War II, all military services made significant strides toward accomplishing genuinely effective close air support.[7] The severe military cutbacks subsequent to World War II revealed the true commitment of each service to close air support. In this environment, the Marine Corps put its confidence on close air support and worked to improve techniques and capabilities in using aircraft in support of infantry marines.[8]

Indeed, before the Korean War, the Marine Corps had developed a truly effective system of close air support.[9] When VMF–214 arrived off the coast of Korea on August 3, 1950, it was there for one function: to use its special training in support of the 1st Provisional Marine Brigade. Unlike the other services that were making do with older aircraft to provide close air support, the Marine Corps was implementing its doctrine.

Ironically, although supporting the ground marines was a long-standing doctrinal position of the Marine Corps, for Corsair pilots who deployed with VMF–214, as well as other marine pilots serving in other squadrons who came later, their previous combat experience in World War II had little to do with close air support. This evolution shows the determination of the Marine Corps to redirect its fighter squadrons toward ground support during World War II and in the subsequent years.

A series of oral history interviews with veteran pilots of VMF–214 in Korea bears this out. Many of the pilots joined the Marine Corps in the first place because of the media attention that marine fighter squadrons gained during the battle for air superiority in the Solomons and Rabaul. Most believed that, by getting into marine aviation, they would have a better chance to fly fighters and shoot down Zeros. Few had any knowledge of the primary mission of marine aviation. They trained with the Navy and became fighter pilots, and many fulfilled their desire for aerial combat. Several had enemy kills, and one, Howard J. Finn, became an ace.[10]

By the time of the Okinawa campaign, the Marine Corps had made significant progress toward an efficient and effective system of close air support. Yet, close air support was a secondary mission for marine Corsair squadrons, which were tasked with protecting the fleet. This irony is evidenced in the pilot interviews. Joe McPhail, a pilot in VMF–323, made only four strike missions of the forty-nine flown at Okinawa; the remainder were combat air patrols over the fleet. McPhail scored two kills at Okinawa and would remark years later that the marines' "main purpose" was protecting the fleet. George Dodenhoff, a pilot in VMF–311, noted that they performed very little close air support. He recalled seeing Navy fighters heading toward the island for air-to-ground work while the land-based marine Corsairs flew out to sea. Guy Washburn, a marine fighter pilot at Okinawa who became Chesty Puller's regimental air officer in Korea, could knowledgeably assert that "at Okinawa, [close air support] wasn't that good."[11]

Although flying close air support was rarely done by marine fighter pilots in World War II, fundamental changes occurred in the war that were critical to the transition leading to Corsair pilots becoming experts in close air support by the time of the Korean War. These changes fell into three broad categories: equipment, carriers, and training.

The most important equipment change was the evolution of the F4U Corsair from fighter to fighter-bomber. The earliest model of the Corsair that marines flew, the F4U–1, was "clean, slick and a straight fighter," as Bruce Matheson, one of Boyington's Black Sheep, characterized it.[12] By early 1944, however, the Corsair began sprouting appendages that gave it the ability to carry air-to-ground ordnance such as bombs and rockets. Additionally, and perhaps most importantly, four-channel radios were replaced with ten-channel sets in later models, such as the F4U–1D, a true fighter-bomber, which marines flew at Okinawa. Another Corsair variant flown at Okinawa, the F4U–1C, presaged the Corsairs flown in Korea; this variant had 20-mm cannon instead of .50-cal. machine guns.[13] The Corsair's proven capabilities as a ground-attack aircraft convinced the Marine Corps to do away with its dive bomber and torpedo bomber aircraft altogether, a process that began even before World War II had ended. By the time of the

July 26, 1951, K–1 Airfield, Pusan, Korea. Joe Murphy, before takeoff on strike to north, at Sangpyong-Ni, VMF–214, F4U–4B Corsair.

August 29, 1951, K–1 Airfield, Pusan, Korea, Joe Murphy, VMF–214, perched on an ordnance trailer.

Korean War, the only combat aircraft that marines flew, except for one squadron that flew the F9F jets, was the F4U–4B Corsair, a true fighter-bomber.

World War II also saw the development of more effective and potent ordnance, for example, variable-timed bombs, air-to-surface rockets, 20-mm cannon, and most importantly for close air support, napalm. A concoction of jellied gasoline, napalm was first introduced to marines during the Marianas campaign when, on July 19, 1944, "an enthusiastic Navy commander arrived on Saipan with an impressive Army Air Forces film showing what happened when napalm powder was mixed with aircraft fuel."[14] A few days later, the Air Forces' P–47 Thunderbolts were dropping napalm-filled wing tanks on Tinian island. Initially it was thought that the best use of the chemical would be to burn off the thick foliage that often hid enemy troops and emplacements.[15] It was not long before Marine Air Group 31 in the Marshall Islands was conducting its own napalm experiments. Soon, napalm became commonplace on World War II battlefields, where it was found to be more tactically effective against troops than against foliage.

Carrier operations marked the second critical development that allowed VMF–214 and other marine squadrons to provide effective close air support in Korea. In the 1930s, marine pilots had been regular members of carrier air wings, but during World War II, the U.S. Navy decided it did not have the time or equipment to qualify marine pilots. Consequently, the vast majority of the marine pilots trained in World War II "had never been aboard a carrier."[16]

Marine ground commanders, dissatisfied with the air support provided by the Navy and Army Air Forces during the Central Pacific drive, clambered to get marine air units assigned once again to carriers. Little progress was made until the waning months of the war, when the Navy acceded to their requests and assigned marine squadrons to escort carriers (CVEs) expressly for providing support for amphibious landings. The marine units did not become operational in time to support any such World War II assaults.[17] The Navy and Marine Corps continued this policy even after the war, thus ensuring that, when VMF–214 and its sister squadron VMF–323 initiated air strikes in Korea in 1950, the squadrons were aboard CVEs and specifically assigned to support the 1st Provisional Marine Brigade.

The third aspect of this close air support (CAS) transition was a commitment to better training and indoctrination of marine fighter pilots in the tactics and techniques of close air support. Fundamental to this indoctrination was reintegrating fighter pilots into the mainstream Marine Corps by reinstituting infantry training for all marine officers. The concept that all marine officers were infantry

August 29, 1951, F4U–4 Corsairs of VMF–214 and VMF–312 (MAG–12) taxiing out for a strike in North Korea, at K–1 Airfield, Pusan, Korea (view to the north)

Oct. 16, 1951, USS *New Jersey,* off the east coast of Korea near Kansong, firing inland. Photo taken on return, by Jeep, from K–18 Airfield to 5th Marines command post at Won-tong-Ni.

officers first was bedrock Marine Corps doctrine before World War II. Would-be marine aviators attended the Basic School, which enforced Marine Corps traditions and infantry training. Additionally, marine aviators regularly served tours in ground billets. The commencement of all-out war, however, and the intense demand for pilots caused this principle to be dropped. Consequently, the entire generation of marine pilots trained in World War II had little or no exposure to the infantry training, traditions, and discipline implicit with being a marine. The concept that marine aviation existed only to support the marine rifleman was foreign to many pilots trained during World War II.

Efforts to introduce its aviators to the ground side of the Marine Corps began even before the war ended. Ad hoc schools were established at East Coast and the West Coast locations, where pilots, fresh from Navy flight school, received training and instruction in the basics of the Marine Corps. Two such pilots, Hyman Kovsky and C. D. Norman arrived at the Marine Corps Air Station in El Toro, California, expecting to be assigned to a tactical fighter squadron. Instead they found themselves bound for Camp Pendleton and put under the tutelage of enlisted marines, "veterans of Guadalcanal," who acted uncomfortably like drill instructors. With all rank insignia removed, the instructors "really put them through the paces." Long hikes, rifle qualifications, crawling through an infiltration range, and plenty of harassment gave the Navy-trained pilots an entirely new perspective on the word *marine*.[18]

Immediately after the war, the Marine Corps reinstituted mandatory Basic School training for all new aviators. Many veterans of the war were assigned to the Junior Course, later named Amphibious Warfare School, where they received a thorough indoctrination in air-to-ground philosophy and tactics. For many seasoned marine aviators, like Major Keller who had attended the Junior Course in 1946, this was the first Marine Corps school they had attended. It was from such schools that the Marine Corps promulgated its air-to-ground team doctrine.[19]

For most Corsair pilots, evidence of the transition from an air-to-air to an air-to-ground mission became apparent in the training they received at the squadron level. This change began before the war ended, hitting the Black Sheep in June 1944 as they trained in California for redeployment to the Pacific. The squadron war diary records that the commanding officer directed his intelligence department to gather all available material on bombing by F4Us and distribute it to his pilots.[20] Subsequently, bombing, strafing, and rocket-firing sorties became part of their regular training regimen. On November 26, 1944, the Black Sheep pilots, still in training, flew their first mission in which a ground coordinator directed an air strike from the ground.[21] Control of air strikes from the ground was a unique aspect of the marine system of close air support.

The marines were the only service that used a ground coordinator, later known as a forward air controller (FAC). They vested their FACs with an exceptional level of authority. FACs served as agents of the ground commanders, usu-

Oct. 9, 1951, 5th Marines command post, northeast of Punchbowl in Soyang River valley (view to southwest). Tactical Air Control Party tent, radio truck, and Jeep (left front).

ally posted at the battalion level. As such, they had direct tactical control over the prosecution of the air strike. They could determine the level of air support needed and then brief the pilot on how the strike was to be conducted.[22] The Marine Corps validated and legitimized the FAC role by ensuring that first-rate pilots served in those billets and, indeed, even made serving as a FAC a career-enhancing experience. The small size of marine aviation ensured that FACs and the pilots overhead often knew one another personally, and because they spoke the same language, air support was enhanced. Furthermore, assigning aviators to FAC roles spurred a multidisciplinary attitude that enhanced better air-ground integration.

Implicit in providing effective air support was actual training with ground units. For marine Corsair squadrons, this began in World War II. Again, VMF–214 is representative of what occurred throughout marine fighter aviation. On the strike in which they first worked with a ground coordinator, the Black Sheep flew support for troops in a practice amphibious landing on San Clemente Island.[23]

Marine squadrons continued this type training after the war. In November 1947, the Black Sheep, operating from the CVE USS *Rendova*, provided close air support for a practice amphibious assault on a Camp Pendleton beach. The next year, VMF–214 participated in another amphibious exercise in which the squadron operated from an expeditionary airfield at Camp Pendleton for an entire month. Both of these exercises provided very appropriate training for the actual wartime conditions that the Black Sheep would face in Korea.[24]

The year 1949 found the Black Sheep participating in a sophisticated war game, the MIKI exercise, in which they flew a variety of missions that included fleet defense, antishipping strikes, and close air support. On the eve of the Korean War, in March 1950, the Black Sheep set a new record for the number of hours flown in one month for a single-engine squadron, amassing more than 3,100 flying hours that month.[25]

In June 1950, the Black Sheep were again aboard the USS *Rendova,* bound for Hawaii, when news arrived of North Korea's invasion of South Korea, and with it came a dramatic change of plans. Commanding general of the Fleet Marine Force, Pacific, Lt. Gen. Lemuel C. Shepherd, Jr., summoned Major Keller, the Black Sheep commander, to his headquarters on Oahu. Keller flew to Camp H. M. Smith where he met with Shepherd's chief of staff, Col. Victor H. Krulak. With full intensity, Krulak asked Keller, "Major, are you ready to go to war?" With all honesty, Keller assured Krulak that VMF–214 was indeed ready to go to war. He was right.

The transformation that occurred in marine Corsair squadrons in the preceding years converted fighter pilots to CAS specialists, and so the Korean War was a conflict that marine aviators were well prepared to fight. Carrier-deployed fighter-bombers flown by experienced pilots who had received extensive training in CAS techniques delivered impressive firepower for infantry units, on time

Nov. 16, 1951, Lt. Gen. Lemuel C. Shepherd, FMFPAC, leaving by helicopter. Col. Richard Weede, CO of 5th Marines, and Lt. Col. Virgil Banning, XO of 5th Marines, shaking hand of general.

and on target. In so doing, the marine air-ground team doctrine was validated as an effective doctrine for battlefield success.

Notes

1. A copy of this dispatch from an unidentified correspondent can be found in the personal papers of Col Frank H. Scribner-Lamson, USMC, in the Personal Papers Collection, Marine Corps Research Center, Quantico, Va.
2. Summary of Monthly Operations, VMF–214, August 1950–November 1951, National Archives and Record Administration (NARA), Suitland, Md. Hereafter, noted as War Diary.
3. Robert Sherrod, *History of Marine Corps Aviation in World War II* (San Rafael: Presidio Press, 1952), pp 427, 430.
4. War Diary, VMF–214, March 1943–March 1945.
5. Robert F. Futrell, *The United States Air Force in Korea, 1950–1953* (Washington, D.C.: Office of Air Force History, 1983); Robert Jackson, *Air War Over Korea* (New York: Charles Scribner's Sons, 1973); and Richard Hallion, *The Naval Air War in Korea* (Annapolis: Nautical and Aviation Press, 1986).
6. James A. Ginther, Jr., "Marine Aviator Number One: Alfred Austell Cunningham and the Development of Early Marine Corps Aviation, 1912–1920" (M.A. thesis, Abilene Christian University, 1993), pp 25–28; "Keith Barr McCutcheon and the Integration of Aviation into the Marine Corps" (Ph.D. diss, Texas Tech University, 1999), pp 13–15; and Edward C.

Johnson and Graham A. Cosmas, eds, *Marine Corps Aviation: The Early Years, 1912–1940* (Washington, D.C.: History and Museums Divisions, Headquarters U.S. Marine Corps, 1985), pp 2–10.

7. See the following for service accounts: Thomas A. Hughes, *Overlord* (New York: The Free Press, 1995), which details close air support after D-Day; Wesley F. Craven and James L. Cate, *The Army Air Forces in World War II* (Boston: Little, Brown & Company, 1950); and *History of the U.S. Marine Corps Operations in World War II* (Washington, D.C.: Historical Division, Hqs, U.S. Marine Corps, 1971).
8. Allan R. Millett, *Semper Fidelis* (New York: Macmillan Publishing Co., Inc., 1980), p 466.
9. The immediate effectiveness of marine close air support in Korea is evidenced in most studies of the war, including Clay Blair's *The Forgotten War* (New York: Times Books, 1987), p 197; David Rees's *Korea: The Limited War* (New York: St. Martin's Press, 1964), p 50; and Roy Appleman's *East of Chosin* (College Station: Texas A&M Press, 1987), pp 105, 338, and his *South to the Naktong, North to the Yalu* (Washington, D.C.: Office of the Chief of Military History, U.S. Army, 1961), p 275.
10. The desire to fly fighters is a recurring theme in the twenty-six interviews with the Black Sheep Korean veterans. See interviews conducted by author with Guy Washburn, Hyman Kovsky, John Barnett, William Dobbins, George Dodenhoff, and Joe McPhail.
11. Benis M. Frank and Henry I. Shaw, Jr., *Victory and Occupation*, vol 5 of *History of U.S. Marine Corps Operations in World War II* (Historical Branch, G–3 Division, Hqs, U.S. Marine Corps, 1968), p 671; Col Joe McPhail, USMC, interview by author, Apr. 19, 1999, Houston, Tex., tape recording; Col George H. Dodenhoff, USMC, telephone interview by author, May 30, 1999, tape recording; and Maj Guy M. Washburn, USMC, telephone interview by author, tape recording, all in the Marine Corps Oral History Collection, Marine Corps Historical Center (MCHC), Washington Navy Yard.
12. Col Bruce J. Matheson, USMC, interview by author, Lubbock, Tex., tape recording, MCHC, Washington Navy Yard.
13. Robert Sherrod, *History of Marine Corps Aviation in World War II* (San Rafael: Presidio Press, 1980), pp 235–36; and Maj. William J. Sambito, USMC, *A History of Marine Attack Squadron 311* (Washington, D.C.: History and Museums Division, Hqs, U.S. Marine Corps, 1978), p 7; Lt Col Emmons S. Maloney, USMC, interview by author, Mar. 15, 1999, Fallbrook, tape recording, MCHC, Washington Navy Yard; and Dodenhoff interview.
14. Henry I. Shaw, Jr., Bernard C. Nalty, and Edwin T. Tumbladh, *Central Pacific Drive*, vol III of *History of U.S. Marine Corps Operations in World War II* (Washington, D.C.: Historical Branch, G–3 Division, Hqs, U.S.

Marine Corps, 1963), p 364.
15. *Ibid.*; Jeter A. Isley and Philip A. Crowl, *The U.S. Marines and Amphibious War: Its Theory and Its Practice in the Pacific* (Princeton: Princeton University Press, 1951), p 333.
16. John P. Condon, *Corsairs and Flattops* (Annapolis: Naval Institute Press, 1998), p 3.
17. *Ibid.*, pp 4–5; Sherrod, pp 329–30; and Frank and Shaw, p 672.
18. Lt Col Hyman Kovsky, USMC, and C. D. Norman, interviews by author, Jan. 16, 1999, Dallas, Tex., tape recording, MCHC, Washington Navy Yard; and Gen Vernon E. Megee, USMC, interview with Ben M. Frank, May 18, 1967, transcript, MCHC, Washington Navy Yard.
19. Lt Gen Robert P. Keller, USMC, interview by author, Aug. 28, 1998, Pensacola, Fla., tape recording, Marine Corps Oral History Collection, MCHC, Washington Navy Yard.
20. War Diary, VMF–214, Jun. 1944, NARA, Suitland, Md.
21. *Ibid.*, October 1944.
22. Allan R. Millett, "Korea, 1950–1953," in *Case Studies in the Development of Close Air Support*, Benjamin F. Cooling, ed (Washington, D.C.: Office of Air Force History, 1990), p 351.
23. War Diary, November 1944.
24. Monthly Narratives, VMF–214, 1947 and 1948, NARA, Suitland, Md., Sgt. Maj. Floyd P. Stocks, USMC, interview by author, Mar. 16, 1999, Sun City, tape recording, MCHC, Washington Navy Yard; and Stocks's Diary.
25. Monthly Narratives, VMF–214, January–June 1950, NARA, Suitland, Md.

The Generals and Close Air Support

William T. Y'Blood

Of all the forms and uses of air power, the one that has been the most contentious among America's armed forces over the years has been that of close air support. The Korean War was no exception. Throughout that conflict, the various commanders of the Far East Air Forces (FEAF) and Fifth Air Force clashed continually with ground leaders over the proper use of aircraft in support of ground operations. One senior U.S. Army officer, in particular, not only became enamored of the Marine Corps style of close air support, but he also sought to control air assets himself.

Close air support, as practiced in Korea, was rooted in Field Manual (FM) 31–35, *Air-Ground Operations*. First published in August 1946, this manual distilled the lessons and procedures learned in World War II, primarily in Europe, by the 12th Army Group and the Army Air Forces' Ninth Air Force. This joint doctrinal publication was in effect when the Korean War began. A second publication, the "Joint Training Directive for Air-Ground Operations" (generally known as the JTD), was issued on September 1, 1950. This directive elaborated upon FM 31–35. Although the JTD was a joint effort, neither the Army nor the Air Force assented to it as official policy. Nevertheless, despite worries by both services, neither really objected to its application in Korea.

Like the other services in Japan at the start of the war, FEAF, under Lt. Gen. George E. Stratemeyer, was an occupation force, and its charter was the air defense of its area of operations, which included Japan, the Ryukyus, the Marianas, and the Philippines. It had many secondary missions, including "air support of operations as arranged with appropriate Army and Navy commanders." Little training, however, had been accomplished with the Army because of the severe budget cuts that followed World War II.

During the early, desperate days of the war, Stratemeyer and his vice commander, Maj. Gen. Otto P. Weyland (who later became FEAF leader), strove to their utmost to provide the ground forces with needed support, using B–26s, B–29s, and even F–82s for close air support. This was not good enough for some in MacArthur's Army-dominated headquarters. They wanted to run the air war from Tokyo. None was more adamant about this than Maj. Gen. Edward M. Almond, MacArthur's chief of staff.

Almond had been a student at the Air Corps Tactical School in 1938, from which he received an aerial observer rating. It appears he emerged from there with a deep-seated belief that the Air Corps (and its descendants) was fixated on air superiority and strategic bombing to the neglect of support of the ground forces. And his time there also seems to have sown the seeds of a conviction that he knew more about how to conduct close air support than did most airmen. These beliefs only blossomed in Korea.

At first, Almond contented himself with just sniping at FEAF for not being more aggressive against the enemy, but he soon decided that he and members of his staff should actually pick targets for FEAF. Unfortunately, no one on his staff had any experience in targeting, and this resulted in choosing targets that were unsuitable for air attack or, far too often, that did not even exist. Weyland took it upon himself to confront Almond on this matter. Almond did not take kindly to being challenged. He ordered Weyland to meet with him and some of MacArthur's staff. The group had hardly gotten seated before Almond began berating the airman. Weyland let him rant, but after one profane outburst by Almond, Weyland cut him off: "General, don't speak to me in that manner, using those words or that tone of voice. You happen to be speaking to your superior officer, and I don't intend to have one more word like that." (Weyland, an Army major general, thus outranked Almond.)

Almond, whose temper was legendary, sputtered and fumed but finally settled down. He was soon off on another tantrum, however. Weyland, who apparently enjoyed baiting Almond, later commented, "I discovered the way to needle him a little bit, and then he would bounce off the ceiling. Then he lost all reason. He wasn't thinking clearly any more. He would lose his train of thought, and he was just so mad." Another member of the group finally prevailed on Almond to leave, and the remaining members were able to reach agreement on the use of FEAF aircraft and targeting. Almond, however, would remain a thorn in the leaders' sides.

In September 1950, Almond now commanded the X Corps, which landed at Inchon. The support he received there from Task Force 77 and the 1st Marine Aircraft Wing evidently confirmed his long-standing belief that the Air Force cared little about close air support. Marine air had always been an integral part of Marine Corps land operations. Usually light in artillery, the marines relied on their own planes, along with their own tactical air control parties (TACPs) and forward air observers (FACs), to provide the necessary close support. This meant that marine aircraft were usually on air alert and could be on a target within a short time. In contrast, because the Air Force flew a wider variety of missions, it preferred to keep its planes on ground alert, which could produce delays in reacting to requests to strike specific targets.

Another factor that seemed to escape the notice of most ground commanders, but not Stratemeyer, concerned the frontage being covered by the aircraft. The FEAF leader argued that the marines were able to have their aircraft overhead seemingly continuously because they had relatively few men in contact with the enemy on a front that extended for only a few miles. On the other hand, FEAF aircraft had to protect 150 miles of front lines. Thus, at Inchon, on a narrow front, Almond was well-served by the marine style of support that was at his call at all times.

Almond also very much liked the idea of acting as his own tactical air commander and of controlling his own private air force, which Inchon gave him the chance to do. He attempted to retain control of the tactical aircraft during the Wonsan landings in October, but this time he was rebuffed. Eventually, he went so far as to recommend that each corps commander should have operational control over a number of aircraft equivalent to one group per division. Moreover, he wanted an air officer on the staff of the corps commander. This officer would command all Air Force units supporting a corps, would determine whether or not an aircraft would fly based on mechanical or weather conditions, would supervise the planning of air operations, and would prepare and supervise the training of the air units under his command. The commander of the tactical air force (that is, Fifth Air Force) would be responsible only for the administrative support of the air units.

Because the Army was then contemplating an expansion of up to one hundred divisions, this would require more than 7,000 aircraft just for close air support. Given the paucity of aircraft at that time, Almond's ideas were sheer nonsense, as many of his contemporaries realized. And the thought of giving up control of its resources to a ground officer was anathema to the Air Force. Nonetheless, Almond continued to press his ideas on close air support up the chain of command.

Although many ground commanders appreciated the support given them by FEAF aircraft, notably the 2d Infantry Division during its terrible ordeal during its battle south of Kunu-ri in early December 1950, others did not. World War II had shown that close air support worked best in fluid situations, when the enemy was on the move. In the static conditions that occurred during the last two years of the Korean War, when the enemy was dug in deeply, artillery fire was more often a better choice than air. Unfortunately, the ground troops had gotten used to having air support virtually on-call, and they were not pleased when the airmen began to seek more lucrative targets behind the lines—in other words, interdiction. The cooperative spirit fostered by the fine support during the first year of the war quickly degenerated into ill feelings, which festered for the remainder of the war. Typical of these sentiments was the following from a regimental commander:

> If you want it, you can't get it. If you can get it, it can't find you. If it can find you, it can't identify the target. If it can identify the target, it can't hit

it. But if it does hit the target, it doesn't do a great deal of damage anyway.

Considering this officer's comments, one might wonder why he would be so desirous of close air support in the first place.

A more vocal division commanders on what he considered the proper use of close air support was Maj. Gen. Gerald Thomas, commander of the 1st Marine Division. He complained to Maj. Gen. Frank Everest, the new Fifth Air Force leader, that his division had taken unnecessary casualties because of poor air support. Everest pointed out to the marine that during December 1950 the five divisions of the X Corps, including the 1st Marine Division, had received 1,664 close air support (CAS) sorties. The marines had received 679 of these, or 40 percent of the total. During the same period, the other two corps in the Eighth Army had received only 335 and 356 sorties, respectively.

These numbers did not impress Thomas, who requested that forty CAS sorties be flown daily exclusively for his division and that they be flown exclusively by the 1st Marine Air Wing. Everest stated he could not justify such favorable treatment to the marines at the expense of other U.N. ground forces. General Weyland and Lt. Gen. James A. Van Fleet, the new Eighth Army commander, concurred as Thomas's request went up the chain of command to Lt. Gen. Matthew B. Ridgway. In his reply to Thomas, the U.N. commander stated, "the request you submitted if approved would occasion so wide a departure from sound practice as well as fair treatment, as to be quite unacceptable." Thomas withdrew his request, but remained intractable on what he perceived as shortcomings in the CAS process.

By this time in the war the front lines had settled into what, after modifications, would become the final armistice line. A period of relative inactivity ensued with both sides content to pursue active defense operations rather than full-blown offensives. Everest thought this would result in fewer calls for close air support and then he could focus more on interdiction. He was wrong. Many division commanders continued to insist on getting their share, whatever that may have been, of close air support. One commander ordered his G–3 (Air) to request fifteen prebriefed flights per day and to find targets to justify this many flights. Another wanted as many air strikes as he could get against targets as small as two- and three-man bunkers. Van Fleet complained that he had to rely on close air support because he was short of artillery tubes. Later research showed that as much artillery and mortar fire was expended in Korea between June 1950 and December 1952 as had been shot in the Mediterranean and Pacific theaters combined during the entire previous war.

The idea of assigning aircraft to corps commanders resurfaced in December 1951 when Van Fleet broached the subject to Everest. The Eighth Army commander proposed assigning one squadron of fighter-bombers to each corps. Corps commanders would control the operations of these squadrons, and Everest would only monitor their use. Everest, naturally, refused, citing the principles in FM 31–35, but he also sensed that Van Fleet may have been pressured from above, probably from Gen. J. Lawton Collins, the Army chief of staff, or Gen. Mark Clark, then Chief, Army Field Forces. Both men had advocated the Army's regaining control of aircraft for close support.

Perhaps hoping to sidestep Everest and Weyland, Van Fleet wrote Ridgway regarding his concerns about the present CAS procedures and his proposal to shift control of the air assets to the corps commanders. Although Ridgway undoubtedly agreed with Van Fleet, he was a joint commander and knew that he would have a hard time selling this to the Air Force. He decided to talk to Weyland. The FEAF leader was characteristically blunt in his assessment. As he recalled later:

> I said, "I was sent over here to run the air, and I wasn't going to be any part of it. Absolutely not." Then I reviewed a little bit about a meeting that was held in Europe right after World War II. General Eisenhower presided, and it had to do with the employment of tactical and strategic air power, the conclusion of which Gen. Eisenhower had apparently concurred in. I may have dolled it up a bit, but he believed in air power under centralized control, which had worked in Europe.... The airmen ran air units, and the ground didn't control it. So I told Ridgway this and, of course, Ike was about to be president. Well, that closed him up quickly. [Actually, at this time, Eisenhower was just campaigning for the presidency.]

Ridgway, a very politically astute individual, decided the time was not yet ripe for such sweeping action and let the matter die. A silver stake had not been driven into the heart of the matter, though, and it would arise again.

In May 1952, Clark replaced Ridgway as the commander of U.N. forces. Van Fleet remained the Eighth Army leader until February 1953 when Lt. Gen. Maxwell Taylor succeeded him. To those ground officers who thought Clark's arrival portended a significant change in CAS policies, disappointment awaited. Clark obviously agreed with Van Fleet about Army control of CAS aircraft, but like Ridgway he was not about to escalate interservice disputes over the issue. Nonetheless, when Van Fleet sent him an almost verbatim version of his message to Ridgway, Clark was interested. Somehow Weyland, though not an addressee, received a copy of the message.

According to Weyland, Clark was a far different opponent than Ridgway, and far more difficult. When Clark called him in to discuss the message, Weyland feigned ignorance. Shown a copy, the FEAF leader put on a furious act, slamming the message down and fulminating about the effrontery of a subordinate Army commander proposing a major reorganization of the theater air forces without even informing the senior Air Force leaders. Weyland continued:

> I said, "This is the goddamnest way to run a war that I have ever heard of." I was really putting on an act. He took it [the message], looked at it, and said, "What a stupid guy. What in the hell? Well, just the same though, I

> think this is a good idea." I said, "I don't. I've been through this racket before. As a matter of fact, I went through it with your predecessor. I won and I'll win again." He said, "Well, now, see here, you know that I'm the commander-in-chief over here, and I want to have consensus.
>
> So I said, "Well, this goes both ways.... You are my boss.... But you are talking a well-known Army line.... I know that you started this back at Fort Monroe.... As long as I'm here, you're going to have to fire me . . .. I'd rather fight the Communists than to fight the United States Army, but if you want to fight, you'll get it." Well, I thought I'd get fired right then. He sat back and was silent. For a moment he got quite pale because he is a very strong-willed and capable guy, and it was in his blood to try and put this over. Well, he subsided and said, "Okay, we will fight the Communists."

Weyland and Clark did agree that the JTD could be improved, and Clark issued a letter concerning air–ground operations. Subordinates were directed to reexamine their positions on close air support and to make every effort to perfect the system. Clark's letter had some positive effect. More ground officers began attending the Fifth Air Force ground operations course in Korea, and attendance by Army and Air Force officers swelled at the Far East Air-Ground Operations School in Japan. The Fifth Air Force also began sending groups of pilots on three-day tours of the front lines, and a traveling Eighth Army–Fifth Air Force indoctrination team proved very successful in spreading the CAS word.

Although these measures were productive, they occurred late in the war. In the following years, CAS doctrine was dissected, studied, analyzed, and redissected by both services. Neither could reach a compromise of a new doctrine. In April 1953, before the end of the war, the Air Force had issued Air Force Manual AFM 1–2, *United States Air Force Basic Doctrine*. After review, this seminal document was officially published in 1955. It immediately ran into strong opposition from the other services, which saw the USAF as interested only in centralized control of an air war. Because of this opposition and because the Air Force appeared to be retreating from a commitment to close air support, the Army swiftly repudiated the earlier JTD. The Air Force, looking to its own future, was itself not sorry to see the JTD disappear. Thus, as historian Allan Millett has written, "For all practical purposes the Army and Air Force had finally found a consensus by agreeing not to agree on what close air support would play in future war."

Note

This paper is based on William T. Y'Blood, *Down in the Weeds: Close Air Support in Korea* [*The Korean War Fiftieth Anniversary, Commemorative Edition*] (Washington, D.C.: Air Force History and Museums Program, 2002).

The Army View of Close Air Support in the Korean War

Donald W. Boose, Jr.

Coordinating air and ground forces effectively has always been a problem since the air force became an independent service. The doctrine and structure of air power have emphasized its capacity to deliver decisive victory independently, rather than through support of land and sea operations.

—Jeremy Black[1]

Because the mission of the U.S. Army is to achieve victory through the conduct of land operations, soldiers inevitably view air operations as being in support of the land mission. This has always produced tension over the issue of close air support, which is the most direct and significant way air forces can support Army forces in pursuit of the Army's primary mission. The Army view of close air support, in the Korean War or any war, was explained to me in the spring of 1967 by MSgt. Rodney Baker while the two of us lay behind a rice-paddy dike in the Mekong Delta. Sergeant Baker said, "I agree with Bobby Kennedy. We should stop bombing North Vietnam." "Why?" I asked. "Because I don't want to waste any of it. I want it all, I want it now, and I want it in that tree line right over there."

That is what ground soldiers directly engaged in combat always want, no matter how much they may agree intellectually with the airmen's logic about the importance of centralized control of air power, the primacy of air superiority, the need for a flexible, multipurpose aircraft that can both control the skies and attack ground targets, and the value of strategic attack and interdiction. Senior Army officers may recognize the legitimacy of the Air Force arguments, but, although they may not want it all, they invariably want control of timely and accurate close air support (CAS) missions. The ground soldiers' perceptions and recurring arguments about close air support have centered historically on the relative priority of close air support among other air missions, the timeliness of response to frontline calls for fire, control by the supported Army units of CAS attacks, and the need for an aircraft specifically designed for and dedicated to the CAS mission. The tension over close air support has always been greater whenever resources are limited. When the Air Force enjoys unchallenged air superiority, plenty of airplanes are available, and all requests can be met. Then the airmen do not mind diverting missions from strategic attack and interdiction to providing close air support to the ground forces, and the soldiers are generally happy with the support. However, when the tempo of ground combat ramps up and fire support assets are in short supply, old arguments reemerge.

All of these issues surfaced during the Korean War. For many reasons, the war brought a long-standing, but quiescent, tension to the fore. It required relearning old lessons on how best to conduct close air support, and it produced a legacy that would contribute to the later reacquisition by the Army of its own CAS capability.

Prewar Doctrine

When the North Korean People's Army attacked across the 38th parallel on June 25, 1950, the U.S. Army and Air Force had in place a doctrine and procedures for conducting close air support. These were set forth in the 1946 version of Field Manual (FM) 31–35 and in a joint training directive (JTD) published a few months after the war began.[2] The doctrine and procedures had been developed largely from the Army and Air Force experience in northern Europe in World War II. The CAS procedures of the European theater of operations were, in turn, based upon the British and American experiences in North Africa and Sicily.[3]

Certain assumptions about air-ground operations that had been derived from the North African experience were reflected in the 1942 edition of FM 31–35. These assumptions were that air and ground units formed a combat team, that air superiority was a prerequisite to effective air-ground operations and must have priority, that aircraft were more vulnerable and costly than artillery, and that the central control of air assets provided the flexibility to "concentrate the air effort at short notice on a particular point or distribute it to many points within a relatively short time." The preferred missions for air-ground operations were interdiction of enemy reinforcements and destruction of enemy mechanized forces on the move. Direct support of ground forces in contact should be considered only when enemy forces could not be "effectively and quickly reached by artillery" and were not "within the effective range of the weapons of ground forces."[4]

The 1946 FM 31–35, which reflected doctrine on the eve of the Korean War, inherited these assumptions and also the view that air and ground forces were separate and coequal forces under a unified commander who alone could make authoritative decisions affecting both forces.[5] It assumed centralized control of all air assets by the Air Force commander in the theater, who in wartime would assign a tactical air force to work in cooperation with a field army. The two headquarters would be collocated and would establish a Joint Operations Center (JOC). The Army element of the JOC (the Air-Ground Operations System

[AGOS]), would receive and evaluate requests for close air support (tactical air requests) from frontline units, and the Air Force element would make the final decisions on the allocation of air assets and, through a tactical air direction system, direct aircraft to the targets. An Air Force tactical air control party (TACP) would direct the actual strikes on the targets.[6] The system, with requests making their way up the AGOS, worked best for preplanned missions and depended on the Army's providing personnel and equipment to establish the necessary communications system and to man the JOC. As had been shown in Europe, and in other theaters in which variations of this system were used during World War II, the system could work effectively, even for emergency calls for fire. However, the feature of centralized control, delays between requests and the actual strikes, and Air Force control over the mission would eventually raise concerns in ground commanders.[7] Some senior commanders also worried that the Air Force might neglect aircraft optimized for the CAS mission in favor of high-performance fighters.[8] One experienced and influential critic was Gen. Mark W. Clark, at the start of the war, chief of Army Field Forces,[9] and in 1952, commander-in-chief of Far East Command (FEC) and of the United Nations Command (UNC). Clark had commanded the U.S. Fifth Army in Italy in World War II. Writing in 1950, he had argued that the command setup for air-ground operations in Italy had been unsatisfactory and remained so:

> I believed then…that ground troops cannot be successful in battle unless adequately supported by combat aviation, and that such planes as are used for this purpose are necessarily auxiliary weapons, as is the artillery, and that they should come under the direct orders of the ground commander. That, in a sentence, is still my belief today.[10]

All of these issues would surface repeatedly during the Korean War. Other problems occurred as well. Close air support is a difficult, complex, and dangerous operation that requires practice for its effective conduct. In the post–World War II era of tight budgets and the Air Force's focus on its strategic mission at the expense of tactical aviation, little emphasis had been placed on air-ground operations, and neither the soldiers nor the airmen were sufficiently practiced in the relevant techniques. All this would have posed obstacles to the effective conduct of close air support in the early days of the war, but the air-ground relationship was complicated by attitudes and perceptions engendered during the Air Force's long struggle to become an independent armed service and the interservice infighting that had occurred during and after the enactment of the National Security Act of 1947, the 1949 amendments to that act, and the efforts to elucidate the roles and missions of the three services.[11] The Air Force leadership saw both the service's future and its justification for independence in its ability to conduct strategic attack. Evidence suggests that the Air Force established the Tactical Air Command out of concern that, if it did not do so, the Army would succeed in gaining control of all tactical air assets.[12] During the Korean

War, especially during the first year, Air Force officers would react with suspicion to criticism and recommendations for changing the CAS system, seeing these actions in light of the roles and missions struggle as attempts to reopen the issue of Air Force independence and control of tactical aviation.[13]

Furthermore, an alternative approach to CAS doctrine and procedures was already available. To the Navy and Marine Corps, close air support was not only an appropriate and suitable use of air power, it was a proper substitute for artillery in amphibious operations. The Navy and marines had devoted considerable effort to developing and practicing effective procedures for close air support and in optimizing aircraft for the ground-attack role. The procedures involved rapid response, from aircraft carriers or from airfields close to the battle area, to requests sent directly from the frontline ground units and involved measures to control the attacks by ground TACPs down to the battalion level.[14]

The Navy and Marine Corps also adhered to a definition of *close* in close air support that was much nearer the frontline troops than the concept held by the Air Force, and it was closer than normally expected by the Army. To the Air Force (and in the prevailing Army doctrine), close air support was to be used for targets that artillery could not effectively engage. Hence, the Air Force's CAS strikes were made at distances of greater than 1,000 yards from the front lines, except in extreme emergencies. To the Navy and marines, for whom close air support supplemented and often substituted for artillery, CAS missions were routinely conducted within 1,000 yards, and sometimes as close as 50–100 yards, of the front lines.[15] The Air Force argued logically that the Navy–Marine Corps system, though suitable and appropriate for amphibious and airborne operations, required air superiority, air bases close to the front lines, and more aircraft and TACPs than could reasonably be provided to Army units in sustained operations.[16] All these arguments had merit, but from the perspective of the soldier on the ground, the Navy–Marine Corps system was very appealing.

Desperate Days: June–August 1950

Immediately after the North Korean attack, Maj. Gen. Earle E. Partridge's Fifth Air Force, the tactical air force stationed in Japan as part of Lt. Gen. George E. Stratemeyer's U.S. Far East Air Forces (FEAF), began conducting air operations, sweeping the North Korean air force from the skies and supporting Republic of Korea (ROK) Army forces. On July 3, 1950, the first Air Force TACPs arrived in Korea. Two days later, U.S. Army forces went into action against the North Koreans; soon thereafter Lt. Gen. Walton H. Walker established the headquarters of Eighth U.S. Army in Korea. Eighth Army and Fifth Air Force constituted the field army and tactical air force that would work together to conduct air-ground operations as envisioned in FM 31–35 and the JTD. General Partridge established a forward headquarters, Fifth Air Force in Korea, and he and Walker began to put the system into effect. The JOC specified by in the doctrine began operations on July 14.[17]

Problems, understandably, arose. Structured primarily for the air defense of Japan, Fifth Air Force had been equipped with short-range jet interceptors and a few all-weather fighters not well-suited for CAS operations. Its light-bomber force was designed for interdiction. The front line changed daily as Eighth Army units fell back in the face of the North Korean attack. Communications were difficult. Eighth Army did not have the assets to establish the AGOS communication net for tactical air requests. The previous failure by both Eighth Army and Fifth Air Force to practice CAS procedures added to the problems. Air Force TACPs had difficulty getting close to the front lines, and, when they did, they were often shot up, leading Fifth Air Force to make use of airborne tactical air coordinators, initially flying in light aircraft and then in fast, tough, and maneuverable T–6 Texan advanced trainers, which became known as Mosquitoes from their radio call sign. Army ground units found that, in the absence of the doctrinally mandated but nonexistent Army radio net, they could send requests for CAS missions directly to the JOC by way of the Mosquito radio net. Though bypassing the various layers of the AGOS, this system was quite satisfactory from the perspective of beleaguered frontline forces. Working with TACPs assigned to every Eighth Army regiment and using their tactical air control radio net as the ad hoc system for Army calls for fire, Mosquitoes became the key element of the Air Force CAS system.[18]

In late July, with the North Koreans threatening to envelop the southern flank of the Eighth Army, General MacArthur directed the aircraft carriers of Navy Task Force 77 (USS *Valley Forge* and HMS *Triumph*) to assist in the support of frontline forces in southwest Korea. Until now, Navy carriers had conducted strikes against targets in North Korea and attempted to interdict North Korean lines of communications. Some problems had arisen in coordinating these earlier operations, and the addition of Navy aircraft, with their different communications systems, doctrine, and procedures, compounded the difficulties.[19] From the perspective of the ground forces, however, the important issue was their exposure to the Navy's version of close air support. Earlier, to overcome the problems of the inability of jet fighters to operate from unimproved airfields in Korea and the consequent short time on station and light bombloads necessitated by operating from Japan, the Air Force had brought into service World War II–era, propeller-driven F–51 Mustang fighter-bombers, well-liked by the ground forces. The Navy's propeller-driven Douglas AD Skyraiders and Vought F4U Corsairs had much larger ordnance loads and could stay on station much longer than Air Force jets could, reinforcing the Army view that purpose-built CAS aircraft—preferably propeller-driven, not jet—were better suited to the Army's needs.[20]

Army perceptions that the Army–Air Force CAS system was flawed increased with the arrival on August 3, 1950, of Brig. Gen. Edward A. Craig's 1st Provisional Marine Brigade, consisting of the 5th Marine Regimental Combat Team and Marine Air Group 33 (MAG–33).[21] Flying from small, escort aircraft carriers stationed close offshore and making use of the Marine Corps CAS system, MAG–33 conducted exceptionally effective operations in support of both marine and Army forces. When supporting the marine brigade, MAG-33 aircraft did not report to the JOC; they used their established air control procedures. When the marine brigade was not in action, MAG–33 furnished its CAS capabilities to the JOC for use in support of the entire Eighth U.S. Army in Korea line. Inevitably, ground forces made unfavorable comparisons between the responsiveness and accuracy of the marine CAS missions and the performance both of the Army–Air Force system and the Air Force pilots.[22]

The situation was aggravated by press articles making these same unfavorable comparisons. General Stratemeyer, who had made every effort to support Eighth Army, including using B–29 strategic bombers in a tactical role, was angered by these reports that he called "reprehensible pieces of carefully contrived propaganda and untruths." He attributed them to the machination of Navy leaders in Washington who, he believed, were trying to discredit the newly independent Air Force. Stratemeyer argued that the marine focus on close air support was possible only because Fifth Air Force controlled the skies and too few personnel, aircraft, and other resources were available to provide the same level of support to all of Eighth Army.[23] In August, Stratemeyer asked General Walker to rebut one of the articles, but he was disappointed with Walker's reply which summarized the Army perspective on close air support in Korea:

> As for the support rendered my troops by the Fifth Air Force, I have every praise for the cooperation and assistance of Partridge and his people and have gone on record in this regard. Without the slightest intent of disparaging the support of the Air Forces, I must say that I, in common with the vast majority of officers of the Army, feel strongly that the Marine system of close air support has much to commend it. Marine aviation is designed, equipped and trained for the sole purpose of supporting Marine ground forces. It operates equally well from land bases or carriers, often permitting support from short distances not possible if there is sole dependence upon land air bases. During training and maneuvers, Marine aviation works constantly with ground units to perfect the communications and coordination so essential in the application of any type of supporting fires, whether delivered by aircraft, artillery, or supporting infantry weapons. Tactical air support parties are available to units down to and including the infantry battalion. In short, although there are probably strong reasons such as governmental economy to the contrary, I feel strongly that the Army would be well advised to emulate the Marine Corps and have its own tactical support aviation.[24]

The X Corps Perspective: September–December 1950

The Eighth Army front line finally stabilized at the end of July. On July 20, Maj. Gen. Otto P. Weyland became vice commander of FEAF, bringing with him his experience as commander of the XIX Tactical Air Command in Europe during World War II. Under Weyland's influence, FEAF overcame many of the earlier problems of air operations.[25] During August and the first two weeks of September 1950, General Walker conducted a tenacious defense of what came to be known as the Pusan perimeter in southeast Korea. Both MAG–33 and Fifth Air Force provided effective close air support in their own ways. In late August, planning began for the amphibious landing at Inchon. This operation and subsequent operations in North Korea would further influence Army perceptions of close air support and involve the most tenacious critic of the Army–Air Force air-ground operations system: Maj. Gen. Edward M. Almond. A graduate of both the Army Air Corps Tactical School and the Naval War College, General Almond had commanded an infantry division in Italy during the final year of the preceding war, a time when CAS procedures had been perfected and air power was abundant. As General MacArthur's chief of staff, he had taken a keen interest in target selection and other aspects of air operations, often to the discomfort of Generals Stratemeyer and Partridge.[26]

Vice Adm. Arthur D. Struble, U.S. Seventh Fleet commander, was overall commander of the amphibious phase of the Inchon operation. General MacArthur gave Almond command of the ground force, called X Corps, an ad hoc unit made up of the 7th Infantry Division, 1st Marine Division, and 1st Marine Air Wing (MAW). The arrangements for air support of the operation were very much to Almond's liking. The Navy controlled the airspace over the amphibious objective area prior to the landing, and it conducted attacks against airfields within 150 miles of Inchon. General Stratemeyer had overall control of the air campaign and was responsible for interdiction operations to isolate the Seoul-Inchon area. He was also responsible for the support of Eighth Army and for other air operations outside the AOA. Marines flying from the escort carriers would provide close air support to the landing force. Once an airfield was captured, the 1st MAW would assume CAS responsibilities and become the X Corps Tactical Air Command.[27]

Simultaneously with the Inchon landing, Eighth Army began its breakout from the Pusan perimeter, with close air support provided by Fifth Air Force. When Eighth Army and X Corps linked up south of Seoul on September 26, 1950, General Walker anticipated that he would take control of X Corps, and General Partridge expected to take operational control of marine aviation operating in Korea. Instead, General MacArthur kept X Corps as an independent force, reactivated Admiral Struble's joint task force, and sent X Corps (now including an additional U.S. infantry division and an ROK Army corps) into northeast Korea while the Eighth Army pushed into the northwest.[28] Reluctant-ly, General Stratemeyer agreed to the continuation of the arrangement whereby the 1st MAW operated as the X Corps "integral supporting air arm," with the proviso that, once the amphibious operation in northeast Korea was completed, FEAF would gain operational control of all land-based air operations in Korea."[29]

Air-ground operations in northeast Korea, with TACPs assigned down to the battalion level and with fast-response marine CAS procedures, convinced Almond of the superiority of the Marine Corps system. He asked Fifth Air Force to provide enough TACPs to outfit every battalion in his U.S. and Korean divisions, a request that prompted General Partridge to visit X Corps headquarters to reiterate the doctrine set forth in FM 31–35 and the JTD, to explain the limitations on the ability of the Air Force to provide TACPs, and to encourage General Almond to provide the resources required to make the air-ground operations system work, including X Corps representation at the JOC. Almond's lack of response caused General Stratemeyer to note in his diary: "General Almond is not a team player and is attempting to control, contrary to all written documents, the Air Force that supports him."[30]

Army dissatisfaction with the existing CAS system went beyond General Almond. General Clark, chief of Army Field Forces, who had been critical of the Air Force system of close air support in his prewar book, continued to examine the issue. In October 1950, he wrote to the Army chief of staff laying out a series of recommendations to improve air-ground operations. The key proposals were for one group (two or three squadrons) of fighter-bombers for each division in combat, the development of aircraft "primarily designed for tactical support roles," and the establishment of a joint air support center where all the services would formulate doctrine, pursue research, and conduct training to perfect close air support.[31] In December, Clark published an article in *Air Force Magazine* publicly calling for aircraft specifically designed for close air support. He countered Air Force arguments about the survivability of such aircraft by saying that the CAS aircraft should be escorted and protected by high-performance fighters.[32] In November 1950, the chief of staff of the Army, Gen. J. Lawton Collins, wrote to the chief of staff of the Air Force, expressing dissatisfaction with the support provided to Army forces. He reiterated Clark's proposals for a fighter-bomber group to be deployed to support each division in an overseas field army and for Army input into the development of CAS aircraft. He further argued that field army commanders and, in some cases, corps commanders should have operational control of "close air support units engaged in providing reconnaissance and fire support to the ground operation."[33]

Interviewed on November 25, 1950, Walker expressed his views on the issue. His comments were interpreted as an endorsement of the Air Force system, and the official Air Force historian quoted the first part of Walker's statement to the effect that, had it not been for the Fifth Air Force, the Eighth Army could not have stayed in Korea.[34] But Walker went on to talk about the Marine Corps system: "It's good, it's excellent, and I would like to have that kind of air support available, too," he said, acknowledging that the marine system was unaffordable for a large army. With regard to the air-ground operations system, he mused:

> I am entirely familiar with 31–35 and am in complete accord with it's [sic] provisions. Now, after I have had an opportunity to examine the subject more thoroughly, maybe, just maybe, I will be in favor of closer control by an appropriate army unit, but I am not prepared to recommend it now. I am thinking ahead, and of the possibility of achieving even closer teamwork such as was accomplished between Artillery and the Infantry when the Artillery was assigned to the Infantry Division.[35]

Walker would never have the chance to "examine the subject more thoroughly." He wrote those words the day before the massive Chinese attacks that would end the U.N. incursion into the north and change the character of the Korean War. A month later he would be dead, killed in a Jeep accident after the headlong withdrawal of the Eighth Army in the face of the Chinese attack.

The withdrawal of Eighth Army and X Corps from North Korea strengthened the widespread view in the Army that the Marine Corps system was superior. Although both Fifth Air Force and Navy and marine fliers provided critical and essential close air support to the retreating forces, delays were often long between the desperate calls for support from Eighth Army units and the arrival of Fifth Air Force fighters on target.[36]

Marine Corps and Navy pilots, flying from carriers and bases near the front, were consistently on target quickly and responsive to the ground units. Much of the problem with the Fifth Air Force operations stemmed from deficiencies in the control system that neither Eighth Army nor the Air Force had ever adequately addressed, but the perspective of the men on the ground was concisely summed up by the historian Allan Millett:

> The December campaign simply reinforced the conviction in X Corps from General Almond to the lowliest rifleman that the Marine system surpassed the Air Force system in every way. If the Chinese intervention had dampened Eighth Army's satisfaction with Fifth Air Force, it sent X Corps' expectations for close air support soaring.[37]

Reorganization and Mobile Warfare

After the withdrawal from North Korea, it was the Air Force and not the marine system that was installed. The 1st MAW was separated from X Corps, coming under General Partridge's operational control in accordance with previously agreed-upon directives. X Corps was subordinated to Eighth Army, ending its 3½-month existence as an independent force.[38]

Over the next 2½ years, in spite of recurring efforts by Army commanders to gain control of a portion of the tactical air assets and to decentralize the air request system and make it more responsive, successive Air Force commanders would successfully rebuff these efforts to change the FM 31–35, JTD system, even while making efforts to improve the responsiveness and effectiveness of the system. Several reasons contributed to this. Army views of Air Force close air support were not all negative. Although both General Collins in Washington and Lt. Gen. Matthew B. Ridgway in Korea had raised questions about the responsiveness of Air Force close air support, neither was prepared to raise the level of interservice conflict, and both viewed close air support in the context of larger issues. The Air Force had also taken measures to improve the standing of tactical aviation within the Air Force and the responsiveness of the CAS system.[39]

Studies conducted by the Air Force and Army during the fall and winter of 1950 had identified shortcomings, but all had generally endorsed the FM 31–35 doctrine and recommended that resources be provided to fully implement the system.[40] These studies were influential in buttressing the Air Force position, but dissenting voices were heard. A study directed by the FEC concluded that the Marine Corps system of close air support was markedly more responsive to frontline commanders, noting that the time from submission of a CAS request by a regiment or division until a Fifth Air Force aircraft was on target was at least 45 minutes, whereas Marine aircraft were on target within 5 to 10 minutes after a request was submitted.[41] At General Almond's direction, X Corps had conducted its own studies which concluded that the Army should have a say in the development of tactical support aircraft, that the primary mission of tactical air units should be tactical air support, that a TACP should be part of the organization of every infantry battalion and higher headquarters, that field army or separate corps commander should have operational control over supporting tactical air units, and that at least one squadron of twenty-four tactical aircraft should be apportioned to each infantry division.[42] The recommendations of the X Corps study reflected the key aspects of a majority Army view of close air support in the Korean War and would, in one form or another, periodically resurface throughout the war.

From January until May 1951, a war of movement raged across Korea as the Chinese pushed deep into the south until the Eighth Army, now commanded by General Ridgway, counterattacked and drove the Chinese north and recaptured Seoul on March 14, 1951. The Chinese launched another offensive in April, but the Eighth Army stopped this attack north of Seoul, went back on the counteroffensive, and by mid-June 1951 was generally north of the 38th parallel.[43] During this time, General Almond made every effort to continue the marine system as a model for controlling CAS missions in X Corps, even after the marines were detached and he lost his own Tactical Air Command. He organized additional, provisional TACPs manned and equipped with Army personnel to supplement those provided by the Air Force in constructing the thirteen TACPs per division that he considered essential. In January 1951, with TACPs at every battalion-sized force, X Corps could handle additional CAS sorties, and Almond asked for additional airborne air controllers and CAS sorties. General Ridgway persuaded Fifth Air Force to honor calls for fire from these "provisional" TACPs.[44]

Although General Ridgway continued to examine the issue of improving the effectiveness of close air support, he did not wholeheartedly endorse Almond's proposals, and he generally supported General Partridge's insistence that Eighth Army follow Air Force doctrine.[45] In February, Ridgway rebuffed requests from Maj. Gen. Oliver P. Smith, 1st Marine Division commanding general, to have the 1st MAW support his division. Ridgway also rejected Smith's later request as acting IX Corps commander for operational control of at least one marine squadron.[46] Smith later raised the issue with Lt. Gen. Lemuel C. Shepherd, commanding general of Fleet Marine Force Pacific, who brought the matter to MacArthur's attention. General Partridge agreed to an informal procedure that provided some marine air support for the marine division, but he refused to place any part of the 1st MAW under ground force operational control. The MAW commander, Maj. Gen. Field Harris, was more sympathetic to Partridge's view than to Smith's, and the new Eighth Army commander, Lt. Gen. James A. Van Fleet, backed Partridge.[47] General Ridgway, now having replaced MacArthur as commander-in-chief of FEC and the UNC, also told Shepherd that "it was obviously unreasonable…to make the Marine Air Wing solely available to the 1st Mar Div when six U.S. Army Divisions, all engaged in a common mission with the 1st Mar Div, could not possibly be given but a small fraction of this support."[48]

In March 1951, Ridgway asked his artillery commander, Brig. Gen. John J. Burns, to examine the overall issue of fire support coordination. Burns formed a board to examine the issues. The Burns Board concluded that the procedures established in the JTD were valid and appropriate to the Korean theater of operations. The board recommended, however, that the air-ground system be linked to the artillery Fire Support Coordination Center system. While TACPs would remain at the regimental level, with four per division, each TACP should have "dependable and immediate communications with the artillery battalion FDC [Fire Direction Center] so that targets can be coordinated for attack by artillery and/or air, when possible from which it can visually control the target area."[49]

On April 14, 1951, General Van Fleet took command of Eighth Army.[50] Van Fleet had risen from regimental to corps command in World War II and, as head of the U.S. Military Advisory and Planning Group in Greece during the Greek civil war, was instrumental in developing the CAS capability of the Royal Hellenic Air Force. Speaking of close air support during the final big offensive of the Greek civil war, Van Fleet would later reminisce that it "was always a joy to see that combined joint effort by three nations and three services."[51] In the same 1973 oral history, Van Fleet claimed to be very satisfied with close air support in Korea, noting in particular the use of B–29s dropping 500-pound bombs within

300 yards of the front line.[52] On May 13, 1951, General Stratemeyer happily recorded in his diary a message from General Van Fleet to his corps commanders and to the ROK Army, directing them to limit CAS requests "in order to provide maximum air effort for interdiction." This was the first time, he reported to the chief of staff of the Air Force, "that such a signal has emanated from the United States Army over here and speaks well for the planning and thinking of Lieutenant General Van Fleet."[53] In fact, Van Fleet's views on close air support were by no means totally aligned with those of the Air Force, and he would, on several occasions, complain about the quality of close air support and request that CAS assets be placed under his operational control.

The period from April to June 1951 saw tough fighting, as the Eighth Army repelled the Chinese spring offensive and then counterattacked to a line north of the 38th parallel. General Almond, who once again had the 1st Marine Division as part of X Corps, conducted a study of CAS operations during that period. He concluded that, although close air support had been good, it was "not adequate due to the average time interval of 67 minutes between front line requests and the delivery of air strikes." He called for air bases to be located closer to the front line, preferably within the corps area, and for all CAS squadrons to be placed under the operational control of the field army commander with further allocation to the corps, depending upon the tactical situation.[54] General Ridgway continued to support the Air Force perspective on the operational control issue, however, particularly as the nature of warfare in Korea now changed profoundly.

Stalemate

In May 1951, after a major strategy review, the U.S. leadership, concluding that any further advances would require the introduction of substantial additional forces, decided to pursue truce negotiations. The rising cost of the war, the success of the UNC counteroffensive, and the failure of their own spring offensives also led the Chinese and North Korean leadership, with Soviet agreement, to seek a negotiated end to the war with the objective of restoring the prewar boundary. Truce talks began on July 10, 1951, and lasted for two years.[55] Although many local attacks, hard fighting, and heavy casualties would be incurred, neither side would undertake another major ground offensive. With the enemy forces dug into fortified positions, CAS attacks became increasingly dangerous and difficult. The Air Force was reluctant to expend aircraft for missions they believed could be better performed by artillery without the risk of losing expensive aircraft and trained crews. More important, General Ridgway saw air power as the one way he could bring the Chinese and North Koreans to the negotiating table in the absence of a major UNC ground offensive. Interdiction and attacking strategic targets became more important than ever.[56]

The CAS issue continued to smolder as personalities changed in Korea. In June, General Weyland took over Far East Air Forces, and Lt. Gen. Frank F. Everest became Fifth Air Force commander. Maj. Gen. Clovis E. Byers replaced

General Almond as X Corps commander on July 15, 1951. As commandant of the Army War College, Almond continued the fight for a decentralized air-request system and operational control of CAS assets by ground commanders.[57]

In August 1951, the new Fifth Air Force commander began focusing his efforts on interdiction, reducing the amount of close air support available for the frontline forces. General Van Fleet was at that time considering a limited-objective offensive and was amenable to Everest's arguments that the stepped-up interdiction would weaken the enemy's ability to respond to the offensive. Van Fleet eventually canceled the offensive, believing that the benefits to be gained weren't worth the probable high cost in casualties, but, because he anticipated only limited offensive operations over the next few months, he agreed with Everest that interdiction should continue to take priority and that ninety-six CAS sorties a day would meet the needs of the Eighth Army.[58]

In September, however, General Van Fleet ordered a limited-objective advance to capture key terrain in the mountainous Punchbowl area of central Korea. Problems with close air support, particularly for the 1st Marine Division in General Byers's X Corps, led Van Fleet to ask the Air Force commanders to review the CAS procedures. In October 1951, Generals Collins and Ridgway visited General Van Fleet in Korea. During their discussions, the Eighth Army commander raised the subject of close air support, and both General Byers, the X Corps commander, and the 1st Marine Division commander argued vigorously for improvements in close air support. Weyland and Everest were willing to make some adjustments that would allow marine aircraft to provide support to the 1st Marine Division, but they remained adamant on the issue of greater authority over close air support by the ground commanders. Historian Allan Millett suggests that General Byers's vigorous efforts to change the CAS system led to his removal from combat command in Korea.[59]

In December 1951, General Van Fleet had become sufficiently disgruntled with the close air support provided to the Eighth Army to make a strong bid to change the system fundamentally. In a memorandum to General Ridgway, he argued that not enough sorties were allocated to close air support, that airfields were too far from the front lines, that the system of JOC control of all missions caused unacceptable delays in responses to calls for fire, that there were too few TACPs, and that no aircraft optimized for close air support had been developed since World War II. He proposed a short-term solution: place three marine squadrons under his operational control with further control decentralized to the corps; locate advance air bases near corps headquarters; and process CAS requests by the corps and use trained Army personnel to control air strikes. In a separate letter intended for Ridgway's eyes only, Van Fleet pointed out that, although he and Everest saw eye to eye on most issues, the Air Force was institutionally unwilling to accept any ground control of air assets.[60]

On January 12, 1952, General Weyland responded to Van Fleet's proposals. He accepted that there could be "modifications and refinements in tactics, in the systems and methods of last-phase control of close air support aircraft, and similar matters," but he insisted that "the air units in Korea must be retained under centralized command and control."[61] At General Ridgway's request, the FEC chief of operations, Brig. Gen. Edwin K. Wright, reviewed the correspondence. He concluded that Weyland's memorandum was "another inflexible expression of the Air Force position" but noted that Weyland had strong support in the recently approved joint regulations on Joint Action Armed Forces. Wright knew "of no ground commander who has taken part in the Korean War who is satisfied that he is getting the best close air support possible" and whose objectives concurred with Van Fleet's. However, he also noted that operations in Korea had been conducted effectively "for the first time under a truly unified command" without serious interservice rancor, and he thought it undesirable to become embroiled in interservice disputes now. He recommended against any action that would be "in violent opposition to the policy of any service" and suggested the correspondence be forwarded to the chief of staff of the Army. General Ridgway wrote on the memo that his decision was not to forward the correspondence to Washington, "but orally to ask WEYLAND to sit down with VAN FLEET and discuss frankly ways of improving tac air support, particularly 'close air [support]'; WEYLAND also to personally acquaint himself with the wide-spread view of ground commanders that tac air support in Korea is NOT as good as it should be."[62] This essentially ended any prospect of fundamental change in the CAS system while also making clear General Ridgway's dissatisfaction.

The new doctrinal statement on Joint Action Armed Forces (JAAF) that General Wright referred to had been issued on September 19, 1951, by the three services to establish "the principles, doctrines, and procedures governing the activities and performance of the Armed Forces when two or more Services or elements thereof are acting together to achieve a common task or mission."[63] The JAAF gave the Air Force primary responsibility, "in coordination with the other Services," to develop "joint doctrines and procedures for close combat air support of ground forces" and to establish and operate a joint tactical air support board in which the other two services would participate. Each service was responsible for providing the necessary "communications, personnel, and equipment" for developing its own relevant "equipment, tactics, and techniques" and for training its own forces in the conduct of "close combat air support of ground forces."[64] The JAAF document also established that when one force was assigned "the sole mission of close support…the supported force will exercise general direction of the supporting force [including] designation of targets or objectives, timing, duration of the supporting action, and other instructions necessary for coordination and for gaining the greatest advantage."[65]

On May 12, 1952, Gen. Mark W. Clark replaced Ridgway as the UNC and FEC commander-in-chief. General Van Fleet renewed his efforts to have some CAS assets placed under Eighth Army operational control, but whereas Clark had previously been a strong advocate for the Army view of close air support, when faced with the responsibilities of a unified commander, like Ridgway, he subordinated his views to the larger issue of effective cooperation among the services. He would later write, "I hadn't come to the Far East to aggravate this basic difference of opinion between the Air Force and the Army. It was my job to work around the fringes of this unsolved problem."[66] There was little change, except for incremental improvement in techniques, in close air support for the remaining year and a half of war.

Conclusion

At the end of the Korean War, the Army view of close air support was mixed. In the minds of those who actually experienced the battlefield, from privates to generals, none questioned the value of close air support to the Army's mission. One veteran of the Pusan perimeter battles wrote:

> Almost every soldier and Marine who fought in Korea in those early days soon "fell in love with" the fighters that swooped in to their aid one time after another. The Corsair and F–51 aircraft were the favorites because they seemed to be able to stay overhead the longest. Jets appeared too fast to the infantryman, but they, too were cheered.[67]

Army participants at a postwar conference on close air support at Fifth Air Force headquarters agreed that the JOC-based system of control of tactical air operations had improved in the course of the war and could be improved further through better communications and more training. They accepted the value of a single air commander for theater air operations, the primacy of air superiority, and the importance of interdiction. But the Army participants, with their Navy and Marine Corps counterparts, made a series of proposals that reflected the key tenets of the Army view of close air support: allocation of some portion of the tactical air effort to the operational control of corps commanders, decentralization and simplification of the air request system, and the provision for TACPs down to the battalion level. The Air Force representatives rejected these proposals or any deviation for the existing doctrine established in the JTD.[68] So the perception lingered in the Army that the Air Force approach to close air support was inadequate and that the Marine Corps system of dedicated CAS assets, decentralized air requests, and battalion-level TACPs was superior for the effective accomplishment of their land warfare missions. That attitude would play an important role in the Army's subsequent efforts to get control of its own, organic close air support.

General Ridgway, who had rebuffed General Van Fleet's attempts to gain Army operational control of CAS assets during the war, wrote in 1956 of the "ticklish problem" presented to him as unified commander in the Far East by the "Army's desperate need for close air support, and the Marine Division's opulence in this respect." He praised the Marines for their willingness to provide close air support to the Army divisions, saying that

> efforts to speed up and improve the use of Air Force planes in close support met with a less cooperative attitude because of policy decisions in Washington.…Requests for air strikes continued to follow the old merry-go-round, up through channels to Army, then to Air Force, and down again. Frequently as a result of this time-consuming procedure, when the planes got there, the enemy had gone.[69]

The link between this experience and postwar events is clear in this statement by Ridgway:

> To do its job on the battlefield…the Army must have the support of combat aircraft that can fly in any kind of weather, under all conditions incident to enemy interference, both in the air and from the ground, and deliver its bomb load, or its rockets, on target with the accuracy of a field gun. If the Air Force should develop such planes, we would be deeply pleased. If they continue to ignore our needs in this respect, we eventually will have to develop them ourselves."[70]

In 1956, Gen. Maxwell D. Taylor, the last commanding general of the Eighth Army in the Korean War, declared to a conference of senior Army commanders that "we haven't had close effective tactical air support; we cannot expect to have it in the future. The high-performance Air Force planes are flying away from us; they have left the battlefield."[71]

The Army would, over the next several decades, through a slow and often uncoordinated process, acquire its own CAS assets. The National Security Act of 1947 that had established the Air Force as a separate service also provided a mandate for the Army's possession of aircraft. When the Korean War began, the Army holdings had been exclusively light, fixed-wing aircraft and a few helicopters for artillery spotting, observation, and liaison duties. The war had seen a substantial increase in the number of helicopters flown by Army pilots and their use in aeromedical evacuation, resupply, and even tactical movements of troops. The major focus of the Army's post–Korean War efforts to acquire aircraft was mobility. Those who worked to secure an expanded role for aviation in the Army were not intentionally trying to replace the Air Force as the provider of close air support. Nonetheless, the perception that the Air Force could not be depended on had an effect in a process that eventually led to the development of Army helicopters with CAS capabilities far transcending the beloved Air Force F–51 Mustangs, marine Corsairs, and Navy Skyraiders.[72]

The bitter interservice rivalries of the late 1940s and early 1950s are muted today, if not entirely absent. Today's doctrine and procedures for unified action and the technological capabilities of all the services provide for a responsiveness, accuracy, and effectiveness of close air support that the Korean War soldiers would envy. Echoes of the old disputes can still be heard, and the Army view of close air support has not fundamentally changed, regardless of the uniform worn by the soldier. Before the 1991 ground offensive began in Afghanistan, television news showed an interview with a Northern Alliance commander who was complaining that he watched U.S. aircraft flying overhead to hit Kabul and Khandahar while he needed the air strikes. To paraphrase his comments: "I want it all, I want it now, and I want it on that ridgeline right over there."

Notes

1. Jeremy Black, "War and Strategy in the 21st Century," Foreign Policy Research Institute Watch on the West, vol 3, no 4 (4 Feb 2002); available via the Internet at http://www.fpri.org/ww/0304.200202.black.warandstrategy21stcentury.html, accessed Apr 15, 2002.
2. Robert Frank Futrell, *Ideas, Concepts, Doctrine: A History of Basic Thinking in the United States Air Force, 1907–1964* (Maxwell Air Force Base, Ala.: Air University, 1971), pp 375-77; United States Army, War Department, Field Manual 31–35, *Air-Ground Operations* (Washington, D.C.: GPO, 1946); and United States Army Field Forces and United States Air Force Tactical Air Command, *Joint Training Directive for Air-Ground Operations* (Fort Monroe and Langley AFB, Va.: Office, Chief, Army Field Forces and Headquarters, Tactical Air Command, Sep 1, 1950).
3. Useful summaries of the development of U.S. CAS doctrine in World War II can be found in David Syrett, "The Tunisian Campaign, 1942–1943"; Alan F. Wilt, "Allied Cooperation in Sicily and Italy, 1943–1945"; Will A. Jacobs, "The Battle for France, 1944"; and Joe Gray Taylor, "American Experience in the Southwest Pacific," all in Benjamin Franklin Cooling, ed, *Case Studies in the Development of Close Air Support* (Washington, D.C.: Office of Air Force History, 1990). See also John T. Greenwood, "Army Ground Forces and the Air-Ground Battle Team, Including Organic Light Aviation," *The Army Ground Forces*, no 35 (Washington, D.C.: United States Army Ground Forces Historical Section, 1948); Futrell, *Ideas, Concepts, Doctrine*, pp 135–38, 173–78; and Riley Sunderland, *Evolution of Command and Control Doctrine for Close Air Support* (Washington, D.C.: Office of Air Force History, 1973), pp 3–25.
4. United States War Department Basic Field Manual 31–35, *Aviation in Support of Ground Forces* (Washington: GPO, 1942), pp 5–6, 9. The doctrine also identified air superiority and interdiction as the first and second priorities for tactical aviation, with close air support a distant third. These priorities were explicitly set forth in Field Manual 100–20, published in July of 1943. United States War Department, Field Service Regulations FM 100–20, *Command and Employment of Airpower*, Jul 21, 1943 (Washington, D.C.: GPO, 1944), pp 10–11; see also Alfred Goldberg and Donald Smith, *Army-Air Force Relations: The Close Air Support Issue*, Project

RAND Report R-906-PR (Santa Monica, Calif.: RAND, 1971), pp 3–4.

5. This assumption of coequality had been first set forth in FM 100–20, which was the turning point in the quest for the Air Force to be recognized as a separate service and coequal with the Army. The first sentence of FM 100–20 reads, in capital letters, "LAND POWER AND AIR POWER ARE CO-EQUAL AND INTERDEPENDENT FORCES: NEITHER IS AN AUXILIARY OF THE OTHER." FM 100–20, p 1.
6. United States Army, War Department, Field Manual 31–35, *Air-Ground Operations* (Washington, D.C.: GPO, 1946), pp 1, 9–15, 28–68. Allan R. Millett explains the Army–Air Force system very clearly in his "Korea, 1950–1953," Benjamin Franklin Cooling, ed, *Case Studies in the Development of Close Air Support* (Washington: GPO, 1990), pp 347–48. This article is the essential beginning to any study of close air support in the Korean War.
7. Goldberg and Smith, *Army–Air Force Relations*, pp 9–10. Allan Millett points out that, before the Korean War, only Maj Gen Clovis C. Byers, commanding general of the 82d Airborne Division, identified these problems during prewar exercises, but all would become issues during the war. Byers would later command U.S. X Corps in Korea. Millett, "Korea," p 349.
8. Earl McClendon, *Army Aviation, 1947–1953*, Air University Documentary Research Study AU-239-53-RSI (Maxwell AFB, Ala.: Air University, 1954), pp 11–13.
9. Army Field Forces was an organization formed in 1948 to supervise all Army training. James J. Hewes, Jr., *From Root to McNamara: Army Organization and Administration* (Washington, D.C.: Center of Military History, 1975), p 170.
10. Mark W. Clark, *Calculated Risk* (New York: Harper & Brothers, 1950), p 161. Clark would express similar views a few months later in an article in *Air Force Magazine*.
11. For an old but still useful study of the pre–Korean War issues of interservice rivalry, see Paul Y. Hammond, "Super Carriers and B–36 Bombers: Appropriations, Strategy, and Politics," in Harold Stein, ed, *American Civil-Military Decisions: A Book of Case Studies* (Birmingham: University of Alabama Press, 1965), pp 465–67. For two service perspectives, see James A. Field, Jr., *History of United States Naval Operations, Korea* (Washington, D.C.: GPO, 1962), pp 21–34; and Futrell, *Ideas, Concepts, Doctrine*, pp 191–201, 251–59.
12. Caroline Frieda Ziemke, "In the Shadow of the Giant: USAF Tactical Air Command in the Era of Strategic Bombing, 1945–1955" (Ph.D. diss., Ohio State University, 1989), p 18; and Herman S. Wolk, *Planning and Organizing the Postwar Air Force, 1943–1947* (Washington, D.C.: Office of Air Force History, 1984), p 128.
13. See, for example, entries in the diary of Lt Gen George E. Stratemeyer in

which he comments on articles that unfavorably compare U.S. Air Force close air support to that of the Marine Corps. Stratemeyer believed the articles were written by the Navy headquarters in Washington to discredit the Air Force. George E. Stratemeyer, *The Three Wars of Lt. Gen. George E. Stratemeyer: His Korean War Diary*, William T. Y'Blood, ed (Washington, D.C.: United States Air Force History and Museums Program, 1999), 110–11, 129–32.

14. Donald William McMaster, "The Evolution of Tactical Airpower—With Particular Emphasis upon its Application by the U.S. Navy and U.S. Marine Corps in the Korean War, 1950–1953" (M.A. thesis, University of Maryland, 1959), pp 107–108.
15. *Ibid.*, 109–10; Robert F. Futrell, *The United States Air Force in Korea, 1950–1953* (Washington, D.C.: Office of Air Force History, 1983), p 705; and Richard Hallion, *The Naval Air War in Korea* (Baltimore: Nautical and Aviation Publishing Company of America, 1986), pp 43–44.
16. Stratemeyer, *Korean War Diary*, 217–18; Gen Otto P. Weyland, the Far East Air Forces commander for much of the Korean War, made similar points and argued for the greater value of interdiction in a summary of Korean War air operations that he wrote soon after the war: Otto P. Weyland, "The Air Campaign in Korea," *Air University Quarterly Review*, vol 6, no 3 (fall 1953): 3–41.
17. Futrell, *Air Force in Korea*, pp 2–3, 6–13, 30–31, 78; Roy E. Appleman, *United States Army in the Korean War: South to the Naktong, North to the Yalu* (Washington, D.C.: GPO, 1961), pp 51, 95–96; and Conrad C. Crane, *American Airpower Strategy in Korea 1950–1953* (Lawrence, Kans.: University of Kansas Press, 2000), pp 24–28.
18. Futrell, *Air Force in Korea*, pp 79–83, 107–109; and J. Farmer and Michael J. Strumwasser, *The Evolution of the Airborne Forward Air Controller: An Analysis of Mosquito Operations in Korea*, Research memo RM–5430–PR (Santa Monica, Calif.: The RAND Corp, 1967), pp 18–26, 32–39.
19. The Navy–Air Force problems involving integration of Navy air into the overall air effort are beyond the scope of this paper. Good descriptions can be found in Hallion, *Naval Air War*, pp 41–45; Futrell, *Air Force in Korea*, pp 48–51 and 114–19; and Field, *Naval Operations*, pp 110–19, 138–44. Two excellent overviews of command relationship issues in the Korean War are Donald Chisholm, "Negotiated Joint Command Relationships: Korean War Amphibious Operations, 1950," *Naval War College Review*, vol 53, no 2 (spring 2000): 65–124; and James A. Winnefeld and Dana J. Johnson, "Korea, 1950–1953: The Renewed Clash of Service Air Command and Control Doctrines," in *Joint Air Operations: Pursuit of Unity in Command and Control, 1942–1991* (Annapolis, Md.: Naval Institute Press, 1993): 39–62.
20. Crane, *Airpower Strategy*, pp 24–27; hqs, X Corps, "Army Tactical Air Sup-

port Requirements," Dec 25, 1950, p 3; and U.S. Army War College Memorandum, "Reply to AFF Letter on Effectiveness of Close Air Support in Korea," Nov 3, 1952, Edward M. Almond Papers, box "Korean War: Tactical Air Support, Combat Notes & Enemy Tactics," file "Tactical Air Support," U.S. Army Military History Institute (MHI), Carlisle Barracks, Pa.; and Uzal W. Ent, *Fighting on the Brink: Defense of the Pusan Perimeter* (Paducah, Ky.: Turner Publishing Co., 1996), pp 52, 121–22.

21. Appleman, *South to the Naktong*, pp 258–59; Lynn Montross and Nicholas A. Canzona, *U.S. Marine Operations in Korea, 1950–1953*, vol 2, *The Inchon-Seoul Operation* (Washington, D.C.: Historical Branch G-3, hqs, U.S. Marine Corps, 1955), pp 104, 167–70.
22. Millett, "Korea," pp 366–68.
23. Stratemeyer, *Korean War Diary*, pp 110–11, 129–32.
24. Quoted in Stratemeyer, *Korean War Diary*, p 132.
25. Futrell, *Air Force in Korea*, pp 52–55.
26. Biography of Lt Gen Edward M. Almond; Edward M. Almond, "Senior Officer Debriefing Program: Conversations Between Lieutenant General Edward M. Almond and Captain Thomas G. Ferguson," 1975, sec 2, pp 65-72, MHI; and Stratemeyer, *Korean War Diary*, pp 44, 68.
27. Field, *Naval Operations*, pp 179–80, 208; Futrell, Air Force in Korea, pp 151–52; Lynn Montross and Nicholas A. Canzona, *U.S. Marine Operations in Korea, 1950–1953*, vol 3, *The Chosin Reservoir Campaign* (Washington, D.C.: Historical Branch, G–3, hqs, U.S. Marine Corps, 1957), pp 13, 31–34.
28. Shelby L. Stanton, *America's Tenth Legion: X Corps in Korea, 1950* (Novato, Calif.: Presidio Press, 1989), pp 119–64; and Field, *Naval Operations*, pp 219–50.
29. Futrell, *Air Force in Korea*, p 202; and CINCFE Msg CX 66169, Oct 11, 1950, quoted in Stratemeyer, *Korean War Diary*, p 234.
30. Stratemeyer, *Korean War Diary*, p 247.
31. Letter from Chief of Army Field Forces to Chief of Staff, United States Army, ATSEC 360(C)(24 Oct 50), "Army Requirements for Close Tactical Air Support," Almond Papers, "Tactical Air Support Studies 1950–51," file "Air Support for Ground Forces," MHI.
32. Mark W. Clark, "What Kind of Air Support Does the Army Want?" *Air Force Magazine* (Dec 1950): 24–25, 52, cited in Futrell, *Ideas, Concepts, Doctrine,* p 308.
33. Memo, Chief of Staff of the Army to Chief of Staff of the Air Force, Nov 21, 1950, "Close Air Support of Ground Operations," Almond Papers, box "Korean War Tactical Air Support Studies 1950-51," file "Air Support for Ground Operations," MHI.
34. Futrell, *Air Force in Korea*, p 146.
35. Glenn O. Barcus, "An Evaluation of the Effectiveness of the United States Air Force in the Korean Campaign," Target Selection and Intelligence, Jan

1951, U.S. Army Military History Research Collection, copy at MHI.

36. Glenn O. Barcus, *Evaluation of the United States Air Force in the Korean Campaign* (hereafter as Barcus Report), vol II, ch 1, "The Air-Ground Team," file K 168.041-1, Air Force Historical Research Agency (AFHRA), Maxwell AFB, Ala., pp 54–55.
37. Millett, "Korea," p 373.
38. *Ibid.*; and Lynn Montross, Hubbard D. Kuokka, and Norman W. Hicks, *U.S. Marine Operations in Korea, 1950–1953*, vol 4, *The East-Central Front* (Washington, D.C.: Historical Branch, G-3, hqs, U.S. Marine Corps, 1962), pp 1–18.
39. Millet, *Korea*, pp 374–78; and Ziemke, *Shadow of the Giant*, 171–74.
40. Summaries of the results of the major Air Force and Army studies are in Crane, *Airpower Strategy*, pp 59–62; Ziemke, *Shadow of the Giant*, pp 164–66, 188–89; and Millett, "Korea," pp 371–72. The most extensive study (*An Evaluation of the Effectiveness of the United States Air Force in the Korean Campaign*, 7 vols, Mar 12, 1951) was conducted by a team headed by Air Force Maj Gen Glenn O. Barcus, who would later take command of Fifth Air Force on May 30, 1952. Another study, intended to be that of an impartial civilian, but directed by the Secretary of the Air Force, was conducted by Dr Robert L. Stearns, president of the University of Colorado ("Korean Evaluation Project: Report on Air Operations, January 16, 1951"). The Army study (Army Air Support Center, ATASC–D 373.21, "Air Support in the Korean Campaign, 1 December 1950") was conducted under the leadership of Brig Gen Gerald J. Higgins.
41. Operations Research Office, Headquarters Far East Command, "Close Air Support Operations in Korea: Preliminary Evaluation," ORO–R–3 (FEC), Feb 1, 1951. A copy is held at the AFHRA.
42. Hqs X Corps, "Army Tactical Air Support Requirements," Dec 25, 1950, MHI.
43. Billy C. Mossman, *United States Army in the Korean War: Ebb and Flow, November 1950 –July 1951* (Washington, D.C.: Office of the Chief of Military History, 1990); and Roy E. Appleman, *Ridgway Duels for Korea* (College Station: Texas A&M University Press, 1990).
44. Ltr, Maj Gen Almond to Gen Collins, Jan 23, 1951; ltr, Maj Gen Almond to Gen Mark W. Clark, Jan 26, 1951; Almond Papers, "Korean War Tactical Air Support Studies 1950–51," file "Air Support of Ground Forces"; and hqs X Corps, "Infantry Battalion Tactical Air Control Parties," Jan 28, 1951, Almond Papers, "Korean War Tactical Air Support Studies 1950-51," file "Battalion Tactical Air Control Parties," MHI.
45. Millett, "Korea," p 378.
46. *Ibid.*
47. *Ibid.*, pp 378–79.
48. Memo, Matthew B. Ridgway, "Summary of Conversation this date with

Gen L. C. Shepherd, USMC, no other persons present," May 24, 1951, Matthew B. Ridgway Papers, box 20, "Eighth Army Correspondence Files," file "Special File April 1951–January 1952," MHI.

49. Matthew B. Ridgway, diary entry for Mar 6, 1951, paragraph 3 on meeting with Gen Partridge (Actg Comdr FEAF) and Gen Timberlake (Actg Comdr Fifth Air Force) and Memo of conversation between Gen Ridgway and Gen Burns, Mar 18, 1951, both in Ridgway Papers, box 20 "Eighth Army Correspondence Files," file "Special File Dec 50–Mar 51;" and U.S. Joint Air Ground Operations Board (EUSAK and 5AF), "Analysis of the Air-Ground Operations System in Korea" (Burns Report), Mar 26, 1951, MHI.
50. Mossman, *Ebb and Flow*, p 366.
51. James A. Van Fleet, "Conversations Between General James A. Van Fleet and Colonel Bruce Williams," 2 vols., Senior Officer Debriefing Program (Carlisle, Pa.: U.S. Army Military History Institute, 1973), the James A. Van Fleet Papers, box "Oral History," pp 45–46, MHI.
52. Van Fleet, "Oral History," p 34.
53. Stratemeyer, *Korean War Diary*, p 513.
54. Hqs X Corps, "Tactical Air Support, X Corps, 10 May –5 June 1951," Almond Papers, "Korean War Tactical Air Support Studies 1950–51," file "Air Support of Ground Forces," MHI.
55. Donald W. Boose, Jr., "The Korean War Truce Talks: A Study in Conflict Termination," *Parameters*, vol 30, no 1 (spring 2000): 102–16.
56. Crane, *Airpower Strategy*, p 76 ff.
57. A substantial part of the extensive Almond Papers at the Military History Institute consist of Almond's directed studies, lectures, and correspondence on the CAS issue. Much of this material is contained in the "Korean War Tactical Air Support" boxes.
58. Walter G. Hermes, *United States Army in the Korean War: Truce Tent and Fighting Front* (Washington, D.C.: Office of the Chief of Military History, 1966), pp 86–87, 105–106.
59. Allan R. Millett, *Drive North: U.S. Marines at the Punchbowl*, Marines in the Korean War Commemorative Series (Washington, D.C.: U.S. Marine Corps Historical Center, 2001), pp 55–57, 59.
60. Ltr, James A. Van Fleet to Commander–in–Chief, Far East Command, AG 370.3 KCG, "Close Air Support," Dec 20, 1951; and ltr, ("Dear Matt"), Dec 20, 1951, James A. Van Fleet Papers, box 84, folder 32, George C. Marshall Library, Lexington, Va.
61. Memo, Lt Gen O. P. Weyland to Gen Matthew B. Ridgway, "General Van Fleet's Letter dated 20 December 1951," Jan 12, 1952, Ridgway papers, box 20, folder "Special File Jan-Apr 51," MHI.
62. Memo, Brig Gen Edwin K. Wright, "Close Air Support" Jan 15, 1952, with hand-written comment by Gen Matthew B. Ridgway, Ridgway papers, box 20, folder "Special File Jan–Apr 51," MHI.

63. United States Departments of the Army, the Navy, and the Air Force, Field Manual 110-5/JAAF/AFM 1-1 Joint Action Armed Forces (Washington, D.C.: GPO, 1951), p v.
64. JAAF, pp 12, 15–16, 20.
65. *Ibid.*, p 36.
66. Mark W. Clark, *From the Danube to the Yalu* (New York: Harper, 1954), p 91.
67. Ent, *Fighting on the Brink*, p 121.
68. Millett, "Korea," pp 394–95
69. Matthew B. Ridgway and Harold H. Martin, *Soldier: The Memoirs of Matthew B. Ridgway* (New York: Harper & Brothers, 1956), p 315.
70. Ibid., pp 314-15.
71. The occasion was an April 5, 1956, Army Commanders' Conference at Fort Bliss, Tex. The remarks are quoted in A. J. Bacevich, The Pentomic Era: The U.S. Army between Korea and Vietnam (Washington, D.C.: National Defense University Press), p 88.
72. For an account of the process whereby the Army gained not only a vast fleet of transport and scout helicopters, but also acquired attack helicopters, see Frederick A. Bergerson, *The Army Gets an Air Force: Tactics of Insurgent Bureaucratic Politics* (Baltimore, Md.: Johns Hopkins University Press, 1980). Bergerson makes the link between the Korean War experiences and Army desires for control of CAS assets on p 52. On p 4 he identifies the armed helicopter as "the ultimate instrument for Army control of close air support." Bergerson's story ends in 1978 with the Cheyenne program. Today's Apache-equipped forces demonstrate that the process continues.

The Close Air Support Controversy in Korea

Capt. Keith F. Kopets, U.S. Marine Corps

The Apple of Discord

Of all the missions flown by the United Nations Command in the Korean War—air superiority, interdiction, armed reconnaissance, and resupply—none caused more discussion and debate in the Far East, Washington, D.C., and the press than did close air support. Of the million-plus sorties flown by the pilots of Far East Air Forces, 123,000 were in close support of ground action, *close* meaning that the strikes required detailed coordination with the infantry and control by a ground or aerial observer.

The strikes themselves were not controversial, except on the few occasions when friendly planes inadvertently strafed or bombed friendly troops. Nor were the strikes novel or innovative: all the American air services in Korea and many of their pilots had experience from World War II in coordinating air attacks with ground action. The Army Air Forces had provided close air support in North Africa, Italy, Europe, and the south Pacific, and the Navy and Marine Corps had done the same in the south, central, and western Pacific. Nor, for that matter, was the controversy in Korea a new phenomenon: during World War II, ground commanders had complained "long and loud" about the quantity and quality of air support they received. They always wanted more, and they always wanted it faster. Speaking from experience, one air commander said, "Hell hath no fury like a…battalion commander suddenly deprived of his air support."[1]

The apple of discord in Korea stemmed from sensationalistic press reporting; lingering interservice bitterness from the 1947 unification hearings and the failed political campaign waged by a group of U.S. Navy officers over the B–36 bomber program; divergent air power philosophies; and a general state of unpreparedness for air-ground operations. This presentation chronicles the close air support (CAS) controversy in Korea; describes the different air-ground operating systems of the U.S. Army, Air Force, and Marine Corps; and referees the debate over which was more effective.

Opening Moves

Lt. Gen. George E. Stratemeyer assumed command of Far East Air Forces in April 1949. A year later, on a Sunday morning, June 25, eight divisions of the North Korean People's Army barreled south across the 38th parallel. General Stratemeyer remained the senior air commander in the Far East until incapacitated by a heart attack in May 1951. His replacement was Maj. Gen. Otto P. Weyland, whose tactical air command covered the Third Army dash across Europe and whom Gen. George S. Patton called "the best damn general in the Air Corps."

The Korean War was the first test of the three-year old independent Air Force. Stratemeyer's largest subordinate command, Fifth Air Force, which Maj. Gen. Earle E. "Pat" Partridge had commanded since 1948, served as tactical air force in Korea and was responsible for planning and implementing close air support for the U.S. Eighth Army, the senior allied ground command in the Far East.[2]

Props versus Jets

Fifth Air Force employed high-performance jets—Lockheed F–80 Shooting Stars and Republic F–84 Thunderjets—as its primary CAS platforms. The limited bomb payload of these aircraft and, more importantly, their runway requirements during the extemporized air war of 1950 caused the Air Force to resurrect the World War II–era, piston-engine North American F–51 Mustang.

The Mustang required less runway, burned less fuel, carried a heavier payload, and could remain on station longer than could the jets. At this stage in the war, the situation in Korea forced the Air Force to keep its jets on strip alert at facilities in Japan, but it could base its Mustangs in Korea. General Stratemeyer, therefore, swapped six squadrons of F–80C Shooting Stars for Mustangs. The Mustangs, with their in-line, liquid-cooled engines and radiators underneath the fuselage, were extremely vulnerable to antiaircraft fire. Jet pilots themselves were not enthused at the prospect of transitioning back to Mustangs. "A lot of pilots," said a member of the 8th Fighter-Bomber Group, "had seen vivid demonstrations of why the F–51 was not a ground-support fighter in the last war and weren't exactly intrigued by the thought of playing guinea pig to prove the same thing over again."[3]

During the Korean War, the Air Force's loss rate of Mustangs was twice that of jets. Marine pilots and naval aviators of the Seventh Fleet also flew close air support using piston-engine, propeller-driven aircraft, and with great results. In fact, Vought F4U Corsairs flew 80 percent of the naval CAS missions during 1950. Their success led to a myth, cited frequently by critics of the Air Force. In actuality, piston-engine aircraft *were not* more effective than jet aircraft in a ground support role, though they seemed to be to casual observers in Korea, especially war correspondents and ground officers. Because conditions in Korea were benign, these World War II aircraft could orbit the battlefield with impunity: Far East Air Forces owned the skies; Seventh Fleet controlled the seas.

Col. Jack R. Cram, a Marine Corps pilot who flew both Corsairs and jets in Korea, said there was no comparison: without question, jets were an improvement on the Corsair. Transitioning from Corsairs to jets, Cram said, was "like going from the Model-T to a Cadillac." Using the dive brake in the jet, he could attack targets at the same speed as if he had been flying a Corsair. He could accomplish his mission twice as fast in a jet than he could in a Corsair, and, absent the vibration and torque from a propeller, he could achieve greater accuracy in hitting his targets with napalm, guns, and rockets than had he been flying a Corsair. Above all else, Colonel Cram emphasized that jets were better air defenders than Corsairs were. "There's no prop job made that can whip a jet," he said.[4]

And jets had already proved their effectiveness during the first few months of the war. After his capture in October 1950, an enemy senior colonel said the Air Force "should use more jets." "Not only did they come in quickly and destroy the target with a great element of surprise," said this former chief of staff of the North Korean 13th Division, "The soldiers feared them because of the great speed and the way the aircraft appeared before the sound of its flight reached them to make them aware of its presence."[5]

Air-Ground Antecedents

> LAND POWER AND AIR POWER ARE CO-EQUAL AND INTERDEPENDENT FORCES; NEITHER IS AN AUXILIARY OF THE OTHER...CONTROL OF AVAILABLE AIR POWER MUST BE CENTRALIZED AND COMMAND MUST BE EXERCISED THROUGH THE AIR FORCE COMMANDER.[6]

These words appeared in capital letters in July 1943 in the opening paragraphs of War Department Field Manual 100–20, *Command and Employment of Air Power*. Many people considered at the time, and still do so today, this field manual to be the Air Force fourteen-page declaration of independence. "In the zone of contact," the manual said, referring to close air support, "missions against hostile units are most difficult to control, are most expensive, and are, in general, least effective."[7] In other words, field artillery was cheaper, faster, and a better source of fire support for the ground commander.

Close air support never ranked higher than third among the tactical priorities of the Air Force, always falling behind air superiority and interdiction. No pilot of any service questioned the need to first gain air superiority, but some did question giving interdiction a higher priority than that given close air support. Air Force officers favored interdiction because it made more sense to them to destroy enemy personnel and materiel before they reached the front, not afterward. Striking the heart of the enemy's industry would starve him into submission, or at least lessen the workload for the infantry.

Unlike the Air Force of 1950, Marine Corps air units had no strategic mission; marine air units had, and still have, purely tactical applications. Because it required a greater amount of training and coordination and carried a smaller margin for error, close air support received more attention from marine pilots than interdiction did. Marine air-ground coordination in Korea was based on two principles:

1. Close air support is an additional weapon for the ground commander to use at his discretion. It neither supplants the other weapons at the ground commander's disposal nor competes with field or naval artillery. The ground commander may employ close air support in either of two ways: against targets his other weapons cannot reach or in conjunction with the ground weapons in a coordinated attack.
2. Timing is of the utmost importance. Ground commanders should have air support readily available. When they call for air support, they should receive it deliberately, accurately, and in coordination with the other assigned units.[8]

Air-Ground Operations, Korea

Fifth Air Force and Eighth Army air-ground operations in Korea followed the dictums of the 1943 manual, *Command and Employment of Air Power*, its August 1946 revision, Field Manual 31–35, *Air-ground Operations*, and the September 1950 *Joint Training Directive for Air-ground Operations,* issued by the Tactical Air Command and Army Field Forces (but not the service headquarters).[9] The post–World War II gutting of the armed forces left neither Fifth Air Force nor Eighth Army prepared for combined operations in 1950. From 1947 to 1950 the Army and the Air Force conducted eight significant joint tactical exercises. All were disappointing.[10] What resulted during the first year of the Korean War was a rigid, bureaucratic air direction system that stressed centralized control of aircraft over response time.

The command and control agency for tactical air operations in Korea was the Joint Operations Center (JOC). It comprised a Fifth Air Force combat operations section and an Eighth Army air-ground operations section.[11] Fifth Air Force essentially ran the JOC and provided liaison officers down to each Eighth Army regiment. The JOC air direction system worked as follows: an Eighth Army maneuver battalion commander requested an air strike through his parent regiment, division, and corps, all the way up to Eighth Army headquarters and the JOC. There, the Eighth Army G–3 (Operations) section air liaison officer consolidated all air requests and identified them to the senior Fifth Air Force representative.

The JOC dispatched strike aircraft to the air liaison officer in the division fire support coordination center, who in turn vectored the aircraft to either an airborne controller or a regimental tactical air control party (TACP), a ground-controlling agency similar to the Rover Joes of World War II. The airborne controllers orbited the battlefield in North American T–6 Texans that answered to the call sign "Mosquito." These spotter craft were similar to the Horsefly Stinson L–5 Sentinel liaison planes that had been used successfully during World War II over another mountainous peninsula, Italy.[12]

According to a senior marine pilot in Korea, a successful CAS system must permit the commander of a battalion to make a request directly to the controlling center and specify the emergency air support he requires; the center must be capable of providing supporting aircraft over the target area within minutes, not hours or days, and it must provide a competent air controller in a forward observation post where he can see the friendly front lines, the aircraft, and the target.[13]

Such were the underpinnings of the Marine Corps air-direction system, under which the TACP of a maneuver battalion requested air strikes directly from a central air control agency, the Direct Air Support Center. The Direct Air Support Center controlled a pool of aircraft (some of which were already airborne in the target area) and directed fighter-bombers to report to the requesting TACP. Intermediate headquarters—regiment and division, for example—monitored air requests and intervened only to cancel strikes when necessary.

The Marines Arrive in Korea

An air-ground brigade of marines arrived in Korea on August 2, 1950, and went into action at Pusan the next day. The 1st Marine Brigade was an air-ground task force built around a reinforced rifle regiment and a composite air group, Marine Aircraft Group 33, featuring two CAS squadrons of Corsairs embarked on the carriers of the Navy's Task Force 77. Its arrival brought another air service to the Far East, with a CAS system and air power philosophy that became the envy of some senior Army officers and a thorn in the side of General Stratemeyer, whose Far East Air Forces had already flown more than 4,000 sorties in close support of the Eighth Army.[14]

One Army regimental commander on the line at Pusan marveled at the marines. "The Marines on our left were a sight to behold," said Col. Paul F. Freeman of the 23d Infantry, "They had squadrons of air in direct support. They used it like artillery. It was 'Hey, Joe—This is Smitty—Knock the left side of that ridge in front of Item Company.' They had it *day and night*. It came off nearby carriers, and not from Japan with only 15 minutes of fuel [remaining] to accomplish its mission."[15]

"Once a Newspaper Touches a Story"

The great American writer Norman Mailer wrote, "Once a newspaper touches a story, the facts are lost forever, even to the protagonists." He may have been writing about the press reporting in Korea. United Press International correspondent Robert Miller wrote a sensationalistic story on August 14 that said, in effect, that marines were providing more effective close air support than the Air

Force was and that Far East Air Forces should emulate the marines. Stratemeyer went through the roof. He called the Miller article "one of the most reprehensible pieces of carefully contrived propaganda and untruths that I have read in my career." Stratemeyer suspected the Navy of subterfuge: "It is my opinion and that of my PIO [public information officer] that this was not only stimulated by Navy sources, but was even prepared by them in detail."[16] Stratemeyer sent a copy of the article to Eighth Army commander Lt. Gen. Walton H. Walker for comment. Walker wrote back on August 18, 1950: "I feel strongly that the Army would be well advised to emulate the Marine Corps and have its own tactical support aviation."[17]

On August 19, Wayne Thomis of the *Chicago Tribune* stirred the pot further with another article claiming the marines had it right and the Air Force had it wrong. Phillip Potter of *The Baltimore Sun* did likewise on August 23. Stratemeyer complained to MacArthur and his superiors back in Washington. The Thomis article "was another step in a planned program to discredit the Air Force and the Army and at the same time…unwarrantly enhance the prestige of the United States Marines," said Stratemeyer. "It is completely unrealistic and plainly dogmatic propaganda and is probably and unfortunately part of a planned conspiracy for the accomplishment of basic changes in the Defense Department."[18]

Marine Aircraft Group 33 and the carrier air wings of the Task Force 77 provided close support for Eighth Army during their defense of Pusan. After Pusan, Marine Aircraft Group 33 served, in effect, as the tactical air force for X Corps during the Inchon landing. After X Corps captured Kimpo airfield, the 1st Marine Air Wing headquarters and a second marine aircraft group moved ashore. The 1st Wing supported the advance of X Corps on Seoul, the corps's landing at Wonsan and its drive along the eastern coast to the Yalu River, and its withdrawal to the port of Hungnam and subsequent evacuation from North Korea. Eighth Army absorbed X Corps in late December 1950; Fifth Air Force did likewise with the 1st Marine Air Wing.

Marine pilots now had to follow the JOC system of close air support. This pleased few and upset many, including Army Lt. Gen. Edward M. Almond who observed marine air firsthand at Inchon, Seoul, and Chosin and whose X Corps had reaped the benefits of the marine air-direction system during the last four months of 1950. Almond had become a disciple and an advocate of marine close air support. He had his staff prepare a study in December 1950. The report, "Army Tactical Air Support Requirements," compared the two systems of close air support used in Korea and came out in strong favor of the marines. Almond's report, however, contained numerous flaws. Supported ground commanders in the Marine Corps did not control their own air. The 1st Marine Air Wing was not an organic unit of the 1st Marine Division. Jets could fly close air support just as effectively as propeller-driven aircraft.[19]

Senior military officers in Washington were already debating the arguments raised by Almond over air-ground operations in Korea. Army Chief of Staff J.

Lawton Collins had written a memorandum to Air Force Chief of Staff Hoyt S. Vandenberg during November: "There is an indispensable requirement for adequate, effective air support for ground operations at all times." "This requirement is currently not being met."[20]

Vandenberg had already dispatched an evaluation team. One of its members was the commander of Tactical Air Command and future commander of Fifth Air Force in Korea, Maj. Gen. Glenn O. Barcus. Dr. Robert L. Stearns of the University of Colorado also served as a member. The evaluation team produced a seven-volume study (*An Evaluation of the Effectiveness of the United States Air Force in Korea*) known popularly as the Stearns-Barcus report. It pronounced the Air Force system of close air support to be completely sound; all it required, according to Stearns and Barcus, was better execution.[21]

Marine commanders believed that, under the new command arrangements of 1951, their pilots were not being allowed to do their jobs. Just as General Stratemeyer had suspected the naval services of subterfuge during the summer and fall of 1950, the marines in 1951 grew suspicious of the Air Force, believing Far East Air Forces was building a case against the existence of marine aviation by having marine aircraft perform the same missions as Air Force aircraft.

Fleet Marine Force Pacific commander Lt. Gen. Lemuel C. Shepherd wrote a letter to the 1st Marine Air Wing commander on April 25, 1951: "Marine Aviation was not bought by the public as a small echo of the Air Force but as a truly professional specialist group.... If we do not realize and fight for this principle, we are helping to write the coroner's certificate for the most powerful close fire support weapon so far devised."[22]

Two days later, on April 27, Shepherd wrote another letter, this time to his boss in the Pacific, Vice Adm. Arthur W. Radford: "We believe in providing for a small number of on-station planes; the Air Force does not. We believe in continuous direct communication between the front line battalion and the controlling air agency; the Air Force does not. We believe that close air support of the front line troops should take precedence over routine interdiction missions; the Air Force does not. We believe these things implicitly, have repeatedly demonstrated their soundness, and adhere to them as principles."[23]

In Hindsight

About to gain legislative protection of its force structure, Marine Corps headquarters chose not to press the issue of close air support in Korea. For their part, the Army and Air Force never did reach a consensus. The issue died on the vine. A series of air interdiction programs in 1951 targeting enemy road networks, rail lines, and bridges and a general destruction campaign from 1952 through the cease-fire diverted aircraft from battlefield support.

So, was there any merit to all the interservice squabbles over close air support? Which method was more effective? Comparisons are not fair to a three-year-old independent Air Force; it had its hands full keeping Eighth Army on the

Korean peninsula during the dark days of summer 1950. Nor is any comparison fair to the marines; their air arm would not have fared as well as it did in Korea without the Air Force first having gained air superiority, then providing vital logistics support to the 1st Marine Air Wing.

In hindsight, the air-ground controversy in Korea boiled down to different philosophies of air power. Thankfully, today's doctrine recognizes the uniqueness of each of the air services and protects their sovereignty.

Notes

This paper is based on Keith F. Kopets, "The Close Air Support Controversy in Korea," *Marine Corps Gazette* (May 2001): 41.

1. Maj Gen Vernon E. Megee, "Tactical Air Support of Ground Forces," *Marine Corps Gazette* (Dec 1955): 33.
2. The basic sources I used for Air Force operations in Korea are Robert F. Futrell, *The United States Air Force in Korea, 1950–1953* (Washington, D.C.: Office of Air Force History, USAF, 1983); Robert F. Futrell, *Ideas, Concepts, Doctrine*, vol 1, *Basic Thinking in the United States Air Force 1907–1960* (Maxwell AFB, Ala.: Air University Press, 1989); and Conrad C. Crane, *American Airpower Strategy in Korea, 1950–1953* (Lawrence, Kans.: University Press of Kansas, 2000). Also useful was Phillip S. Meilinger, *Hoyt S. Vandenberg: The Life of a General* (Bloomington: Indiana University Press, 1989).
3. Quoted in Futrell, *Air Force in Korea*, p 112.
4. Col Charles L. Banks, USMC, and Col Jack R. Cram, USMC, "Win Place and Show for the Jets," *Marine Corps Gazette* (Dec 1951): 15–17.
5. Quoted in Futrell, *Air Force in Korea*, p 133.
6. FM 100–20, *The Command and Employment of Air Power* (1943), quoted in James A. Huston, "Tactical Use of Air Power in World War II: The Army Experience," *Military Affairs* 14 (winter 1950): 167.
7. FM 100–20, quoted in Huston, "Tactical Use of Air Power in World War II," p 168.
8. Lt Col Keith B. McCutcheon, "Close Support Aviation," McCutcheon Papers, Marine Corps Research Center, Quantico, Va. McCutcheon published this document as "Close Air Support SOP," *Marine Corps Gazette* (Aug 1945): 48–50. Also see James A. Ginther, "Keith Barr McCutcheon: Integrating Aviation into the United States Marine Corps, 1937–1971" (Ph.D. diss, Texas Tech University, 1999), pp 38–52; and Maj. Charles W. Boggs, Jr., *Marine Aviation in the Philippines* (Washington: HQMC, 1951), 56–106.
9. Futrell, *Ideas, Concepts, Doctrine*, pp 173–78; Allan R. Millett, "Korea, 1950–1953," in B. Franklin Cooling, ed, *Case Studies in the Development*

of Close Air Support (Washington, D.C.: Office of Air Force History, USAF, 1990), pp 347–48.
10. Millett, "Korea," p 349.
11. Futrell, *Air Force in Korea*, pp 78–79.
12. Millett, "Korea," pp 375–76. On the "Rover Joe" and "Horsefly" air direction systems of World War II, see Alan F. Wilt, "Allied Cooperation in Sicily and Italy, 1943–1945," pp. 208–11, 217–18; and W. A. Jacobs, "The Battle for France, 1944," pp 273–74, in B. Franklin Cooling, ed, *Case Studies in the Development of Close Air Support* (Washington, D.C.: Office of Air Force History, USAF, 1990).
13. Megee, "Tactical Air Support," p 15.
14. I used the following basic sources on the operations of the marines in Korea: Lynn Montross, et al., *U.S. Marine Corps Operations in Korea, 1950–1953* (Washington, D.C.: Historical Division, HQMC, 1954–1972); Malcolm W. Cagle and Frank A. Manson, *The Sea War in Korea* (Annapolis, Md.: Naval Institute, 1957); James A. Field, Jr., *History of United States Naval Operations in Korea* (Washington, D.C.: GPO, 1962); Richard P. Hallion, *The Naval Air War in Korea* (Baltimore, Md.: Nautical & Aviation Publishing, 1986); Millett, "Korea, 1950–1953," pp 345–405; and Allan R. Millett, *In Many a Strife: General Gerald C. Thomas and the U.S. Marine Corps, 1917–1956* (Annapolis, Md.: Naval Institute, 1993).
15. Quoted in Lynn Montross and Capt. Nicholas Canzona, *The Pusan Perimeter* (Washington, D.C.: Historical Division, HQMC, 1954), p 243.
16. William T. Y'Blood, ed, *The Three Wars of Lt. Gen. George E. Stratemeyer: His Korean War Diary* (Washington, D.C.: Air Force History and Museums Program, 1999), p 110.
17. *Ibid.*, p 132.
18. *Ibid.*, pp 128–29.
19. X Corps, Army Tactical Air Support Requirements (1950–51), Gen. Edward M. Almond Papers, U.S. Army Military History Institute (USAMHI), Carlisle Barracks, Pa (Hereafter Almond Papers).
20. Memo, J. Lawton Collins to Hoyt S. Vandenberg, Nov 21, 1950, subj: Close Air Support of Ground Operations, in "Tactical Air Support Files," Almond Papers. Also see Office, Chief of Army Field Forces to C/S, USA, memorandum: "Army Requirements for Close Tactical Air Support," October 24, 1950, in "Tactical Air Support Files," Almond Papers.
21. Millett, "Korea," pp 371–72; Y'Blood, passim; and Crane, *American Air Power Strategy in Korea*, pp 60–61.
22. Lt Gen Lemuel C. Shepherd, CG, FMFPac to Maj Gen Field Harris, CG, 1st MAW, April 25, 1951, in FMFPac, "Report of Observations of CAS in Korea," 7 May 1951, Korean War Collection, Marine Corps Historical Center (MCHC), Washington, D.C.
23. Shepherd to Radford, April 27, 1951, MCHC.

Air Interdiction and Bombardment

Air Interdiction and Bombardment in the Korean War

Edward J. Marolda

The strengths and weaknesses of air power, especially its components of interdiction and bombardment, were clearly revealed in the Korean War. On the positive side, the readiness, flexibility, and forward-basing of U.S. and allied air units prevented the communist North Korean forces from destroying the U.N. ground army in South Korea and seizing the entire peninsula. Only one week after the enemy's combat divisions stormed across the 38th parallel, strike aircraft from one American and one British aircraft carrier bombed targets in and around Pyongyang, the capital and war-making center of North Korea. In the months that followed, U.S. Air Force and Royal Australian Air Force units based in Japan and U.S. naval air forces operating from carriers pummeled communist tracked and wheeled vehicles moving toward Pusan and supply points behind the lines. Simultaneously, allied air forces seized control of the skies over and around the Korean peninsula, a control that was sorely tested by MiG–15s from 1951 to 1953 but was never lost. The presence in the combat theater of a powerful U.N. air and sea armada also discouraged Chinese communist and Soviet activity in the waters surrounding the peninsula. Assured of protection from above, U.N. ships for three years deployed badly needed reinforcements and supplies to South Korea from ports worldwide. Bombardment and interdiction enabled allied forces to mount the masterful amphibious assault at Inchon free from air opposition and then to protect the beachhead from enemy counterattacks. Fire from above fueled an increasingly disorganized flight of the North Korean army back across the 38th parallel in the autumn of 1950.

Following entry into the war of the People's Republic of China and stabilization of the fighting front around the 38th parallel, U.N. air forces focused on the road and railroad system of North Korea, reducing the amount of enemy supplies reaching the fighting front. Later, Air Force, Navy, Marine Corps, and allied bomber and attack squadrons destroyed power-generating facilities, industrial plants, dams, fuel and supply depots, and other vital resource centers. Eventually, bombs from the sky knocked out irrigation dams, causing the flooding of great swaths of North Korean farmland. Without this massive sustained air effort, many more tanks, artillery pieces, and small arms—and much more ammunition, fuel, construction material, rations, and other vital supplies—would have reached communist troops entrenched on the 38th parallel. And U.N. casualty figures might have been astronomical.

U.N. air power, however, failed to live up to the promises of its most ardent advocates. Preventing air power from enabling the allies to win the war or even end it on favorable terms were politically driven restrictions in this first limited war of the Cold War era; confused command and control procedures at the theater, operational, and tactical levels; interservice rivalry; and inadequate aircraft, weapons, munitions, and other resources. The enemy's actions were certainly no less relevant to frustration of the U.N. air campaign. Chinese and North Korean forces became adept at defending and repairing critical transportation assets, moving troops and supplies at night, and stockpiling fuel, ammunition, and other materials close to the relatively static front line. The Asian communist countries, which learned in Korea how to deal with America's preponderant air power, used that knowledge with devastating effect to American fortunes a decade later during the Vietnam War.

Despite its flaws, U.N. air power was essential to the preservation of the Republic of Korea during its 1950–1953 trial by fire. U.N. air forces afloat and ashore, along with allied ground and naval contingents, defeated one communist offensive after another. These U.N. battlefield successes finally convinced the communist leaders in Moscow, Beijing, and Pyongyang that military force would not gain them victory. Air power, primarily American, once again proved to be an indispensable weapon in the arsenal of modern warfare.

The U.S. Navy's Air Interdiction Effort during the Korean War

Jeffrey G. Barlow

In June 1950, the definition of interdiction was "to prevent or hinder, by any means, enemy use of an area or route."[1] It is important to note that the air interdiction mission had been granted to the U.S. Air Force as part of its primary responsibility to "furnish close combat and logistical air support to the Army" under the 1948 terms of the roles and missions agreements among the military services. According to these agreements, the U.S. Navy had only a collateral function in interdiction, and then only after the Joint Chiefs of Staff had authorized it.

The first carrier operations in Korea were the strikes by aircraft from the USS *Valley Forge* sent against the Pyongyang area on July 3 and 4, 1950. North Korean airfields were struck on the morning of July 3; from the Navy's perspective, however, these morning strikes constituted attack operations rather than interdiction operations because they were directed against fixed shore targets such as supply facilities, oil refineries, and military installations not directly related to enemy transportation.[2]

On August 3, several senior Air Force officers and some junior naval aviators held a conference at the headquarters of Far East Air Forces (FEAF) to improve coordination of the Korean air effort and to establish naval air target priorities. The Navy priorities informally agreed upon were, first, close support (under the tactical control of Fifth Air Force), second, close interdiction of key enemy transportation in areas south of 38 degrees north latitude (targets coordinated with Fifth Air Force), and third (when the situation dictated), the attack of key transportation facilities north of 38 degrees that were assigned to FEAF bomber command (and coordinated by FEAF headquarters).[3] In the days after this meeting, FEAF agreed to provide the Navy with selected Air Force targets and maps of areas located between 37 and 38 degrees north latitude. FEAF also furnished the Navy with the bomb command master list plan.[4] Thereafter, although during the fall of 1950, carrier aircraft took part in an increased interdiction effort, the effort proved intermittent and not normally run according to a predetermined interdiction plan.[5] The Air Force interdiction plan in the first few months of the war generally concentrated effort upon North Korea's four main lines of communication: the east coast route (Ch'ongjin–Hungnam–Wonsan–Samchok–Kyangju); the west coast route (Sinuiju–Sinanju–Pyongyang–Sariwon–Seoul) and its alternate (Sakchu–Chongju–Sinanju–Pyongyang); the north central spur (Kanggye–Huichon–Sinanju); and the south transverse route (Seoul–Wonju–Andong–Kyongju).[6]

In early November, in response to the changing tactical situation due to the communist Chinese forces' entry onto the battlefield, Gen. Douglas MacArthur called for a maximum air effort. On November 6, FEAF commanding general George E. Stratemeyer ordered FEAF bomber command to destroy six of seventeen international bridges spanning the Yalu River between Manchuria and North Korea. Because the FEAF B–29 bomber force was unable to cover the entire target set, MacArthur asked Adm. C. Turner Joy, Commander, U.S. Naval Forces Far East, to assign some of the bridge targets to the carriers of Task Force 77.[7] Beginning on November 9, aircraft from the carriers USS *Valley Forge,* USS *Philippine Sea*, and USS *Leyte* struck the bridges over the Yalu. During the course of eight days (November 9, 10, 12, 14–16, 18, and 21), AD Skyraider attack planes and F4U Corsair fighter-bombers while covered by their escorting F9F Panther fighters struck the assigned bridges. In 593 sorties against these very difficult targets, carrier aircraft used 500-, 1,000-, and 2,000-pound bombs to drop the spans of three of the bridges, including the very important highway bridge at Sinuiju, and to damage another four.[8]

Despite such successes, the Navy's assessment of the interdiction effort after the first five months of war was a qualified negative. Although the Air Force–Navy effort may have hindered the enemy's use of certain routes, it failed to prevent the large-scale reinforcement of the North Koreans by the Chinese communists.[9] As veteran operations evaluation group analyst John Coyle noted:

> The general impression gained is that these [North Korean and Chinese] troops, while they did take advantage of all available methods for troop transport and resupply, are much less dependent upon volume of supply than are U.S. forces. As long as they have ammunition and are maneuvering at a rate adequate to prevent complete exhaustion of local food sources, they seem able to exist for months as a reasonably aggressive fighting force.[10]

On December 15, General Stratemeyer promulgated FEAF interdiction campaign No. 4. This plan combined a scheme to collapse the North Korean railroad network with an effort of intensive armed reconnaissance. To facilitate this campaign, North Korea was divided into eleven zones.[11]

The North Korean rail system at the beginning of 1951 consisted of six rail lines crossing into the country from Manchuria; three entered in the western portion and three entered in the eastern portion of the peninsula. On the western side, three single-line tracks ran from the northern border down to the city of Sinuiju. From there, double-line tracks ran southeast to the North Korean capital of Pyongyang and then to the fighting front. On the eastern side, the three single-line tracks came together near Kilchu and merged into a single track running south to Kowon where the rail line divided; one line headed west toward Pyongyang, and the other continued south, along the east coast, to Wonsan. Below Wonsan was a second rail split; one track headed southwest toward the South Korea capital of Seoul while the other continued along the east coast.[12]

On January 15, 1951, the Fifth Air Force commanding general, Earle E. "Pat" Partridge, requested that the Navy begin cutting rail lines along the eastern side of the peninsula. Seventh Fleet commander Vice Adm. Arthur D. Struble initially demurred, telling Generals Earle E. Partridge and Matthew B. Ridgway that the aircraft carriers could be better used for close air support of allied troops. But Struble was overruled, and on January 29 the carriers of Task Force 77 began launching strikes against the east coast rail lines as its second priority.[13]

On February 15, FEAF asked the Navy to assume temporary responsibility for interdiction of the northeast coastal route because the Air Force withdrawal from Kimpo and other forward air bases made it difficult for Fifth Air Force planes to hit targets there because of their limited range. Vice Adm. Joy accepted this assignment for his carriers the next day, though it meant foregoing close air support missions in support of the Eighth Army. Ten days later, the Navy assumed this east coast railroad interdiction effort as a continuing responsibility.[14] In March, the Air Force formally turned over the responsibility for interdiction in the three easternmost zones—F, G, and H—that extended from Wonsan up to the Siberian frontier.[15]

The railroad interdiction effort proved a formidable task because the target set included 956 bridges and causeways, 231 tunnels, and some 1,140 miles of track.[16] The actual routes to be cut, a much smaller subset, were determined by studying the route system and, on the basis of detailed photographic coverage, choosing vulnerable points. Once a bridge had been cut by an air strike, new photographs of the site were taken every fourth day to determine when repairs to the bridge would require a new attack.[17]

From February through June 1951, aircraft from Task Force 77 flew 5,321 armed reconnaissance and interdiction sorties.[18] Successful bridge attacks during the February 24 through June 16 period numbered 74 initial railroad bridge breaks and 76 rebreaks, and 69 initial highway bridge breaks and 40 rebreaks.[19] As a rule, Task Force 77 found that, to achieve one initial break of one span of a railroad bridge, four Skyraiders, each loaded with three 2,000-pound bombs (with a 0.01 sec., nose fuze setting and a nondelay tail fuze) and four F4Us, each loaded with one 1,000-pound bomb (with similar fuzing) were required.[20] The campaign of rail cuts proved surprisingly effective in reducing the rail traffic on the east coast routes. Whereas these routes had been carrying a high of 65 percent of Korea's total rail traffic in February 1951, the total had fallen to 48 percent in March and to just 32 percent in April.[21]

The attention paid to highway bridges and roads from June though August 1951 followed the decision by Fifth Air Force to institute Operation Strangle, the second of three interdiction campaigns pursued during 1951. Initiated by Maj. Gen. Edward J. Timberlake, temporary commander of Fifth Air Force in late May 1951, it was at the request of the commanding general of Eighth Army.[22] Under this plan, Task Force 77 was assigned interdiction responsibilities for the two center areas of the eight interdiction areas established. As discussed in the third report of the Korean War evaluation by the commander-in-chief of the Pacific Fleet, "this primary mission of interdiction has presented the most serious problem—how to hinder, if not prevent, by the use of 150 aircraft operating at the most three days out of four and by naval gunfire along the coast the movement of enemy supplies through an area extending 300 miles from the North Korean border to the bombline and inland from the east coast to the center of North Korea."[23]

The eastern road net in North Korea included some 2,000 miles of roads. These paralleled the railroad in most areas and connected rail heads and rail junctions by direct routes.[24] From June through December 1951, aircraft of Task Force 77 flew 12,730 armed reconnaissance and interdiction sorties.[25] The effects of Operation Strangle (which ran through August) did not prove particularly impressive. As the Pacific Fleet's third interim evaluation report noted: "The chief success of the highway interdiction program was to divert traffic to secondary roads and suppress movement by day. Ninety percent of the vehicle sightings continued to be made at night throughout Korea."[26]

The most important development in the 1951 interdiction program of Task Force 77 was the switch, on approximately October 1, from bridge-breaking to track-cutting efforts. In eight days of strike operations from October 18 through 31, carrier aircraft achieved 490 cuts in the main line running from Ch'ongjin to Samdong-ni, forcing the North Koreans to abandon hundreds of railroad cars. Similarly in November, Task Force 77 planes claimed 922 track cuts and 44 railroad bridges destroyed, despite below-average flying conditions.[27] In January 1952 a more concentrated destruction of rail beds in selected areas replaced the system of scattered track cuts over a wide area. On occasion, this increased the time from two or three days to eight to ten that certain lines were out of commission.[28]

The Navy was forced to conclude that the interdiction effort was ineffective overall. As the Pacific Fleet evaluation report for the second half of 1951 stressed, "In spite of persistent and damaging air attacks and naval bombardment the Communists in North Korea have kept their armies adequately supplied. The enemy has combined a well organized logistical supply system with an increasingly effective air defense and supply route repair and maintenance program."[29]

During most of the first half of 1952, Task Force 77 concentrated its interdiction efforts on cutting tracks and destroying rail beds. From January through May 1952, Navy carrier aircraft flew 11,315 armed reconnaissance and interdiction sorties.[30] During these five months, Navy aircraft achieved 10,561 railroad track cuts.[31] In June, however, Task Force 77 temporarily switched its emphasis from track cutting to mass, coordinated attacks on key enemy targets including major rail and transportation centers, power complexes, and supply and troop concentrations. This change in targeting was forced by the realization in late spring 1952 that the communists not only were able to maintain their frontline positions but also had been able to accumulate sufficient supplies in the forward area to pose a serious offensive threat to U.N. forces. Accordingly, it was thought that continued destruction of enemy rails was less damaging than direct destruction of military materiel.[32] One of the principal targets struck in June was the Suiho hydroelectric plant, the fourth largest such facility in the world.

Despite these efforts, the Pacific Fleet fourth interim evaluation report was forced to conclude that "the objective of the interdiction campaign has been to decrease significantly the combat potential of the Communist forces. This was not accomplished, nor was there any prospect in June 1952, after two years of war, that it would be accomplished with the forces available and the effort applied. The interdiction campaign has not prevented the enemy from maintaining a firm line of defense across Korea, from adequately supplying his forces of over 900,000 men in Korea, or from developing the capability of launching and sustaining a general offensive."[33] During the second half of 1952, the only new development of importance in Task Force 77 offensive operations was the Cherokee strike. The brainchild of Seventh Fleet commander, Vice Adm. "Jocko" Clark (himself, part Cherokee Indian), the Cherokee strike was a prebriefed strike against a specific target in front of friendly ground positions in direct support of the Eighth Army. It generally targeted enemy supply storage, personnel bunkers, and artillery positions. Formally begun in October 1952, the strikes were in large part the inevitable outgrowth of a target shortage brought about by the abandonment of the unsuccessful interdiction campaign against enemy lines of communication and an increasing shortage of North Korean industrial and other high-value targets.[34]

During the latter half of 1952, the Navy, Marine Corps, and Air Force continued to conduct coordinated, maximum-effort air strikes on major enemy targets. Some thirty such attacks were executed against North Korean power, manufacturing, mining, and rail centers by the end of the year.[35]

Cherokee strikes continued to be the primary offensive attacks employed by Navy carriers during the final six months of the war. The success of individual missions, however, was often clouded by an inability to assess the damage that resulted from the strikes.

The U.S. Navy role in air interdiction during the Korean War, like that of the U.S. Air Force, was a mixture of bright hopes and darkening reality. Despite the heroic efforts of thousands of allied aviators, interdiction's promise of throttling the enemy's supply lines went unrealized. The allied coalition never had the aerial strength that would have been required to cut off the enemy's frontline troops from their military supplies.

Notes

1. Joint Chiefs of Staff, *Dictionary of Military Terms for Joint Usage*, First Revision (June 1950), quoted in Commander In Chief U.S. Pacific Fleet Interim Evaluation Report No 2—16 November 1950 to 30 April 1951, vol 2, section entitled Project No 1.A.2.d. Combat Operations Section Naval Air (Other than Marine Air)—INTERDICTION, p. 634; CINCPACFLT Interim Evaluation Report—Korean Conflict Files, Operational Archives [hereafter cited as OA], Naval Historical Center.
2. For a discussion of what constituted an attack operation from an interdiction operation, see Commander In Chief U.S. Pacific Fleet Interim Evaluation Report No 1—25 June to 15 November 1950, vol 3, section entitled Project No 1.A.2.e. Combat Operations Section Naval Air Operations—ATTACK, p 309; CINCPACFLT Interim Evaluation Report—Korean Conflict Files, OA. Strikes on the afternoon of Jul 3 and 4, however, were directed against Pyongyang's railyard and rail and road bridges over the Taedong River. These were classic interdiction targets. Malcolm W. Cagle and Frank A. Manson, *The Sea War in Korea* (Annapolis, Md.: Naval Institute Press, 2000), p 38.
3. Memo, CG, FEAF, to Comdr Naval Forces Far East, subj: "Target Arrangements with Navy," AG 7692, Aug 5, 1950, printed as Appendix 3 to Commander in Chief U.S. Pacific Fleet Interim Evaluation Report No 1—25 June to 15 November 1950, vol 3, section entitled Project No 1.A.2.d. Combat Operations Section Naval Air Operations—INTERDICTION, p 298; and CINCPACFLT Interim Evaluation Report—Korean Conflict Files, OA.
4. Interim Evaluation Report No 1, Project No 1.A.2.d.—INTERDICTION, p 286.
5. *Ibid.*, p 282.
6. *Ibid.*, p 281.
7. Robert F. Futrell, *The United States Air Force In Korea, 1950–1953* (Washington, D.C.: Office of Air Force History, 1983), pp 223–24; and Cagle and Manson, *Sea War in Korea*, p 224.
8. Cagle and Manson, *Sea War in Korea*, pp 226–27; and Chief U.S. Pacific Fleet Interim Evaluation Report No 1—25 June to 15 November 1950, vol 3, section entitled Project No 1.A.2.e. Combat Operations Section Naval Air Operations—ATTACK, pp 310–11 and Appendix 4 "ATTACKS AGAINST SINUIJU BRIDGE," p 322.
9. Interim Evaluation Report No 1, Project No 1.A.2.d.—INTERDICTION, p

287.

10. Memo for File by John Coyle (OEG), subj: "Weapon and Target Selection for Interdiction," Jan 19, 1951, p 300; Appendix 4 to Interim Evaluation Report No 1, Project No 1.A.2.d.—INTERDICTION.
11. Futrell, *The United States Air Force In Korea*, p 317; and Eduard Mark, *Aerial Interdiction: Air Power and the Land Battle in Three American Wars*, Special Studies (Washington, D.C.: Center for Air Force History, 1994), pp 293–95.
12. Cagle and Manson, *Sea War in Korea*, p 231.
13. *Ibid.*, p 230; Interim Evaluation Report No 2, Project No 1.A.2.d.—INTERDICTION, p 656.
14. Interim Evaluation Report No 2, Project No 1.A.2.d.—INTERDICTION, 656, and msgs printed in Appendix 1, pp 687–89.
15. Mark, *Aerial Interdiction*, p 297.
16. Cagle and Manson, *Sea War in Korea*, p 231.
17. Interim Evaluation Report No 2, Project No 1.A.2.d.—INTERDICTION, p 659.
18. *Ibid.*, totaled from table on p 644.
19. *Ibid.*, totaled from table and accompanying text, p 661.
20. *Ibid.*
21. *Ibid.*, p 657.
22. Mark, *Aerial Interdiction*, pp 289–90, 304. An earlier Operation Strangle had occurred during the fighting for Italy in World War II.
23. Commander In Chief U.S. Pacific Fleet Third Evaluation Report 1 May–31 December 1951, Chapter 10—INTERDICTION, p. 10-17; CINCPACFLT Interim Evaluation Report—Korean Conflict File, OA.
24. *Ibid.*, pp 10–21.
25. *Ibid.*, totaled from table, pp 10–25.
26. *Ibid.*, pp 10–45.
27. *Ibid.*, pp 10–47.
28. *Ibid.*, pp 10–50.
29. *Ibid.*, pp 10–52.
30. Totaled from table in Commander in Chief U.S. Pacific Fleet Interim Evaluation Report No 4, 1 January 1952–30 June 1952, Chapter 3—Carrier Operations, pp 3–63; CINCPACFLT Interim Evaluation Report—Korean Conflict File, OA.
31. *Ibid.*, totaled from Figure 45, pp 3–73.
32. Interim Evaluation Report No 4, Chapter 3—Carrier Operations, pp 3–77.
33. Ibid., pp 3–61.
34. Commander in Chief U.S. Pacific Fleet Interim Evaluation Report No 5, 1 July 1952–31 January 1953, Chapter 3—Carrier Operations, pp 3–85; and CINCPACFLT Interim Evaluation Report—Korean Conflict File, OA.
35. Ibid., pp 3–9.

British Commonwealth Carrier Operations in the Korean War

Commander David Hobbs, MBE Royal Navy

In 1950, the Royal Navy was still recovering from a shortage of manpower after the World War II drawdown. Few ships had their war complement embarked, although those deployed to the Far East were more capable than those on the home station. Naval air squadrons were short of aircrew, and maintainers and were still using stocks of obsolete wartime aircraft because production of new types progressed slowly. Fortunately, a number of people with war experience had been retained, and the Far East Station covered a vast area with significant responsibilities.

With a great deal of British help, the Royal Australian Navy had formed its Fleet Air Arm in 1948 and had only recently taken delivery of its first carrier and embarked air group. Many of its aircrew had wartime experience with the Royal Navy or Royal Australian Air Force.

The Royal Canadian Navy had also recently formed its Fleet Air Arm with a light fleet carrier on loan from Britain, but did not deploy it to Korea. A potential plan to embark a Canadian Sea Fury squadron in a British carrier was never acted upon.

The Outbreak of War

After its surprise attack on June 25, 1950, the North Korean People's Army (NKPA) advanced, almost at will, through the South Korean defenses. On June 27, President Syngman Rhee and his government left Seoul, and it must have seemed to the communist commanders that the war was already won. However, they neglected to account for a factor that was to prove their ruin: sea power. The reaction of the United Nations to this aggression was swift and unambiguous, allowing allied navies to exert relentless pressure on North Korea.

In the summer of 1950, the British Far East Station commander Adm. Sir Patrick Brind flew his flag at a shore headquarters in Singapore. Much of the operational fleet, fortuitously, was in Japanese waters under the operational control of Rear Adm. Sir William G. Andrewes, Flag Officer Second-in-Command

Far East Fleet (FO2 FEF), in the cruiser HMS *Belfast*. They had recently participated in a number of exercises with U.S. Navy (USN) warships, under the command of Vice Adm. C. Turner. Joy, Commander, U.S. Naval Forces Far East (COMNAVFE). The British task force included the light fleet carrier HMS *Triumph*, the cruiser HMS *Jamaica*, and a number of destroyers, frigates, and logistic ships, plus a hospital ship.

Hearing of the invasion, Admiral Andrewes sailed on his own initiative at 0130 on June 26, ordering his force to concentrate in southern Japanese ports. On June 27, the U.N. Security Council had described the NKPA attack as "a breach of world peace" and authorized member nations to assist the Republic of Korea. On June 27, in the House of Commons, Prime Minister Clement Attlee announced Britain's decision to support the Security Council resolution. The next day, he announced that British naval forces in Japanese waters were placed at the disposal of U.S. authorities to act on behalf of the U.N. Security Council. The Canadian government immediately offered naval support, followed on June 29 by the governments of Australia and New Zealand. Orders from the Admiralty were sent directing the Commander-in-Chief Far East "to place the Royal Navy at present in Japanese waters at the disposal of the US Naval Command." Admiral Brind had already offered the use of his fleet to Admiral Joy for "any humanitarian mission" and warned Admiral Andrewes that he might soon be called on for action under the U.N. charter.

Commonwealth naval units were rapidly assimilated into the U.S. command structure. COMNAVFE Admiral Joy placed Admiral Andrewes in command of Task Group 96.8, the West Korean Support Group, which comprised mainly Commonwealth and allied ships. Rear Adm. John M. Higgins, USN, was placed in command of the mainly USN East Korean Support Group. HMS *Triumph* joined Task Force 77 of the U.S. Pacific Fleet off Okinawa, where Rear Adm. John M. Hoskins, USN, commander of Carrier Division 3 in USS *Valley Forge* took tactical command of the force. Planning for a combined strike against targets in North Korea began at once, and the task force moved to the operating area. American signal procedures were adopted immediately, and no difficulties were found in working with the USN. Rear Admiral Andrewes later wrote that "it all seemed so familiar as it was just what we had done so often before during the exercises in March with very similar forces." Also, it was only five years since the U.S. and British Pacific fleets had worked together so successfully in the final phase of the war against Japan.

The First Carrier Strike

The first naval air strikes of the war were flown between 0545 and 0615 on July 3 from USS *Valley Forge* and HMS *Triumph*. Eight Corsairs, sixteen Skyraiders, and twelve jets from *Valley Forge* attacked Pyongyang and other airfield sites, destroying fifteen to twenty aircraft on the ground and two in the air. Armed with rockets, twelve British Fireflies and nine Seafires from the *Triumph* attacked

Haeju airfield and damaged hangars and buildings, but no aircraft were sighted. All aircraft returned safely; flak had been negligible, but some aircraft demonstrated slight damage from small arms fire.

After 1945, both navies had been at pains to work out common operating procedures, and these, enhanced by cross-deck operations in the recent exercises, worked well. On July 4, aircraft from the *Valley Forge* attacked two gunboats in the Taedong estuary, destroyed one small railway bridge, damaged another, and destroyed fifteen railway locomotives and a significant amount of rolling stock. Aircraft from *Triumph* attacked the railway between Yonan and Haeju, scoring two hits on a bridge. The planes also attacked targets of opportunity that included a column of marching troops. Two American and one British aircraft experienced damage from flak.

The choice of targets for the British aircraft was severely limited by the poor combat radius of the early version of the Fireflies of *Triumph*'s 14th Carrier Air Group (CAG) and the limited strike capability of the Seafire 47, which was primarily an air defense fighter. The Fleet Air Arm suffered its first casualty of the war on July 28. A U.S. Air Force B–29 shot down, for unapparent reasons, Commissioned Pilot White of 800th Naval Air Squadron, in his Seafire. A USN destroyer picked up White from his dinghy, who was suffering burns, and transferred him to HMS *Triumph* later in the day. Commenting on the incident, COMNAVFE later said that the calculated risk of damage to friendly forces must be accepted.

Carrier Operations

Like all wars in the modern era, this was a maritime war with the United Nations utterly dependent on the sea for the transport of troops, supplies, and, to a very large extent, air support. Control of the sea allowed the establishment and maintenance of a firm beachhead around Pusan. USS *Philippine Sea*, a more potent strike carrier, replaced HMS *Triumph* in Task Force 77. After repairs to its leaking stern gland, *Triumph* joined the West Coast Task Force, in which British and Australian carriers were to operate for much of the remainder of the war. Although less capable than her USN counterparts, *Triumph* played a key role in the war by being in the right place at the right time, and her contribution was, thus, more significant owing to the proximity of her location. *Triumph* also played a small part during the landings at Inchon in the covering force that transformed the war. Her elderly air group had by then become increasingly difficult to maintain, and she was due for replacement.

A sister ship, HMS *Theseus*, carrying the 17th CAG and equipped with squadrons of very capable Sea Fury and Firefly FR5 aircraft, relieved the *Triumph.* Her squadrons were kept busy flying combat air patrols over shore forces, strafing mine-laying junks, and supporting troops ashore. By November, it seemed the war was nearly over, and *Theseus* was allowed to leave the combat zone when U.N. forces moved close to the Yalu River. She was hastily recalled

HMS *Theseus*

when Chinese troops infiltrated into Korea and struck hard at U.N. ground forces.

A pattern of operations emerged in which the British carrier off the west coast alternated with a USN light carrier, and friendly rivalry led to a constant improvement in the warfighting capability of both navies. When not on patrol, the British ship would return to the Commonwealth base port at Sasebo to take on replacement aircraft and ammunition and allow rest and recreation for the ship's company. A patrol typically comprised ten days at sea with a day in the middle for refueling and rearming.

Theseus operated throughout the bitterly cold winter of 1950–1951 despite gales, hail, snow, and poor visibility. In December, the air group was able to fly on only seventeen days, but it managed 630 accident-free sorties. By February 1951, the sortie tally had risen to 1,500, a testament to the ruggedness of the aircraft and skill of the pilots. In 1950, the 17th CAG was awarded the Boyd Trophy, instituted by Rear Adm. Sir Denis Boyd, the wartime captain of HMS *Illustrious* during the famous World War II attack on the Italian fleet in Taranto harbor. The trophy is awarded for the most outstanding feat of naval aviation in a given year. Until his death in 1965, Admiral Boyd usually presented the trophy in person.

As spring succeeded winter, less wind and a heavy swell gave deck landings a lively interest, but the accident rate remained commendably low. Aircrew morale was further bolstered by the loan of a USN helicopter to replace the obsolete Sea Otter biplane flying boat for combat search-and-rescue (SAR) duties. In its first few weeks of operation, the helicopter rescued five aircrew within minutes of ditching.

HMS *Unicorn*

This is an appropriate point to mention the maintenance carrier HMS *Unicorn* that served throughout the war in support of the operational carriers. She ferried hundreds of replacement airframes from the main British bases at Singapore and Hong Kong, used her extensive workshops to repair battle-damaged aircraft, and transported thousands of Commonwealth troops to and from Korea. On one sortie, she even bombarded NKPA shore positions with her four-inch guns. Despite her largely second-line tasking, she had a fully functional flight deck, and replacement pilots often used her for landing practice. She also acted as a spare deck for the operational carriers. Replacement aircraft were ferried from the United Kingdom to the Far East in the light fleet carrier HMS *Warrior*.

In April 1951, HMS *Glory* relieved *Theseus*, which by then had launched 3,500 operational sorties in eighty-six flying days over seven months. The light fleet carriers were built to austere specifications in World War II, and many disadvantages, such as lack of speed, liveliness in rough weather, and recurrent trouble with the single catapult, plagued them. Despite that, these ships succeeded in operating with an intensity and skill that Rear Adm. Alan K. Scott-Moncrieff, who had relieved Rear Admiral Andrewes as FO2 FEF on his promotion to vice admiral, was able to report to his commander-in-chief as being praised highly by the USN.

HMS *Glory*, another of the ubiquitous light fleet carriers, carried the reformed 14th CAG which was equipped with Sea Furies and Firefly FR5s that were to be the standard Commonwealth carrier fighter-bombers for the rest of the war. Her first patrol coincided with the Chinese spring offensive when the 1st Battalion of the Gloucestershire Regiment was almost annihilated defending a position on the Imjin River, and the British 27th Brigade and the U.S. 5th Cav-

HMS *Glory* with Sea Furies of 801 NAS and Fireflies of 821 NAS, Korea 1952/53

alry Regiment fought memorable delaying actions near Kapyong. In the summer, talks about an armistice began, and the land war became static, based on lines of trenches reminiscent of World War I.

In September 1951, *Glory* was relieved by HMAS *Sydney*, the first Commonwealth carrier to go into action and a great credit to the Royal Australian Navy. Her squadrons were equipped with the same type of aircraft as her British sister ships, and indeed many of her replacement aircraft came from British Far East reserve stocks, lent to the Australian ship while she was in the war zone. Aircraft maintained the coastal blockade and kept a watchful eye on the buildup of Chinese troops by rail and road. During October, *Sydney* had to move away from the war zone to avoid Typhoon Ruth, but she still encountered storm-force seas that destroyed six aircraft in the deck park.

HMAS *Sydney* in heavy seas in Typhoon Ruth off Sasebo, Japan.

In four months of operations, while *Glory* was being refitted in Australia, *Sydney*'s 21st CAG flew 2,366 sorties in 43 operational flying days. Casualties included three pilots killed and fifteen aircraft lost. In January 1952 *Glory* relieved her, and she fell back into the routine as if she had never been away. Flying operations now included the defense of allied-occupied islands off the west coast as well as interdiction, spotting for naval bombardment, blockade enforcement, and close support of the Commonwealth Division. By the end of her second deployment in the war zone, *Glory* completed nearly 5,000 operational sorties for the loss of nine aircrew and twenty-seven aircraft. Her Sea Furies, armed with two 500-pound bombs, had become deadly accurate dive-bombers, using a 45-degree dive technique.

For the remainder of the war, *Glory* alternated in the operational area with yet another light fleet carrier, HMS *Ocean*. The summer of 1952 saw the appearance of the first communist jet, the MiG–15, engined with a copy of the Rolls-Royce Nene turbine. The MiGs had a considerable edge in performance over the Sea Fury, but fortunately their pilots did not. Sea Fury sections stayed together, kept their eyes peeled, used the available cloud cover, and survived. Some did more than that. A veteran pilot from World War II, Lt. Peter "Hoagy" Carmichael, and his flight from 802d Naval Air Squadron of HMS *Ocean* shot down a MiG–15 on August 9, 1952. They inconvenienced several others.

Carmichael recalled after the war that ox carts were among the main road objects to target, saying it was amazing how many exploded when you hit them with cannon fire. This was a manifestation of the allied policy of interdiction, in which both heavy bombers of the USAF and the carrier fighter-bombers, armed with bombs and rockets, attempted to halt enemy troop and supply movement. The effort was not entirely successful, and the communist forces were able to launch a large-scale offensive in the spring of 1953, as the possibility of a truce became stronger with the hope of making it appear as if the United Nations was suing for peace to avoid defeat. During this final period, Sea Furies and Fireflies covered large areas of the country, attacking anything that moved, and much that did not. For a time, three night-fighter Fireflies were put ashore at the request of the U.S. Fifth Air Force to counter nighttime nuisance raids by communist propeller-driven aircraft. In this role, they operated with success from an airstrip south of Seoul.

At last, on July 27, 1953, an armistice was signed at Panmunjon. For some months after the war, light fleet carriers continued to operate close to Korea in case hostilities resumed. These included a tour by HMS *Warrior*, returned to operational duties after her time as a ferry carrier, and HMAS *Sydney*, which left Korea for the last time in June of 1954.

Of all the Commonwealth carriers in the Korean War, HMS *Glory* saw the most action. She equaled the record of 123 sorties in a single day set by HMS *Ocean*, a feat that involved every pilot, including Commander "Air" flying four sorties and which resulted in the destruction of seven bridges, twenty-eight buildings, and five ox carts. After leaving the United Kingdom in May 1951, she steamed 157,000 miles and flew 13,700 sorties, of which 9,500 were operational. Her aircraft destroyed 70 bridges, 392 vehicles, and 49 railway trucks for the loss of 20 aircrew. Weapon expenditure for this ship alone totaled 278 1,000-pound bombs, 7,080 500-pound bombs, 24,328 3-inch rocket projectiles, and 1,441,000 rounds of 20-mm cannon ammunition.

HMS *Glory* Roll of Honor

Sorties

Sorties flown from HMS *Glory* were of many types. In July 1951, attacks concentrated on railway trucks, junks, and barracks, and several "moving haystacks" caught fire after being hit. In September 1951, her aircraft achieved a new record of 66 offensive and 18 defensive sorties in a day with 100 percent serviceability, In February 1952, *Glory*'s aircraft operated in defense of allied-held islands including Cho-do and Paengnyong-do. In March 1952, Lieutenant Fraser's Sea Fury suffered an engine failure "slotting" to starboard of the carrier. After ditching, he was immediately rescued by the USN helicopter on plane-guard duty, which returned him to deck in less than two minutes, quicker than he would have been there if he had been in his own aircraft. In March 1953, *Glory*'s aircraft equaled the record of 123 sorties in a single day set by *Ocean*.

People

Although individual accounts of war operations are beyond the scope of this paper, I have selected two as being illustrative of the Commonwealth carrier operations. Sub Lt. Neil MacMilland and CPO Hancox of the Royal Australian Navy were shot down in their Firefly near Sariwon, north of Haeju. Sea Furies from the HMAS *Sydney* were in the air and were sent to provide cover because the downed aircraft was well inside enemy territory. The carrier captain found it difficult to make the decision to send the SAR helicopter, on loan from the USN with a USN crew, because it was doubtful it could fly the seventy-five miles and clear enemy territory before nightfall, but he approved the sortie, and the helicopter set off. Meanwhile, Meteor fighters of 77 Squadron RAAF joined the Sea Furies, and the downed aircrew helped to keep the encircling enemy troops at bay with their Owen submachine guns. At 1715, the Meteors had to go, but the Sea Furies, flown by Lieutenants Cavanagh and Salthouse, decided to stay despite being low on fuel. At 1725, the helicopter arrived, having flown at 120 knots, some 20 knots above the accepted legal maximum, and landed. Its observer, CPO Gooding, jumped out and shot two enemy soldiers who had crept to within fifteen yards of the downed aircraft. An hour later, the helicopter, with the two rescued aircrew, and still escorted by the Sea Furies, landed at Kimpo airfield, just as darkness fell.

During a patrol by HMS *Glory* in January 1953, a different form of interdiction was tried. With the rivers and ground both frozen hard, road transport could easily drive around any bomb damage. It was well known that railway bridges

Korean War Rescue by David Marshall. Sub Lt MacMilland and CPO Hancox (with Owen submachine gun) dash under fire for HMAS *Sydney*'s rescue helicopter. Overhead, Sea Furies ride cover above the downed Firefly.

were always quickly repaired, so attacks were directed at railway lines at inaccessible parts of the routes. Thirty-three cuts were made, and repair activity was initially slow. On January 5, a Sea Fury piloted by Lt. D. G. "Pug" Mather was hit by enemy flak after an attack on a railway line north of Chaeryon. The plane caught fire, and Mather bailed out, but the other pilots in his section failed to see where he landed. After aircraft searched for him for ninety minutes without success, a USAF helicopter, escorted by two Sea Furies, went to the scene. Unfortunately, bad weather forced it to turn back, and Mather was taken prisoner by the NKPA. One of the escorting Sea Furies, flown by Sub Lt. B. E. Rayner lost radio contact and was never seen again. Later in the day, a Sea Fury flown by Sub Lt. B. J. Simonds, Royal Naval Volunteer Reserve, spun from 3,000 feet and exploded on hitting the ground. Lieutenant Foster landed his Sea Fury with wheels up at Paengnyong-do after experiencing a rough-running engine and electrical failure. On the next day, a Firefly flown by Lt. W. R. Heaton was hit by flak and ditched north of Kirin-do. He was rescued from his dinghy by a USAF helicopter from Paengnyong-do.

Some Lessons Learned

Photography was used extensively, being particularly useful for harbor reconnaissance in the enforcement of the blockade and for assessing the results of interdiction missions. In mid-1952, a photo interpretation officer was appointed to the operational carrier. His services were described as invaluable, and the hundreds of images he obtained, when expertly interpreted, revealed many ingeniously camouflaged targets.

The value of the helicopter in the combat SAR role was amply demonstrated on land and at sea. Used to guard planes during flying operations, the helicopter was unrivaled for efficiency by day, but a carrier still required destroyer escort at night. At different times, Royal Navy aircrew were rescued by helicopters operating from bombarding cruisers at Wonsan and Inchon, from the minesweeping tender, from USAF airfields, and from their own carriers as well. Their effect on morale was important, but their limitations had to be appreciated. These included a small radius of action, made even smaller by strong headwinds and a reliance on dead-reckoning navigation with its potentially large errors. Instrument flying capability was minimal, and the range of the VHF radios was limited. For these reasons, the ubiquity of basing was an important factor, and some of the aircrew who were rescued would not have been recovered if only the carrier-borne helicopters had been available.

HMS *Ocean* instituted predawn missions which proved very productive because its aircraft found enemy transport that was still on the move. Many trucks were destroyed in these raids, and the experience gained by aircrews from this type of operation was of great value. The enemy was not slow to react, however, and *Glory*'s aircraft soon had difficulty finding targets after the enemy introduced a simple but effective air-raid warning system: warning fires were lit

Dragonfly onboard HMS *Theseus*.

HMS *Unicorn* (left) and HMS *Ocean* at Kure, Japan, 1952/53.

on the ground, appearing from two to three miles ahead of the aircraft. On looking back, pilots could see a long line of fires stretching behind them. A low approach was then adopted to deceive the enemy radar, but the foggy season intervened before the effectiveness of this method could be fully gauged.

In general, Royal Navy pilots had not been trained in night landing techniques. Consequently, night interdiction was not possible throughout the war.

Command and Control

It was clear from the outset that the United States would bear the heaviest share of the fighting, and because a U.S. command structure existed in Japan, it was natural that naval contributions from the Commonwealth navies should fit into the same command structure. Operational command had the most significance because the British Far East Fleet had its own logistics and type support structure able to support the Australian, Canadian, and New Zealand units because all operated ships and equipment of British manufacture. Throughout the war, personal relations between American and British officers were effective and cordial. Misunderstandings and differences of outlook were inevitable, but they were always overcome. Many arose simply because of the difficulty of arranging verbal contact with the American operational commanders, most of whom exercised their commands afloat. In contrast, the three British admirals who acted as FO2 FEF during the war exercised their command from Sasebo in Japan, only traveling to the operational area with a small staff on special occasions.

The chief difference between the American system and the British system lay in the rigidity of the former. Orders were extremely detailed, and direct communication on a junior level with another service or even task force was frowned upon. All communication was supposed to go up the chain of command, through to the top, and come down again. *Information* addressees did not take action until told to *comply* by the immediately superior authority, even when it was obvious that such action was imperative. Practically no discretion was left to the man on the spot. By comparison, in the command structure of the British Commonwealth, anticipation and initiative were expected and exercised. USN ships attached to the West Coast Blockade Group very much appreciated the reduced reliance on signals, instructions, and demands for situation reports. Later relations between the USN and the Royal Navy benefited greatly from the perceptions of mutual confidence that grew from these operations.

Another difference was the USN rule that the officer in tactical command of

HMAS *Sydney*, Sasebo, Japan 1953.

a carrier task force or group must himself be an aviator. It accepted that less efficient antiaircraft and anti–surface weapon screening and coordination between forces might result, and the Royal Navy view was that nonflying factors might suffer in consequence. The fact that none of the British flag officers were aviators made it difficult for the Seventh Fleet commander to understand how they could command a task group that contained two light fleet carriers. At one stage, it was suggested that the light fleet carriers should be removed from Task Force 95 and, although continuing to operate in the same area in the Yellow Sea, placed under the command of Task Force 77, the heavy carriers, which usually operated in the Sea of Japan. The British vetoed this.

Communications

The rigidity of the U.S. system of command threw a heavy strain on communications. Operation orders and plans reached prodigious dimensions and contained so much detail that, from a British perspective, "some of the wood could not be seen for the trees." Time was wasted while orders were passed down the long chains of command and Americanisms (for example, RFS, or ready for sea) initially caused confusion. On the whole, Commonwealth warships had little difficulty in using the U.S. system, but they had to augment their equipment and manning levels to cope with the increased traffic.

The strain on communications was amplified by the large number of situation reports, reports of intentions, action taken, and so on required from ships at sea by U.S. commanders. Great importance was placed on operational summaries intended for the benefit of the press. This was something new to the British at the time, although it was to become familiar to a later generation during the Falklands War.

British Perception of the Interdiction Campaign

Complete interdiction of a battlefield has always proved difficult, but circumstances in Korea seemed to offer special opportunities. The complete blockade enforced by the overwhelming U.N. naval forces entirely ruled out supply by sea; the meager rail and primitive road communications of North Korea seemed vulnerable to the almost undisputed U.N. air power. Additionally, important road and rail centers on the east coast were open to naval bombardment. The vulnerability of the railways seemed to be enhanced by the large number of bridges and tunnels necessitated by the mountainous terrain of North Korea. For example, the eastern network, the scene of most of the naval interdiction effort, included 956 bridges and causeways, 231 tunnels, and 1,140 miles of track.

After the limitation of the Chinese offensive, the main effort of U.N. air operations was directed at interdiction. This was the primary responsibility of the U.S. Fifth Air Force, supported by allied contingents and all available naval and U.S. Marine Corps aircraft. Efforts of the USAF and USN were never coordinated at the theater level due to the lack of a unified joint command. Gradually,

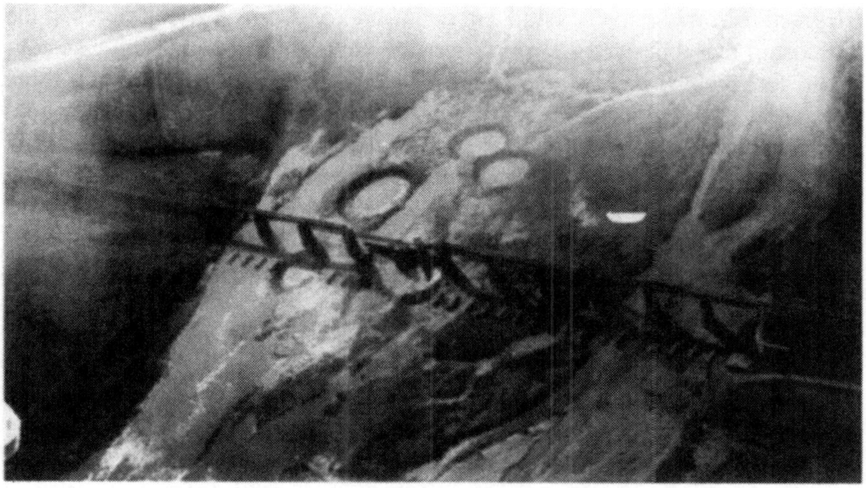

Bomb damage to a bridge in Korea

it came to be accepted that, broadly speaking, the USN would deal with the east coast railway and highway systems, and the USAF would deal with the west coast, where it interacted with the Commonwealth carrier efforts. Except when circumstances dictated other temporary uses of aircraft, this policy continued for twenty months. Immense damage was unquestionably inflicted on the enemy communications systems, and all movement by rail or road was confined to the hours of darkness, but full interdiction of the battlefield was never achieved. Throughout the campaign, the communists were always able to launch an offensive if they wished to.

The causes of this failure, in British eyes, were primarily due to inhibitions accepted by the United Nations for political reasons, but tactical and operational conditions were also partly to blame. With respect to political considerations, the ban on sources of supply in Manchuria robbed aircraft of targets that might well have been decisive. The static war, accepted during the protracted armistice negotiations, enabled the communists to keep their strongly fortified front lines sufficiently supplied to a degree they could never have achieved in a war of movement. The enemy was allowed to fight on his own terms, and many of the advantages possessed by the allies were negated.

When it was initiated in January 1951, the object of the interdiction campaign was to impede the communist advance. Though this line of reasoning was undoubtedly justified, Vice Adm. Arthur D. Struble, Seventh Fleet commander of Carrier Task Force 77, opposed it because he believed his aircraft would be better used to provide close air support for the army. Continuation of the interdiction campaign throughout the long armistice negotiations savored dangerously of trying to win the war by air power alone, while the army and navy were relegated to comparatively static and defensive roles. It is difficult to resist the conclusion that this strategy, which certainly suited the communists, was continued for too long and that better results would have been obtained if a more aggressive strategy had been implemented in which the three services would have worked together in the closest cooperation in support of one another. With hindsight, had the U.N. forces exerted the mobility and flexibility given them by their command of the sea and air, the enemy could have been forced into a war of movement that he could not sustain. This might well have compelled the enemy to accept more satisfactory armistice conditions at an appreciably earlier date.

Summary and Comment

At the outset, Admiral Andrewes had stated that it would be wrong to regard a single light fleet carrier as representative of what naval aviation could achieve in any theater. Even taking into account the conditions under which the war was fought, the endless coastline around a narrow peninsula, and the lack of naval and air opposition, Commonwealth carriers performed remarkably well. The intensity of flying, the operational lessons, and the length of the war, throughout which the Commonwealth maintained a carrier on station, brought many squadrons and their people to a high pitch of professionalism and efficiency that was matched in few other arms of the British services. In turn, this participation produced a corps of experienced aircrew and maintainers well equipped to handle the new generation of aircraft, such as the Buccaneer, and to use the new equipment and techniques being developed in the United Kingdom that would revolutionize carrier aviation.

The light fleet carriers provided the most conspicuous aspect of Commonwealth operations in the Korean War. Their performance, admitted on all sides to be outstanding, was possible only because of the lack of serious naval and air opposition. Had these existed on an appreciable scale, more ships would have been needed, and a greater effort would have been required for fighter defense and escort, likely to the detriment of offensive operations. The results achieved were the product of hard work, much improvisation, and, in some cases, the driving of machinery beyond the limits for which it was designed.

The signing of an armistice on July 27, 1953, ended hostilities that had lasted 1,128 days and involved naval forces from Australia, Canada, Colombia, France, the Netherlands, New Zealand, the Republic of Korea, Thailand, the United Kingdom, and the United States. The seal of royal approval was set on the Commonwealth effort two days after the armistice was signed when the following message from Her Majesty the Queen to the Board of Admiralty was signaled to the Fleet, "Please express to all serving in Commonwealth Fleet my deep appreciation of the splendid service they have given throughout the fighting in Korea."

Statistics

During the war, seventy-six ships of the Commonwealth navies and their fleet auxiliary services served in the combat area for varying periods. The thirty-two warships of the Royal Navy included five carriers, six cruisers, seven destroyers, and fourteen frigates. The nine warships of the Royal Australian Navy included one carrier, four destroyers, and four frigates. Their combined casualties totaled 191.

Serving afloat in Korean waters were 17,000 officers and men of the Royal Navy, Royal Marines, and Royal Fleet Auxiliary Service, and 4,300 more served ashore in Japan. One hundred and sixty-five officers and men were decorated for gallantry, and 289 were mentioned in dispatches. British warships steamed a total of 2,100,550 miles and used 632,150 tons of fuel. Carrier aircraft dropped 15,200 bombs of various sizes and fired 57,600 rockets and 3,300,000 rounds of 20-mm cannon ammunition in 23,000 operational sorties.

Among the 4,507 officers and men from the Royal Australian Navy who served afloat in the war zone, 57 were decorated for gallantry. Australian warships steamed more than 419,000 miles, and Australian carrier aircraft dropped 802 bombs of various sizes and fired 6,359 rockets and 269,249 rounds of 20-mm cannon ammunition during a total of 2,366 sorties.

Searching for Lucrative Targets in North Korea: The Shift from Interdiction to Air Pressure

Conrad Crane

A half century ago in Korea, the staff of the Far East Air Forces (FEAF) conducted the first systematic American study of the best way to apply air power to produce a negotiated settlement in a limited war. As the conflict and truce talks continued through 1952, the stalemate on the ground and ineffectiveness of air interdiction inspired Brig. Gen. Jacob Smart, FEAF deputy commander for operations, to look for a better way to apply his resources. He directed two members of his staff, Col. R. L. Randolph and Lt. Col. B. I. Mayo, "to devise ways and means of exerting maximum pressure on the Communist Forces in North Korea through optimum application of FEAF effort." Smart was frustrated by the lack of U.N. progress in ending the war, and his subordinates' mission was "truly a search for new ideas." Randolph and Mayo began by examining the course and results of the interdiction campaign, which had been focused on enemy railroads since August 1951. The objective remained to cut rail lines completely at selected points and force the enemy to use roads as the primary channel of supply. Planners then hoped that Fifth Air Force aircraft could cause enough attrition of enemy trucks so that frontline armies could not be supplied, thus subjecting them to "unbearable pressure, despite the lack of offensive ground action." It had not worked, despite more than 15,000 rail cuts and at least partial destruction of 199 bridges. Enemy repair efforts, night movement, and attacks by MiG–15 jet fighters had foiled FEAF efforts to close transportation routes. Randolph and Mayo also pointed out that the enemy's entire daily requirement of mortar shells could be carried by a single truck or one hundred coolies with A-frames and that it would be virtually impossible to stop all such traffic with aerial interdiction. In addition, FEAF had suffered heavy losses: 243 aircraft destroyed and 290 heavily damaged, while only 131 replacements had been received. The two staff officers looked for a way to reapply American air power to bring real pressure on the communists to conclude an armistice.[1]

Brig. Gen. Jacob Smart was the FEAF staff officer most responsible for developing and implementing the Air Pressure campaign. He had also devised the concept and written the plan for the mass raid on the Ploesti oil refineries in Romania in 1943. He eventually earned four stars and commanded Pacific Air Forces.

Their staff study was finished on April 12, 1952, and it recommended that any air resources beyond those required to maintain air superiority "be employed toward accomplishing the maximum amount of selected destruction, thus making the Korean conflict as costly as possible to the enemy, in terms of equipment, supplies, and personnel." Targets were prioritized on the basis of the effect their destruction would have on the enemy, their vulnerability to available weapons, and the probable cost to FEAF of attacking them. Suggested objectives included hydroelectric plants (if they were cleared for attack by the Joint Chiefs of Staff [JCS]), locomotives and vehicles, stored supplies, and even buildings in cities and villages, especially in areas that were "active in support of enemy forces." Based on the study, Smart planned to deemphasize interdiction to concentrate on the new target systems, aiming to "bring about defeat of the enemy as expeditiously as possible" rather than "allowing him to languish in comparative quiescence while we expand our efforts beating up supply routes." He knew the enemy was well dug in and under no real pressure on the front line, and it needed very few supplies to sustain operations during the stalemate anyway. Smart also believed attacks should be scheduled "against targets of military significance so situated that their destruction will have a deleterious effect upon the morale of the civilian population actively engaged in the logistic support of the enemy forces." He knew that selecting those targets that would influence enemy decision makers would be difficult, not only for operational reasons but because it was not known who those key decision makers were nor how their minds worked.[2]

The initial determination of the United Nations Forces Commander and U.S. Far East Commander Gen. Matthew Ridgway to influence negotiations with air power had been tempered by his disappointment in the results of the interdiction campaign and early battles with the JCS about bombing North Korean ports and the capital of Pyongyang. He also appeared hesitant to risk anything that might cause the communists to break off the peace talks. They had already used air attacks on the negotiating site as an excuse to do that twice, once with apparently faked evidence and another time because of an actual U.N. bombing error. In May 1952, Ridgway's successor, Gen. Mark Clark, was not as skeptical about the efficacy of air power nor as reluctant to confront the JCS, all of whose members were also increasingly frustrated by the seemingly interminable armistice discussions. Clark described his previous experience bargaining with the communists (when he was the American high commissioner for Austria) as "two years of head-knocking with the Russians to teach me what it is that Communists respect: FORCE." The new commander might also have been more realistic in his expectations about interdiction. Ridgway had commanded a division and corps in northwest Europe in the final drive against the Germans in World War II and had seen the obvious effects of allied air power on enemy fuel and transportation infrastructures in forcing final victory. Clark had commanded an army in Italy when the original Operation Strangle had caused the Germans great logistical difficulty and produced some battlefield success, but it failed to bring swift victory in a deadly struggle in mountainous terrain. When FEAF commander Lt. Gen. O. P. Weyland and General Smart approached their new boss with their air pressure strategy, they were pleasantly surprised to find a willing listener. Weyland dealt with Clark personally from then on with photographs and plans for all significant air operations, thus keeping the Far East Command staff "out of the target selection business" and strengthening Clark's belief in the importance of hitting targets in enemy rear areas.[3]

Soon after the staff study was completed, the FEAF Target Committee began discussing ways to initiate the new destruction campaign. By early July, the members agreed that a revised target attack program had to be developed to reflect the new destruction priorities. Smart cautioned everyone that the modifications should be referred to as "not a major change in policy, but rather a shift in emphasis from delay and disruption operations to destruction." This terminology was intended to prevent arousing "further Army desires for close air support" as well as controversial newspaper headlines.[4]

The FEAF directive outlining the policies of the new air attack program was published in the second week of July. Three major factors shaped the directive, the first being that the communists had massed "considerable air power" in the Far East that could be used offensively against U.N. forces at any time. The second was that the enemy's major source of supply was off limits to air attack and that transportation routes from his sanctuaries used for meeting his small supply requirements were relatively short. The final factor was that, with a stabilized front, friendly ground forces needed only minimal close air support. The first priority for FEAF air action remained air superiority, followed by "maximum selected destruction," and then direct support of ground forces. Specific targets within the second, destruction, category were prioritized as follows:

1. aircraft
2. serviceable airfields
3. electric power facilities
4. radar equipment
5. manufacturing facilities
6. communication centers
7. military headquarters
8. rail repair facilities
9. vehicle repair facilities
10. locomotives
11. supplies, ordnance, petroleum, lubricants
12. rail cars
13. vehicles
14. military personnel
15. rail bridges and tunnels
16. marshaling yards
17. road bridges

The new directive still required that sufficient attacks be maintained against the rail system to prevent it from being able to support "extensive sustained enemy ground operations."[5]

Hitting Power Plants and Cities

The first major target for the escalated air campaign would be North Korean hydroelectric plants. In March, Ridgway had rebuffed a Fifth Air Force and FEAF request to attack them by stating that intelligence did not justify destroying targets that functioned primarily in the civilian economy and that their destruction would not hasten communist agreement to U.N. armistice terms. He would sanction attacks only if negotiations were hopelessly deadlocked or broken off. To prepare for April discussions with the JCS, U.S. Air Force headquarters in Washington queried FEAF about "the feasibility and desirability" of attacking the installations, also as a possible response to a breakdown or continued deadlock in armistice talks. In preparing a response, FEAF asked its Bomber Command what it would take to destroy the targets. It received a rather gloomy reply that discussed the problems inherent in conducting night bombing so far from navigation beacons and predicted anywhere from nine to twenty-nine days to achieve 50 percent destruction of each facility. Fifth Air Force was more optimistic, however, and FEAF told USAF headquarters that they could accomplish the mission in two or three days, relying heavily on fighter-bombers. A May message from the JCS, probably intended to goad Ridgway into action, reminded him that their most recent directives specifically prohibited attacking only the Suiho Dam on the Yalu; the other power facilities were beyond the restricted areas. On June 11, 1952, Weyland sent Clark a plan to bomb all complexes except Suiho. In the meantime, USAF Chief of Staff Gen. Hoyt Vandenberg was shepherding the removal through the JCS of all restrictions on attacks against Yalu River hydroelectric installations. Far East Command received notification of this in time to add Suiho to the target list, and Clark approved the attack for June 23 or 24, when Navy carriers were available to hit eastern objectives.[6]

The addition of Suiho presented a number of difficulties to FEAF planners beyond just its location on the Yalu River in MiG Alley. It was a massive structure, the fourth largest dam in the world, and beyond the capabilities of FEAF to destroy. Even the smaller dams turned out to present similar difficulties. Smart reviewed techniques used by RAF dambusters in World War II, but he discovered the USAF could not emulate them. As a result, penstocks, transformers, and power distribution facilities were targeted at Suiho and the other hydroelectric sites, not the dams themselves. The difficulty of completely destroying those diverse objectives limited the long-term effects of the eventual attack to some extent. However, a successful strike against the Suiho complex was seen as critical to applying effective pressure on communist decision makers. While most of the output from the other hydroelectric facilities was for domestic use, planners knew that much of Suiho's power went to China.[7]

The operation began on the afternoon of June 23, and this raid on Suiho bears special mention as a model of interservice cooperation. It began with 35 Navy F9F Panther jets suppressing enemy defenses, followed by 35 Skyraiders with 5,000-pound bombloads. All had been launched from Task Force 77 of the Seventh Fleet which was operating for the first time with four fast carriers. Ten minutes later, 124 F–84s of the Fifth Air Force hit the target, while 84 F–86s flew protection for the whole operation. Within four days, 546 Navy sorties and 730 by Fifth Air Force fighter-bombers had destroyed 90 percent of North Korea's electric power potential. Early in the war, such joint air operations would have been impossible. With interservice relations poisoned in the aftermath of the "Revolt of the Admirals," the Navy and Air Force seemed incapable of overcoming interoperability problems occasioned by different doctrines and technologies. Eventually, each air service was given its own separate sphere of action in Korea. But by 1952, the personal relationships that Generals Clark and Weyland developed with Vice Adm. Joseph "Jocko" Clark of the Seventh Fleet produced an atmosphere that encouraged more cooperation.[8]

The effective air attacks on North Korean power facilities would not have been possible without the participation of the carrier-borne Panthers and Skyraiders of Task Force 77.

The attacks had many repercussions besides a reduction in the output of Manchurian industries. The effect on North Korea was immediately apparent to American POWs, who never got to see the end of any of the propaganda films they were subjected to that summer "because in no instance did the electric power hold out for the full showing." In Parliament the British Labor Party denounced the bombings as a provocation that could lead to World War III, and only Prime Minister Winston Churchill's announcement that he was appointing a British deputy for the U.N. Command in Korea mollified them. Secretary of Defense Robert Lovett publicly endorsed this addition to General Clark's staff; he also provided the press with the misleading explanation that the JCS had given special permission on the basis of purely military considerations to allow the raids on the hydroelectric plants. American newspapers were not fooled and speculated that the attacks which had "plunged much of North Korea and a good part of Manchuria into darkness and industrial paralysis" were the start of a new "get tough" policy to break the stalemate over POW treatment at the peace talks. Some congressmen even questioned why the plants had not been bombed earlier. Both Churchill and Lovett denied that the attacks signified any change in U.N. policies.[9]

The next sign of increased air pressure was an all-out assault on Pyongyang, which the JCS cleared for attack in early July. Operation Pressure Pump on July 11 involved 1,254 sorties from Fifth Air Force, U.S. Navy, U.S. Marine Corps, Republic of Korean, Australian, South African, and British aircraft by day, and fifty-four SHORAN-directed B–29s at night. Psywar leaflets, warning civilians to leave the city, were dropped before the strike as part of Psychological Operation Blast, designed to demonstrate the omnipotence of U.N. air power and disrupt industrial activity in the city. Radio Pyongyang was knocked off the air for two days, but, with power restored, announcers stated that the "brutal" attacks had destroyed 1,500 buildings and inflicted thousands of civilian casualties. Intelligence sources reported that one extra benefit from this attack was a direct hit by an errant B–29 on an air raid shelter used by high-ranking officials that resulted in between 400 and 500 casualties. The effort was repeated on August 29 in an operation called All United Nations Air Effort which involved more than 1,400 sorties and had a special purpose: "to achieve psychological benefit from our ability to punish the enemy through airpower" during the Moscow conference between the Chinese and Russians. General Smart also scheduled additional attacks on targets in the far northwest of the peninsula to further "display the effect of our airpower" to the attendees.[10]

The way these raids were perceived in different parts of the world reveals much about how the efficacy of American air power was viewed. The British press emphasized the multinational composition of the strike force and gave equal coverage to North Korean accusations of nonmilitary damage. It also noted the irony that antiaircraft guns surrounding the "undefended city" claimed to have downed ten U.N. aircraft. *The New York Times* observed, with some optimism and surprise, "the signs are that, in spite of the bombing, the enemy has become more eager for a ceasefire." An Asian delegate to the U.N. summed up the fears of his bloc, "It seems to me to be a dangerous business, this policy of

These leaflets dropped as part of Psychological Operation Strike warned civilians to stay away from military facilities that might be bombed. The bomb craters in the marshalling yard in Pyongyang attest to the ultimately unsuccessful efforts to cut off railroad traffic in North Korea.

mass air attacks while the truce talks are going on. Knowing the Chinese, I think it likely that they would regard the signing of an armistice under such military pressure as a loss of face." Chinese representatives in Delhi characterized the recent air attacks as "19th century gun boat tactics," and assured Indian diplomats that the operations would have no effect on communist forces or negotiators. American press coverage played up the massive power of the raids along with the fires and explosions they caused among stockpiled communist supplies. It also highlighted the heavy defenses of the "peaceful city" and pointed out that civilians had received ample warning about the bombing via leaflets. Newsreels portrayed "a relentless attack on the city's rich military targets" by U.N. fighter-bombers of five nations, using film footage provided by the Department of Defense. As with the hydroelectric complex attacks, American newspapers perceived the air activity as part of "a new initiative intended to demonstrate to the Communists that they have nothing to gain and much to lose by prolonging the present deadlock."[11]

Pyongyang was not the only North Korean city or town attacked during the air pressure campaign. A FEAF operational policy directive dated July 10, 1952, outlined the new air attack program to all subordinate units, and they moved swiftly to comply. Task Force 77 also participated. In the latter half of 1952, Navy and FEAF aircraft conducted more than thirty joint "maximum-effort air strikes" against key industrial objectives. Targets included supply, power, manufacturing, mining, oil, and rail centers. On July 20, Fifth Air Force B–26s began using incendiary and demolition bombs in night attacks on enemy communications centers as part of Operations Plan 72–52 to destroy "supply concentration points, vehicle repair areas and military installations in towns where damaged buildings were being utilized." To increase the effect of the air attacks, beginning on July 13, Psychological Operation Strike dropped warning leaflets on seventy-eight towns, advising civilians to distance themselves from military targets. Illustrations depicted North Korean transportation routes and support facilities. The text announced that the U.N. Command knew where all military targets were, but it wanted to protect innocent civilians who were advised to leave immediately with their families and friends and to stay away from the danger area for days because of delayed-action bombs. In addition to the 1.8 million psywar leaflets dropped by Fifth Air Force between July 13 and 26, Radio Seoul broadcast a series of warnings before each night attack, advising civilians in the specific target area to seek shelter. Newsreels called the bombing operation a warn 'em, sock 'em campaign. An August 5 press release from Lt. Gen. Glenn Barcus, commander of Fifth Air Force, announcing widespread attacks and explaining that the radio notices and leaflet campaign were a "concerted humanitarian effort at reducing civilian population casualties" still brought protests from the State Department, which feared the warnings and bombing operations might be exploited by enemy propaganda and would harm the U.N. position in world opinion. Weyland, who believed that few useful targets remained in North Korean cities and towns anyway, relayed the State Department and General Clark's concerns about the press release to the embarrassed Barcus, who said he got the idea from Weyland's own public information officer.[12]

The press releases stopped, and the mass strike warnings were curtailed, although civilians were occasionally still given advance notice of some raids. But the bombing of North Korean towns and cities continued unabated. Even the B–29 Superfortresses of FEAF Bomber Command joined in the attacks on communication centers. By early 1953, Bomber Command considered small cities and towns "the last currently vulnerable link in the supply and distribution system for the communist armies." Intelligence reported them all taken over as sup-

Although the insufficient night capabilities of the B–26 Invader limited its effectiveness for transportation interdiction, it performed better against stationary communication centers.
By the end of the war, most North Korean villages resembled this destroyed supply center in the environs of Pyongyang.

ply and troop centers, and they were too heavily defended for daylight attacks by lighter bombers. Contrails and bright moonlight that aided enemy night interceptors limited allied operations along the Yalu River to one week a month, so the medium bombers spent most of their time hitting airfields and communication targets in the rest of North Korea.[13]

The Search for Targets Continues

General Clark was very pleased with the strikes against the hydroelectric plants and Pyongyang and was anxious to continue the campaign of air pressure. Weyland gave him a detailed briefing on FEAF target selection in late July, explaining that they did not expect to find any targets in North Korea that were comparable in importance to the power facilities. The key military installations in most towns and cities had already been hit, and "incidental to the destruction of those military objectives," in Weyland's estimation, "the destruction of the towns and cities ranged from forty to ninety per cent." He said he could wipe out the rest of the urban areas, but he was loathe to do so because they were "primarily residential." Clark agreed, saying that he did not himself "want to recommend the complete destruction of these towns." Weyland then covered the remaining target possibilities: Rashin, Sinuiju, Uiju, and some metallurgy plants and installations. Clark offered to check into remaining JCS restrictions about the port of Rashin, and he also agreed to study a memorandum from Weyland, who asked that the JCS give the Far East Commander authority to conduct preemptive strikes against Manchurian airfields "if it became evident that the Communists were about to launch a major attack against our installations." Weyland did not expect Clark to submit the request, nor for the JCS to grant it, but Clark did authorize photoreconnaissance missions by an RF–80 and two RF–86s over Manchurian airfields that were flown on August 1.[14]

Some members of the FEAF staff remained skeptical about the shift from interdiction to destruction, most notably Brig. Gen. Charles Banfill who was Weyland's Deputy for Intelligence. In late August, Banfill sent General Smart a detailed memorandum outlining the reasons why "factors restricting the successful application of this program are of such a nature as to make results commensurate with the cost extremely doubtful." The enemy had moved most industrial facilities into a "safety zone" in the northeast which was heavily defended and out of range for Fifth Air Force fighter-bombers and SHORAN stations. Other smaller targets had been moved underground. The principal sources of supply and most important strategic targets, however, were outside Korea's borders. Banfill lamented, "We are somewhat in the position of trying to starve a beggar by raiding his pantry when we know he gets his meals from his rich relatives up the street." He was concerned that, while FEAF aircraft searched for the few lucrative targets to destroy, unrestricted enemy transportation was allowing communist forces to increase their artillery fire by a factor of ten and to triple U.N. casualties. He concluded, "Although rail interdiction may not prove decisive, statistical evidence indicates that immediate resumption of the rail interdiction program is warranted."[15]

General Smart sent back an equally detailed reply explaining his rationale for the new program. While conceding that "the majority of medium bombardment targets remaining throughout North Korea appear to be of marginal value," he argued that attacking them was still more useful than interdiction. Political and military restrictions combined with a static battlefront made an effective program of interdiction "almost impossible of execution." Smart continued that the new policy had elicited "a more telling response from the enemy," as evidenced by "references to our 'savagery' by even the Communist armistice delegation."

He interpreted the increase in enemy artillery fire as "a retributive reaction to our present pattern of air action, rather than the expenditure of a handy surplus accumulated since the curtailment of our interdiction program." If that were true, goading the enemy into action would increase supply requirements and generate some "truly remunerative air targets." He concluded, "I feel that the purpose of any air action is to bring about defeat of the enemy as expeditiously as possible, not merely to complicate his maintenance of a position in which demonstrably he not only can support but actually can replenish himself, despite our efforts to prevent his doing so." However, interdiction was just deemphasized, not prohibited, and air pressure was applied "against an expanded target spectrum."[16]

Once in a while during 1952, FEAF did manage to find some lucrative industrial targets to hit. Mining facilities were attacked, and strikes were conducted against the remnants of North Korean industry that were mostly concentrated along the Soviet and Manchurian frontier. As Banfill had pointed out, many of these targets were beyond the range of Fifth Air Force jets. When Bomber Command conducted its last great daylight raid of the war against the Kowon marshaling yard in October, Banshee jet fighters from Navy carriers had to serve as escorts. Usually, however, naval aircraft acted alone to hit such objectives. The largest carrier strike of the war occurred in September when 142 planes from three carriers destroyed the Aoji oil refinery and attacked other industrial targets at Munsan and Ch'ongjin. These were in an area less than five miles from Manchuria and within eleven miles from the USSR, and the raids caught enemy fighters and the flak defenses completely by surprise. This time the British were notified a few days before the attacks, and they agreed the objectives were "good military targets."[17]

In his messages to the JCS in late 1952, General Clark continued to emphasize "firmness in negotiations to be supported militarily by continued heavy bombing attacks." The JCS agreed that "the principal factor favorable to the UNC [United Nations Command] in the present military situation on Korea is the air superiority which the UNC forces hold over North Korea." This air superiority deprived the communists of the ability to support larger forces, enabled outnumbered U.N. ground forces to hold their positions, and constituted the most potent means to perhaps pressure the enemy into agreeing to acceptable armistice terms. The chairman of the JCS, Gen. Omar Bradley, and General Vandenberg even proposed to try to intimidate China with a mass B–29 raid aimed at Shanghai. The formation would come close enough to get picked up on radar and then "veer off about fifteen miles away and fly down the coast." The State Department discouraged it, however, fearing that such a "show of force might boomerang" with allies and world opinion. At the same time, agencies in Washington and the Far East continued to worry about the communist air buildup that threatened U.N. air superiority. The Central Intelligence Agency noted an increase in aircraft based in Manchuria and declared, "Soviet participation in enemy air operations is so extensive that a de facto air war exists over North

Korea between the U.N. and USSR." Ironically, by mid-1952, coordination between the Chinese Air Force and its Soviet mentors had almost completely disintegrated, but concerns that the Russians were really running the communist air war became great enough in the Department of Defense that the Secretaries of the Air Force and Army tried to persuade the State Department to allow more publicity about Soviet personnel fighting directly against American forces. Planning also continued about actions to be conducted if negotiations should break down or if the war should escalate. Far East Command and the JCS considered air options including attacks on the USSR, the use of atomic or chemical weapons, and bombing of Chinese airdromes and communication centers.[18]

In the meantime, Far East Command and the JCS remained alert for any signs that the campaign of air pressure might be working. In September, Clark transmitted an intelligence report to the JCS that stated bombing was breaking down civilian morale in North Korea. Cities and towns that had been subjected to U.N. air attacks were "bordering on panic." Civilians who had joined labor battalions because of job and food shortages or conscription were now deserting to return home. They believed the air attacks were really the prelude to a U.N. general offensive to end the war. The report also noted that the North Korean government was afraid air attacks would motivate many civilians to join U.N. guerrillas. Further information provided to the FEAF Target Committee added that the communist government had to send special agents to help control the unrest in those cities hardest hit by U.N. air strikes. Clark's optimistic assessment was seconded by the ambassador to Japan, but one "ancient report" was not enough to persuade the State Department or JCS that an armistice was imminent. They continued to look for other signs that air pressure was producing results. Initial optimism waned as peace talks dragged on through 1952 and into 1953, and the search continued for some way to apply more effective air power to produce an acceptable armistice.[19]

Attacks on Irrigation Dams

Clark and his subordinates continued to grapple with how best to execute this new concept of "employing air forces as the single strategic offensive in a war" by seeking new targets. The JCS supported their efforts and, except for delaying an attack on a major supply complex at Yangsi because a prisoner exchange facility was nearby, approved all of Clark's target requests, including more attacks on hydroelectric plants. The JCS did, however, prohibit any public statements announcing the intent of such operations to pressure the communists into an agreement, fearing that, if communist prestige became "seriously engaged," they would find it difficult to accept any armistice. High-level statements had to treat the air attacks as routine operations "based upon solely military grounds." Ironically, as the raids were directed more and more at achieving a political settlement, the less this could be admitted to the public as justification for them.[20]

Destroying the last major target system in North Korea would be hard to justify to world opinion as "solely military." In March 1953, the FEAF Formal Target Committee began to study the irrigation system for 422,000 acres of rice in the main agricultural complexes of South Pyongan and Hwanghae. The deployment of North Korean security units to protect key reservoirs from guerrillas during the growing season indicated the importance of those targets to General Banfill. His staff estimated that denying the enemy the rice crop from the area would cause a food shortage, overwhelm transportation routes due to the necessity of importing rice from China, and require the diversion of troops for security and repair efforts. Clark advised the JCS that, if the peace talks experienced a prolonged recess, he planned to breach twenty dams to inundate the two areas and destroy an estimated 250,000 tons of rice, "thereby curtailing the enemy's ability to live off the land and aggravating a reported Chinese rice shortage and logistic problem."[21]

This was not the only proposal to escalate the air war. As a means to ratchet up pressure if necessary, Weyland retained a Bomber Command attack for possible later use that "would effectively [have] obliterated what remains of the city of Pyongyang." He also appears to have doubted the military utility of the attack, just as he was "skeptical of the feasibility and desirability" of the attacks on the rice irrigation system. However, his planners convinced him to authorize attacks on three dams near important railways with the effect of washing away the lines as part of the interdiction program, even though among themselves they considered that rationale a "mode of deception" to deceive the enemy about the true objective of destroying the rice crop. Fifth Air Force fighter-bombers hit the Toksan and Chasan dams in mid-May, one of the most vulnerable times for newly planted rice, followed by Bomber Command night SHORAN missions against Kuwonga Dam. Clark informed Washington that these missions had been "as effective as weeks of rail interdiction."[22]

The JCS quickly approved the bombing of two more dams by fighter-bombers to inundate jet airfields at Namsi and Taechon. The draft armistice agreement provided that the number of combat aircraft allowed within Korea for each side could not exceed the number in place on the effective date of the armistice, and Clark worried that the communists intended to sneak high-performance aircraft into North Korea immediately before that date, possibly taking advantage of marginal weather during the rainy season. His intelligence had noted an increased pace of airfield construction and "frantic repair efforts" after raids. Smart suspected that the airfields were just decoys to distract U.N. bombers from more valuable targets, but Bomber Command hammered them by SHORAN at night while fighter-bombers hit them by day. Clark knew that further dam attacks risked a negative reaction from allies and might affect the armistice negotiations, but he and Weyland believed the missions had to be conducted to eliminate the airfields.[23]

Contrary to Clark's expectations, the dam attacks attracted very little notice in the world press. American newspapers were preoccupied with the exploits of

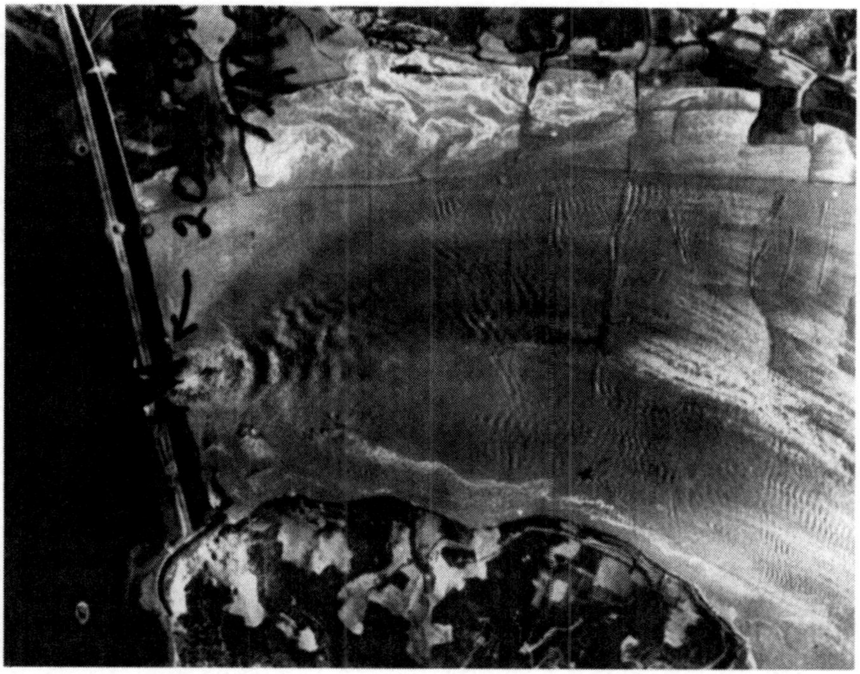

FEAF fighter-bombers tore this 200-foot breach in Chasan Dam and sent water into the streets of Pyongyang. Eventually, North Korean countermeasures reduced the effect of such attacks.

the jet aces, and each MiG that was downed received more coverage than any bombing raid. The biggest war story in May was whether Capt. Joseph McConnell or Capt. Manuel Fernandez would hold the record for air-to-air victories. FEAF press releases dutifully reported attacks by F–84s on the earthen dams, mentioning that the Kuwonga Dam which had been hit by B–29s was close to key rail and road bridges. North Korea decried "barbarous raids on peaceful agricultural installations" or attacks on water reservoirs that were not military objectives, but no one seemed to notice. Perhaps like the boy who cried wolf, the communist complaints about U.N. air atrocities were just not being taken seriously anymore. Or maybe, because no mention was made about targeting rice crops, reservoirs did not seem to merit any consideration in the press as a particularly promising or questionable objective.[24]

FEAF press releases did not mention naval air operations. Instead, the activities of Navy and marine pilots were covered in the combat summaries provided by Far East Naval Forces. Although relations between General Clark's and Admiral Clark's airmen remained cordial, each side continued to fight its own separate air war. By June 1953, however, the Navy was coordinating on joint target selection with Fifth Air Force, now commanded by Lt. Gen. Samuel E.

Anderson. He was impressed enough with the Navy's cooperation to request their representation on the FEAF Formal Target Committee. Weyland indicated that he could not order the Navy to participate because the carrier aircraft were not under his operational control, but he told Anderson to invite the Navy to send a representative from the joint operations center to attend future meetings. Because the armistice was signed a few days later, the offer was never extended. Ironically, as service cooperation increased in Korea, the air staff in Washington was gathering combat data emphasizing the superiority of land-based over carrier-based aircraft to counter Navy attempts to increase the budget priority for aircraft carriers. Using numbers of sorties and tonnages of bombs dropped in Korea, USAF operations analysts argued that their jets and propeller-driven planes were far more cost-effective than those of their naval counterparts.[25]

Those last few FEAF Formal Target Committee Meetings were dominated by discussion about how best to exploit the possibilities of the dam attacks. New ideas included proposals to use delayed-action bombs to deter repair efforts and to drop leaflets blaming the continuing air attacks, and the loss of water for irrigation, on the Chinese communists. Weyland was adamant that the dam attacks were for interdiction purposes and vetoed a proposal by Smart for a psywar campaign warning farmers and populations below all the dams in North Korea of their imminent destruction. Although Weyland and Clark justified the dam attacks as interdiction raids, neither their planners nor the communists perceived them that way. The Toksan and Chasan attacks did flood two key rail lines and many roads, but they also inundated nearby villages and rice fields. The flash flood from Toksan "scooped clean" twenty-seven miles of river valley, and both raids sent water into the streets of Pyongyang. Bomber Command delayed its attack long enough that the North Koreans were able to develop countermeasures, and they were able to avoid the catastrophic results of the first two raids by lowering the water level in the reservoir. This tactic also worked for the last two dams. The communists put more than 4,000 laborers to work repairing the Toksan Dam and placed antiaircraft defenses around it. Weyland was amazed at the speed of their recovery operations. Only thirteen days after the strike, they had completed a temporary dam and all rail repairs. When Clark queried him as to what targets were left to exert more pressure for an armistice, the all-out blow on Pyongyang was all that came to mind. Clark had Weyland prepare a message for the JCS to get approval for the raid, but it was never sent.[26]

The resort by the United Nations to such extreme measures as the dam attacks might have alarmed the enemy enough to influence their negotiating position to some degree. Although there is no evidence that warnings from the Eisenhower administration that the United States was prepared to lift restrictions on nuclear weapons ever reached leaders in the Soviet Union or China—and the President's own remarks at a July 23, 1953, National Security Council meeting imply that he did not think the communist agreement was a product of those threats—signs were obvious that U.S. patience was wearing thin and the war might expand if it continued. The number of unsanctioned sorties by eager F–86 pilots crossing the Yalu to hunt for MiGs increased. Even if notice about the possibility of the use of American atom bombs was never transmitted through diplomatic channels, rumors about Eisenhower's threat to "raise the ante unless a cease fire was negotiated" were rampant throughout Korea and would have been picked up by the communists from spies or POWs. Many other factors besides military pressure were involved in the communist decision to sign the armistice. The death of Stalin and continuing instability within the Kremlin combined with riots in Czechoslovakia and East Germany gave the Soviet Union plenty of incentive to disengage from Korea, and these events shocked China as well. Late gains on the ground against South Korean troops allowed the communists to save face while making concessions for the armistice. Further delays might also allow South Korea's unpredictable Syngman Rhee to further disrupt peace efforts and lead to more heavy casualties from artillery and bombing.[27]

Instead of influencing armistice talks with any specific bombing operation, the major contribution of air power probably resulted from the accumulative massive punishment it delivered to Chinese armies and North Korean towns throughout the course of the war. Eighteen of twenty-two major cities were at least half obliterated by bombs, and most villages were reduced to "a low, wide mound of violet ashes." That is what the North Koreans remember most about American air power, and North Korean programs to develop missiles and weapons of mass destruction have been motivated to a large extent by the desire to deter any future applications of "air pressure."[28]

Notes

Most of this material comes from Conrad C. Crane, *American Air Power Strategy in Korea, 1950–1953* (Lawrence, Kans.: University Press of Kansas, 2000), and is used with permission of the publisher. The views expressed herein are those of the author and do not purport to reflect the positions of the U.S. Army War College, the Department of the Army, or the Department of Defense.

1. Interview of Gen Jacob Smart, USAF (Ret), by Conrad Crane, Nov 2, 1997, Arlington, Va., with changes provided by letter from Gen Smart on Nov 29, 1997; and Col R. L. Randolph and Lt Col B. I. Mayo, Staff Study for Deputy for Operations, FEAF, "The Application of FEAF Effort in Korea," Apr 12, 1952, in FEAF Historical Division, *FEAF Operations Policy, Korea, Mid-1952*, Mar 1955, file K720.01, 1952 (addendum), Air Force Historical Research Agency (AFHRA), Maxwell AFB, Ala.
2. "The Application of FEAF Effort in Korea"; and Smart interview with Crane.
3. Matthew B. Ridgway, *The Korean War* (New York: Da Capo, 1986), pp 200, 202, 244; General Mark W. Clark, *From the Danube to the Yalu* (Blue Ridge

Summit, Pa.: Tab Books, 1988), p 3; and ltr, Weyland to Vandenberg, Sep 15, 1952, box 56, the Papers of Hoyt Vandenberg, Manuscript Division, Library of Congress (MD/LC), Washington, D.C. For more on interdiction operations in Italy and northwest Europe in World War II, see Eduard Mark, *Aerial Interdiction: Air Power and the Land Battle in Three American Wars: A Historical Analysis* (Washington, D.C.: Center for Air Force History, 1994), pp 141–57.

4. Extracts from FEAF Target Committee Meeting Minutes, 1952, in *FEAF Operations Policy, Korea, Mid-1952.*
5. Fifth Air Force Air Attack Program, in *Fifth AF Intelligence Summary, 16–31 July 1952*, file K730.607, AFHRA. Some confusion surrounds the actual date of the directive; some sources attribute it to Jul 10, and others to two days later.
6. *History of the Far East Air Forces, January–June 1952*, vol I, pp 41–48, file K720.01, AFHRA; msg, VCO 118 CG, FEAF to HQ USAF, Apr 29, 1952, sec 96, and msg, JCS 908100, JCS to CINCFE, May 6, 1952, sec 97, box 39 and JCS 1776/297 with attachments, Jun 19, 1952, sec 104, box 40, Geographic File, 1951–53, 383.21 Korea (3-19-45), Records of the Joint Chiefs of Staff (JCS), Record Group (RG) 218, National Archives (NA) II, College Park, Md.; msg, CG FEAF to CG FEAF BOMCOM, Apr 10, 1952, with Apr 16 reply, file B–17961, box B200, the Papers of Curtis LeMay, MD/LC; and msg, JCS 95977, JCS to CINCUNC, Jul 10, 1951, in U.S. Dept of State, *Foreign Relations of the United States, 1951,* vol VII, *Korea and China* (Washington, D.C.: USGPO, 1983), part I, pp 646–47.
7. Entry for Jun 11, 1952, Weyland Memoranda for Record, 52/06/01–52/12/31, file 168.7104–6, AFHRA; and Smart interview with Crane.
8. Memo, Operations Evaluation Group Representative to Commander Task Force 77, subj: The Suiho Power Plant Attack 23 June 1952, 13 Aug 52, in Commander in Chief U.S. Pacific Fleet, *Interim Evaluation Report no 4, 1 January 1952–30 June 1952*, ch 3, Carrier Operations, pp 3-122–3-126, Naval Historical Center, Washington, D.C.; and Robert F. Futrell, *The United States Air Force in Korea 1950–1953* (Washington, D.C.: USGPO, 1983), pp 487–89. For more on interservice relations and operations, see Crane, pp 28–30, 137, 156, 162.

9 Maj Gen William F. Dean, *General Dean's Story* (New York: The Viking Press, 1954), p 263; "Labor Protests at Bombing on the Yalu River: Mr. Churchill Denies Change of Policy," *The Times of London* (Jun 25, 1952): 2 (also see continued coverage of Parliamentary debates the next day); "Speculation Links raid to Truce Talks," and "New Initiative in Korea," *The New York Times* (Jun 24, 1952): 3, 28; and Austin Stevens, "Lovett Says the Joint Chiefs Authorized Air Blow at Yalu," *The New York Times* (Jun 25, 1952): 1, 3.

10. Memo, Maj Gen Herbert Thatcher to Gen Nathan Twining, Jul 1, 1952, with attachments, file OPD 384.5 Korea (Jul 22, 1950), sec 2, box 904, Records of Headquarters, USAF, RG 341, NA II; Futrell, 516–17, 525; Stephen E. Pease, *Psywar: Psychological Warfare in Korea, 1950–53* (Harrisburg, Pa.: Stackpole Books, 1992), pp 82–84; entry for Jun 25, 1952, Weyland Memo for Record, file 168.7104-6, 52/06/01–52/12/31; memo, Brig Gen Jacob Smart to CG, Fifth AF, subj: Targets in Pyongyang, *History of the Far East Air Forces, 1 July–31 December 1952*, vol II, file K720.01; and minutes of FEAF Target Committee Meetings for Aug 12 and 21, 1952, file K720.151A, 22 Jul–16 Dec 1952, AFHRA.
11. "Chinese Accuse US Pilots: Raid Across Yalu Reported," and "Korean Negotiations," *The Times of London* (Jul 14, 1952): 6–7; "Asians in UN Fear Raids Harm Truce," *The New York Times* (Jul 12, 1952): 2; telegram, Holmes to Dept of State, Jul 23, 1952, in *Foreign Relations of the United States, 1952–1954,* vol XV, *Korea* (Washington, D.C.: USGPO, 1984), part I, p 419; Lindesay Parrott, "Long UN Air Raid Pounds Pyongyang and Reds' Build-up," *The New York Times* (Jul 12, 1952): 1–2; Parrott, "Heaviest Air Blow of War Smashes Red Korea Capital," *The New York Times* (Aug 30, 1952): 1–2; Universal International Newsreels, vol 25, no 582, Jul 28, 1952, RG 200, NA II; and "New Initiative in Korea," *The New York Times* (Jun 24, 1953): 28.
12. Intelligence Summaries for 16–31 July 1952, pp 57, 74–76, and for 1–15 August 1952, containing copies of the STRIKE leaflets, *Fifth Air Force Intelligence Summaries*, file K730.607; and *History of 3rd Bombardment Wing, 1 July 1952–31 December 1952*, pp 5–10, file KWG-3-HI, AFHRA; Commander in Chief, U.S. Pacific Fleet, *Evaluation Report no 5, Interim, 1 July 1952–31 January 1953*, pp 3-93–3-95, U.S. Naval Historical Center; Pease, pp 82–84; Universal International Newsreels, vol 25, no 596, Sep 15, 1952, lead story, RG 200; Futrell, pp 518–19; and entries for Jul 28 and Aug 7, 1952, Weyland Memoranda for Record, 52/06/01–52/12/31, file 168.7104-6, AFHRA.
13. Entries for Sep 14–22, 1952, LeMay Diary #4, box 103; ltr, Brig Gen W. P. Fisher to LeMay, Mar 6, 1953, FEAF folder, box B84, LeMay Papers; msg, CG 1583, LeMay to Clark, Aug 30, 1952, Records of General Headquarters FEC, SCAP, and UNC, Office of the Chief of Staff, Chief of Staff subj files 1945–52, TS Personal File for 1949-1952, box 3, Records of United States Army Commands, 1942–, Record Group 338, NA II.
14. Entries for Jul 24 and 28, and Aug 1, 1952, Weyland Memoranda for Record, file 168.7104-6, 52/06/01–52/12/31, AFHRA.
15. Memo, Banfill to Deputy for Operations, subj: Utilization of Air Power in Korea, Aug 29 1952, *FEAF Operations Policy, Korea, Mid-1952*, file K720.01, 1952 (Addendum), AFHRA.
16. Memo, Smart to Deputy for Intelligence, subj: Utilization of Air Power in

Korea, Sep 16, 1952, *FEAF Operations Policy, Korea, Mid-1952*, file K720.01, 1952 (Addendum), AFHRA.

17. Richard Hallion, *The Naval Air War in Korea* (Baltimore, Md.: Nautical and Aviation Publishing Company, 1986), pp 135–36; memo of conversation by Allison, subj: General Clark's Request to Bomb Targets in Korea near Manchurian and Soviet Borders, 26 Aug 52, *FRUS, 1952–1954,* vol XV, *Korea*, part I, pp 458–59.
18. See documents in *FRUS, 1952–1954,* vol XV, *Korea*, part I, pp 39, 436–42, 470, 527–28, 575, 650; and Shu Guang Zhang, *Mao's Military Romanticism: China and the Korean War, 1950–1953* (Lawrence: University Press of Kansas, 1995), pp 180–81.
19. *FRUS, 1952–1954*, vol XV, *Korea*, part I, pp 466–69, 475, 514–19; and minutes of FEAF Target Committee meeting, Sep 24, 1952, file K720.151A, 22 Jul–16 Dec 1952, AFHRA.
20. "Staff Study of Intelligence Requirements by Cdr, FEAF for the Present and the Future," p 5, *History of the Far East Air Forces, January–December 1953*, vol III, part 1, file K720.01, AFHRA; memo by Maj Gen Lee, May 4, 1953, and Summary Sheet by Lt Col Kidd, Apr 28, 1953, subj: Air Attacks Against Targets in Korea near the Manchurian Border, with attachments, file OPD 384.5 Korea (22 Jul 50), sec 3, box 906, RG 341; msg, JCS 915579, JCS to CINCFE, Aug 8, 1952, Geographic File, 1951–53, 383.21 Korea (3-19-45), sec 109, box 40; and msg, C 62275, CINCFE to JCS, May 6, 1953, with attached memo for General Bradley, Incoming Messages, February 11–May 31, 1953, box 7, RG 218.
21. Minutes of the FEAF Formal Target Committee Meeting for Mar 24, 1953, with inclosure, *FEAF Bomber Command History, January–27 July 1953*, vol III, file K713.01-39, AFHRA; and msg, C62419, Clark to JCS, May 14, 1953, Incoming Messages, February 11–May 31, 1953, box 7, RG 218.
22. Minutes of the FEAF Formal Target Committee Meetings for 7 April, 12 May, and 26 May 53, *FEAF Bomber Command History, January–27 July 1953*, vol III, file K713.01-39, and entries for 7 May and 8 May, Weyland Memoranda for Record, vol IV, 53/01/01–53/07/31, file 168.7104-7, AFHRA; and msg, 62451, Clark to JCS, 16 May 53, Incoming Messages, February 11–May 31, 1953, box 7, RG 218.
23. Msg, CX 62662, Clark to JCS, 27 May 53, Incoming Messages, February 11–May 31, 1953, box 7, RG 218; msg, CX 62983, Clark to JCS, Jun 11, 1953, with JCS reply, JCS 941184, Jun 11, 1953, sec 130, box 44, Geographic File, 383.21 Korea (3-19-45), RG 218; Smart interview with Crane; and msgs, Clark to JCS, CX 62901, 8 Jun 53, CX 62960, Jun 10, 1953, and CX 63033, Jun 13, 1953, Incoming Messages, June 1–July 31, 1953, box 8, RG 218.
24. As an example of the McConnell-Fernandez coverage, see Robert Alden, "Sabre Jets Score 12 Mig Bag in Day," *The New York Times* (May 19,

1953): 3. For press releases by both sides on the dam attacks, see the official reports of Korean action that were always on page 2 of *The New York Times* (May 15, 17, 18, and 23, 1953).

25. Minutes of FEAF Formal Target Committee Meetings for 23 June and 22 July 53, *FEAF Bomber Command History, January–27 July 1953*, vol III, file K713.01–39, AFHRA; memo, Maj Gen Lee to DCS/Operations, subj: Carrier Forces Versus Land Based Forces, Feb 13, 1953, with inclosures; memo for General Vandenberg from W. Barton Leach, Mar 11, 1953, with inclosures; memo, Col Wallace Barrett to Leach, subj: Carrier Operations in Korea, Mar 30, 1953; and memo for Gen Vandenberg from Leach, Mar 31, 1953, folder 7C, box 84, Vandenberg Papers.
26. Minutes of FEAF Formal Target Committee Meeting for 26 May 53, *FEAF Bomber Command History, January–27 July 1953*, vol III, file K713.01-39, AFHRA; entries for May 21 and 26, and Jun 16 1953, Weyland Memo for Record, vol IV; and Quarterly Review Staff Study, "The Attack on the Irrigation Dams in North Korea," *Air University Quarterly Review* IV (winter 1953–54): 40–61.
27. William Stueck, *The Korean War: An International History* (Princeton: Princeton Univ. Press, 1995), pp 326–30, 341–42; and ltr to author from Brig Gen Theo. C. Mataxis, May 12, 1998. After the war, Eisenhower did become convinced that his threats had been successful. In early 1965, President Lyndon Johnson discussed the growing problem in Vietnam with Eisenhower, and the general remarked that he had ended the war in Korea by having the word passed through three different channels "telling the Chinese that they must agree to an armistice quickly, since he had decided to remove the restrictions of area and weapons if the war had to be continued." Notes by Andrew Goodpaster of a meeting between Johnson and Eisenhower, Feb 17, 1965, from the LBJ Library, copy furnished by Charles F. Brower IV.
28. Crane, pp 168–69; and Selig Harrison, "The Missiles of North Korea: How Real a Threat?" *World Policy Journal*, 17 (fall 2000): 13–24.

Air Power Coordination during the Korean War

Vice Adm. Jerry Miller, USN (Ret.)

Air power coordination during the Korean War can be summarized as being nonexistent during the early phases, subject to geographic determinants for much of the rest of the war, and outstanding during the final month. At the opening of the Korean War in June 1950, the U.S. Navy had one World War II aircraft carrier deployed in the western Pacific. The embarked air group consisted of two propeller aircraft squadrons and two jet squadrons. This was the beginning of jet aviation for the Navy, and operational accidents were not uncommon. Squadrons equipped with propeller aircraft could carry large amounts of ammunition and ordnance, highly suitable for support of the ground troops struggling in the Pusan perimeter, but Navy aircraft could not communicate with the ground troops. Forward air control was in short supply.

The U.S. Air Force had been forging ahead with its jet aircraft program. Units of the Fifth Air Force based at Itazuke Air Base in southern Japan were flying the relatively new jet-powered Lockheed F–80 Shooting Star. It had a short range and could not carry much ordnance. Just flying from Japan to the Pusan perimeter consumed much of the aircraft's fuel, and it arrived on station low on fuel and with only a small amount of ordnance to use in support of the ground troops. The need for immediate target assignment added to the urgency of the situation and confusion in communications.

On July 5, barely two weeks after the beginning of hostilities, a Joint Operations Center (JOC) opened at Taejon in South Korea to provide improved close air support for U.S. ground forces. However, communications were limited. As a result, the emergency, or guard channel, was used a great deal to direct aircraft to suitable target areas. A lot of support from Navy aircraft flying circles in the sky was lost to the ground troops simply because of poor communications and lack of a coordinated attack plan.

Forward air controllers used small liaison aircraft to direct F–80 strikes in support of ground troops, but T–6 Texan trainer aircraft were brought in quickly as replacements because the small liaison aircraft were vulnerable to enemy antiaircraft fire. Communication between these aircraft and U.S. Navy units was difficult. As a result, coordinating the limited amount of available air resources that were available was impossible.

On July 14, a Fifth Air Force–Eighth Army JOC began functioning at Taegu. The next day, Navy carrier aircraft on missions over Korea began to report to the center for coordinated air support. On July 22, the USS *Boxer* arrived in the area with 145 Air Force World War II F–51 propeller fighter-bomber aircraft. At about the same time, the USS *Philippine Sea* arrived, after an emergency deployment from San Diego. This added two more propeller and two more jet fighter-bomber squadrons to the total air arsenal. Ground support capability improved, in potential at least. However, poor communications and the lack of a coordinated air plan still prevented the most efficient use of this increasing air support.

Propeller-driven aircraft with a large ordnance load and an ability to remain over the troops for a long period were the most suitable characteristics for support of the ground campaign. Jets were required for dealing with the MiG fighters and maintaining air superiority. Flak suppression, that is, confronting ground antiaircraft weapons, also became a major mission for the jets, at which they performed well.

On July 24, the Fifth Air Force moved its advance headquarters from Japan to Taegu in South Korea, locating it next to the U.S. Eighth Army headquarters to ease communications and improve coordination. However, no Navy or Marine Corps representatives were present at the headquarters. At about this time, the Far East Air Forces (FEAF) also established a provisional combat cargo command to coordinate logistic operations that were supplying all the units preparing for the Inchon amphibious landings. However, General MacArthur blocked FEAF's efforts to be assigned sole responsibility for all air raids over North Korea. The proposed change in authority for the use of air power might have helped coordination, but it was not to be approved because of anticipated opposition from Navy and marine air units. Interservice rivalry, particularly among air units, was apparent.

During the amphibious landings at Inchon in September, two Navy carriers provided most of the air power that supported the troops who were making the landings. No close coordination with Air Force units was required. The Navy units, now augmented by marine aviation, flying another propeller-driven aircraft from World War II, the Vought F4U Corsair, operated in whichever region needed support. The Air Force was busy building up its forces in country while supplying support as requested, but little coordination existed between Air Force and naval units. Units were later assigned specific geographic areas in which to conduct operations, thereby providing some form of coordination and separation of forces.

During the latter part of 1950, coordination by geographic areas was continued. Navy and marine aircraft covered the marines and X Corps as they withdrew from the Chosin Reservoir and were evacuated by sea at Hungnam. The Air Force supported the Eighth Army, which was withdrawing down the western side of Korea from its forward advancement close to the Yalu River. Little communication occurred between the two ground forces. It was almost as though two separate ground campaigns were being fought, with separate air forces providing cover.

Following the Chosin Reservoir operation, Task Force 77 sent a senior air group commander to Fifth Air Force headquarters to help coordinate Air Force and Navy air operations. When some special support by the Navy was required, such as the escort of a B–29 bombing mission, this liaison officer was the medium of communications with Task Force 77. This temporary liaison post was later changed to a permanent position with a senior Navy captain in place. However, as a rule, the Navy operated in eastern Korea, the Air Force operated in western Korea, and marine aviation operated wherever marine ground forces were located.

In mid-1951, the Air Force devised the short-range navigation (SHORAN) bombing system, initially using B–29 bombers. SHORAN used radio navigation beacons and extremely accurate maps for getting bombs on the targets to avoid the limitations of visual and radar bombardment. Eventually, the SHORAN technique was modified to include Air Force tactical aircraft and Navy Task Force 77. Pilots using the system would check in with a SHORAN ground controller on an assigned frequency, and the flight leader would report the composition of his flight and specific ordnance being carried. Equipped with appropriate ballistic tables for each type of aircraft and knowing the specific ordnance items carried, the ground controller would vector the attacking aircraft to the target area, putting them on a specific altitude, air speed, and heading. At the proper time, a countdown would begin, with all aircraft releasing their ordnance simultaneously. This may not have been the most accurate form of bombing, but it did provide bombs over the bomb line in cases in which weather might otherwise have forced a mission to be scrubbed. SHORAN provided for coordination in delivery of ordnance under adverse weather conditions, and it could be considered to be a significant step in bringing together Navy and Air Force units in support of troops on the ground.

Eventually, as the Fifth Air Force continued its buildup of air power in country, a coordination center was established in Seoul. It served essentially to coordinate Air Force units and did not initially include Navy and Marine Corps aviation, except for special missions arranged through the Navy liaison office in the center. Coordination was provided between units of Bomber Command and the Fifth Air Force, but coordination between the services was still accomplished principally by geographic assignment. Navy units would operate in a designated part of the theater; Air Force units, in another; and Marine Corps, wherever marine ground forces were operating. Occasionally, a Navy fighter unit would be assigned to cover an Air Force bombing formation, attacking targets in northeast Korea that were too distant for adequate Air Force fighter coverage. These were specially arranged missions with prior coordination and appropriate message traffic. In late November 1951, the Combined Command for Reconnaissance Activities in Korea was established as part of an effort to at least coordinate the gathering of intelligence that, in turn, would provide a common intelligence database for all combatants to use.

In June 1953, the imminence of an armistice became obvious. The communists launched some aggressive ground campaigns to gain the most favorable positions possible, positions they would take to the negotiating table for argument. The Eighth Army was under severe attack. The commander of the U.S. Seventh Fleet, Vice Adm. "Jocko" Clark, sent out a message to the carriers stating that now was the time for all good naval aviators to come to the aid of the Eighth Army. He was so determined that there would be coordination for maximum efficiency that he agreed to have his air units, specifically Task Force 77, take target assignments from Fifth Air Force headquarters, a command arrangement that had been denied by General MacArthur in the early days of the war. To implement this arrangement, Admiral Clark dispatched two carrier squadron commanders to Fifth Air Force headquarters in Seoul with instructions to take orders from the Air Force, which would now be directing carrier attack sorties. By that time, the carriers could provide 500 attack sorties daily. These sorties were in addition to the Navy air defense sorties that continued to be flown over the task force, just in case a stray MiG might become too curious.

The first coordination problem faced by the Navy squadron commanders upon arrival in Seoul had to do with secure communications. Sending attack orders to the carriers meant that the orders had to be encrypted, which meant delay. To ensure the timely arrival of orders, planning for each day's events required scheduling Navy sorties two days in advance, not the best arrangement for a coordinated effort. Newly arrived squadron commanders from the fleet fixed this problem immediately by stating they would take their chances with no encryption. Target assignments were passed in the clear. The first step in coordination was recognized. Now, at least, every one was operating from the same clock.

Coordinated attacks for each day were developed at a planning conference held at 1300 the day preceding execution. Emergency air support requests were handled immediately, but interdiction and other ground support were planned more deliberately. Target materials and requests for support were reviewed. Assignments were made to units by organizational components, with orders to attack the following day. The Navy received first priority, selecting those targets and air support requests that were deemed most suitable for attack by Task Force 77. Other elements of the total air power structure were then given their assignments. Included at the table were combat veterans from each air component. The B–29 bomber force had a representative, as did the B–26 night attack units. Marine aviation had a representative as did Air Force tactical units. Most impressive by this time was the magnitude of the F–86 fighter force, which received their MiG Alley assignments at this coordination planning conference. Because those at the table had already participated in combat during the Korean War, they were very familiar with the weapons systems involved. Hence, these daily conferences were conducted in a highly professional manner and seldom lasted more than one hour. Literally hundreds of sorties were allocated each day for a single coordinated air plan. Messages to combat units went out immediately after each meeting, ensuring adequate time for preparation by those who would actually conduct the air missions the next day.

The efficiency of the professionals at the planning table, working with a vast array of requests for air support, was admirable. They made the assignments quickly, putting their targeting messages into the communications hopper, and then starting to work on the requests coming in for more air support. The lesson has been proved time and again: combat experience provides the professional expertise needed for efficient coordination.

The British air unit presented a special problem, however. It operated from a small British carrier in the Yellow Sea. By this time, massive numbers of U.N. sorties were flown over the bomb line each day. It was absolutely essential that participating aircraft be equipped with an identification, friend or foe system, but the British aircraft were not so equipped. Further, their aircraft had a maximum airborne time of seventy-five minutes. Task Force 77 sorties were running ninety minutes for the jets. To solve the coordination problem, the British were given a section of the bomb line near the western shore and were told to develop their own targets and attack plans, a solution that worked quite well. However, when Jocko Clark sent out his call for sailors to come to the aid of the Eighth Army, the British reacted in their typical admirable fashion with an all-out effort, pushing the weather on the first launch with something less than satisfactory results. Further, exhibiting the typical British pride in combat, they insisted on having a bigger piece of the action. They wanted to be in the middle of the mix of various aircraft over the bomb line, being kept under control by a good identification, friend or foe system. Because Navy Task Force 77 coordinators were responsible for the assignment of British air, discussions were spirited between the British liaison officer and the Navy coordinators in Fifth Air Force headquarters. British gung-ho spirit was well-recognized and appreciated, but British forces remained in their own previously assigned area. What was not needed at that time in the air coordination process was some gallant Brit being bagged by an Air Force F–86 or U.S. Navy fighter.

This was the way the air war ended. The Fifth Air Force did a superb job of bringing literally thousands of sorties to the front each day in a coordinated attack while maintaining air superiority with its massive fighter sweeps up MiG Alley. What a pity that something even remotely similar was not available in southern Korea during the days of the Pusan perimeter in 1950. It could have prevented many U.N. force casualties while contributing to the destruction of the enemy.

Dinner Remarks

Lt. Gen. Robert P. Keller, USMC (Ret.)

While I strongly acknowledge and applaud the valor and combat accomplishments of all members of the U.S. armed forces, my talk tonight will focus mainly on the United States Marine Corps. As some of you may know, my experience in World War II was in flying the F4U-1 Corsair in the northern Solomon Islands. I had taken command of Marine Fighter Squadron 223 while still a twenty-three-year-old major. Our mission spectrum in the northern Solomon Islands and the Rabaul, New Britain area, late in 1943 and during the first half of 1944, included two air-to-air dogfights with Japanese fighters, during which I shot down one in flames and damaged two others. Mostly, however, my squadron escorted bombers of both the Army Air Forces and the Marine Corps as they attacked a variety of targets, flew combat air patrols over Navy surface forces, and expended bombs and .50-cal. machine gun fire on a considerable extent of Japanese positions, impedimenta, and installations. We did not have occasion to operate directly in support of ground marines engaged in battle.

After finishing this tour of duty and returning stateside, I transitioned into the Grumman F7F2–N twin-engine night fighters, better known as Tigercats. We deployed in July 1945 to cover the planned invasion of Japan. While we were still at sea, the atom bombs were dropped on Hiroshima and Nagasaki, bringing matters to a swift conclusion before our new aircraft could enter combat. I commanded Marine Night Fighter Squadron 533 for a relatively brief time while on Okinawa, before deploying the squadron to north China early in October. Once again, I had no occasion to support our marines engaged in ground combat.

In August 1949, after completing the Air Command and Staff School at Maxwell Air Force Base, Montgomery, Alabama (which I enjoyed very much), I became the executive officer of Marine Corps Fighter Squadron 214 at Marine Corps Air Station, El Toro, near Santa Ana, California. By now, the U.S. armed forces had been greatly reduced in the post–World War II environment. Still, VMF–214 had twenty-four Corsairs and plenty of available aviation fuel, so we flew a great deal through all of the appropriate tactical maneuvers. This included working frequently and closely with ground-based marines in combat-oriented exercises.

Left to right: Fred Gutt, Charles Lindbergh, and Major Keller, CO of VMF–223. Lindbergh flew three combat missions with VMF–223, over Rabaul, New Britain, in the Chance-Vought F4U–1. (April 1944, Green Island, South Pacific)

During March 1950, for example, the squadron logged 3,136 hours, averaging 90-plus hours of productive training per pilot. I personally flew 108 hours. Over this period, VMF–214 also had short stints both on the fleet aircraft carriers and the smaller escort carriers.

Now we approach the Korean War period. Commencing on June 18, 1950, I led the squadron on a summer training cruise involving Navy Reserve Officers Training Corps midshipmen. We were aboard the CVE USS *Badoeng Strait* when the North Koreans attacked the South on June 25th. The training task force was a few days short of Honolulu. I received a message on June 28 to fly ashore and report to the commanding general, Fleet Marine Forces Pacific. The first question asked of me was "How ready are you for combat?" I affirmed my squadron was fully ready.

The squadron then became part of the 1st Provisional Marine Brigade, consisting mainly of a less than full-strength marine regiment and a marine air group, plus some reinforcing elements. Totaling about 6,500 men, all were assembled on the West Coast and set sail from San Diego in the middle of July.

On August 1, VMF–214 flew ashore to Itami Air Base, Japan. We stretched our wings for a couple of days, and then on the afternoon of August 3 we launched our twenty-four Corsairs—in three flights of eight—to rendezvous with the CVE USS *Sicily* in the Tsushima Straits. We landed aboard at 1630 and loaded eight Corsairs with rockets, bombs, and 20-mm rounds for our wing guns. We then launched the attack. This was the initial Marine Corps combat effort of the Korean War. I led it.

We hit equipment, railroad cars, and such personnel as we could ferret out in Chinju and Sinban-ni, off the southwest corner of the Pusan perimeter. Thereafter, my wingman and I landed at Taegu to talk with Air Force and Army members of the Tactical Air Control Center, whose call sign was Mellow Control. After exchanging information and receiving a briefing on the situation as they

First USMC combat effort of the Korean War, 3 Aug. 1950. Eight F4U–4B Corsairs launched from USS *Sicily*, CVE–118, in the Tsushima Straits. Major Keller led the first division of four aircraft in an F–4U #8, pictured here leading the formation. Their targets were supplies, equipment, and personnel in the Chinju and Sun Ban Ni areas.

saw it, we went back to the *Sicily*. Over the next two days, *Sicily* steamed west, then north, around the Korean peninsula, along the way striking a considerable variety of targets of opportunity. The North Koreans learned that a new element had entered the fray.

Thereafter, our aircraft carrier joined with the *Badoeng Strait*, which had VMF–323 aboard. This small task group supported the ground-based marines who now had moved into contact with the enemy. We became a truly effective air-ground team, with other brigade air elements launching from bases ashore both in Korea and Japan.

The battle got real tough, and it stayed that way. Our ground marines were like a fire brigade—going to where the conflict was the worst, quelling it, then heading off to another crisis. Their supporting air guys performed superbly. We flew often and targeted the opposition wherever it appeared. In doing so, we helped save the lives of a multitude of our own marines as well as soldiers of the U.S. Army and Korean forces. Because we were always only minutes away from crisis points, we could remain on station for an hour or two, as necessary, and then return to the ship to rearm, relaunch, and return. This was when I first fully comprehended the complete meaning of the term *marine air-ground team*.

Then came the Inchon landing in September. Two marine fighter squadrons aboard the *Sicily* and *Badoeng Strait* as well as Air Force elements, Navy aircraft from fleet carriers, naval gunfire, and a variety of special units prepared the way. Everyone continued to provide support after the marine and army ground forces had landed. It was a grand team effort by all U.S. services, plus some allied participation.

Seoul was captured after hard fighting, and the North Koreans retreated pell-mell, heading back above the 38th parallel. Bob Keller had now been fully baptized as a marine in the crucible of tough, team conflict.

Early in November, VMF–214 moved ashore to operate from Wonsan in northeast Korea. Within a week, I was detached and ordered to Seoul to become a member of the Fifth Air Force–Eighth Army Joint Operations Center. After fifteen active months in the squadron, I had become the representative of the commanding general, 1st Marine Aircraft Wing.

Maj. Gen. Earle Partridge, commanding general of Fifth Air Force, and Maj. Gen. Field Harris, commanding general of 1st Marine Aircraft Wing, reached agreement that the marines could direct their own aircraft to targets, while keeping the Fifth Air Force informed. This arrangement was in response to the fact that communications across the Korean peninsula between the two headquarters were relatively unreliable. My primary duties were to advise about marine air capabilities and actions.

Then, the Chinese suddenly entered the battle in large numbers and the United Nations forces commenced their withdrawal. While this was in progress, on December 23, orders came for me to return to the United States for assignment as close air support officer at the recently established Tactics and Techniques Board in the Marine Corps Development Center, Quantico, Virginia. It was an appropriate slot for me.

Forty-one years later, a marine who was involved in Operation Desert Storm wrote some words that pretty much sum up the way I had felt following my Korean War experience, all those years earlier. I quote:

> One night during one of [our] combined arms raids, I heard over our radios the voice of the F/A–18D FASTFAC pilot telling the "wolfpack" pilots: "hurry up! They are attacking our Marines" as he watched muzzle flashes of the Iraqi artillery firing at our ground raid force. That was one of the most poignant moments of my life. I never take this Air-Ground team for granted. Such teamwork doesn't just happen—and it can't be legislated by Congress or created by some "instruction." Nor can it really be explained why it's like it is. But, the result is a marvelous marriage, more powerful than the sum of the parts, where a Marine's most sought after privilege is to be able to fight for another Marine.

Countless heroic actions occurred during the next three years of conflict in Korea that involved a very large number of other fighting men. We marines recognize and honor them. We just try to do whatever our job may be, the best possible way we can. Each of our nation's services has its own ethos. With all of us

General Anderson and Mrs. Keller pin on stars during Maj. Gen. Keller's promotion to lieutenant general. (Photo by L/Cpl J. Burke, Defense Dept)

operating together at our very best, no other opposing force or forces can prevail.

One more word: our wives and loved ones have the exceptionally difficult and distressing task of enduring while their men proceed in harm's way, fighting for our national welfare. My dear wife, Lucille, faced up magnificently to this challenge during three wars for me, and one for each of our two sons. She has been superb. I know that you ladies here this evening have done as she did. Bless you.

Keynote Address

An Infantry Platoon Leader in the Korean War

Brig. Gen. Philip L. Bolté, USA (Ret.)

What can a former grunt tell you? Let me talk from the perspective of a former infantry platoon leader who only started learning lessons in Korea and learned much more later. One of the things I learned was that, in large part, military activity is a function of money spent earlier.

Prewar Budgets and Interservice Rivalry

In the late 1940s, President Harry S. Truman severely restricted military spending, requiring it be held at about $15 billion annually. The national strategy was predicated to deter and/or defeat the Soviet Union by launching massive nuclear air strikes against its cities if Soviet forces invaded Western Europe. The role of the U.S. Army was to guard our air bases and occupy territory after the war.

With restricted budgets in place, interservice problems were serious and worsening: the U.S. Air Force declared it needed seventy first-line aircraft groups to carry out its assigned missions. The U.S. Navy wanted to build a supercarrier to launch aircraft armed with atomic weapons, for which the Air Force saw no need. The Army and the Air Force believed that the U.S. Marine Corps was too big, particularly Marine Corps aviation which some thought should be eliminated altogether. Almost everyone agreed that the Army needed eighteen divisions, but they knew the number requested was too large for the President's budget.

Two momentous events occurred in 1949. The North Atlantic Treaty Organization was born, thereby making the ground defense of Western Europe a part of the national strategy of the United States. And the Soviet Union exploded an atom bomb, ending the American monopoly and prompting the issuance of a new national security memorandum that concluded the military budget should be *tripled.* Unfortunately, it was too late to do much by June 1950, when war broke out in the Korean peninsula.

Korean War Started

Much has been written since of the untrained and unfit American troops who fought in Korea. A recent case study of one regiment might lead to a reconsid-

2dLt. Philip L. Bolté and Platoon Sergeant Raymond Caroll, 2d Platoon, Co I, 7th Cavalry Regiment, 1st Cavalry Division (Infantry), Yongbyon, North Korea, November 1950.

eration of that conclusion: it suggests that the more serious problems in the Korean War may have concerned understrength units and weapon shortages. One area was divisional strength. All but one division in Japan had two battalions in each of the three infantry regiments instead of the usual three. Normal structure called for each division to have a heavy tank battalion plus a tank company in each infantry regiment. Instead, the divisions in Japan had only one tank company, and it was equipped with only light tanks. Ammunition and weapons were in seriously short supply, and many weapons were unserviceable as well. The significance of this situation was that the Army could neither employ normal tactics nor rely on fire support.

Additionally, the Army believed that the Air Force concentrated too much on its long-range bomber fleet to the detriment of providing close air support. In response, the Air Force cited the testimony of Lt. Gen. Walton H. Walker, Eighth Army commander, who said that without air support he could not have held the Pusan perimeter. It is also true, however, that early in the war, Brig. Gen. John H. Church, the first American commander on the ground, called for a halt to all air strikes south of the Han River because of the large number of strikes being made against friendly forces, particularly against the Republic of Korea army.

The Argyll and Sutherland Highlanders

I was first exposed to this problem in Japan while on my way to Korea, where I met a lieutenant from the Argyll and Sutherland Highlanders. Curiously, he was wearing a U.S. uniform and rank. Later, I learned the details of his experience. He had lost everything when he was wounded in a friendly-fire air strike.

In late August 1950, two battalions of the 27th British Brigade left Hong Kong and arrived in Pusan. By mid-September, the Eighth Army started its breakout of the Pusan perimeter. On September 23, the Argylls were ordered to attack Hill 282 as part of the pursuit of North Korean forces. B and C companies attacked and took the hill. C company started toward Hill 388, which dominated their position, and the Argylls called for an air strike on Hill 388. Let me read what happened from the official U.S. Army history:

> Just after noon the Argylls heard the sound of approaching planes. Three F–51 Mustangs circled Hill 282, where the British displayed their white recognition panels. The enemy on Hill 388 also displayed white panels. To his dismay, Captain Radcliff, of the tactical air control party was unable to establish radio contact with the flight of F–51s. Suddenly, at 1215, the Mustangs attacked the wrong hill; they came in napalming and machine-gunning the Argyll position.

The tragedy was over in two minutes. The survivors were unable to hold the hill and withdrew at 1500. The next day, a count showed two officers and eleven men killed, four officers and seventy men wounded, and two missing—a total of eighty-nine casualties. Of this number, approximately sixty were caused by the mistaken air strike.

Lesson Learned

Fast forward to the Arab-Israeli War of 1973. An American team was immediately dispatched to Israel to work with the Israeli Defense Forces and record some of the lessons learned from that war. One of the most important was the need to have a reliable identification system for friendly forces. The Israeli Defense Forces has subsequently installed such a system on its armored vehicles.

However, you will recall that in Desert Storm a significant number of U.S. casualties were caused by so-called friendly fire, including air attack. With nothing better on hand, U.S. forces had painted infrared-sensitive Vs on vehicles—hardly a sophisticated identification, friend or foe system.

Did we relearn the lesson? Well, if we marched off to a conventional war tomorrow, the troops would again be painting Vs or adopting some similar solution. What we have learned—fifty years after the war in Korea, thirty years after the 1973 Yom Kippur War, and ten years after the Persian Gulf War—is that millions of dollars are spent in research and development and promises of some super identification, friend or foe system to be incorporated "some day." Perhaps the real lesson is that we do not learn all we could from history.

Personal Anecdote

My father, Maj. Gen. Charles L. Bolté, was Army deputy chief of staff, G–3 (training and operations). In November 1950, he traveled to Japan and Korea. I was pulled away from my platoon and told to report to Eighth Army Advance headquarters in Pyongyang. Getting there was quite a challenge. As Lt. Gen. William H. Tunner of the Far East Command Air Force reported, my dad got an ass-chewing from me. I told him, "It seems as if the greatest country in the world could find enough food and winter clothing for the small number of people we have fighting here." General Tunner said he would fly a Berlin airlift if he could get the crews for his airplanes. Apparently my father pulled the right switches because Tunner said he got a go-ahead for more flights and for the support he needed.

Air Reconnaissance and Intelligence

Air Reconnaissance and Intelligence

R. Cargill Hall

Although its technology has changed markedly in the last fifty years, the functions of intelligence and air reconnaissance have remained essentially unchanged. Properly collected, analyzed, and disseminated, all-source intelligence provides strategic indications and warning of hostile action and knowledge of the kinds and disposition of an adversary's weapon systems and order of battle. And air reconnaissance still leads the fight; it finds the enemy and identifies the targets. But if the attention of a nation's leaders is focused elsewhere, or if denial and deception successfully cloak a threat, military intelligence can be easily misread—or ignored entirely. The sudden, unexpected North Korean attack on the Republic of South Korea on June 25, 1950, shocked and completely surprised American leaders. The country's intelligence establishment, military and civil, not only failed to recognize the telltale signs of an impending invasion, it was woefully unprepared to conduct operations in the Korean peninsula on the far reaches of the Pacific rim. As Jack Finnegan makes plain in his essay, the U.S. Army at the outbreak of hostilities possessed essentially *no intelligence assets* in Korea, and that included the near-total absence of area maps, photo interpreters, and linguists proficient in Korean. For all practical purposes in 1950, U.S. forces committed in Korea fought in an intelligence vacuum, in a virtual terra incognita.

The conceit of military commanders also weighs heavily in the market for discounted or misinterpreted intelligence. If military leaders at the Pentagon in Washington, D.C., schooled in World War II, supposed that the Korean peninsula was unsuited to and would not see armored warfare, others in theater believed that Chinese communist threats to intervene in the Korean War were a bluff. The latter miscalculation, made just five months after the war's unexpected outbreak, resulted in a second intelligence failure of even greater magnitude. In Patrick Roe's assessment, that failure entirely changed the outcome of the war and its effects remain with us today. As U.N. forces neared the Chinese border in October and November 1950, the Chinese People's Liberation Army, using denial and deception most effectively, surreptitiously moved into North Korea in extremely large numbers without heavy equipment, and, avoiding main roads, largely under the cover of darkness. In Tokyo, General of the Army Douglas MacArthur, the United Nations commander, and his intelligence chief analyzed reported contacts and order of battle misinformation, and estimated the number of Chinese communist military in North Korea as a token force comprised of no more than a few divisions. Late in November, with some nine armies in the field, communist China entered the Korean War directly, and within a few days, U.N. forces in North Korea were in full retreat. In the event, Roe explains, the previously ignored military tactics of the Chinese dictator Mao Tse Tung and the historic writings of General Sun Tzu emerged as subjects worthy of study.

On the invasion of South Korea in June 1950, U.S. Air Force officials in theater found themselves equally unprepared and ill-equipped to conduct air reconnaissance over the peninsula. The flying service possessed only one tactical reconnaissance unit, the 8th Tactical Reconnaissance Squadron (TRS) based in Japan, equipped with twenty-five RF–80 Shooting Star jet aircraft. Moreover, the solitary reconnaissance technical squadron, also based in Japan and responsible for processing and interpreting aerial film, the 548th Reconnaissance Technical Squadron (RTS), possessed insufficient trained photo interpreters to handle the rush of combat film. And the U.S. Army, which was supposed to provide photo interpreters to cover its needs, had none to offer. In the months that followed, as Samuel Dickens describes the actions and events, the Air Force moved aircraft and trained personnel into Japan and Korea as rapidly as possible. The Strategic Air Command sent RB–29s and RB–45C reconnaissance bombers into the theater. The service also moved the 363d RTS to Taegu, South Korea, in

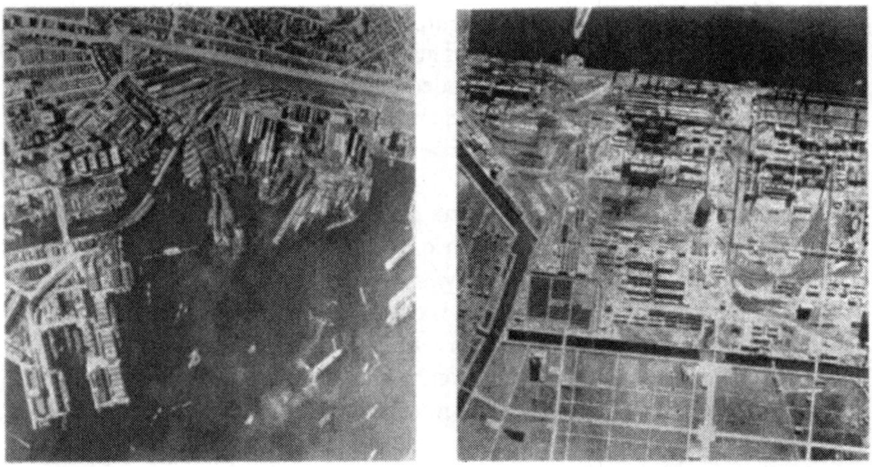

An RB–26 of the 12th Tactical Reconnaissance Squadron photographed Vladivostok harbor at low altitude at night using flash bombs during the first week of October 1951.

October 1950 to provide the Army and the Air Force with photo interpreters on site. Eventually, in early 1951, the 8th TRS inactivated when the 67th Tactical Reconnaissance Wing activated and moved to South Korea with three flying squadrons: the 12th TRS equipped with RB–26s for nighttime photoreconnaissance; the 15th TRS daytime photoreconnaissance also equipped with RF–80s and, by 1952, in possession of a few RF–86s; and the 45th TRS equipped with RF–51 Mustangs and later with RF–80s.

By the end of 1951, eighteen months after the start of hostilities, the U.S. Army and Air Force had sufficient intelligence and aerial reconnaissance assets in place to support U.N. combat operations at least adequately. But by this time, as Finnegan tartly observes, the maneuver phases of the Korean War had ended, and the opposing forces occupied essentially static positions on or near the 38th parallel, a situation in which the value of intelligence and aerial reconnaissance to combat operations is rather more circumscribed than it might be on a fluid battlefield. During the conflict, however, Air Force tactical reconnaissance aircraft made a number of noteworthy contributions. If they missed the movement of Chinese communist troops into North Korea in late 1950, a subject that is still hotly debated,[1] they definitely captured on film the first MiG–15 aircraft to be stationed there in late 1951. Moreover, with the Chinese intervention in the war, President Harry Truman in December 1950 approved military aerial overflights of the Soviet Union and mainland China, an activity that subsequently provided American leaders with reliable strategic intelligence. During the war, as Dickens points out, select members of the tactical reconnaissance squadrons in theater periodically conducted these Top Secret missions. Indeed, Sam Dickens piloted a reconnaissance overflight of the Soviet port of Vladivostok and environs with the 15th Tactical Reconnaissance Squadron in 1954, *after* the Korean War ended,

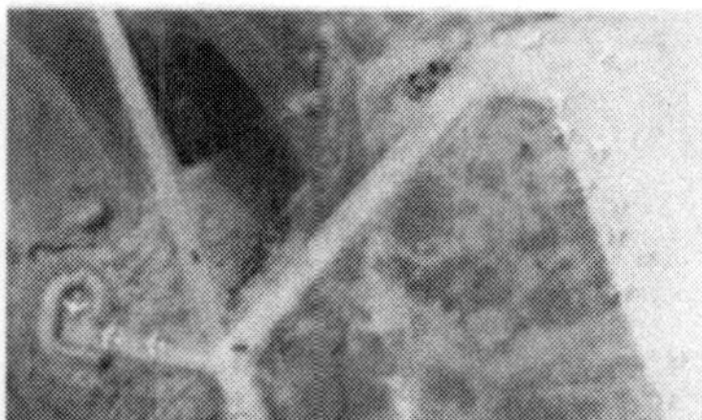

Uiju Airfield on the south bank of the Yalu River, near Sinuiju, North Korea. On November 9, 1951, an RF–80 of the 15th TRS provided this first confirmation of MiG–15s deployed in Korea. Enlargement showing some of the MiG–15s at Uiju. These Soviet aircraft soon caused this region to be termed "MiG Alley."

when President Dwight Eisenhower made Truman's wartime overflight precedent peacetime national policy.[2] Altogether, the papers presented by Jack Finnegan, Pat Roe, and Sam Dickens contribute to the literature and our appreciation of intelligence and air reconnaissance as it was practiced, and malpracticed, in the Korean War.

Notes

1. A number of contemporary photo interpreters claimed to have examined aerial reconnaissance film in October and November 1950 that showed Chinese troops crossing the Yalu River into North Korea, and to have passed that film with flash reports to command authorities at Far East Command. See, for example, Frederick R. Sager, "Photo Interpreting in Asia," in R. Cargill Hall and Clayton D. Laurie, eds., *Early Cold War Overflights, 1950–1956: Symposium Proceedings* (Washington, D. C.: National Reconnaissance Office, 2003).
2. See the symposium proceedings, *Ibid.*

The Intelligence War in Korea: An Army Perspective

John Patrick Finnegan

Many intelligence reports are contradictory, even more are false, and most are uncertain.

—Karl von Clausewitz

The whole *art of war consists in getting at what is on the other side of the hill.*

—Duke of Wellington

It is excusable for a general to lose a battle; it is unpardonable for a commander to be surprised.

—Frederick the Great

The Korean conflict was primarily a ground war, and in intelligence, as in other areas, the Army took the lead. The U.S. Army served as executive agent of the Joint Chiefs of Staff (JCS) in prosecuting the war, and the Army thoroughly dominated the United Nations Command (UNC) throughout the course of the conflict. As a result, the key intelligence decisions—assessments and misassessments—were made by commanders and G–2s in olive drab. Moreover, the Army provided most of the collection assets fielded by the armed services. Under Korean conditions, however, Army and Air Force intelligence operations were deeply intertwined. The U.S. Army depended on the U.S. Air Force to conduct photoreconnaissance missions, interpret the resulting imagery, and insert locally recruited Army agents deep behind enemy lines.

The war in Korea did not begin auspiciously for the intelligence community. Neither the Army nor the Air Force was prepared to meet a Korean contingency, and the intelligence arms of both services had been allowed to atrophy in the aftermath of World War II. The newly established national-level intelligence agencies (the Central Intelligence Agency [CIA] and the Armed Forces Security Agency [AFSA]) had concentrated their efforts on the Soviet Union. Once deployed to Korea, however, the Eighth Army cobbled together an intelligence architecture, despite severely limited resources and an almost complete lack of Korean linguists. American commanders were able to obtain enough intelligence on the intentions and dispositions of their enemy to parry every attack against the defensive perimeter that had been set up around the port of Pusan. The invading North Korean forces were checked and driven back in disarray. However, at the end of November 1950, while apparently on the verge of total victory, the UNC forces in Korea were routed by an army of 300,000 Chinese who had crossed the Yalu River undetected by aerial reconnaissance and slipped wraithlike through the forested mountains of North Korea.

The high-technology assets upon which the UNC had relied to provide indications and warning—Air Force photoreconnaissance and national and service signals intelligence—had been thwarted by a low-technology enemy whose light infantry force presented few detectable signatures. Realizing it was operating in an intelligence vacuum, the Army mounted deep-penetration human-intelligence (HUMINT) missions, using Air Force assets to parachute agents in blind drops behind enemy lines. Army intelligence improved only after the performance of combat intelligence had been upgraded and tactical signals intelligence units were fielded, and when Chinese forces, augmented by artillery, armor, and radio nets, provided a more detectable target array. By mid-1951, when most elements of a revamped Army–Air Force intelligence structure were at last in place, the maneuver phase of the Korean War ended and truce talks were underway. For the final two years of the war, the mission of Army intelligence was to secure tactical advantage rather than ward off operational surprise.

The First Surprise

The traumatic experience of the Korean conflict was a watershed in the evolution of Army intelligence. Within six months, the Army found itself confronted with two major intelligence disasters: it was caught unprepared by the initial North Korean invasion of June 1950, and was again caught unprepared by the massive Chinese intervention in November of the same year. Once again, skeptics felt free to say that military intelligence was an oxymoron.

The sudden outbreak of the Korean War on June 25, 1950, came as a shock to U.S. leaders. At first glance, this seems hardly surprising because, since the onset of the Cold War, the nation's intelligence assets had been targeted almost exclusively against the Soviet Union, the major potential antagonist. Furthermore, intelligence responsibilities in the Far East were badly fragmented. MacArthur's Far East Command (FECOM), the major theater headquarters in the area, no longer had any jurisdiction over the Korean peninsula: authority over that area had devolved to the Korean Military Advisory Group (KMAG) after the last American occupation forces left in mid-1949. Because the KMAG had no positive collection capability, Korea was pretty much an intelligence vacuum. Maj. Gen. Charles Willoughby, MacArthur's G–2, did maintain a residual intelligence organization in Korea, the Korean Liaison Office (KLO). However, the reports generated by this small office received little attention in a preoccupied Tokyo.

The Republic of Korea (ROK) sources that supplied the KLO with information were considered of dubious credibility. Similar reports submitted by a CIA cell and an Air Force Office of Special Investigations (OSI) team that also remained in Korea were likewise disregarded. By 1950, ample intelligence existed that North Korea had positioned its forces forward, built up the necessary logistics structure to support an attack, and cleared civilians from its border areas—all prime indicators of a possible impending invasion. What this amounted to was less than completely clear. Both sides had initiated border clashes. Although the North Korean destabilization campaign against the South had failed, it seemed more likely in 1950 that the North would turn to political initiatives rather than to embark on a military adventure.[1]

The Army's evaluation of the situation was that the small North Korean army, though well armed and well motivated, did not have the superiority of forces necessary to conquer its neighbor. Its overt preparations were misinterpreted as a standing threat to increase pressure on its rival. Warnings from ROK sources that an attack was imminent were discounted as unreliable. Moreover, the information received was often conflicting. Intelligence officers back in Tokyo had heard "wolf" cried too often to believe anything was actually going to happen.[2]

Army intelligence had misjudged the situation. The course of events in Korea in 1950 was determined by the top leadership of the Soviet Union and North Korea, and it was shaped by the nature of the relationship between the two countries. Having prepared for an invasion of South Korea, Kim Il Sung had repeatedly sought Stalin's approval, but he had repeatedly been turned down. Eventually, reassured by promises of quick and decisive victory and perhaps influenced by Dean Acheson's declaration that Korea was not part of America's first line of defense, Stalin changed his mind. Now free to act, Kim Il Sung ordered the tanks to roll. There was simply no collection mechanism then available that could have accurately predicted this sequence of events and provided policymakers with the information they needed.

The advance of T–34 tanks across the 38th parallel thus came as a strategic surprise. Stalin was no doubt equally surprised by the swift and violent American reaction. The Korean War played out in ways unanticipated by either of the superpowers. Once uncertainty about the adversary's intentions had been dispelled, however, military intelligence was confronted by tasks that lay more within its capabilities. But America found that, in the field of intelligence, as in almost everything else, five years of peacetime neglect and limited budgets had left its forces ill equipped to meet the challenge of war.[3]

Far East Command Assets

FECOM controlled the first intelligence assets brought to bear, and on paper, they were substantial. In Japan, MacArthur's intelligence chief, Maj. Gen. Charles Willoughby, had more than 2,500 intelligence personnel at his disposal. These elements were organized to support an army of occupation, however, not a fighting command. The largest single intelligence component within FECOM was the 441st Counter Intelligence Corps (CIC) Detachment targeted against Japanese subversive elements and reporting to MacArthur in his capacity as Supreme Commander Allied Powers, not as head of FECOM. The four Army divisions in Japan were without organic CIC detachments of their own. A large military intelligence service company of Japanese interpreters supported the 441st CIC Detachment, but only two Korean linguists were at G–2's disposal. FECOM's Technical Intelligence Section had been discontinued in 1949. The photo intelligence (PHOTINT) capability of the command had shriveled. When the UNC was formed in July 1950, it inherited only what FECOM had on hand.[4] Army cryptologic resources in the Far East were equally lacking. Unlike other assets in the theater, these were not under MacArthur's direct control. The Army Security Agency (ASA), the Army's signals intelligence and communications security organization, exercised control over its worldwide elements structured through a vertical, stovepiped command. ASA maintained a theater headquarters in Tokyo (ASA Pacific) that commanded two companies and two detachments in the Far East along with several major installations.[5] But these ASA units were trained and equipped for fixed-site operations and could not easily be shifted to the field.

At the national level, available intelligence support to prosecute a land battle on the far margins of the Pacific Ocean was equally thin. The intelligence community, whose capstone was the CIA headed by Rear Adm. Roscoe Hillenkoeter, had focused almost all of its efforts on the Soviet Union. The CIA was a bifurcated organization with responsibilities both for collating intelligence and for running special operations. Until the Korean War, the agency's special operations (directed by the Secretaries of State and Defense, not by Hillenkoeter) had mostly involved combating Soviet subversion in Europe. Neither the CIA director nor his agency were major players on the Washington scene.[6]

The Army was equally unprepared to meet the intelligence challenge. In particular, its signals intelligence and security architecture was in a state of flux. In 1949, ASA had been eviscerated, losing most of its personnel and responsibilities to a new centralized AFSA that integrated Army, Navy, and Air Force cryptologic assets. AFSA conducted research and analysis and exercised operational control over ASA fixed sites, but it was hardly prepared to deal with a Korean contingency. In fact, only one analyst worked on the North Korean problem, and AFSA had "no Korean typewriters, books on the Korean language, or Korean dictionaries." On paper, ASA was now responsible for providing support to the Army's forces in the field with deployable tactical units. But the assets did not exist.[7]

In the aftermath of World War II, the Army had at least maintained sizable organizations for cryptology and counterintelligence.[8] These served identifiable functions during the occupation and Cold War. However, other Army intelligence disciplines suffered almost complete neglect. The Military Intelligence

Training Center that had produced the Army's combat intelligence specialists during World War II shut down as soon as the guns had stopped firing. What little intelligence training remained was left to the Army General School. In 1950, the Army had prepared tables of organization and equipment for cellular intelligence units that would bring together photo interpreters, translators, prisoner-of-war interrogators, and order-of-battle specialists. But the units had yet to be formed. In any case, the language skills needed to operate in Korea were lacking throughout the Army.

The deficiencies in all of the nation's military intelligence capabilities were made starkly evident in July 1950 when the United States committed combat forces to Korea. Though the occupation of South Korea had ended only a year previously, the U.S. troops that deployed to the peninsula found themselves fighting in what for all practical purposes was terra incognita. Not only did they lack the linguistic capabilities to exploit their enemies' weaknesses or even to communicate with their ROK allies, they were also dependent on outdated Japanese maps. (Air Force bomber crews at first found themselves attacking nonexistent targets.) Because Army leaders had concluded that the Korean peninsula was unsuitable for armored warfare, they failed to furnish our ROK allies the tanks or the antitank weapons needed to counter the North Korean T–34s that were sweeping southward. Initially, U.S. troops were not much better off as missiles from their 2.36-inch rocket launchers bounced harmlessly off these well-armored Soviet tanks, even though the tanks were of the World War II era.

The Army's communications security posture was equally deficient. The chief of the ASA complained that U.S. troops were committing "about 400 violations a minute." Commanders were transmitting their orders over the radio in the clear, but fortunately the North Koreans failed to exploit the situation. The Army used the SIGROD electromechanical cipher machine to safeguard its high-level radio communications. During the course of the long retreat from Seoul to the Pusan perimeter, SIGRODs were successively destroyed by the embassy in Seoul, by KMAG at Suwon, and by the Eighth Army west of the Naktong River before they could fall into enemy hands. But the incendiary destruction devices did not always work as well as they were supposed to. Here again, the North Koreans failed to exploit the situation because the invaders ignored the enigmatic half-charred machines they discovered.[9] The real security threats to U.S. forces manifested themselves in the counterintelligence arena. On the Korean peninsula, the endless columns of refugees that poured through U.N. lines were laced with infiltrating enemy soldiers and intelligence agents. In Japan, much of the sizeable Korean community favored the Kim Il Sung regime. As a result, the base areas for American forces swarmed with enemy agents whose activities the 441st CIC Detachment was hard put to suppress.[10]

The Eighth Army Effort: Only the Agent Loss Rate Fulfilled Expectations

Despite multiple handicaps under which it was forced to labor, the Eighth Army in Korea nevertheless cobbled together enough of a intelligence structure to cope with the immediate threat. The KLO that Willoughby established was already in place on the peninsula, and it was quickly augmented. The 441st CIC Detachment provided an attached CIC detachment to each of the American divisions and higher formations as soon as it deployed. (By the end of September, almost 240 CIC personnel had been transferred from Japan to Korea.) Because of the imperatives of the combat situation, these detachments devoted most of their energies to the collection of positive intelligence utilizing HUMINT. ASA Pacific provided cryptologic/signals intelligence (SIGINT) support from the outbreak of hostilities, although the first eight-person ASA liaison element did not arrive in country until mid-September. The Army also took under its wing a specialized Korean SIGINT detachment with unique language and technical capabilities. Because of limited Air Force reconnaissance assets and a complete lack of Army photo interpreter units, Army divisions used their light aircraft to collect imagery and the divisional signal companies to process the film and produce PHOTINT. Finally, the CIA provided Eighth Army headquarters with an additional intelligence collection element.[11]

The Army's largest and most visible (if not necessarily most productive) intelligence effort in the early stages of the Korean War was in HUMINT. An organization quickly developed around the nucleus of the KLO, with personnel from the 441st CIC Detachment. To execute its mission, the KLO hastily recruited Korean peasants, provided them with sketchy training, and airdropped them behind enemy lines with instructions to return with intelligence reports. Few did. In addition, KLO set up tactical liaison offices (TLOs) at division level to recruit Koreans as line crossers to gather clandestine HUMINT. Although it operated in support of Eighth Army and its tactical commanders—the TLOs, in fact, were described by one officer as simply glorified reconnaissance units—the whole structure remained firmly under Willoughby's control.[12] Agent casualties were high, and the quality of intelligence produced was unsatisfactory. As the military expert and author S. L. A. Marshall observed grimly, "Only the loss rate [of agents] fulfilled expectations." But, in the early stages of the war, these methods seemed to be essential. Nonetheless, the KLO attempted to improve the collection situation as early as August 1950. One basic problem was that both agent insertion techniques employed by the KLO—parachute drops and line crossings—were intrinsically hazardous, and even parachute agents had to exfiltrate through enemy lines to return with their reports. The KLO devised the idea of using small boats, both to land its agents behind enemy lines and to retrieve them, thus bypassing the dangers of the fighting front. However, the cooperation of the ROK Navy was necessary for this effort, and this was difficult to obtain.

The idea was temporarily abandoned in September 1950 when the needs of the forthcoming amphibious operation at Inchon absorbed all available shipping.[13]

Determined American fighting men, supported by this jury-rigged intelligence system and its mixed bag of assets, sufficed to save the Eighth Army from defeat during its darkest days as it manned the defenses of the Pusan perimeter. By exploiting North Korean communications, Eighth Army commander Gen. Walton H. Walker was able to parry every enemy attack, dispatching units like fire brigades to threatened sectors of his line. However, at this point, the intelligence that would have allowed Walker and his commanders to make an accurate assessment of the enemy's steadily weakening force level along the Naktong River was just not there. The fact that the Eighth Army was actually facing an outnumbered foe did not become apparent until the United Nations was able to break out of the peninsula, capture masses of knowledgeable prisoners, and count the number of enemy dead. Intelligence support for MacArthur's strategic landing behind enemy lines at Inchon, however, proved superior. With the help of Korean partisans, the CIA and U.S. Navy reconnoitered the port before the assault, determining that the landing approach was practicable and that the port of Inchon itself was held by only a small force of second-line troops.[14]

In this operation, intelligence served as shield as well as sword. Preparations for such a massive assault were too big to be hidden, and the staging areas in Japan were under observation by hostile eyes. The 441st CIC Detachment scooped up numerous enemy agents, arresting the head of the main North Korean spy ring in Japan less than a week before the landings. However, the real security of Operation Chromite was provided by the unexpected audacity of the plan itself. Although it was clear an armada was being assembled to strike somewhere in Korea, it was generally assumed that any landing would occur at a less risky site far to the south of the actual objective.[15]

The overwhelming victory of U.N. forces in the aftermath of the Inchon landing appeared to obviate the need for intelligence. Additionally, the very success of U.N. forces exacted a price: intelligence elements repeatedly had to displace to keep up with the pace of the advance, which disorganized the intelligence structure and impaired its operational capabilities. At the time, this did not cause great concern, as in the old and complacent adage: you don't need intelligence when you're winning. With the North Korean army in a state of rapid collapse, intelligence work was becoming the task of performing an autopsy on an expired enemy. A party of CIC agents with strong military escort—Task Force Indianhead—scoured the wreckage of Pyongyang for documents of intelligence interest as soon as the North Korean capital had been liberated.[16]

By the fall of 1950, additional intelligence assets were rather belatedly entering the theater. ASA deployed a tactical unit in Korea in October, shipping a company all the way from the United States. Moreover, back in the United States, a mobilization of intelligence resources accompanied the military buildup. President Truman had decided to replace Admiral Hillenkoeter as director of Central Intelligence with the forceful and prestigious Gen. Walter Bedell Smith, who had been Eisenhower's chief of staff. Smith moved to expand and revamp the CIA, bringing its special operations elements firmly under his control. Focus on the Korean problem at the national level was at last producing results. The armed services were doing their part. New intelligence units were rapidly organized, although it would take some time before they trained and deployed, and many were slotted to support NATO elements in Europe rather than U.N. forces in Korea.[17]

Intelligence Failures

Even as U.N. forces advanced, however, the inadequacy of their intelligence support became increasingly apparent. The X Corps landing at Wonsan on the east coast of Korea was impeded by the unexpected discovery that the port was heavily mined. At the end of October, Chinese forces popped up, savaged the Eighth Army advanced formations, and then mysteriously disappeared. Commanders were uncertain what to make of this. At the beginning of November, the appearance of MiG–15 jets above the Yalu revealed another intelligence shortfall. Air Force intelligence had underestimated the performance characteristics of the new Soviet interceptors. With its swept wings, the MiG could fly higher and faster than almost anything in the U.N. inventory. It could be effectively challenged in air-to-air combat only by the small number of advanced F–86 fighters available to the Far East Air Forces. Additionally, the sudden appearance of the MiGs gave rise to the potentially disconcerting question as to who was flying them: neither North Korea nor China was supposed to have a jet air force.[18]

In short, by November 1950, divided and overextended U.N. forces were conducting aggressive military operations while they lacked adequate intelligence collection mechanisms, appropriate linguistic skills to deal with contingencies, accurate maps, or any situational awareness of what was occurring outside the Korean peninsula. The UNC chose to ignore the implications of these shortcomings. Like their Japanese counterparts after Pearl Harbor, America's policymakers found themselves overcome by what was later termed the victory disease. With eyes wide shut, the UNC drove its forces on toward the Yalu, was strategically surprised by a major Chinese communist intervention at the end of November, and reeled backward in defeat.

The strategic surprise that befell the UNC was perhaps the most obviously telegraphed surprise in the history of American arms. In October, Zhou Enlai, the foreign minister of the People's Republic of China, had publicly announced that China would enter the war if U.S. forces crossed the 38th parallel. Anti-American demonstrations had swept through China as MacArthur's forces neared the Yalu, and American intelligence was all too painfully aware that some 400,000 troops of China's best combat element, the Fourth Field Army, had been concentrated just across the Yalu River in Manchuria.[19]

In Tokyo, at command headquarters, all of these warning indicators were dismissed or disregarded. Because the United States and the People's Republic of China had no diplomatic relations, Zhou Enlai's message had been conveyed through the government of India. However, the United States distrusted the reliability of India's ambassador to China, who was pegged as a leftist sympathizer. If Zhou had actually issued such a warning, it was probably a mere bluff, an empty threat, made to salvage Kim Il Sung's tottering government at no cost to China. Likewise, the demonstrations (which were actually intended to mobilize public support for war) could be ignored. China was a land of paper dragons and firecrackers; the communists were always mobilizing crowds and issuing extravagant and meaningless denunciations of something or other. Troop movements into Manchuria also could be readily explained as a matter of Chinese forces simply returning to their home bases following the successful termination of the Chinese civil war.

The completely unexpected appearance of Chinese formations in North Korea at the end of October should have called MacArthur's intelligence assessments into question. Military intelligence had discovered the Chinese presence in the simplest way possible: by finding that U.S. and ROK forces had taken Chinese prisoners. The meaning of all this remained enigmatic, however. The Chinese forces soon disengaged, and the Chinese prisoners of war, when interrogated, claimed they were members of special military units that at first were assumed to be only token cadres from the Fourth Field Army. Washington analysts thought the Chinese initiative had been limited to "piecemeal commitments of small forces" from diverse units, with the belief being that the Chinese were trying to maintain "the fiction of volunteer forces" while pretending that they were present in greater strength than was the case. The first-phase offensive did not shake the underlying assumptions of the UNC. Neither did the discovery that 30,000 maps of Korea had been sent to cities along the Manchurian–Korean border. Although the intelligence apparatus realized the Chinese most certainly had the military capability for a full-scale intervention, it doubted they would pursue such a course as winter began. If the Chinese had failed to intervene in August, when the Eighth Army was trapped in the Pusan perimeter and intervention could have been decisive, it appeared irrational for them to intervene when North Korea had been broken. It seemed plausible to assume that the Chinese presence in Korea was in the nature of a face-saving gesture.[21]

Catastrophe: The Reason Why

The massive intervention of thirty People's Liberation Army divisions in the second-phase offensive dramatically underscored the catastrophic failure of UNC intelligence. The whole set of self-serving assumptions about the nature and likelihood of the Chinese threat came crashing down like a house of cards. The UNC had been confident that any large-scale movement of Chinese troops into Korea could be detected; that such a movement could be smashed by air power; and that, in any case, an underequipped army of Chinese coolies could be easily met and disposed of by the forces in place. This interlocking belief system was overturned at a blow.[22]

First, the ability of MacArthur's intelligence collection systems to provide early warning was grossly overestimated. When Maj. Gen. Pang Ho San's forces first streamed across the Yalu in mid-October 1950, the limited aerial reconnaissance assets of the United Nations found themselves in the wrong place at the wrong time. Photoreconnaissance aircraft were committed to flying daylight missions to assess bomb damage of the ruins of North Korean factories. Once Chinese forces had appeared on the battlefield, the Air Force turned its attention to evaluating the success of its bombing campaign against the exit points of major bridges along the Yalu. By this time, the Chinese were already on the other side. Once across the river, the People's Liberation Army was able to slip through the mountainous Korean terrain. Normally moving only at night, observing perfect march discipline, and presenting minimal signatures to technical collection systems because they lacked vehicles and radios, the Chinese light infantry was able to remain effectively invisible until the moment they chose to attack. Air Force efforts to mount night reconnaissance missions over North Korea were thwarted by terrain and adverse weather.[23]

Second, what could not be discovered could not be hit. U.N. fighter-bombers had operated against North Korean columns with devastating effect during the first part of the war. Based on this experience, MacArthur had declared that any attempt by the Chinese to intervene would be met with the "greatest slaughter." Light infantry sifting through and around the rugged hills of Korea provided far less lucrative targets than tanks and trucks traveling on roads. Finally, intelligence officers simply lacked a basic understanding of the way in which the Chinese force structure interacted with their choice of tactics. On paper, Chinese divisions looked like weak and underequipped versions of their Soviet and North Korean counterparts, lacking vehicles and heavy weapons. But this lack of materiel actually facilitated the infiltration tactics at which the Chinese were so adept. The People's Liberation Army's approach to war reflected its guerrilla roots; its tactics followed Mao's simple dictum: "Enemy advances, we retreat; enemy halts, we harass; enemy tires, we attack; enemy retreats, we pursue." Unfortunately, as one historian has pointed out, the writings of Mao were unavailable to Western analysts in 1950. Lured on by the belief that the enemy was in no condition to resist, MacArthur launched his Home for Christmas offensive and marched his armies into a gigantic trap.[24]

In the ensuing military debacle, U.N. forces found themselves not only beaten but also blinded. East of the Taebaek Mountains, X Corps was tightly gripped by the enemy until it found sanctuary in the perimeter around Hungnam. However, to the west, the Eighth Army found itself fleeing an invisible foe. In the aftermath of the second-phase offensive, the Chinese People's Liberation Army had broken off contact, leaving Eighth Army completely in the dark as to where the enemy was or what forces were comprised by its order of battle. At this critical juncture, the UNC turned once more to HUMINT to meet its pressing need for intelligence.

But the KLO organization (now officially titled the Far East Command Liaison Group, Korea) was unprepared to meet the demand. No agent assets were in the areas in which the Chinese were advancing. Further, the KLO had no radios suitable for agent work, and none of its parachute agents were trained in radio operation anyway. In a desperate attempt to clarify the tactical situation, the KLO was reduced to dropping twelve two-man agent teams equipped with smoke grenades north of U.N. lines to establish the location of the Chinese forces. Only a few teams ever managed to send back signals, and none reported any enemy activity. When Lt. Gen. Matthew Ridgway assumed command of the Eighth Army, the only information about the strength and disposition of the enemy that his intelligence was able to provide was a map with "a big red goose egg . . . with '174,000' scrawled in the middle of it" somewhere north of his lines.[25]

Reshaping the System

In the first part of the Korean War, each party had achieved major strategic surprises as their armies swept up and down the length of the Korean peninsula. After the Chinese intervention, in the second stage of the war, both armies became locked in battle on a fluctuating fighting line in the vicinity of the 38th parallel. Attacks and counterattacks mounted by both sides in this constricted zone of ground combat achieved local success but failed to fundamentally alter the strategic balance. Once truce talks had established the approximate boundaries of any future territorial settlement between the parties, the nature of the war changed. On the ground, it became a grinding attritional struggle of artillery duels and small-scale battles fought over the possession of individual hills. At the strategic-operational level, it evolved into a series of tactical problems. Inevitably, these changes were reflected in the nature of the intelligence requirements of the Eighth Army. An irony of the war is that the UNC did not acquire a mature intelligence architecture until its leaders determined to cease major ground operations in the Korean theater.

The last days of December 1950 proved to be a milestone both for the Eighth Army and for military intelligence. When the Eighth Army finally regrouped following its long retreat from North Korea, what had been a blurred intelligence picture began to gain focus. Military intelligence no longer had to play a guessing game about the possible intentions of enemy forces of undetermined strength and location. Now the Chinese forces were countable and pressed up against the Eighth Army front lines. The very success of Chinese forces had increased their vulnerability to technical methods of intelligence collection: as the Chinese army advanced, it lost its cloak of invisibility. The People's Liberation Army needed columns of supply trucks to sustain its advance and quantities of artillery to break through the Eighth Army's defensive lines; it had to use radio communications to coordinate its operations, and these things could not be hidden. The North Koreans had not improved their operational security, and they unintentionally provided U.N. intelligence with valuable information on their Chinese guests.[26]

Short of a full-scale Soviet intervention and a consequent nuclear war, the enemy's opportunity to mount further strategic surprises was sharply diminished. The flanks of the Eighth Army were securely protected by seas under the complete control of U.N. naval forces. Although the allied front lines were shaky and overextended, the rugged nature of the terrain canalized the possible enemy axes of advance in more or less predictable ways. Finally, once locked in face-to-face combat, the Eighth Army was able to form a better idea of its foe. (This knowledge did not extend to enemy command relationships. The Eighth Army leadership seems to have been under the impression that the Chinese People's Volunteers were led by Marshal Lin Biao, rather than by Peng Dehuai.)[27]

General Ridgway not only saved the Eighth Army, but, in doing so, he helped establish the preconditions for more effective intelligence support. "Infantry," as an analyst wrote at the time, "is the antenna of combat intelligence." At the beginning of 1951, the Eighth Army's frontline troops had practically abandoned this elementary approach to intelligence collection. On a flying visit to Korea, the Air Force chief of staff, the West Point–trained Gen. Hoyt S. Vandenberg, concluded that the Army had forgotten how to execute ground patrols, and he personally led a ground reconnaissance mission deep into no-man's land. Ridgway reversed the situation. Ordering his troops to undertake aggressive patrolling, he quickly established the location and disposition of the enemy. Prisoners captured during these operations provided a wealth of information. Chinese troops, it developed, received elaborate briefings by their leadership on the roles and missions assigned to them by their higher command.[28]

Other collection assets remained limited. In February 1951, the first sizable group of Army photo interpreters finally arrived in Korea and was integrated with Fifth Air Force personnel into a joint photo center. This by no means provided a complete solution. The Air Force, which controlled the reconnaissance platforms, had its own priorities for taking photographs. Moreover, Chinese infantry continued to show a disconcerting talent for invisibility from the air; Ridgway discovered this by personally making an aerial reconnaissance mission along the front lines. Even when the Air Force took the photos the Army wanted, severe distribution problems occurred. Eighth Army units repeatedly overran enemy positions before the imagery of their assigned objectives trickled down through the system to the users.[29]

The 442d CIC Detachment: Line Crossers, Salamander, Aviary

Ground patrols could reveal what was going on only near the front lines, and technical collection systems had their own limitations. To meet its intelligence requirements, the UNC relied on an expanded program of clandestine HUMINT.

The Army, the CIA, and ROK forces all contributed. On December 20, the Army activated the 442d CIC to assume operational control of the KLO central office and the division-level TLOs. Between January 1951 and the first armistice negotiations in June, the 442d achieved significant accomplishments regarding agent insertion, communications, and training.[30]

Until early 1951, agent insertions had been accomplished by line crossings and parachute drops. At the TLO level, hundreds of Korean peasants were sent to gather limited information about enemy dispositions in front of the U.N. lines. The KLO, using Air Force C-47s controlled by the Eighth Army Special Activities Mission, also had line-crossers. Under Operation Aviary, it paradropped smaller numbers of Korean agents on long-range collection missions. Both insertion techniques resulted in heavy attrition of agents. During night drops, parachute agents were routinely deposited miles from their intended objectives by untrained aircrews. To remedy this situation, the 442d began to supplement its ground and parachute insertion methods by using boats to land agents behind enemy lines, a course first suggested in the summer of 1950.[31]

Confronted by an unacceptable loss rate among their line crossers, TLO teams from the 3d and 25th Infantry Divisions began transporting agents by small boat around the enemy's flank on the west coast of Korea. At the same time, the 442d CIC Detachment headquarters element implemented a much larger program of amphibious espionage that was assigned the codename Salamander. This involved the use of Korean-manned fishing boats to insert long-range agents deep within enemy territory. Salamander operations were initially conducted from the numerous islands off the west coast of Korea and located behind enemy lines. (The CIA made its own agent insertions from the east coast.) These islands were rendered more or less secure from hostile attack by the U.N. naval blockade, and many were already in the hands of anticommunist North Korean partisans.[32]

The first Salamander operations were mounted from the island of Paengyong-do, just below the 38th parallel. They soon moved to a more advanced base at Cho-do, strategically located just five miles off the North Korean coast. The position gave 442d agents access to the entire west coast of Korea up to the Yalu River. To complement this operation, the 442d later initiated plans to establish an east coast Salamander base on the bleak and inhospitable island of Yo-do. This move not only would provide intelligence coverage of another enemy flank but would allow agents to provide extensive lateral coverage of North Korean positions because they could land on one coast and exfiltrate on the other. Salamander was not without its operational difficulties, however, because the native fishing boats used by the operation were small and unseaworthy, so the 442d quickly took steps to secure fast American craft.[33]

Agent communications were also improved. Until the end of December 1950, radios had been unavailable, and the 442d's agent handlers were forced to wait until an agent actually returned to his base before they could procure any intelligence gained. The situation gradually improved in 1951. Radio teams equipped with SCR–300 walkie-talkies were provided for both Aviary and Salamander operations. The use of voice radio allowed agents to furnish Army intelligence with information on a real-time basis. However, this was not a panacea. Voice radio had its limitations; its short range meant that relays had to be used—Salamander agents passed their messages through the Cho-do base—or that aircraft had to hover in the immediate area of the agent radio teams, risking compromise of the mission. An additional complication was that some of the Air Force crews providing communications support to Aviary operations were inexperienced, flying the mission for an average of only two weeks. Many agent radio teams were lost. Continuous-wave radios, with their longer range, would have helped, but no agents had yet been trained in Morse code.[34]

Now the agents were provided with at least some minimal training. In March 1951, the 442d set up a training school at Pusan capable of providing groups of twenty agents with a basic two-week instruction course. (The facility moved to Taegu in June.) After completing training, new agents went to the TLO teams and the 442d central office. Unsurprisingly, American intelligence personnel rated the new breed of agents as "far superior" to their predecessors. For one thing, the new agents appeared to be enthusiastic and had "a basic idea of the mission." Better training, however, seems to have been partially offset by increased enemy security measures. Line crossing continued to be a hazardous operation, and agents were captured at increasing rates, although a large number of detained agents were able to escape and return to U.N. lines. Overall, the new recruitment and training program made replacements easier to obtain.[35]

Overcoming Adversity

Despite the improvements in its collection capabilities, the UNC fought the maneuver phase of the war in Korea between June 1950 and November 1951 with marginal intelligence capabilities. Its in-theater assets were inadequate; only 7 percent of Eighth Army personnel assigned to intelligence positions had any prior training or experience in the field. Language problems persisted; after a year of fighting, the Army Language School had succeeded in training only approximately one hundred Korean linguists. This meant that almost all counterintelligence and HUMINT operations had to be conducted through interpreters of varying abilities. Even some of its intelligence successes reflected an ad hoc approach in perhaps the most unusual undercover mission of the Korean War: the surgeon general of FECOM personally made a clandestine landing behind enemy lines south of Wonsan in March 1951 to track down rumors of a plague epidemic.[36]

Whatever its deficiencies, UNC intelligence proved adequate to successfully prosecute combat operations during the most active phase of the Korean War. After taking over Eighth Army, Ridgway was at least able to get a handle on the strength and disposition of the enemy forces to his immediate front. The enemy's strategic reserves, however, largely continued to be an unknown quantity. From January to November 1951, Eighth Army was able to mount a series of limited offensives that diminished the enemy's forces and steadily repelled them beyond the 38th parallel. During the same period, the Eighth Army withstood four major enemy offensives. Although U.N. troops were forced to yield ground, they were never strategically surprised or caught out of position. Once the shock of the initial Chinese intervention had passed, the adverse conditions under which the U.S. Army had been forced to fight the Battle of the Bulge in World War II did not recur in Korea. Altogether, intelligence acquitted itself better than might have been expected. The only embarrassing shortfall came in counterintelligence when the prisoner-of-war insurrection at Koje-do took FECOM by surprise.

The UNC intelligence activities in the air war proved equally productive as the war progressed. Battle damage assessment presented the usual problems. However, Army (and later Air Force) intelligence was able to track enemy aircraft on the ground and in the air through various technical means. As always, military intelligence was better at bean counting than at soothsaying. In March 1951, intelligence confirmed that Russian pilots were flying the jet aircraft encountered over the Yalu. This fact was not broadcast to the world; even the CIA's Top Secret Special Estimate of August 1951 stated only that the jets were of "undetermined subordination." In spring 1951, aerial photography discovered that the enemy was preparing advanced bases in Korea that could be used to provide air cover for the forthcoming spring offensive. This allowed UNC bombers to neutralize the fields just before they were occupied, thus depriving Chinese armies of a key asset.[37]

A Different Set of Challenges

In July 1951, armistice negotiations between the UNC and the North Korean and Chinese forces began. These proved inconclusive, but major fighting sputtered to a halt in November as both parties agreed on a tentative military demarcation line separating North and South Korea. The Korean War thus shifted from a war of maneuver to one of stalemate. On one hand, the intelligence challenge diminished. On the other, the nature of the intelligence target progressively changed. In the summer of 1951, the North Koreans belatedly began to improve their communications security, reducing the information flow available to the intelligence units. At the sane time, the Chinese forces began to offer a much higher signature profile as their armies obtained Soviet equipment and were reconfigured for trench warfare. New artillery, tank, and antiaircraft units appeared in the theater, and radio communications were used on a large scale. In any case, as the war progressed, the intelligence assets available to the UNC increased. As a result of the nation's mobilization, the necessary intelligence units finally had been organized, trained, and fielded, although all the intelligence support elements would not be in place in Korea until the fall of 1952.[38]

In July 1951, the Army reorganized its clandestine HUMINT organization. As a result of its decision to gradually return all CIC personnel to their normal duty assignments, the Army deactivated the 442d CIC Detachment. The intelligence corps personnel and assets transferred to a new organization based on a table of distribution and allowances, the 8240th Army Unit, which also included a headquarters element in Tokyo and a logistical element in Sapporo, Japan. The former KLO/TLO organization now became officially known as the Far East Command Liaison Detachment, Korea.[39]

The new HUMINT unit now had at its disposal a number of agent nets. These consisted of permanent agent organizations behind enemy lines that were linked to headquarters by radio control and were supplied and reinforced by Salamander and Aviary operations. These nets were now entrusted with a portion of the training function. Agent communications were further improved. By the summer of 1951, the Army at last found it possible to establish a ten-week Morse code course for agents, which permitted the nets to use long-range, continuous-wave radios in addition to their existing voice transmitters.[40]

By the fall of 1951, the FECOM Liaison Detachment began to reevaluate its procedures for inserting long-range penetration agents. The Salamander operation, which used boats to land and retrieve agents, had been very successful. By contrast, the Aviary program, which paradropped agents deep within enemy territory and then required them to return to U.N. lines on their own, produced far less satisfactory results. Although Aviary operations were intensively pursued—111 agents were paradropped during a single month—the rate of return was discouragingly low. At one point in October, the Liaison Detachment contemplated reducing its airborne operations by 50 percent, but it decided to adopt a new technique. Dropped in teams close behind enemy lines, agents would be wearing enemy uniforms and carrying small arms. In this way, they could impersonate enemy patrols and, if necessary, shoot their way back to the safety of U.N. lines. This tactic, along with better screening of agents and increasingly specific intelligence assignments greatly reduced losses and gave Aviary a renewed viability.[41]

The Army's clandestine HUMINT effort in Korea had now become part of a wider secret war, waged on an extensive but uncoordinated basis. In parallel with the Liaison Detachment's operations, the U.S. Eighth Army was supporting a growing partisan effort from the same Korean west coast islands that served as Salamander bases. These islands also provided bases for various clandestine operations undertaken by the U.S. Air Force, which used them to gather intelligence and to support the escape and evasion of downed fliers. The CIA was another player in the secret war.[42]

Combined Command for Reconnaissance Activities, Korea

To better coordinate these fragmented efforts, a new theater-level structure was created on December 10, 1951, the Combined Command for Reconnaissance Activities, Korea (CCRAK). (Some thought the initials stood for Covert, Clandestine, and Related Activities, Korea.) CCRAK was an umbrella organization established to impose a type of centralized control on the secret activities of the armed services, the CIA, and our ROK allies. Army counterintelligence, however, which also produced some positive intelligence from interrogating refugees and suspected enemy agents, was not in the CCRAK reporting chain. One knowledgeable Army officer dismissed CCRAK as "a hodgepodge intelligence operation." Concurrently, the partisan warfare efforts previously conducted by the Eighth Army were resubordinated to the Liaison Detachment.[43]

The Liaison Detachment became a miniature Army version of the World War II Office of Strategic Services. Its responsibilities included secret intelligence and special operations. This was the first time these functions had been combined in a single Army organization, but the arrangement had a certain logic to it. In accordance with existing doctrine, it moved control of partisan warfare from the field army to the theater level. The reorganization also provided the Liaison Detachment with a partisan force that could protect the detachment's island bases and provide it with supplementary intelligence reports. Finally, the Liaison Detachment was now in a position to prevent partisan operations from inadvertently jeopardizing intelligence activities.[44]

The increase in the Liaison Detachment's responsibilities brought a concurrent increase in its personnel. In February 1952, the detachment had 150 assigned or attached personnel on board; this figure continued to grow until the Liaison Detachment reached a strength of 450 by the time a cease-fire was finally concluded in the summer of 1953. (Many of these personnel, however, were engaged in partisan or psychological warfare operations rather than engaged in intelligence.) By that time, the Liaison Detachment's Intelligence Division controlled five separate intelligence commands, each allotted its own geographic area of responsibility. The five commands directed the activities of no less than seventeen separate agent nets and 2,100 agents. The CIA's HUMINT effort in Korea was even larger.[45]

The nature of the game meant the structure was not perfect. The necessity of setting up a clandestine organization in a denied area under wartime conditions had forced compromises in the administration and caliber of recruited agents. (Until 1953, the pay of TLO agents was less than that of day laborers working for the Eighth Army, so the latter deficiency is particularly unsurprising.) Some nets produced only inconclusive results, and nothing indicates that any were able to supply high-level intelligence on enemy plans. Nevertheless, by the end of the war, the Liaison Detachment had become the chief producer of HUMINT for the whole CCRAK organization, furnishing as many as 1,000 intelligence reports a month. This input was particularly important because, once the Chinese armies had gone to ground in the trenches, prisoners of war were very hard to obtain.[46]

Upgrading Military Intelligence

Other intelligence and security disciplines were greatly strengthened during the long period of the Korean War that lasted from the first armistice proposals in mid-1951 to the final conclusion of hostilities in July 1953. The military intelligence service units called for by Army doctrine finally materialized. The first platoons and detachments arrived in Korea in 1951. By 1953, the Eighth Army was supported by the 502d Military Intelligence Service (MIS) Battalion, which comprised five separate MIS companies and ten numbered MIS platoons. The photo intelligence situation also improved. In July 1952, an engineer aerial photo reproduction company arrived in Korea, at last providing the Eighth Army with the capability to copy and disseminate aerial imagery in a timely fashion. In September, the creation of a joint Army–Air Force element within the UNC Joint Operations Center improved scheduling of reconnaissance missions.[47]

The ASA was at last able to field the tactical support force it had envisioned before the war. Two ASA "communication reconnaissance" battalions arrived in Korea in June 1951, and the 501st Communication Reconnaissance Group, tasked with coordinating all ASA activities in country, deployed to the theater the next month. Eventually, this unit exercised command and control over the 301st, 303d, and 304th Communication Reconnaissance Battalions (respectively assigned in a direct support role to X, I, and IX Corps) and five companies assigned functional missions. By the time the war ended, some 1,600 ASA personnel were stationed in Korea. Under conditions of trench warfare, ASA found it possible to exploit low-level voice transmissions and enemy landlines. Ultimately, low-level voice intercept became the Army's most productive source of tactical intelligence. Teams of native speakers working as Department of the Army civilians manned twenty-two listening posts housed in bunkers along the Eighth Army front lines.[48]

An Evaluation

Dissatisfaction with the performance of military intelligence remained. As might be expected, a great deal of finger-pointing followed any unexpected Chinese intervention. General MacArthur, in Tokyo, blamed officials in Washington for their failure to provide him with intelligence on enemy intentions. In turn, Washington blamed MacArthur: as theater commander, he should have been aware of what was going on in his own area of responsibility. MacArthur's G–2, General Willoughby, came in for particularly heavy criticism. It was charged that his situation assessments had been Pollyannaish and that he had told MacArthur only what he thought the commander had wanted to hear. Two successive commanders of the Eighth Army, Generals Ridgway and Van Fleet, thought the Army intelligence system was not responsive to their requirements. Van Fleet complained that, even after two years of warfare in Korea, Army intelligence had not achieved the standards of World War II, a deficiency he blamed on "neglect, disinterest, and possible jealousy" in the five years between the two wars.[49]

In the case of the Chinese intervention, it must be said that Washington and MacArthur blamed each other for not knowing the unknowable. Accurate intelligence could have been divined only from mental telepathy or from physical assets that did not exist. No intelligence means whatsoever can ever readily determine key decisions that are secretly made and result from interactions between and among dictatorial leaders in closed societies, especially when the leaders involved keep changing their minds. Intelligence can begin to provide insights only when decisions are debated, communicated, and acted upon. Only at that point can the traditional intelligence disciplines of HUMINT, PHOTINT, and SIGINT be called into play. To accomplish the mission, however, the necessary collection assets must be in place initially.

The Chinese Communist Party leadership discussed the advisability of military action in Korea. No U.S. agents were among its members, although rumors of these discussions did reach the ears of the U.S. consul in Hong Kong. Zhou Enlai publicly communicated the ultimate Chinese decision, but policymakers discounted his statements. Deployment orders to commanders were not accessible to U.S. intelligence. As a practical matter, lacking a vast network of agents strung out along the Yalu River, intelligence about Chinese armies crossing into Korea could have been acquired only by aerial reconnaissance. Because the skies of Manchuria were off-limits to American combat aircraft, the Far Eastern Air Force had limited reconnaissance assets, and North Korea's border stretched for 450 miles. In addition, Chinese armies showed a marvelous talent for effectively disappearing. The intelligence failure of October–November 1950 thus did not turn on poor assessments. Rather, it resulted from a combination of deficiencies: the exceedingly modest capabilities of a fledgling CIA, the general drawdown of military forces and their intelligence and reconnaissance assets before the war, and MacArthur's own uninformed overconfidence in the capabilities of his forces.

Other criticisms of the performance of intelligence need to be put into perspective. The World War II combat experience of Ridgway, Van Fleet, and Mark Clark had been gained in a European battlefield environment shaped by the availability of Ultra, the Top Secret, high-level intelligence gained from the successful exploitation of German machine ciphers. Transmitted down to army level through a specialized dissemination system, Ultra effectively made much of the decision-making of the German high command completely transparent. As lower-level commanders, neither Ridgway nor Van Fleet would have had direct access to the source, but it would have been clear to them that their own high command would have known as much about the enemy as the enemy himself did. In Korea, the Special Security Officer network that distributed the most sensitive intelligence extended down to corps commanders, but it failed to provide the insights into enemy thinking that had been available during World War II. However, the German and Japanese communication systems had their own unique vulnerabilities in World War II that were not necessarily duplicated by those of other antagonists. In the Korean War, it appears, signals intelligence provided no magic bullet.

Additional useful comparisons can be made between World War II and the Korean War. In the European theater of World War II the United States enjoyed the fruits of collaboration with its British allies, who had been working the intelligence problem for years, whereas the ROK was not in a position to provide the United States with much sophisticated assistance. Moreover, in World War II, Germany was the main enemy in the West, and the bulk of resources could be committed to the intelligence effort against it. The Korean War remained peripheral to America's larger strategic concerns. And finally in World War II one should not overlook the fact that American intelligence enjoyed a long lead time before it had to become fully operational in the European theater. The Army was able to deploy the required intelligence assets in Korea only after truce talks had begun and the maneuver phase of the war was coming to an end.

Two other conditions distinguish the practice of intelligence in Korea from that in World War II Europe. One could essentially go into the streets of any large city in the United States and find Americans fluent in any needed European language. This was not so during the Korean War when the Army found it first had to deal with Korean and then with Mandarin Chinese. Second, one should also note that the long delay involved in organizing, training, and fielding conventional intelligence units presumably led to the Army's developing its own clandestine HUMINT operations in Korea. Large numbers of agents could be hastily recruited in theater and sent on missions with minimal instruction. These operations incurred horrendous Korean casualties, posed intrinsic counterintelligence problems (in a country without records, it was hard to check on the bona fides of recruited agents), and produced intelligence of highly mixed value. However, the absence of alternatives seems to have left intelligence officers with no other choice.

In retrospect, then, once the shock of the Chinese intervention had passed, intelligence support to the Eighth Army appears to have been at least minimally adequate. It was certainly adequate enough to help sustain the Eighth Army advances and repel repeated enemy attempts at mounting a major offensive. Ironically enough, after the war had turned into a stalemate, intelligence support improved as specialized intelligence units at last entered the theater. As the system matured, it was able to track the enemy with greater precision. By August 1952, synergistic employment of various disciplines, especially traffic analysis, was finally able to solve the problem of enemy reserve forces, as the United Nations gained the ability to trace the movements of enemy armies rotating into and out of the Korean peninsula. When the war finally came to its close in 1953, the UNC ironically had at its disposal the intelligence information it needed.[50]

Notes

1. Bruce W. Bidwell, "History of the Military Intelligence Division, War Department General Staff," (U.S. Army Center of Military History, unpublished ms), vol VII, ch II, pp 20–21, and ch III, p 22; Matthew M. Aid, "US Humint and Comint in the Korean War: From the Approach of War to the Chinese Intervention," *Intelligence and National Security* (winter 1999): 33–37; and John R. Singlaub, *Hazardous Duty: An American Soldier in the Twentieth Century* (New York: Summit Books, 1991), pp 156–66.
2. James F. Schnabel, *Policy and Direction: The First Year—United States Army in the Korean War*. (Washington, D.C.: Office of the Chief of Military History, 1972), p 64.
3. On the overall unreadiness of the Eighth Army in the summer of 1950, see Clay Blair, *The Forgotten War: America in Korea, 1950–1953* (New York: Times Books, 1987), pp 48–50.
4. US Army Intelligence Center, "History of the Counterintelligence Corps," vol 1, "Introduction and Background" (unpublished ms, 1959), p 101; Office of the Chief Of Staff, G-2, GHQ, FEC, "Historical Report, I January 30 October 1950," p 103, RG 338, NARA; Assistant Chief of Staff, G-2, "Summary of Major Activities Relating to the Korean Conflict, 25 June 1950–8 September, 1951," U.S. Army Center of Military History; and Aid, "US Humint and Comint," p 43.
5. Army Security Agency, Pacific, Summary Annual Report, Fiscal Year 1951, p 2, Army Cryptologic Records Center. The units were the 111th and 126th Signal Service Companies and the 50th and 51st Signal Service Detachments.
6. Ray S. Cline, *The CIA Under Reagan, Bush, and Casey* (Washington, D.C.: Acropolis Press, 1981), pp 119, 123, 129.
7. Aid, "US Humint and Comint," p 25; and History Office, National Security Agency (NSA) Fact Sheet, "SIGINT and COMSEC Help Save the Day at Pusan," undtd.
8. John P. Finnegan and Romana Danysh, *Military Intelligence: Army Lineage* (Washington, D.C. U.S. Army Center of Military History, 1998), p 112.
9. Army Security Agency Staff Meeting Notes, 14 Nov 50, Archival Files, Army Cryptologic Records Center; and Finnegan and Danysh, *Military Intelligence*, p 114.
10. Roy E. Appleman, *South to the Naktong, North to the Yalu, United States Army in the Korean War* (Washington, D.C.: Office of the Chief of Military History, 1961), p 199.
11. US Army Intelligence Center, "History of the Counterintelligence Corps," vol 1, "Introduction and Background" (unpublished ms, 1959), pp 105–06; U.S. Army Intelligence and Security Command (INSCOM) History Office Fact Sheet, ASA Units in Korea; John Milmore, "Communications Intelli-

gence in the Korean War," unpublished ms, undtd, INSCOM History Office Files; and John G. Westover, *Combat Support in Korea* (Washington, D.C.: Combat Forces Press, 1955), pp 102–03. At the time, it could take up to eight days for Air Force imagery of the fighting front to reach Army commanders.

12. S. L. A. Marshall, *The River and the Gauntlet: Defeat of the Eighth Army by the Chinese Communist Forces, November 1950, in the Battle of the Chongchon River, Korea* (New York: Morrow, 1953), pp 3–4; author's interview with Russell K. Leick, San Antonio, Tex., 20 January 1985; and Aid, "US Humint and Comint," pp 41–42.
13. Marshall, *The River and the Gauntlet*, p 5; and 442d Counter Intelligence Corps Detachment Historical Report, I, March 1951, NARA. Among other hazards, returning agents ran the risk of being mistaken for enemy infiltrators and shot by troops from their own side. Ed Evanhoe, *Dark Moon: Eighth Army Special Operations in the Korean War* (Annapolis, Md.: Naval Institute Press, 1995), p 13.
14. Tom Johnson, "The Korean War—The Cryptologic Story," History Office, NSA, June 2000, pp 4–5; and Joseph C. Goulden, *Korea: The Untold Story of the War* (New York: McGraw Hill, 1983), pp 204–05.
15. Robert Leckie, *Conflict: The History of the Korean War, 1950–1953* (New York: G.P. Putnam's Sons, 1962), p 131; and Goulden, *Korea: The Untold Story of the War*, p 205.
16. Memo, GHQ, FEC, Military Intelligence Section, 6 Feb 51, subj: After Action Report, Task Force INDIANHEAD, INSCOM History Office Files.
17. Cline, *The CIA Under Reagan, Bush, and Casey*, pp 130–135; and Finnegan and Danysh, *Military Intelligence*, p 116.
18. Malcolm W. Cagle and Frank A. Manson, *The Sea War in Korea* (Annapolis, Md.: U.S. Naval Institute, 1957), pp 133–34; Robert F. Futrell, *The United States Air Force in Korea, 1950–1953* (Washington, D.C.: Office of Air Force History, 1983), pp 219, 222–23; Report SS 1940, Annex 3, Archival Files, Army Cryptologic Records Center.
19. Schnabel, *Policy and Direction*, pp 197, 241.
20. *Ibid,* p 198.
21. Appleman, *South to the Naktong, North to the Yalu*, pp 753, 761–64; and History Office, NSA Release, "COMINT and the PRC Intervention in the Korean War," pp 17–18.
22. Schnabel, *Policy and Direction*, pp 277–78.
23. Appleman, *South to the Naktong, North to the Yalu*, pp 769–70; Goulden, *Korea: The Untold Story of the War*, p 328; and Futrell, *The United States Air Force in Korea*, pp 228–30, 545. Gen MacArthur used his personal plane to conduct a visual reconnaissance mission along the Yalu River. Flying at 5,000 feet, he saw nothing in the way of enemy forces. Clayton James, *The Years of MacArthur*, vol. 3., *Triumph and Disaster, 1945–1964* (Boston:

Houghton-Mifflin, 1985), p 534.

24. Eliot A. Cohen and John C. Gooch, *Military Misfortunes: The Anatomy of Failure in War* (New York: Vintage Books, 1991), pp 176–78; Goulden, *Korea: The Untold Story of the War*, p 310; and Schnabel, *Policy and Direction*, p 278.
25. Memorandum for Record, Far East Command Liaison Group, 17 December 1950; Command Report, 442d CIC Detachment, 1 March 1951, RG 319, NARA; and Matthew B. Ridgway, as told to Harold H. Martin, *Soldier: The Memoirs of Matthew B. Ridgway* (New York: Harper, 1956), p 205.
26. History Office, NSA Release, "Korea," p 55.
27. T. R. Fehrenbach, *This Kind of War: Korea—A Study in Unpreparedness*, (New York: MacMillan, 1963), p 528. Marshal Lin Biao commanded the Fourth Field Army, which provided the forces for the initial Chinese intervention. A hypochondriac, he remained safely on the Chinese side of the Yalu.
28. Billy C. Mossman, *Ebb and Flow, November 1950–July 1951, U.S. Army in the Korean War* (Washington, D.C.: U.S. Army Center of Military History, 1990), p 183; Schnabel, *Policy and Direction*, p 327; S. L. A. Marshall, *Pork Chop Hill: The American Fighting Man in Action, Korea, Spring, 1953* (New York: William Morrow and Company, 1956), p 31.
29. Futrell, *The United States Air Force in Korea*, pp 547–48.
30. GO 86, GHQ FEC, 8 December 50, AMENDED by GO 87, GHQ FEC, 11 December 50; Foreword, Historical Report, 442d CIC Detachment, 1 March 1951; Command Report—December 1950, 442d CIC Detachment, RG 319, NARA.
31. Because of the limited availability of aircraft, agent drops were often combined with propaganda leaflet missions. The Aviary personnel who carried out these risky night missions were known to have a certain indifference as to what was dropped where; as one officer commented, "It doesn't make any difference if we're off a few miles. The main thing is to get these 'gooks' on the ground. They'll find their way back." Evanhoe, *Darkmoon*, pp 85–86, 89. Command Report—December 1950, 442d CIC Detachment, RG 319, NARA; and author's interview with Winston J. Morgan, 30 January 1985, San Antonio, Tex.
32. Historical Report, 442d CIC Detachment, 1 March 1951, RG 319, NARA.
33. Historical Reports, 442d CIC Detachment, April 1951, May 1951, June 1951, RG 319, NARA.
34. Memorandum for Record, Far East Command Liaison Group, 17 December 1950; Command Report—December 1950,442d CIC Detachment; Historical Reports, 442 CIC Detachment, April, June 1951, RG 319, NARA
35. Historical Reports, 442d CIC Detachment, April 1951, May 1951, July 1951, RG 319, NARA.
36. Bidwell, "History of the Military Intelligence Division," vol VII, ch VIII, p

25; James L. McNaughton, "A History of the Korean Language Program at the Defense Language Institute" (Defense Language Institute, unpublished ms, October 1990), p 3; and John Toland, *In Mortal Combat: Korea 1950–1953* (New York: William Morrow and Company, 1991), pp 316–19.

37. Report SS 1940, Annex 3, Archival Files, Army Cryptologic Records Center; and Futrell, *The United States Air Force in* Korea, pp 300–307.
38. Johnson, "The Korean War—The Cryptologic Story," p 9.
39. GO 53, GHQ FEC, 24 July 1951; Historical Report, Far East Command Liaison Detachment, Korea (FEC/LD(K)), 8240th Army Unit, 1 August 1951.
40. Historical Report, FEC/LD(K), 1 November 1951, RG 319, NARA.
41. Historical Reports, FEC/LD(K), 1 August 1951, 1 November 1951, RG 319, NARA
42. *Guerilla Warfare and Airpower in Korea, 1950–1953* (Maxwell AFB, Ala.: Aerospace Studies Institute, 1964), pp 64–72; and Alfred H. Paddock, Jr., *US Army Special Warfare: Its Origins: Psychological and Unconventional Warfare, 1941–1952* (Washington, D.C.: National Defense University Press, 1982), p 103.
43. *Guerilla Warfare and Airpower in Korea,* p 86; Paddock, *US Army Special Warfare*, p 103; and Singlaub, *Hazardous Duty*, pp 181–82.
44. *Guerilla Warfare and Airpower in Korea*, p 86.
45. Historical Report, FEC/LD(K), I April 1953, RG 319, NARA.
46. *Ibid.*; Walter G. Hermes, *Truce Tent and Fighting Front, U.S. Army in the Korean War* (Washington, D.C.: Office of the Chief of Military History, 1966), p 292.
47. *Directory and Station List of the United States Army* (Washington, D.C.: Department of the Army, June 1953), pp 548–49; and Futrell, *The United States Air Force in Korea*, pp 552–53.
48. INSCOM History Office Fact Sheet, ASA Units in Korea; History Office, NSA Release, "Korea", pp 46–48. For an example of the type of intelligence provided by LLVI, see Hermes, *Truce Tent and Fighting Front*, p 384.
49. Bidwell, "History of the Military Intelligence Division," vol VII, ch VIII, p 51. Previously, Ridgway had noted that "We have a curtain beyond the range of our immediate combat development activities which I find extremely difficult to pierce." Roy E. Appleman, *Ridgway Duels for Korea* (College Station: Texas A&M Press, 1990), p 312. The charge was later echoed by the distinguished military historian Max Hastings, who concluded that "throughout the war United Nations intelligence about Chinese and North Korean strategic intentions remained very poor." Hastings, *The Korean War* (New York: Simon and Shuster, 1987), p 244.
50. History Office, NSA Release," Korea," p 52.

The Ghost Armies of Manchuria

Maj. Patrick C. Roe, USMC (Ret.)

The surprise appearance of Chinese Communist Forces (CCF) in late October 1950 and their major offensive in November was a nearly disastrous intelligence failure. Gen. Omar Bradley called it the worst failure since the Battle of the Bulge. Bradley underestimated it. The Battle of the Bulge was a temporary setback in what was otherwise a successful war. The battles in North Korea totally changed the course of our effort in Korea. They ended one war, the war against the North Korean Army, a war which had been won, and opened another war, one in which we settled for an armistice at the 38th parallel. The changed outcome of the war has had effects that remain with us today.

Intelligence Resources

At division level and below, intelligence was principally based upon the reports of patrols, frontline units, prisoner interrogation, reports by both strike aircraft and light observation aircraft, and occasional translation of captured documents, sources all with a classification no higher than Secret. In northeast Korea, the reports of civilians provided much useful information but they were not given much credence at higher levels.

Production of combat intelligence was severely hampered by the lack of the needed intelligence teams, another casualty of the lean postwar years. Prisoner interrogation, normally a very productive source, was crippled by lack of Mandarin-speaking personnel. Interrogation had to be done through interpreters, Mandarin speakers were scarce, and those available had difficulty understanding CCF military terms.

At Eighth Army and X Corps—particularly at the Far Eastern Command—other sources of information had a higher and perhaps more restrictive classification. The Central Intelligence Agency (CIA), for example, produced Intelligence Memoranda and National Intelligence Estimates at the Secret level as well as a Top Secret Situation Summary that contained all-source intelligence.[1] The Top Secret versions were made available to Maj. Gen. Charles A. Willoughby, Gen. Douglas MacArthur's G–2.

Other sources of information available at theater level included information from the Chinese nationalists on Taiwan, the U.S. Consul in Hong Kong, other diplomatic sources, and covert agencies. Information from nationalist sources, forwarded directly to Far Eastern Command by the U.S. military attaché in Taipei, was suspect. Col. James Polk, Willoughby's executive, reported, "No one trusted what they produced because it was invariably biased or self serving."[2] The Communist takeover on the mainland had drastically limited American covert assets there, although the nationalists still had some contacts. In Korea, Willoughby had established the Korea Liaison Office (KLO) in the summer of 1949 with the mission of penetrating North Korea's governmental, military, and industrial organizations.[3] The reports of KLO agents were available to Eighth Army and X Corps. KLO agents occasionally provided some useful information, but they were not especially successful.[4] They failed to give warning of the initial North Korean attack in June and again failed to warn of the arrival of Chinese forces in Korea in October and November.

The Far Eastern Command Daily Intelligence Summary lists a Far Eastern Command Survey Group, the cover name for what apparently were agents controlled directly by Willoughby. This was probably the remnant of the Navy external survey group established in Manchuria after the close of World War II, which, in turn, was the remnant of a network established by Adm. Milton E. Miles in China to assist in landings that were then planned on the Chinese mainland. During the immediate postwar period, the Navy external survey group operated closely with the consulate in Mukden. The activities of this group were the cause of the arrest, detention, and trial of consul Angus Ward and his expulsion, along with the other American members of the consulate, in September 1949.

Aerial Reconnaissance

General MacArthur believed that aerial reconnaissance would warn of any large-scale Chinese intervention. Meeting with the U.S. ambassador to Korea on November 17, MacArthur stated he was sure "the Chinese Communists had sent 25,000 and certainly no more than 30,000 soldiers across the border ... they could not possibly have got more over with the surreptitiously covert means used. If they had moved in the open, they would have been detected by our Air Force and Intelligence."[5] But the economy years had robbed the Air Force of much of its reconnaissance capability. Aside from the Mosquito AT–6, the airborne controllers at Fifth Air Force had no visual reconnaissance capability. Much of the focus of the three available photoreconnaissance squadrons concentrated on the Yalu River crossings, where air efforts sought to prevent the Chinese from crossing. What photoreconnaissance capability remained was limited to areas immediately adjacent to the main roads that the Chinese avoided. A further limitation was a shortage of photo interpreters to read what coverage was available. Not until November 21 did MacArthur order the FEAF to conduct intensive reconnaissance of the area between Eighth Army and X Corps. By then, most of the CCF reinforcements were already in place.[6]

Signals Intelligence

Far and away, the most important source available at the Far East Command, and possibly in Washington, was signals intelligence supplied by the Army Security Agency (ASA) units deployed in the Far East and the Armed Forces Security Agency (AFSA), precursor of the National Security Agency (NSA). NSA has only recently released some general information on signals intelligence during the Korean War, very little on methods, and none at all on actual product. With all sources of information on intelligence production in the Korean War being, like the NSA releases, limited and fragmentary, the complete picture may never be known. Still, relying on what NSA has made available, together with a close scrutiny of intelligence reports and other material available in the National Archives and at the MacArthur Library in Norfolk, Virginia, and by making some elementary conclusions, a fairly good picture can be developed, and flaws, detected.

The very successful and highly prized signals intelligence system developed during World War II had been reduced, as had much of the rest of the armed forces. Intercept facilities in the Pacific region were relatively few. Efforts were focused on the Chinese communists' activities and the Huk rebellion in the Philippines. After World War II, ASA had collected some Chinese civil communications. Beginning in March 1950, after the communists seized power, cryptologic efforts against mainland Chinese targets were intensified. But it took nearly two more years to develop effective processing of Chinese military messages.[7] In the meantime, efforts continued against Chinese civil plain-text messages. That effort produced intelligence on the Chinese economy and on the transportation, logistics, and positions of military units.[8] Before the Korean War, AFSA employed eighty-three analysts against the People's Republic of China. By November 1950, the number was 131, and by February 1961, it was 156, plus additional part-time assistance.[9]

At the start of the war, two fixed ASA stations and three mobile units were performing fixed-station missions in the Pacific. They were the 8069th Army Administrative Unit (AAU), Clark Field, Fort Stotsenberg, Philippine Islands; the 8621st AAU, Tokyo, Japan; the 111th Signal Service Company, Okinawa, Japan; the 126th Signal Service Company, Kyoto, Japan; and the 51st Signal Service Detachment, Chitose, Japan.[10]

The 50th Signal Service Detachment, whose mission was to monitor U.S. forces to enforce communication security, was diverted to wartime support. Provisions were made to provide signals intelligence capabilities to both the Eighth Army and X Corps. The 60th Signal Service Company from Fort Lewis, Washington, arrived in the Far East in early October and was assigned to support the Eighth Army. A provisional unit, the 226th Signal Service Company, and the 2d

Signals Intelligence Unit were attached to X Corps.[11] In Tokyo, Far East Command was also provided with intelligence developed by the British monitoring facilities in Hong Kong.[12]

The initial communications intelligence product was the result of plain-text intercepts and traffic analysis. In fact, at many points in the conflict, traffic analysis, that is, examination of message externals, often constituted the only form of signals intelligence for Americans. Because of problems with mountainous terrain, no steady or reliable information was available from direction finding, which had been an important source of intelligence in World War II. Not until 1952 could traffic analysis detect from military communications when communist Chinese units entered and left Korea. Much of the initial reconstruction of the People's Liberation Army (PLA) order of battle (OB) came from traffic analysis.[13]

ASA units also encountered problems finding Chinese linguists. The large Chinese population in the United States produced few candidates because most American-born Chinese spoke a southern dialect rather than the Mandarin used by the PLA radio operators. To fill the need, a number of Chinese Nationalists from Taiwan were hired as civilians to work with ASA, although some special training was needed to acquaint them with the differences in military vocabulary between the nationalists and communists.[14]

Reading the plain-text traffic produced some useful information and some misleading information. Early in the war a message from Shanghai identified General Lin Biao as the commander of PLA forces that would intervene in Korea. Lin Biao declined the opportunity to command in Korea, and Peng Dehuai took his place. Yet intelligence agencies throughout the war, and some histories afterward, continued to list Lin as the PLA commander. Late September traffic carried the information that Zhou Enlai, the PRC foreign minister, had notified neutral diplomats that China would intervene in Korea if U.N. forces crossed the 38th parallel. That information arrived in Washington by the diplomatic route as well. And as early as July, translation and analysis of civil traffic indicated that elements of the Chinese Fourth Field Army had moved into Manchuria. Later, in September and October, traffic analysis provided information that these forces had continued to move toward the Sino-Korean border. As will be seen, this was only partly correct and ultimately quite misleading.

Estimates of Growing CCF Strength

The Far East Command Daily Intelligence Summary reported increasing CCF strength in Manchuria, some of it near the Yalu border. On September 21 it stated that 35 divisions in 9 armies were confirmed and that an additional 24 divisions in 8 armies were possible. The October 5 summary stated that 38 divisions in 9 armies were confirmed and an additional 24 divisions in 8 armies were possible. By October 24 it confirmed 44 divisions in 11 armies and thought 18 divisions in 6 armies were also possible.[15]

By early October, intelligence officers in Washington, who had previously warned of Chinese intervention, began to have second thoughts. Agencies differed over the strength estimates of PRC units. CIA analysis tended to think that a signals intelligence reference to an army element meant the army had moved intact. Military intelligence officers began to doubt that entire armies had relocated. On October 4, the Army's G–2 issued an estimate saying although China's entry was not "wholly to be discounted," the evidence was insufficient to indicate such a development was "either highly probable or imminent." On October 5, the Watch Committee, a group chaired by the CIA, ventured that even though the PRC had a large force on the border, intervention was less likely than it had been earlier. The committee noted that Beijing's propaganda supporting North Korea had diminished and the PRC leadership probably did not want to expose China to retaliatory U.S. air strikes.[16]

In response to a request from President Harry Truman, the CIA issued an estimate October 12 stating: "While full-scale Chinese Communist intervention in Korea must be regarded as a continuing possibility, a consideration of all known factors leads to the conclusion that barring a Soviet decision for global war, such action is not probable in 1950. During this period, intervention will probably be confined to continued covert assistance to the North Koreans." One of the reasons given was: "From a military standpoint the most favorable time for intervention in Korea has passed."

Evaluation of CCF Strength

On October 24, MacArthur ordered all units "to drive forward with all speed and with full utilization of all their forces" toward the Yalu. The next day, the Eighth Army along the Chongchon and Republic of Korea (ROK) forces on the road to Chosin collided with what were believed to be advance elements of the PLA. Over the next two weeks, United Nations Command (UNC) forces in the west, widely scattered with limited logistic support, were driven back to bridgeheads along the Chongchon River.

Three CCF armies of three divisions each, totaling approximately 35,000 men per army, had begun entering western Korea on the night of October 20. Just before they entered Korea, those three armies were redesignated. The 38th Army became the 54th Unit, the 39th became the 55th, and the 40th became the 56th. The divisions in each army were referred to as the 1st, 2d, or 3d Battalion of that unit. Some prisoners captured in the subsequent fighting gave unit identifications accordingly, but not all prisoners got the word. A reinterrogation report by the 164th Military Intelligence Services (MIS) Detachment on November 8 reported on nineteen Chinese prisoners of whom twelve reported they belonged to a division in the 40th Army, six reported they belonged to the 39th Army, and one reported, the 66th Army. Six mentioned belonging to some "unit": three identified the 56th Unit; two, the 55th Unit; and one was from some unknown unit.[17] Review of twenty-three prisoner of war reports found in the Eighth Army War

Diaries for the period October 25 through November 6 finds that only eight of those interrogated mention membership in a task unit. Nevertheless Tarkenton, the Eighth Army G–2, and Willoughby stuck with the "unit" theory for the next three weeks. It led to a drastic underestimation of the Chinese strength.

Further study of those twenty-three interrogation reports shows something else quite interesting. Individuals with the closest ties to the Communist Party were more likely to give the deceptive "unit" identification. The former nationalists, and there were quite a number of them, were more likely to give their proper unit identification. That would lead to the conclusion that some of the prisoners were specifically briefed to be captured with misleading stories. Later in the war the Chinese did brief soldiers to be captured so they could bring instructions to the prisoner of war compounds.

Persistence in the "unit" theory seems to indicate that Willoughby and Tarkenton had some other source that outweighed the evidence from prisoner interrogations, a source that was purposely misleading. Overlooked in the various estimates was the puzzle of finding task force "units" opposite Eighth Army in northwest Korea, but fully formed regular divisions opposite X Corps in northeast Korea.

On November 7, both in the east and in the west, the Chinese broke off their attack and mystifyingly receded into the hills. The following day, the Defense Investigative Service estimated total CCF strength in Korea to be the 54th, 55th, 56th units at 9,000 each, division-sized, in western Korea, and the 124th Division, at 6,700, in northeast Korea, for a total of 33,700.[18] The mystery was why, with such huge strength in Manchuria, so little was in Korea? Imaginative rationalizations appeared.

At a meeting of the Joint Intelligence Indications Committee, agency representatives puzzled over the "lack of aggressiveness" on the part of the PRC forces. The intelligence officers who thought only elements of armies had deployed to Manchuria now used the same reasoning to estimate how many troops participated in the First Phase Offensive. The Watch Committee believed the Chinese had made only "piecemeal commitments of small forces...from various divisions of three different armies." The committee reasoned the PRC wanted to promote "the fiction of volunteer forces but also...to create the impression of greater strength than was actually present."[19] That was the opposite of what the Chinese successfully tried to achieve—make a large force look small.

The CIA believed that while huge forces in Manchuria were capable of halting the UN advance or forcing withdrawal to defensive positions farther south, their initial effort was only to halt the U.N. advance and keep the North Korean regime in-being on Korean soil.[20] In an estimate on November 24, the CIA believed the Chinese would, simultaneously, maintain Chinese–North Korean holding operations in North Korea, maintain or increase their military strength in Manchuria, and seek to obtain U.N. withdrawal from Korea by intimidation and diplomatic means.[21]

Willoughby's conclusion was that the units in contact had been token forces, only the vanguard of CCF forces tasked with the mission of holding off U.N. forces, while the remainder crossed into Korea.[22] On November 25th, with the Eighth Army's renewed offensive underway, he estimated the enemy strength in Korea as 46,693 to 70,935 in 12 divisions with an additional reconstituted North Korean strength of 82,779. He reported further:

> There are some indications that point to the possibility of a withdrawal of Chinese communist Forces to the Yalu River or across the border into Manchuria. In unconfirmed reports, heavy casualties and the lack of a will to fight are given as possible reasons for such a move. Equally unconfirmed reports furnish a possible link with political factors which might well be influential in making such decisions. The lull in fighting along most of the front, and the actual loss of contact in some sectors might well be indications that such an operation is underway. The report of the return by the Chinese Communist of twenty-seven American PWs to UN lines could also be interpreted as a possible indication that the Chinese have plans to withdraw from Korea.[23]

Those "unconfirmed reports" were very likely from plain-text intercepts and deliberately deceptive.

In fact, the Eighth Army was facing a total of six armies, eighteen divisions, a total strength of some 220,000 to 240,000. In the east, three new armies of the 9th CCF Army Group, with twelve divisions totaling 150,000 men, had entered Korea undetected and were poised to assault the 1st Marine Division and then the remainder of X Corps. That evening, the Chinese struck Eighth Army in full force. Two days later the Chinese offensive began at Chosin.

The Chinese Deception Plan

Historians have concentrated on the unreadiness of American military forces. Equally unready, perhaps even more so, were the Chinese. The PLA was exhausted from twenty-two years of war. It was huge in number but poorly armed and equipped. It has been described as a World War I army without the trucks or artillery. Within the PLA, the ability of the army to fight a modern military force was debated fiercely. The solution to the problem was typically and traditionally Chinese, a coordinated campaign of deception, as expected from dedicated students of General Sun Tzu. The objective was to make the initial forces in Korea appear much smaller than they were and, when the main offensive was launched, make the available forces look much larger than they were.

The keystone to the plan was to capitalize on American technological advantage and provide misleading OB information by simulating the presence of various units through false radio traffic. General Nie Rongzhen, the PLA's acting chief of staff during the Korean War, had practiced a variation of that technique in the Wutai Mountains of North China while withdrawing before a Japanese offensive in the spring of 1941. Willoughby's identification of the units assembling in Manchuria had to have come from traffic analysis by ASA units. Had that information come from an agent network, or a highly placed agent, such a source would surely have warned of large forces crossing into Korea. Plain-text traffic supplemented the effort.

To make that deception work, the next most important supporting element was total secrecy of movement. By moving only at night and maintaining a draconian march discipline, the communists were able to deploy some 220,000 men in western Korea and 150,000 in northeast Korea, without revealing their strength. To achieve further mobility, they left behind much of their artillery and other heavy equipment. Until the actual offensive began, they totally escaped observation by aircraft. It was a superlative achievement.

Deceptive prisoners briefed to give misleading unit designations supplemented the signal deception effort. The misleading "unit" designation caused intelligence officers to drastically underestimate the size of Chinese forces in Korea. One prisoner, captured on November 6, could have explained the deception. Liu Piao-wu was a company cultural officer and explained that the change of designation had been made just before the Chinese entered Korea, changed specifically to confuse the Americans. The reinterrogation of nineteen prisoners on November 8 confirmed what Liu said. Only six of them stuck to the "unit" designation. The rest gave a regular regimental and division designation. Still, Tarkenton and Willoughby stuck by their original estimates.

Further causing confusion was the Chinese withdrawal, starting on November 6. Frontline troops in the Eighth Army were startled to see columns of Chinese retreating into the hills. On the road to Chosin, the 124th Division withdrew, and we secured the Funchillin Pass. In Washington, D.C., the chairman of the Joint Chiefs of Staff (JCS), General Bradley, thought perhaps the Chinese had only intervened in moderate numbers and that these few had suffered such a bloody nose that they may have lost the taste for battle. It was classic Chinese communist guerrilla tactics of luring the enemy in deep. General Peng Dehuai, the Chinese commander, told his officers, "In order to catch a big fish you have to let the fish taste your bait."

Reinforcing the belief that the PLA was of limited strength and preparing to withdraw was the release of twenty-seven U.S. prisoners just before the Chinese commenced their offensive on November 26. Later in the war, release of prisoners came to be recognized as an indication of an impending Chinese offensive.

Capping the deception plan was a diplomatic ruse. At the United Nations a resolution had been introduced calling on China to withdraw. The Chinese were invited to come to the United Nations and participate in the discussion. They declined, but did accept a previous invitation to debate U.S. "aggression" in the Taiwan Straits. The delegation departed Beijing on November 15 and was due in New York on the 19. Pannikar, the Indian ambassador to China, reported they were empowered to discuss the entire question of Korea. This led to some relaxation of concern; a political settlement might be possible. But the Chinese delegation dawdled along the way and did not reach New York until after the Chinese counteroffensive had commenced; it then delivered a blistering condemnation of U.N. action in Korea. There is little doubt that the delegation represented a bit of misdirection, part of the overall deception plan.

In the days leading to resumption of the UNC advance, the basic assumption was that while there were huge forces in Manchuria, CCF forces in Korea were only modest. If the Chinese chose to intervene by reinforcing those forces, the reinforcement would become known, it would take time, and time would be allowed to reevaluate the UNC plans. So the size and strength of the Chinese November offensive was a stunning surprise to the troops in the field, to Tokyo, and to Washington.

In the following days, Willoughby, the Army's G–2, and the CIA all assumed that the rest of the Chinese forces in Manchuria were pouring across the border to reinforce those CCF units already in Korea. Gen. Charles L. Bolté, the Army G–3, thought that with no reinforcement available we should withdraw from Korea. The UNC force could be destroyed—the entire U.S. ground establishment. General MacArthur told the JCS that unless ground reinforcements of the greatest magnitude were promptly supplied to him, the U.N. command, which was "mentally fatigued and physically battered," would be forced into successive withdrawals or into beachhead bastions, with little hope of anything but defense. Unless some positive and immediate action was taken on our part, he could only foresee "steady attrition leading to final destruction."[24] He told Gen. J. Lawton Collins that without air attacks against China and no reinforcement, UNC forces would have to be withdrawn from Korea and that it "should be done as soon as possible." MacArthur thought the CCF force in contact or available numbered more than 500,000, was backed by the entire war potential of the PRC, and was reinforced with rehabilitated North Koreans numbering 100,000, all supported by the logistic and advisory assistance of the USSR.[25]

Willoughby's estimate of enemy strength jumped dramatically from his November 25 estimate. On December 6, he estimated 429,381 CCF and North Korean People's Army troops present, in contact, or on the immediate front of U.N. forces. He noted that the remaining eight CCF armies with twenty-four divisions, 204,000 troops, located along the Yalu were available as strategic reserve, with two more armies along the far northeastern border. He reported to the Department of the Army, "The bottomless well of CCF Manpower in Manchuria continues to overflow into Korea with an unrelenting surge."[26]

By December 9, Far Eastern Command had identified nine armies, 20th, 26th, 27th, 38th, 39th, 40th, 42d, 50th, 66th, believed to total twenty-seven divisions, with the possibility that two more armies, the 24th and 30th, were already in Korea, and that an additional two, the 25th and 37th, would soon appear. These latter four, not in contact, would probably have been identified through traffic analysis. He thought the total might be 268,000 CCF troops in immediate contact with U.N. ground forces, with a minimum of 550,000 additional within supporting distance, and an additional 200,000 expected soon to augment the 550,000. "From the above figures it can be readily ascertained that over a million CCF troops are poised as a threat to UN ground forces. This total does not include 160,000 North Korean troops (presently estimated) or 370,000 CCF militia in Manchuria." They pointed, he believed, "to the probability of unlimited Chinese commitment."[27] Plans were underway for the withdrawal of all UNC troops from Korea.

The Reality

What was the reality of the situation? In his book *Mao's Military Romanticism,*[28] Shu Gang Zhang has made an exhaustive study of Chinese records and compiled the Chinese OB at various points during the war. It is perhaps the most authoritative OB available. A comparison of the CCF units in Korea that Zhang reported with the estimates in Willoughby's reports gives a picture of the actual Chinese situation.

Of the CCF armies that Willoughby reported to be in Manchuria in late October, four—the 38th, 39th, 40th, and 42d—together with two armies Willoughby had not identified—the 50th and 60th—took part in the Chinese first-phase attack. Those same six, with three more that had not been identified to be in Manchuria at that time, took part in the second-phase attack in late November, an attack by thirty divisions, approximately 370,000 men.

The Chinese received no more reinforcements until March of the following year when three other armies identified to be in Manchuria in October, together with three more that had not been previously identified, appeared. By August 1952, another army, plus three more previously unidentified, appeared. But eight of those October armies identified in Manchuria, an estimated 200,000 men, never appeared in Korea during the entire war, and given the difficulties the Chinese had of supporting their armies in Korea, may well have never been in Manchuria. Of the four armies Willoughby reported in his summaries of December 9, the 25th and 30th were never in Korea during the war, and the 24th and 37th appeared much later. So, twelve CCF armies did not exist, at least then, eight from the October 24th report and another four from the December 9 report. They were the Ghost Armies of Manchuria.

Even more confounding, by December 12, the three armies, twelve divisions, of the 9th CCF Army Group were out of action, devastated by their fight with the 1st Marine Division, by air attacks, and by the terrible cold.[29] Song Shilun, the 9th Army Group commander said he needed 60,000 replacements. Not until April of the following year did one army, the 26th from the 9th Army Group, appear on the line.[30]

The Eighth Army was withdrawing south before the six armies of the 13th CCF Army Group. Originally numbering 240,000 men, it had suffered heavy casualties. The 38th, 39th, and 40th Armies had suffered 15,000 casualties each.

The 42d, 50th, and 60th lost about 5,000 each, for a grand total of 60,000. Rather than being driven south by more than a million men, the Eighth Army was fleeing from eighteen tired, primitive, understrength, and poorly supplied divisions, totaling no more than 180,000 men but reinforced by a small group of Chinese radio operators pretending to be the oncoming Ghost Armies of Manchuria.

No doubt the Chinese—knowing of U.S. reliance on signals intelligence—set out carefully and craftily to turn that technological advantage against us. Just as the initial view of the Chinese was that they were poor fighters with no staying power, American hubris could not believe that such a group they thought so primitive could even think of, much less mount, such a deceptive campaign. It was a textbook application of the lessons of Sun Tzu:

> When you are near make yourself look far away
> When you are big make yourself look small
> When you are small—make yourself look big.

In the first-phase offensive, the Chinese used deceptive unit identifications, making divisions look like battalions. In the second phase, they made six armies look like twenty. They succeeded all too well.

Notes

Based on Patrick C. Roe , *The Dragon Strikes and the Korean War* (Navato, Calif.: Presidio Press, 2000)

1. "COMINT and the PRC Intervention in the Korean War" National Security Agency. No date. pp. 10–11. This is apparently a declassification of an article in *Cryptologic Quarterly* a Top Secret publication of NSA now available on the NSA web site. Hereafter referred to as COMINT.
2. Interview with Polk quoted in Blair, Clay. *The Forgotten War: America in Korea, 1950–1953.*, New York: Random House, 1987 p 337.
3. Report by Lt. Col. Leonard J. Abbot to Willoughby, May 18, 1951, MacArthur Library RG 23 Folder 2.
4. Eighth Army PIRs No. 82, 89, and 90 dated 2, 9 and 10 Oct 50, I Corps PIR 54, Nov 8, 1950 and Eighth Army SitRep SitRep 292 101520 Nov 50 all contain reports of covert agents.
5. Schnabel, James F. and Robert J. Watson. *History of the Joint Chiefs of Staff: The Joint Chiefs of Staff and National Policy.* Vol. III *The Korean War.* Part 1. Wilmington, Delaware: Michael Glazier, 1979 pp. 308–309.
6. Futrell, Robert F. *The United States Air Force in Korea: 1950–1953.* Washington: Office of Air Force History. 1983. Revised edition.
7. Hatch, David A. and Robert Louis Benson *The Korean War: The SIGINT Background.* October, 2000. National Security Agency. p. 12. This is a preliminary monograph on signals intelligence during the Korean War avail-

able on the NSA web site. Hereafter cited as NSA Monograph.
8. COMINT p 10.
9. David A. Hatch and Robert Louis Benson, *The Korean War: The SIGINT Background*, p. 8. (National Security Agency, nd.) Hereafter referred to as NSA Monograph.
10. Deptar msg W97801 2 Dec 50 to CINCFE NAR.
11. NSA Monograph p 8 and Annex A, Task Orgn to Open O No. 6, X Corps 14 Nov 50 NAR.
12. JCS to CINCFE 20 Mar 51, RG 90 MCAL.
13. COMINT p 9 and NSA Monograph pp 8, 14.
14. NSA Monograph p 14.
15. FEC DIS 2934, 2948, 2967.
16. COMINT p 15.
17. 8A PIR 119 8 Nov 50—PW Interrogation Report 164th MIS Det—correction sheet.
18. FEC DIS 2982 8 Nov 50.
19. COMINT p 15.
20. CIA National Intelligence Estimate 8 Nov in FRUS p 1101.
21. CIA National Intelligence Estimate 24 Nov 50 in FRUS 1220 ff.
22. DIS 2983-2986.
23. FEC OIS 2999, Nov 22, 1950.
24. FEC msg C-50332 to JCS 3 Dec 50.
25. Memo for Gen Collins 4 Dec 50.
26. DA Telecons 4099 6 Dec 50 and 4105 7 Dec 50.
27. FEC DIS 3013 9 Dec 50.
28. Zhang, Shu Guang. *Mao's Military Romanticism:China and the Korean War, 1950–1953* .Lawrence: University Press of Kansas, 1995.
29. Li, Xiaobing and Glenn Tracy (trans.) "Mao Telegrams during the Korean War: October-December 1950" *Chinese Historians* Vol V. No. 2 (Fall 1992).
30. *An Evaluation of the Influence of Marine Corps Forces in the Course of the Korean War (4 Aug 50–15 Dec 50)* 2 vols. U. S. Marine Corps Board 1952.

USAF Reconnaissance during the Korean War

Samuel T. Dickens

The date was June 25, 1950. The American people were shocked to learn that the North Korean army had massed its forces and rolled across the 38th parallel, which since World War II had served as the artificially devised demarcation line, into South Korea. President Harry Truman responded forthrightly to the surprise assault by having our ambassador to the United Nations (U.N.) urge the Security Council to respond to this unprovoked aggression. With the council's unanimous approval, the United Nations engaged in a police action to stop the belligerent force. Fortunately, the USSR representative was absent from the Security Council and unable to stop the resolution; unfortunately, the United States was ill-prepared for war.

In Japan, our armed forces were engaged in occupation of the Japanese mainland after Japan's formal surrender in September 1945. Essentially, no preparation had been made for war. The overall commander of our forces, Gen. Douglas MacArthur, who was primarily engaged in the formidable task of transforming the Empire of Japan into a democratic society, was quickly named commander of the U.N. forces. Ground troops were immediately committed to the Korean peninsula to bolster the rapidly retreating South Korean and U.S. military forces. The situation was critical, and the North Koreans rapidly drove back the South Korean army and the U.S. Army forces (deployed from Japan) to the southern tip of the Korean peninsula, which became known as the Pusan perimeter.

U.S. Air Force airlift, well experienced after the massive effort to relieve besieged Berlin, swung into action and delivered the most urgent supplies from the United States. A sealift effort followed as well. Those early forces were desperately buying time, maintaining a foothold in Korea, until the major deployment of forces and logistics came on-line.

Critical to our military response was information regarding the disposition of the attacking forces, their major lines of attack, the size of their forces, and their major military equipment, armor, artillery, and supply lines. The North Korean attack moved so swiftly that response plans were overtaken by events. Intelligence information was desperately needed, so USAF reconnaissance aircraft were quickly deployed from central Japan to Itazuke Air Base (AB) on Kyushu Island, Japan, the base closest to Korea.

The only tactical reconnaissance unit based in Japan was the 8th Tactical Reconnaissance Squadron (TRS) equipped with twenty-five RF–80 single-engine jet aircraft. The RF–80, derived from the F–80 (the first truly operational jet aircraft of the USAF), was well-equipped with cameras adequate to the task. The first combat mission of the Korean War fell to Lt. Bryce Poe II, who flew from Itazuke AB across the straits to South Korea. Lieutenant Poe was no novice to reconnaissance, having flown his RF–80 in Top Secret missions over the Vladivostok area of the Soviet Union. Immediately, the RF–80s began to photograph every airfield in North Korea.

The demand for accurate intelligence information was a top priority. In the fast-moving and fluid operations, reconnaissance included visual as well as photographic collection. Rapid film processing and immediate photo interpretation were critical, but the sheer amount of work quickly exceeded the capabilities of the 548th Reconnaissance Technical Squadron. Joint doctrine established that the Army would provide their own photo interpreters to provide intelligence analysis specific to Army needs within a joint organization. However, the army had no available photo interpreters, and the joint organization did not exist. Therefore, individuals throughout every area of operations, Army and Air Force, handled the initial operations in an ad hoc, emergency manner, which required extraordinary initiative.

It is difficult today to imagine the confusion, and yet determination and commitment of our armed forces. The understrength, ill-equipped, and insufficiently trained Army troops were determined to hold the perimeter against overwhelming odds and not be driven into the Sea of Japan. The USAF was involved with close air support and interdiction missions attempting to stem the flow of North Korean men and equipment that were besieging the perimeter. A major problem was the short range of the F–80 and RF–80 aircraft that had to operate from Japan because no suitable bases were available within the perimeter.

In the demobilization subsequent to World War II, the USAF had declined to forty-eight groups by the time the Korean War broke out. Its personnel strength of 411,277 officers and men represented less than 18 percent of its wartime strength. Later, the USAF chief of staff, Gen. Hoyt S. Vandenberg called it a shoestring Air Force. Requests for more F–80Cs, F–82s, B–26s, B–29s, C–54s, F–51s, C–47s, RF–51s, and RF–80s could be met only piecemeal.

One can only marvel at the ability of U.S. forces to hold the perimeter, while forces were being moved from the United States by ship and air to provide more muscle to our limited capabilities. Meanwhile, General MacArthur developed an audacious plan involving a strategic envelopment of the North Koreans that, although exceedingly risky, proved to be masterful in planning and execution. The very high tides at Inchon, on the west coast of Korea, a few miles from Seoul, made the planned amphibious operation problematic. RF–80 aircraft took dicing shots (low-level photo missions with cameras aimed obliquely through the nose of the aircraft) that enabled our skilled photo interpreters to determine accurately the height of the sea wall and the exact times and extent of the tides. The amphibious operation proved a stunning success. U.S. forces broke out of the Pusan perimeter, and the combined penetration and successful envelopment from the Inchon beachhead broke the North Korean attack, allowing U.N. forces to push repel enemy, northward up the peninsula.

USAF reconnaissance assets now included the Strategic Air Command (SAC) reconnaissance bombers, RB–29s, relegated to medium status with the now-operational B–36 heavy bomber. Navy reconnaissance jet aircraft operated from aircraft carriers, and Marine Corps reconnaissance aircraft were later based on land. The traditional reconnaissance effort was augmented by other intelligence-gathering efforts from slower flying C–47s and C–46s, which were sometimes operated openly by the USAF and at other times, by clandestine organizations. Prisoner interrogation provided another form of collecting useful information, fitting into the effort to produce an accurate picture of the enemy's capabilities. Nevertheless, the bulk of all intelligence information was collected, produced, and interpreted by the USAF.

Principal USAF reconnaissance assets included the RB–29, RB–45, RF–80, RF–51, and RB–26. With the exception of the RF–80 and RB–45, these aircraft had major roles in World War II. Providing airfields suited for these jet aircraft posed a major problem that proved so serious that one F–80 fighter squadron converted to F–51 Mustangs simply to provide close air support flying from the short, dirt runways available in Korea. The construction of adequate runways and support facilities was a major activity.

RB–29s provided photoreconnaissance that allowed the B–29s to bomb strategic targets in North Korea. In a short time, it was determined that strategic bombing was no longer needed because no more targets remained. This was before dams and hydroelectric generating plants became targets later during the war. After September 26, 1950, all B–29 bombing missions were directed against tactical targets.

The demobilization of the armed forces in the five years after World War II had significantly reduced our capabilities to effectively wage war. New aircraft were entering production—the F–86, F–84, RF–84F, B–47, and RB–47—but we began fighting the war with World War II equipment. Already, we had forgotten the lessons learned in that war. All the tactical training and coordinated efforts relating to tactical air forces in the support of army units had to be relearned. Individual units had established standards of proficiency, but the bare-bones budget did not allow for joint exercises. The call-up of reserves with World War II experience lessened the learning curve, but time for training was not available; experience in combat and necessity accelerated coordination of the required team effort.

Another major factor limited our fighting capabilities in Korea. The invasion of South Korea seemed to presage an all-out communist effort in Europe. Consequently, the Joint Chiefs of Staff sought to limit the movement of men and equipment to fight in Korea. All subsequent military events in Korea needed to be viewed through the prism that Korea was considered as likely to be only the first phase of a major conflict with communist forces worldwide.

Deployment of tactical reconnaissance units to Korea had the 8th TRS (RF–80s) arriving at Taegu, South Korea, on October 2, 1950, and the 162d TRS (RB–26s) arriving from Langley AFB on October 8, with both supported by the 363d Reconnaissance Technical Squadron, which had also urgently deployed from Langley. These units formed the 543d Tactical Support Group. In November 1950, the 45th TRS, recently activated with RF–51 Mustangs, joined the 543d Group.

Besides the critical shortage of reconnaissance aircraft, the shortage of experienced intelligence experts, that is, photo interpreters, posed a daunting task. Since no reserve photo interpreter organizations had been created after World War II, training new photo interpreters was the only way to reduce the workload.

General Vandenberg told Lt. Gen. George Stratemeyer, commander of Far East Air Forces (FEAF), that to be effective, tactical operations required the interdiction of targets that were the sources for supplies, ammunition, and troops. B–29s of the 22d and 92d Bombardment Groups deployed to Japan for operations against North Korea, augmenting three other groups already available. Industrial centers of Wonsan, Pyongyang, Hungnam, Ch'ongjin, and Rashin were identified as targets. Their selection was based on their falling into one or more of the following categories: port facility, railroad head, petroleum production and storage site, aircraft factory, armament manufacturing, chemical and light-metal plant, and hydroelectric facility.

Three of the bombardment groups were dedicated to strategic targets; the other two were used for interdiction. The FEAF Target Section had not prepared target folders for North Korea prior to the Korean War. Old target folders and photography were discovered at Guam, and these materials, combined with the efforts of the RB–29s of the 31st Strategic Reconnaissance Squadron, produced the radarscope photography to meet the demand. The 548th Reconnaissance Technical Squadron handled the photofinishing and photo interpretation. Of forty-six strategic bombing attacks, bomber crews lacked adequate photography and radarscope intelligence for only one target.

After the bombing of the Fusen hydroelectric plant on September 26, 1950, the Joint Chiefs of Staff informed General MacArthur that all the strategic targets had been eliminated and that all further medium bomber missions would be for interdiction supporting his tactical operations in the field.

On October 18, 1950, the 31st Strategic Reconnaissance Squadron reported that some seventy-five fighters were seen at Antung, the Manchurian air base immediately across the Yalu River, which formed the border between China and Korea. An RF–80 pilot spotted fifteen propeller-driven Yak aircraft at Sinuiju, in

North Korea, and these were quickly attacked by F–80 fighter-bombers which strafed the field and destroyed or damaged seven of the aircraft. One of the F–80s was shot down by gunfire from across the Yalu. Before another attack by F–80s, the surviving Yaks had flown north. At this time, six Russian-made MiG–15s flew into Korea, the first sighting of these jets. Shortly thereafter, U.S. Army and Republic of Korea units approached the Yalu.

As the result of a paper transaction, the 31st Squadron returned to the United States and the 91st Strategic Reconnaissance Squadron replaced it on November 16, 1950. According to historical analysis, neither air nor ground reconnaissance hinted at the major deployment of Chinese troops immediately north of the Yalu as they grouped for an assault on U.N. forces. Much of this oversight is explained by the severe limitations placed on photoreconnaissance after the attack by two MiG–15s on an RB–29 of the 31st Strategic Reconnaissance Squadron near Sinuiju on November 9, 1950. The aircraft crash-landed at Johnson AB, Japan, killing five crewmembers. After this incident, RB–29s were ordered not to approach the Yalu, leaving those missions to the RF–80s flown by the 8th TRS, which was operating from Taegu, well down the peninsula. Gen. George C. Kenney had speculated that the first sign of Chinese communist entry into the Korean War would be observed through air operations. The introduction of the MiG–15s proved his prescience.

As General MacArthur's forces approached the Yalu, the prevailing intelligence assumptions were that the deployment of Chinese forces on the border were to ensure no incursions into Manchuria. However, on November 26, Chinese forces aggressively attacked in an effort to envelop and destroy the U.N. forces.

Various explanations have been given for this intelligence failure. RB–29 reconnaissance flights had been prohibited from approaching the Yalu since November 9, leaving photo coverage to the 8th and 12th TRSs. Joint doctrine called for three daytime reconnaissance squadrons: two would provide visual reconnaissance, and one, photography in advance of an army. Although demands from the Army and Air Force were extensive, the 8th TRS was not overtaxed, as neither the Army nor the Air Force was capable of interpreting all photography speedily because of the shortage of qualified photo interpreters. In fact, the Air Force provided photo interpretation for the Army, which was actually an Army responsibility. The 8th TRS photography focused on the Yalu River crossings, with the 12th TRS flying a few night reconnaissance missions. Fog greatly hindered night photography.

Photo interpreters analyzing reconnaissance missions were frustrated over a reported intelligence failure. They had reported on masses of Chinese troops crossing the Yalu River in the vicinity of Sinuiju, and they noted major stockpiles of equipment concentrated there. Although they had submitted these findings as special intelligence reports, to their chagrin, no bombing raids were scheduled.

On December 15, the first F–86s arrived in Korea, forming the 4th Fighter Interceptor Wing stationed at Kimpo AB (K–14) outside Seoul. The F–86s escorted RF–80s that flew photo missions in the Sinuiju, Sinanju, and Antung areas of operations. Throughout December, reconnaissance confirmed the extension and improvement of runways at Antung in North Korea. At Dairen AB, the Soviets had some 400 to 500 aircraft. The RF–80, limited to Mach 0.8—considerably slower than the speed attainable by the MiG–15s—had to be escorted by F–86s on missions along the Yalu in the area now being called MiG Alley. On December 4, MiGs boxed in an RF–80 and its F–80 escort and damaged both aircraft with 23-mm cannon fire; both planes were fortunate to return to base.

As a result of MiG attacks on RB–29s, the 91st Squadron took control of two RB–45 jet reconnaissance aircraft on January 31, 1951. They had been assigned to Reconnaissance Detachment A of the 84th Bombardment Squadron. Although at first successful in outrunning the MiGs, they too had difficulties. In one attack on April 9, an RB–45 sustained a number of hits, but it successfully returned to base. On June 1, all unescorted Bomber Command aircraft were prohibited from operating in the vicinity of the Yalu and MiG Alley. Then in October, all RB–29s were prohibited from operating in northwest Korea, and the 67th Tactical Reconnaissance Wing (TRW) assumed that photoreconnaissance responsibility. All RB–45 daylight operations ceased after another close call from MiGs on November 9.

During the early part of the Korean War, just two squadrons were performing the tactical missions of visual reconnaissance and photoreconnaissance: the 15th Tactical Reconnaissance, Photo-Jet; and the 12th TRS, Night-Photo, operating from Taegu. By December 1950, the 45th TRS (flying RF–51 Mustangs) joined the reconnaissance effort.

As the demand for reconnaissance grew, it became apparent that the effort had to be coordinated. Some of the supporting units were in Japan. Col. Karl L. "Pop" Polifka, a noted reconnaissance expert from World War II, was brought in to form the newly activated 67th TRW on February 25, 1951. The 8th TRS was redesignated the 15th TRS, while the 12th TRS continued on, as did the 45th TRS. The support elements making up the wing were brought in from Japan.

The 15th TRS was responsible for covering all airfields and lines of communication in the northern part of North Korea, responding to tasking by the Army as well as the USAF. The 12th TRS had the same responsibility, but it was limited to night operations. The 45th TRS provided reconnaissance forward of the Army's front lines. Their job was to learn the features and terrain in front of Army units and, from that familiarity, identify changes signifying enemy movement and emplacements.

In March 1951, Fifth Air Force devised a target location system implemented by the 45th TRS which operated at first light every morning. Night operations would suggest possible locations of enemy trucks and troops that would be trying to conceal themselves as dawn broke. The RF–51s would then be on hand to direct fighter-bomber attacks. These were called Circle 10 missions because the Mustangs flew in a circle roughly ten miles in diameter around the suspected area. When the Mustangs identified the targets, they called in F–80 and F–84 attacks.

By mid-April, RF–51s flew in pairs with one providing top cover to clear the lower-flying aircraft and provide early warning on any enemy antiaircraft fire. This useful tactic was later employed by the 15th TRS and was continued by the 45th TRS when they relinquished their Mustangs for RF–80s.

Throughout February, March, and April, reconnaissance confirmed that North Korean airfields had been readied for aircraft arriving from Manchuria. Photo interpreters discovered that the North Koreans were destroying buildings on either side of a paved road running through Pyongyang and turning it into a 7,000-foot runway. The RF–80s also identified a rapid effort to improve the airfield at Sinuiju. Attacks soon left the runways cratered.

On July 1, Colonel Polifka was killed while flying a combat mission. In his short time as wing commander, he had coordinated the various tactical reconnaissance elements, enhancing their ability to respond rapidly to the reconnaissance requirements called for by the USAF and U.S. Army. In late August, the 67th TRW was able to deploy to Kimpo AB from Taegu, from southern to central Korea, which reduced the time and distance it needed to operate in the northern reaches of the peninsula, up to the Yalu. This reduction was of particular significance for the jet aircraft.

One squadron, the 15th TRS flying the RF–80, was now conducting all the daylight photography in North Korea above the battle line. The missions in MiG Alley to determine the status of airfields were increasingly hazardous despite escorts of sometimes as many as sixteen F–86s. The faster F–86s would provide top cover by weaving back and forth over the slower RF–80s, but MiG–15s diving from higher altitude often penetrated the protective screen of F–86s and were able to fire upon the RF–80s. Additionally, FEAF was tasking the 15th TRS with Top Secret missions which required overflights of Manchuria and mainland China across the Yellow Sea.

By June 1951, the communists realized the futility of operating aircraft from their airfields in North Korea and proceeded to build additional airstrips near Antung, just north of the Yalu River. Soon, some 300 MiG fighters were operating from these bases. Intelligence, based on photography, determined that the MiG–15 buildup of 445 aircraft in June 1951 had increased to 525 by September. For comparison, only 89 F–86s were based in Korea at the same time. By December, however, 127 F–86s were in Korea, the 51st Fighter Wing now having joined the 4th Fighter Wing in combat.

In July 1951, fighter-bombers, though escorted by F–86s, were attacked by MiGs. They escaped, but that same month one RF–80 was badly damaged during an attack. Photo missions were rescheduled time and again to secure coverage in MiG Alley. In November, pilots of the 15th TRS were attacked eleven times by MiGs, all, while being escorted by F–86s. In September, an RF–80 pilot spotted construction of a new airfield at Samcham, about thirty miles northeast of the Sinanju airfield, and the new airfield was immediately targeted for attack by B–29s. RF–80 pilots of the 15th TRS were taking prestrike photos and following up with poststrike photography immediately after bombing missions. The processed film was delivered immediately, with mission results, to allow for a subsequent air strike the same day, if one were needed.

It is difficult today to appreciate the conditions that reconnaissance pilots were subjected to when flying the RF–80. The engine thrust was just over a paltry 3,800 pounds. Additional thrust was obtained during takeoff by spraying a water-alcohol mixture over the centrifugal flow engine, but this lasted for only a few seconds. Navigation was strictly nap-of-the-earth piloting, with pilots using map of various scales to locate assigned targets; the scales included 1:500,000, 1:250,000, and 1:62,500. A radio compass was useful for navigation over South Korea and Japan. Some of the RF–80s had manual canopies; others had no ejection seats. At times, the sliding canopies had to be closed by the crew chief. Cabin pressurization was notoriously poor with these older aircraft, and the cabin pressure at times gave a higher reading than the altimeter. There were no viewfinders to identify targets; pilots aligned themselves directly over the target by banking the aircraft, looking down, and maneuvering the aircraft visually for alignment.

Pilots used forecast winds at altitude to determine ground speeds and to establish the intervalometer settings for the camera to provide adequate overlap of exposures. All this required excellent pilotage to reach the target and good aircraft handling. The requester determined the scale of photography. This required that the necessary focal length of the camera be selected as well as the altitude flown. Usually another pilot, in a companion RF–80 or F–80, would fly above and slightly behind to spot enemy aircraft and antiaircraft artillery fire.

The commander of the 67th TRW requested that a few F–86s be modified to carry cameras. When forwarded to the United States, these requests were rejected because RF–84Fs were to replace the RF–80s. But the RF–84s never came. The 15th TRS commander, working with other pilots in the squadron, prepared a mockup of the nose section of an F–86 fitted with a horizontally mounted camera shooting through a mirror angled at 45 degrees for vertical photography.

The wing commander supported this effort to FEAF, and six F–86As were identified in a project called Honey Bucket for modifications in Japan. General Vandenberg, during a visit to the Far East, strongly supported the effort and directed that kits be prepared by North American Aviation to expedite the conversion of these F–86As to a reconnaissance version. The first RF–86A arrived at Kimpo AB in December 1951 and was flown by a 15th TRS pilot who had previously flown the F–86. Following several camera test flights in South Korea, the first RF–86A combat missions were flown in January 1952. Early photography was not very satisfactory for two basic reasons: the vibration of the mirror, and the reversed image. These factors demanded that the film receive special handling for processing and expert photo interpretation because of the blurred images.

Other reconnaissance elements transferring to the operational control of the 67th TRW in May 1951 were Firefly C–47s. These aircraft had been first used in January 1951 to drop flares to help identify trucks and trains. Their efforts were combined with the flare drops of RB–26s searching for targets at night, bringing in B–26s for night interdiction.

At one time, Firefly aircraft with RB–26s operated at night in MiG Alley to identify trucks and trains. The slow C–47 Firefly aircraft were quickly restrained to a lower latitude, away from the area of MiG operations, because the risk was considered too great. Another time, the Firefly aircraft flew north, armed with specially designed tacks to drop at extremely low altitudes over roads used by enemy trucks. One C–47 almost ran into three enemy tanks after dropping eight tons of these roofing nails. Calling in B–26s, the C–47 pilot overflew the road again, dropping flares for the attack. The trucks stalled by punctured tires were then attacked. On one such mission, thirty-eight trucks were destroyed.

The Firefly C–47s were so successful that twenty C–46s were requested to be assigned to the 67th TRW. This was denied because of a shortage of flares. Sometimes the Marine Corps night fighters would work with the USAF Firefly aircraft and, after the trucks were illuminated, would attack with 500-pound bombs and 20-mm cannon.

Both the RB–26s and RB–29s had problems with the flash bombs used to illuminate targets for night photography. A new system of cartridge-ejection illumination was problematic because the defect rate was high. This system required flying at 3,000 feet, but, given the mountainous terrain and intense ground fire, this was too low for sustained operations. Subsequently, the combination of the M–46 photoflash bomb and night cameras solved the problem when photographs were taken at 7,000 to 8,000 feet. However, to use SHORAN navigational aids, the aircraft needed to operate at still higher altitudes. The M–120 photoflash bomb was then introduced to provide illumination up to 25,000 feet, but when photography was attempted at 14,000 feet, the cameras did not produce the desired results. Thus, the RB–26s had to fly at lower altitudes without the benefit of SHORAN for navigation.

The RB–29s operated at 20,000 feet for safety as well as effective use of the SHORAN navigation equipment. The M–120 photoflash bombs were supposed to be effective, but large-scale photography could not be obtained with the focal length of the cameras that the planes carried. Finally, a camera with a shorter focal length was used and exposures were triggered by the light of the photoflash bombs.

The RB–45s were not effective at night because opening the bomb bays to drop the photoflash bombs produced vibrations that made the photography ineffective.

Essentially, by June 1952, the 67th TRW was providing all the prestrike and poststrike photography required by the strategic bombers.

A decision was made to strike North Korean power complexes virtually simultaneously, but initially planners hesitated to target the dam at Suiho because it was so close to MiG Alley. Other dams to be attacked included Chosen 3 and 4, Fusen 1 and 2, and Choshin 1 and 2. This effort necessitated USAF and Navy fighter-bombers as well as B–29s attacking at night. Two RF–80s, escorted by F–86s, photographed the results two hours after the attack and confirmed extensive damage. North Korean electric power had been reduced by 90 percent when eleven of the thirteen plants were rendered unserviceable. MiGs had not entered the fray.

The 67th TRW established a targets section in the Technical Reconnaissance Squadron. Targets were not in short supply, as evidenced by the fact that the squadron had a backlog of 300 sites by November 1952. Daily intelligence reports and photographs were provided to Fifth Air Force Intelligence from both the 67th TRW and the 91st Strategic Reconnaissance Squadron. In fact, the greatest problem was the ability of Fifth Air Force to properly interpret, process, and assign target missions.

The 67th TRW was responsible for keeping close watch over all major airfields and main lines of communication in North Korea, for identifying targets for interdiction, and for providing visual and photoreconnaissance in front of Eighth Army units, including mosaic coverage in depth of the front, prestrike photography, and poststrike (bomb damage) photography. Photography for the Eighth Army extended fifteen to twenty miles in front of each corps. Visual reconnaissance sightings were reported directly by the pilot to fire-support coordination centers.

The biggest problem for providing adequate, timely photo intelligence to forward Army units was the shortage of qualified Army photo interpreters. The breakdown of responsibilities between the Army and the Air Force was clearly spelled out in joint documents, but the Army could not produce the photo interpreters. It fell to the Air Force to supply the personnel, within its own limitations of qualified photo interpreters.

The 67th TRS continued to produce more photography and intelligence information than could be used, despite being handicapped with older aircraft. After losing five RF–51 Mustangs to ground fire while conducting visual reconnaissance missions, the Mustangs were restricted to 6,000 feet. The Mustang, with its radiator slung on the fuselage beneath the aircraft, was particularly vulnerable to ground fire because a single enemy round that penetrated the radiator could drain all the coolant and cause the engine to seize.

In July 1952, the Eighth Army introduced the 98th Engineer Aerial Photo Reproduction Company, giving it a capability of handling 5,900 negatives and producing 25,000 prints daily. Eighth Army stated that it needed from Air Force reconnaissance 4,900 negatives daily when it was engaged in fighting, and 3,600 negatives when it was static. In September 1952, Eighth Army agreed to the establishment of a Reconnaissance Branch in the joint operations center, which eventually resulted in the Army's reducing its need for photographic coverage.

The Eighth Army demand for photographs did not vary regardless of weather or the fewer daylight hours during winter. This resulted in 30 percent of the Fifth Air Force effort being dedicated to Army front lines. The Army wanted 3,600 daily negatives at a scale of 1:6,000 or 1:7,000. These had been the preferred scales during World War II, but they proved problematic for the faster jet aircraft still equipped with World War II cameras. Installation of image motion compensators on the cameras provided a workable solution. The army requested oblique photography at a scale of 1:3,000, but because of the high aircraft loss rate, Lt. Gen. Glenn O. Barcus in October 1952 prohibited reconnaissance aircraft from operating below 9,000 feet when within 30,000 yards of the front lines. Over heavily defended areas, such as Pyongyang, aircraft would have to remain above 12,000 feet.

The Far East communist aerial order of battle in mid-1952 included some 7,000 aircraft: 5,000 Soviet, 2,000 Chinese, and 270 North Korean. Antung was the principal airfield, but several satellite airfields were located nearby. Other aircraft were located in the Mukden and Changchun area as well as the Port Arthur–Dairen group, and Peiping-Tientsin and Tsingtao group.

These airfields were photographed not only by RF–80s but also by the RF–86s assigned to the 15th TRS. One pilot, Lt. Mele Vojvodich, flying an RF–86 Sabre, spoke of flying an almost weekly coverage of the MiG–15 airfields in the Antung complex. He also flew at least one mission up to the Harbin area. Although spotted by MiGs, he was able to outrun them, first at altitude, and then down on the deck. Subsequently, he was awarded the Distinguished Service Cross for his RF–86 missions. Lt. Tom Gargan, who also flew both the RF–86 and the RF–80, was also awarded the Distinguished Service Cross for an RF–80 mission after completion of his tour, ending with the armistice on July 27, 1953.

Although F–86s from the 4th and 51st Fighter Wings escorted some of these reconnaissance missions, the number of aircraft drew too much attention and led to photo mission aborts. Tactics varied. Sometimes an RF–86 was accompanied by a single F–86, and at other times ,by more escorts. Occasionally, the escort had to break off to engage a MiG, leaving the RF–86 behind.

When the F–80 fighter wings gave up their aircraft for more modern straight-winged F–84s, the 15th TRS was able to incorporate a number of F–80Cs into the squadron. These aircraft were modified to carry one vertical camera with a 24-inch focal length. In August 1952, the 45th TRS gave up its RF–51 Mustangs, and RF–80s from the 15th TRS were made available. Then both the 15th and 45th had a mixture of RF–80As and RF–80Cs, with the 15th TRS also having some five RF–86As. Both squadrons then participated in visual and photo missions.

Covert intelligence reported the presence of a political school in North Korea for training subversives to penetrate into South Korea. The facilities were confirmed through photography, and on October 25, 1952, the 1,000-man school providing a six-month training course was attacked and virtually destroyed.

In December 1952, RB–26s worked with B–26s to locate train traffic. When RB–26s spotted trains, they would illuminate them with flares, and the B–26s would attack. In Operation Spotlight on December 30, four locomotives were destroyed and one was damaged in a marshaling yard. Firefly aircraft also participated in these operations. Thirty-three locomotives were destroyed in January 1953, and twenty-nine, in February. Roads were also blocked, and the vehicles in the resulting traffic jam would be destroyed. In January and February of 1953, 5,432 vehicles were destroyed.

General Barcus, commander of Fifth Air Force, expressed concern over the possibility of an enemy air offensive on January 5, 1953, when Il–28 twin-jet medium bombers were introduced into Manchuria. These aircraft occasionally flew parallel to the Yalu River within Manchuria, not crossing into Korea, and they could have provided an important night attack capability.

On January 12, 1953, an RB–29 was shot down during a night mission while it was dropping leaflets along the Yalu. MiG aircraft carrying external fuel tanks engaged U.S. Marine Corps fighter-bombers, Royal Australian Air Force Meteors, and RF–80s in late March 1953 in the Chinnampo area south of Pyongyang, North Korea's capital. This was an unusual departure from their typical sorties, when they stayed within MiG Alley, close to Manchuria.

In the spring of 1953, the 15th TRS exchanged its RF–86A models for the newer version, the RF–86F. Its ability to carry four drop tanks (instead of the previous two) significantly increased its range and made it much easier to make deep penetrations into Manchuria to overfly and photograph airfields.

In April 1953, reconnaissance revealed communist efforts to make a number of airfields operational, undoubtedly in preparation for the truce. Gen. Otto P. Weyland, commander of the Far East Forces, also anticipating an imminent truce, waited until June 10 before ordering attacks. Foul weather created delays before the airfields could be attacked, but every airfield except one was considered unusable by June 23. Clearing weather revealed rapid progress by the communists to again make these airfields serviceable. Forty-three MiGs were photographed at Uiju, a sod field, and twenty-one conventional aircraft were discovered at Sinuiju.

On July 12, 1953, an RF–80 reconnaissance flight revealed the communists' preparation for an attack on the relatively stabilized front. They had chosen the cover of bad weather, but all Fifth Air Force resources were available to respond. B–29s used SHORAN to attack eighty-five targets that had been previously identified through reconnaissance photography. Forty-three percent of air sorties flown in July, involving 3,385 sorties, provided close air support for the Army. On July 20 and 21, B–29s in night sorties attacked all these airfields. These were followed by fighter-bomber attacks continued until July 23.

The truce was to take effect at 2200 on July 27, 1953. The 67th TRW mounted a maximum effort to photograph every airfield in North Korea and in Manchuria that posed a potential threat to U.N. forces. All the airfields in North Korea were shown to be unserviceable for jet aircraft. Several RF–86 missions were flown into Manchuria to determine the aerial order of battle. One mission photographed airfields in the distant Harbin area.

A pilot of the 45th TRS, flying an RF–80, was killed flying a sortie near the Yalu River. He was the last man killed in combat during the Korea War. The mission he was unable to complete was quickly undertaken by pilots in the 45th TRS, who returned to Kimpo at dusk. An RB–26 flew the last combat sortie of the Korean War.

The first combat mission of the Korean War was flown by Lt. Bryce Poe II of the 8th TRS in an RF–80. The last was flown by an aircrew of the 12th TRS, who returned to base by 2200 on July 27, 1953. Tactical reconnaissance had fulfilled its enduring motto, First and Last Over the Target.

Robert F. Futrell, in his outstanding book, *The United States Air Force in Korea,* sums up the contribution of tactical reconnaissance:

> Despite the fact that the 67th Tactical Reconnaissance Wing was handicapped by the failure of USAF reconnaissance systems to keep pace with the requirements of the jet air age, it nevertheless far outstripped all existing reconnaissance performance records. In Europe during World War II the highest number of sorties flown in any month by a Ninth Air Force reconnaissance group was 1,300 in April 1945. In Korea the 67th flew 2,400 sorties in May 1952.

From D-Day to V-E Day in Europe, the sortie rate of the average Ninth Air Force reconnaissance group was 604 sorties a month, but in the twelve-month period of April 1952 through March 1953 the 67th Group averaged 1,792 sorties per month. During comparable periods, the photo group that supported the U.S. Third Army in Europe made 243,175 negatives; the 67th Group in Korea made 736,684. Still, the Eighth Army stated that only 75 percent of their needs were being met, even though more reconnaissance missions were flown during the Korean War than ever before.

USAF reconnaissance played a vital role in securing the intelligence that was so crucial to both Eighth Army and USAF operations in Korea. The political constraints that prevented the allies from pursuing military operations into Manchuria against the Chinese, effectively providing them a sanctuary, placed a significant burden on all planning and was a challenge to intelligence collection. This was only mitigated by the Top Secret overflights of RF–80s and RF–86s from the 15th TRS. Despite extraordinary burdens resulting from the rapid downsizing of reconnaissance units after World War II, USAF reconnaissance more than met the needs of the Eighth Army and the bombing requirements of the U.S. Air Force.

Independent of what could be identified as conventional missions, USAF reconnaissance activities were Air Force special operations during the Korean War. Typically, their activities were so shrouded in secrecy that only recently have the security wraps been removed. These activities were directed by Far East Command and included selected elements of the USAF. Often activities were melded into or were provided the cover of secrecy by association with normal or routine combat operations.

Various units provided a variety of clandestine activities. These included the training in intelligence reporting and subsequent insertion into North Korea of parachute-dropped Koreans from C–46 and C–47 aircraft. Low, night-flying C–46s and C–47s provided direct intelligence on Chinese forces moving from Manchuria to attack Army forces in early December 1950. Other units prepared and dropped leaflets in psychological warfare programs. Firefly operations previously described were subsequently assigned to the Special Forces. The USAF activities in these operations were organized as B Flight, 6167th Operations Squadron, Fifth Air Force, on April 1, 1952. The flight was equipped with B–26s, C–46s, and C–47s.

Another unit was Subdetachment K of the 607th Counter Intelligence. While stationed at Kimpo AB in 1950, MSgt. Don Nichols trained and worked with South Koreans who successfully penetrated North Korea and persuaded a North Korean pilot to defect with an Il–10. Nichols successfully completed a number of intelligence operations that could only be considered coups, such as securing a Russian T–34 tank and parachuting men into North Korea to acquire target information. By March 1951, Nichols's unit was redesignated the 6004th Air Intelligence Service Squadron. Other USAF units were involved in helicopter and crash rescue boat activity that at times could serve as further means of providing valuable intelligence.

In July 1952, the 581st Air Resupply and Communications Wing arrived at Clark AB in the Philippines from Mountain Home AFB, Idaho. The wing flew twelve modified B–29s, four C–119s, four SA–16 amphibian aircraft, and four H–19 helicopters. Its mission was aerial introduction, evacuation, and resupply of guerrillas, and aerial delivery of psychological warfare propaganda. All units maintained a high degree of readiness and alertness after the July 27, 1953, truce. Reconnaissance units were kept busy flying along the eastern and western coasts of North Korea. RF–80s and RF–86s used oblique photography to record ground activity, and RB–45s were also very much involved. Although these flights were maintained three miles off the coast of North Korea, on occasion they tangled with MiGs.

The success of the RF–86 in combat and its ability to take photographs deep into Manchuria and China led to an improved version of the RF–86F capable of carrying twin forty-inch cone vertical cameras. On March 1, 1954, the 15th TRS deployed to Komaki with its RF–86Fs and RF–80s. There, eight of the newly modified RF–86Fs were waiting. Within a few short weeks, the 15th TRS was involved in a series of Top Secret missions that carried over into 1956. More than forty successful sorties were flown over various airfields in the Soviet Union, China, and North Korea, without a single loss. Each of these Top Secret missions was personally approved by President Dwight D. Eisenhower.

Sources

This paper draws heavily on Robert F. Futrell's outstanding and comprehensive *The United States Air Force in Korea, 1950–1953*, to provide a timeline of military actions from the beginning of the war on June 25, 1950, until the truce on July 27, 1953. Reconnaissance events are juxtaposed with certain other military activities for sake of continuity. This paper neither pretends to provide an analysis of overall USAF strategy nor list the total sequence of military actions. Rather, it presents an overall view of the role of USAF reconnaissance, its problems, and its accomplishments with the inclusion of a number of specific missions that exemplify the role of reconnaissance during the war in Korea.

USAF records: correspondence between Far East Air Force and 67th Tactical Reconnaissance Wing, 1951–1953.

Interviews with RF–80 and RF–86 pilots who flew combat missions during the Korean War, conducted between 1985 and 2002.

B. Hardy and D. Hall, *Photographic Reconnaissance and Interpretation During The Korea War* (private printing, 2002).

Michael E. Haas, *Apollo's Warriors* (Maxwell AFB, Ala.: Air University Press, 1997).

J. Foss & M. Brennan, *Top Guns* (New York: Pocket Books, 1991).

Robert F. Futrell, *The United States Air Force in Korea, 1950–1953* (Washington, D.C.: Office of Air Force History, 1983).

J. Stewart, *Airpower—The Decisive Force In Korea* (New York: D. Van Nostrand Co., Inc, 1957).

K. D. Watson, *The 67th Tactical Reconnaissance Wing 1953 Year Book* (Nagoya, Japan, 1953).

Logistical Support of Air Operations

Introduction to the Logistics Panel

Roger G Miller

After World War II, the United States faced a series of major challenges. The most significant change from the prewar era was that U.S. foreign policy commitments now extended around the world, and a military presence had to be in place to make those policies effective. For the first time in history, the nation required a peacetime military force and a supporting infrastructure capable of operating in a global arena. Further, the advent of new technologies such as jet propulsion, rocketry, and nuclear weapons required dramatic changes in doctrine, organization, and equipment. Finally, the military itself had to undergo transformation. The exponential growth of air power and intensive wartime experience with the joint chiefs organization and unified theater commands ultimately led to a unified Department of Defense in 1947.

The challenges that demanded a significantly modernized and expanded military force flew in the face of the traditional U.S. reaction to victory. No sooner had Germany and Japan surrendered than the American public demanded that the mighty force which had achieved the victory be dismantled, that its men discharged, that their weapons mothballed or destroyed, and that the industrial infrastructure which had permitted the victory be reoriented to peacetime production. Thus, the transformation of the U.S. military into a modern, global force in the late 1940s had to be accomplished in the face of severe constraints and miserly budgets. Ultimately, the years between World War II and the Korean War saw the greatest period of retrenchment and subsequent peacetime military expansion in U.S. military history. The Korean War would in so many ways provide a proving ground for this new force.

Below the level of the services, unification came slowly. The earliest and best-known effort came in air transport. The USAF Air Transport Command and U.S. Navy's Naval Air Transport Service combined to form the Military Air Transport Service in June 1948. This effort, however, still failed to unify all military air transport under one organization. The Air Force continued to maintain a significant number of troop carrier units for tactical support of the Army, and the Navy continued to maintain several transport units to meet its own requirements. Otherwise, unification failed to include the logistical systems supporting each of the individual services which manned and operated their own logistical systems and supported the other services in their own spheres of action; that is, the Air Force provided air support, the Army, land support, and the Navy, sea support. Success thus depended upon coordination and cooperation even within a theater.

Today, we have four presentations that explore significant elements of airborne, seaborne, and land-based logistics during the Korean War. William Suit notes that the logistics of the new service, the U.S. Air Force, went far beyond efforts to keep its own fueled and armed combat aircraft in the skies over Korea. The Air Force provided direct operational support to Army and marine units in combat. Air logistics was thus an essential element of the Korean War, given the tremendous distances, difficult terrain, primitive transportation network, and immediate demands of combat.

Thomas Wildenberg then explores the U.S. Navy's experience using underway replenishment to keep carrier task forces operating at sea for extended periods. Ship-to-ship refueling was a routine matter by 1950, as Wildenberg notes, but the need to transfer huge amounts of munitions and other cargo required to keep a task force operational provided serious challenges for the U.S. Navy.

James A. Ginther, in turn, explores an emerging new technology in his review of the use of helicopters under combat conditions. Helicopters first saw practical use in the China-Burma-India theater during World War II. In Korea, the U.S. Marine Corps began exploring a new tactical doctrine of vertical envelopment, which included the delivery of equipment and supplies under combat conditions.

Finally, Benjamin D. King examines the performance of U.S. Army ground transportation on the Korean peninsula. Transportation, King notes, was a critical matter during the Korean conflict, especially in theater where the terrible terrain, primitive conditions, and shortage of local resources provided unique problems for U.S. Army logisticians.

U.S. Air Force Korean Logistics

William W. Suit

Although the preponderance of air power history focuses on the planning and execution of combat missions, the vast majority of U.S. Air Force personnel who contributed to the Korean War effort served in a support function: training, medicine, intelligence, security, or communications. The contributions of mechanics, civil engineers, and supply officers often went unnoticed, but no combat sorties could have been flown without the support of the logistical tail that began at the war materiel production facilities and ended with the flightline support crews. This article aims to give the reader an appreciation for the effort required to place fueled and armed combat aircraft into the skies over Korea.

North Korea's invasion of South Korea surprised the United States and its allies, all of whom were minimally prepared for the ensuing air war. At first, the U.S. Air Force, U.S. Navy, Royal Australian Air Force, and the British Royal Navy scrambled to throw their available aircraft into the fight. During the first critical weeks, the contribution of the U.S. Air Force's Far East Air Forces (FEAF) proved crucial in halting the North Korean onslaught, and throughout the war the FEAF continued to provide the bulk of the personnel, aircraft, and logistics that composed the United Nations (U.N.) air forces. As the war progressed, efforts to move tactical air units to Korea were hampered by the paucity of adequate airfields, port facilities, and ground transportation in South Korea. Much of what did exist was damaged or destroyed during the first seven months of the war, as the warring armies and U.N. tactical air units moved up and down the peninsula. Accordingly, the Air Force, with Army assistance, repaired and upgraded the few airfields that existed, built additional runways, and established a logistics pipeline. All this was done as FEAF competed for resources with an American-led and -financed, but European-centered, large-scale rearmament effort. Thus, even at the height of combat, the Air Force committed no more than one-fourth of its rapidly expanding resources to FEAF, which included the Fifth Air Force (in Japan), Thirteenth Air Force (Philippines), and Twentieth Air Force (Okinawa and the Marianas).[1]

Because the United States faced no military threat after World War II, the country rapidly demobilized, leaving mountains of air-war materiel strewn about the globe and tens of thousands of aircraft stored around the country. At the same time that the Air Force was dismantling its stock of piston-engine aircraft, it was embarking on the development of a smaller atomic and jet air force. In 1947, the newly created Air Force numbered 339,000 military personnel and employed an additional 111,000 civilians, down from 2.3 million and 410,000, respectively, three years earlier. Aircraft on hand had fallen from a World War II high of 78,000 to 23,000 in 1947, and most of these were in storage.[2] From a logistics viewpoint, the Air Force faced two primary tasks: culling the vast store of materiel left over after the war and equipping itself with modern aircraft and support equipment. But these efforts were hampered at first by the mass postwar exodus of skilled support personnel from the Army Air Forces and then by a precipitous drop in defense spending.

The bulk of the materiel in Europe, mostly in the United Kingdom, had been declared surplus and sold for token sums. The situation in the Pacific was more complicated. At the beginning of the Korean War, vast stores of materiel remained scattered across the region at locations like Guam, the Philippines, Australia, New Guinea, and Japan. In the continental United States (CONUS), the Air Force rapidly reduced its depot structure, but in 1950 its warehouses still bulged with war surplus.[3]

The President's Air Policy Commission (also called the Finletter Commission) and the Congressional Aviation Policy Board (or the Brewster Committee) had recommended that the Air Force establish a minimum of seventy combat groups (or wings), equipped with new aircraft, to meet the nation's security needs. By 1950, a lack of funds compelled the Air Force to scale down its procurement program to provide for only forty-eight groups. With limited funding available and development-to-production lead times growing, an all-jet combat fleet appeared to be many years away.[4]

In June 1950, FEAF possessed approximately 1,200 aircraft, many of which were not even operational. Primarily organized and equipped as an air defense force, the FEAF air fleet consisted of the North American F–51 Mustang piston-engine fighter, the Lockheed F–80C Shooting Star jet fighter, the North American F–82 Twin Mustang, the Douglas B–26 Invader twin-engine light bomber, and the Boeing B–29 Superfortress bomber. The task of supplying the FEAF with the aircraft and war materiel required to fight in Korea fell to Air Materiel Command (AMC), Far East Air Materiel Command (FEAMCOM), and the maintenance, supply, and transportation units within FEAF. Moreover, during the opening days of the war, FEAF fought with the men and materiel it had on hand because it took several weeks for supplies from the United States to reach Japan. After helping sweep the North Korean air force from the skies, the F–80Cs, the most numerous aircraft type in FEAF, proved unsuited for the vital tasks of interdiction and close air support. The F–80Cs had a limited range, were not equipped to carry both bombs and external fuel tanks, were not equipped with pylon bomb racks, and could not operate easily from austere airfields in Korea. To meet the pressing need for ground-attack aircraft during the early months of the war, FEAF stopped reassembling and overhauling incoming F–80Cs and began returning mothballed F–51s and B–26s to combat condition. Additional F–51s and B–26s soon began arriving from the United States, and once the necessary parts were acquired, FEAMCOM began modifying F–80s to extend their range and increase their weapons load capacity.[5]

The U.S. Air Force had been an independent service for only three years when the Korean War began, and it was in the process of developing the next generation of aircraft, weapons, and support equipment. Except for the dramatic decline in support activity, the basic Air Force logistics function had changed little from that of its predecessor Army Air Forces. AMC, commanded by Lt. Gen. Benjamin W. Chidlaw[6] and headquartered at Wright-Patterson AFB, Ohio, served as the primary logistics support organization for the Air Force. The command performed several major logistics functions: supply, maintenance, modification, repair, and materiel acquisition. AMC headquarters, through its subordinate regional procurement units, negotiated and managed major contracts for goods and services, including aircraft purchases and modification projects. The command operated a network of air materiel areas (AMAs) and specialized supply depots in the CONUS. The AMAs and depots comprised supply warehouses that stored spare parts and specialized equipment and operated large industrial facilities for the overhaul, repair, and modification of aircraft.[7] The Sacramento AMA, located at McClellan AFB, California, was the focal point for materiel support to FEAF units. The Air Force also maintained two overseas depots: one at RAF Burtonwood, England; the other at FEAMCOM Air Base (AB), Tachikawa, Japan. FEAMCOM, a FEAF subordinate unit commanded by Brig. Gen. John P. Doyle,[8] operated the air depot in Japan and served as the in-theater materiel support organization for FEAF. The Air Force utilized a three-tier system for aircraft and equipment maintenance: an organization, a field, and a depot level. Under this system, a squadron's ground crews conducted flightline inspections, preventive maintenance, and minor repairs. Field maintenance included repairs that required fixed shops, specialty skilled personnel, and heavy precision tooling, all of which was performed at the air base level. Depot-level maintenance included aircraft, equipment, and component overhaul and modifications performed at a CONUS AMA or at one of the overseas depots. Organizationally, the Air Force employed a standard wing/base structure that assigned a maintenance group, a supply group, and an airdrome group (later renamed air base group) to each wing or major base. The supply groups (or squadrons in some cases) in FEAF requisitioned supplies through FEAMCOM, which procured materiel from AMC and, when considered time-critical or cost-effective, from local suppliers. The U.S. Army Japan Logistics Command provided FEAF with common supplies such as boots, clothing, and tents.[9]

Responsibility for intertheater and intratheater transportation was divided among several organizations. The Military Sea Transportation Service directed sealift activities among the United States, Japan, and Korea, utilizing both U.S. Navy and contractor vessels. The Military Air Transport Service (MATS) was responsible for airlift between the United States and Japan. MATS provided the bulk of the aircraft for this intercontinental air link, but it augmented its own fleet of aircraft by contracting with commercial air carriers. The Combat Cargo Command (later renamed the 315th Air Division [Combat Cargo]) served as the in-theater air transport provider.[10] Several allied air force transport units served under the 315th Air Division. The Theater Air Transport Board allocated the limited air cargo capacity available in the FEAF theater among the using services.[11] The U.S. Army Military Railway Service supervised railroad operations in Korea, but South Korea's National Railway, under contract to the U.S. Army, ran the trains and accomplished much of the necessary repair work. The Japanese had originally built the Korean rail system and thus served as a source of replacement parts and equipment. The U.S. Eighth Army provided most motor transport among the port facilities, supply depots, and Fifth Air Force units in Korea. The Army also used helicopters to deliver supplies and personnel to remote locations.[12]

AMC responded to the sudden demand for aircraft, equipment, and supplies by first drawing heavily on World War II surplus. By November 1950, AMC depots and private contractors had modified and reconditioned more than 400 mothballed aircraft for FEAF and transferred an additional 275 aircraft from CONUS-based units. The Air Force preferred to transport fighter aircraft to Japan aboard Navy carriers.

Unfortunately, when shipped, many aircraft were secured to the upper decks of freighters and tankers where they were exposed to corrosive sea air and saltwater spray. Covering the aircraft with grease and rubber-coating them limited, but did not eliminate, salt corrosion. The first 147 F–51s arrived in Japan aboard the carrier USS *Boxer* in late July 1950. The AMAs installed ferry fuel tanks on longer-range aircraft, such as B–26s and the Douglas C–47 Skytrain which island-hopped to Japan.[13] To meet Korean War and Mutual Defense Assistance Program (MDAP) materiel demands, the command rebuilt its procurement, maintenance, modification, and supply organizations and its infrastructure. Existing supply and maintenance depots expanded operations, and several facilities that had closed after World War II were reactivated. Command personnel strength almost doubled, peaking at 192,000 in 1953.[14] Aircraft procurement funding jumped from $1 billion in 1950 to $10 billion by 1952. American aircraft manufacturers responded by producing thousands of modern jet aircraft, both for the U.S. armed forces and for distribution to allies through the MDAP.[15] Surplus stocks of ammunition and bombs provided an immediate supply source of certain types of munitions, but munitions manufacturers had to rapidly increase the production of napalm tanks, phosphorous bombs, and ground-attack rockets to meet air armament requirements. Given time to organize, both AMC and its industrial partners were soon supplying both the U.S. Air Force and its allies with substantial quantities of modern air war materiel.

FEAMCOM operated a major supply and maintenance depot at Tachikawa AB, Japan, on the site of a former aircraft company industrial facility. FEAMCOM also maintained an aircraft assembly base at Kisarazu AB, on Tokyo Bay; the Tama Arsenal near Tokyo; and the Yamada Reserve Aviation Ammunition depot on Kyushu.[16] In June 1950, the main activity at the FEAF depot facility involved preparing F–80A and F–80B fighters for return to the United States and preparing recently arrived F–80Cs for service with FEAF units that were converting from the older F–80s and F–51s to the newer jet fighter. Preparing new fighter, liaison, and forward air control (FAC) aircraft for Korean combat remained a major task throughout the war. Early 1950s fighter aircraft did not have the range to island-hop across the Pacific; not until the end of the war were fighters, such as the Republic F–84 Thunderjet, capable of aerial refueling and making direct flights to Japan from the United States. Throughout the war, partially disassembled aircraft arrived by ship and were unloaded at Yokohama, Japan. Loaded on barges, they were transported across Tokyo Bay to Kisarazu where they were reassembled and made combat-ready. Almost all aircraft shipped to Japan suffered some degree of salt corrosion damage which had to be repaired upon arrival.[17]

One of the major responsibilities of the Tachikawa depot involved installing the modifications and upgrades to improve the performance of FEAF aircraft or correct defects identified after the aircraft arrived in theater. Some of the modifications performed in Japan included replacing tail booms of the Fairchild C–119 Flying Boxcar; installing pylon bomb racks and wing tanks with increased fuel capacity on F–80s; replacing leading-edge wing slats on the North American F–86 Sabre; installing reconnaissance cameras on F–86s; and, toward the end of the war, modifying F–80s and F–84s for in-flight refueling. Upgrading in-theater aircraft to correct safety problems or improve reliability and performance directly affected combat effectiveness. The most notable example involved replacing the wing leading-edge slats on F–86Es and F–86Fs with extended solid leading edges. This relatively simple modification reduced drag and increased the F–86E's ceiling by 4,000 feet, increased high-speed maneuverability, and improved the aircraft's rate of climb. FEAMCOM's 13th Maintenance Group (MG) also performed airframe and equipment overhaul, minor engine overhaul (jet engines were returned to AMC depots for major overhauls), and battle-damage repair. Much of FEAMCOM's specialized vehicle maintenance was done under contract by the Showa Aircraft Company at the facility-designated Area A of FEAMCOM AB. Showa Aircraft provided the labor, but FEAMCOM provided the equipment because the equipment previously owned by both the Showa Aircraft Company and Tachikawa Aircraft Company had been confiscated as war reparations after World War II. The depot also modified ground equipment. For example, the 13th MG modified and installed photographic equipment in portable vans and trailers to provide operational bases with on-site photofinishing capability. It also modified more than one hundred Jeeps to carry twelve-channel VHF radios and generators for use by Tactical Air Control Party (TACP) ground crews. Utilizing these semimobile radios, TACPs worked closely with Army artillery units to provide battlefield support by coordinating air strikes. In addition, the 13th MG repair shops overhauled and repaired numerous components such as propellers, brakes, radios, and powered ground equipment.[18]

As FEAMCOM expanded its maintenance and modification activities, the command turned to the Japanese labor pool for skilled and relatively low-paid workers. The FEAMCOM work force eventually grew to over 6,300 Americans, both military and civilian, and 16,500 Japanese. (FEAFCOM was later renamed Far East Air Force Logistics Force, or FEALOGFOR.) Japanese seamstresses repaired flight clothing and parachutes, foundry workers produced castings that machinists fashioned into aircraft components, and sheet-metal workers repaired the battle-damaged skins of combat aircraft flown to Japan for repair. FEAMCOM also employed Japanese engineers, draftsmen, tool and die makers, supply managers, and many other skilled workers and laborers at its depot and munitions facilities.[19]

The lack of transportation, frequent relocations, and poor weather took a toll on aircraft operating from forward air bases in Korea. As has been observed, existing Air Force operational procedures required that field-level maintenance be performed at the base or wing level. Theoretically, this included groups and wings deployed to forward operating bases in combat zones. However, that system did not work well in Korea because field-level maintenance required the use of heavy support equipment and machines: 2,000 short tons of supplies and equipment for a jet fighter wing and 2,700 short tons for a conventional light bomber wing. During the first year of the war, when the tactical wings were constantly on the move, the equipment often failed to arrive at the forward operating bases, and when it did, it may not have been unpacked because the bases lacked hangars and structures to house the tools and equipment, or because the units relocated quickly. Not surprisingly, much equipment was abandoned, pilfered, lost, or ruined by exposure to the weather. Until the fighting front stabilized, FEAF units in Korea rarely possessed enough building materials, supplies, spares, machinery, or equipment to adequately establish the necessary supply systems and maintenance facilities to conduct effective field-level maintenance. Acquiring sufficient spare parts for new types of aircraft, such as the various F–84 and F–86 models, proved particularly difficult.

Because the new aircraft types had accumulated limited service time and because the operating conditions in Korea were unusually severe, AMC and the manufacturers could not accurately predict spares requirements based on past consumption. As a result, depots quickly depleted their stocks of particular items, and the manufacturers had to rush production, often shipping items directly to FEAMCOM. A case in point involved the bulky and expensive F–86 external wing tanks. These tanks were originally designed as ferry tanks with the expectation that they were reusable items. The Air Force, therefore, acquired only a limited stock. However, F–86s had to carry the tanks to reach MiG Alley near the North Korean–Chinese border, and the pilots had to jettison them before engaging the MiG–15s in combat. Inevitably, the stock of external tanks vanished, and during January and February 1952 the 4th and the 51st Fighter Wings had to curtail F–86 combat operations. Fortunately, production of the fuel tanks eventually caught up with consumption. Also, few airfields possessed adequate hangars which forced many ground crews to perform maintenance outdoors with only rudimentary windbreaks as shelters against the winter weather. Thus, forward-deployed aircraft received just enough maintenance and repair to keep them flying, and aircraft combat readiness rates declined rapidly.[20]

Fifth Air Force flying units learned to alleviate the poor maintenance support situation at the air bases in Korea by locating their heavy field maintenance equipment at a secure rear area base in Japan and periodically flying their aircraft back to the equipment for intermediate and major inspection and repair.[21] The experiences of the 27th Fighter Escort Wing and the 49th Fighter Bomber Wing provided an example of the practicality of this arrangement. The 49th Wing moved to Taegu in October 1950, where, in harsh weather and without having adequate shelter or equipment, it attempted to perform field-level maintenance on its F–80s. The wing sent ten F–80s back to the FEAMCOM depot in March 1951 for inspection and repair. The aircraft were in such poor condition that each required an average of 7,500 man-hours to recondition. By comparison, the 27th Wing moved to Taegu in December 1951 but left its intermediate and major maintenance assets at Itazuke AB. By shuttling its F–84s back to Japan for intermediate and major inspection and repair, the 27th managed to keep forty-eight F–84s in commission at Taegu at all times, and none of its aircraft deteriorated as badly as had the F–80s of the 49th Wing. This disparity in maintenance results caught the attention of Fifth Air Force logisticians. Similar positive results occurred when the 452d Bombardment Wing moved to Pusan East (K–9) in May 1951 but left its major maintenance capability at Miho AB in Japan. The 3d Bombardment Wing moved its entire maintenance capability to Kunsan in August 1951. (Both wings flew B–26s.) From July through December 1951, the in-commission rate for the 3d Wing dropped from 78 percent to 65 percent, and its monthly flying hours dropped from 5,425 to 3,904. For the 452d during the same period, its in-commission rate rose from 57 percent to 82 percent and its flying hours per month rose from 3,884 to 4,612. The Fifth Air Force soon realized that the aircraft receiving rear-area maintenance maintained higher in-commission rates, suffered fewer accidents and mission cancellations, and completed more flying hours than aircraft receiving forward-based field maintenance. Consequently, FEAF established Rear Echelon Maintenance Combined

Operation (REMCO) operations at air bases in Japan for most Korea-based fighter and fighter-bomber units. REMCOs combined the field maintenance activity for two or more wings at a single base. In this way, the wings could divide base support, supply, and maintenance responsibilities, thus reducing manpower and equipment requirements. REMCOs performed all major inspections on aircraft and accomplished all field-level maintenance, including minor engine repair, battle damage repair, and modifications in compliance with technical orders. Maintenance crews organized aircraft and engine maintenance production lines to better exploit available hangar space, machinery, and skilled technicians.[22] Free from the need to perform field maintenance, forward-based maintenance units performed only organizational maintenance, such as preflight and postflight inspections, arming and servicing aircraft, emergency engine replacements, and one-time flight repairs. The Fifth Air Force established REMCO facilities for F–80s at Tsuiki (then in January 1952 for F–86s), for F–84s at Itazuke, and for B–26s at Miho.[23]

Transports and medium bomber units experienced many logistics difficulties similar to those of the fighters and light bombers. Fortunately for the maintenance crews, the bulk of the transport aircraft operated from the relative comfort of Japan, and all of the B–29s operated from Okinawa, Guam, or the Japanese main islands. The 315th Air Division's three troop carrier wings (TCW) were headquartered in Japan, at Tachikawa AB, Ashiya AB, and Brady AB. Troop carrier detachments eventually operated from six additional bases in Japan and eight in Korea. The 315th experienced serious maintenance difficulties with the relatively new C–119s and the new Douglas C–124 Globemaster IIs that were rushed to Korea without sufficient spares or trained repair personnel.

The 403d TCW, operating C–119s from Ashiya, serves as a case in point. Two factors contributed to the near cessation of C–119 operations in the summer of 1952. First, the C–119s were not designed to operate from rough fields; nonetheless, early in the war they continuously flew heavily laden into and out of crude forward-area strips where the aircraft were literally shaken apart. Second, the 403d received abysmal spares support and inadequate theater maintenance. As a result, during June and July 1952, the wing managed to keep only between 23 and 28 of its 71 active C–119s in commission. The problem was alleviated after AMC established an emergency spares replenishment program, and the war-weary C–119s were rotated out and replaced with newer aircraft. By June 1953, the in-commission rate for the 403d Wing C–119s had climbed to 78.8 percent.[24]

Even with the accompanying maintenance difficulties, moving aircraft units as close as possible to the fighting front greatly increased their combat efficiency. Fortunately, the Air Force quickly cleared the South Korean skies of enemy aircraft. This allowed the Fifth Air Force to establish forward operating air bases in South Korea that remained free from the threat of air attack. Concurrently, FEAF moved as many tactical air units as space would allow to existing airfields on Kyushu, placing the aircraft as close as possible to Korea. From these Japanese and Korean bases, the fighters and light bombers could range farther north while carrying more bombs and less fuel. However, the geography and the very limited transportation infrastructure in South Korea created major obstacles for U.N. military forces trying to rush personnel and materiel into Korea. South Korea possessed only one high-capacity, deep-water seaport, Pusan, and one other large seaport capable of handling coaster-sized ships, Inchon.

When Inchon was liberated in September 1950, two main rail lines (one double and one single track) connected Pusan and Seoul via different routes. A rail line and a highway connected Inchon and Seoul. The mountains that ran north and south along the length of the peninsula dictated that the rail lines follow circuitous routes with numerous steep grades, bridges, and tunnels, thus limiting the freight capacity of the trains. Outside the few major cities, paved roads were virtually nonexistent, restricting the movement of supplies by truck. Rice fields covered most of the flat lowlands and the terraces of the river valleys. These fields were flooded during the summer growing season. Furthermore, at least initially, the North Korean transportation infrastructure was superior to that of the South. As the war intensified, however, most of the North's railroad marshaling yards, bridges, seaport facilities, and airfields were badly damaged by FEAF air interdiction before and during the breakout from the Pusan perimeter, necessitating their repair as the U.N. forces swept north. The cold and snowy Korean winters complicated any in-country movement and slowed all forms of transportation.[25]

The situation for logistics personnel in Korea proved extremely difficult. The first Fifth Air Force flying units to arrive in Korea lacked the necessary support personnel and equipment to sustain combat operations. To meet immediate maintenance, supply, and munitions support needs, FEAMCOM established the Korea Air Materiel Unit (KAMU) at Taegu, South Korea, as a temporary forward-based organization to augment the 6131st Tactical Support Wing. KAMU consisted of two field maintenance units, three depot support units, and one ammunition supply squadron. These units dispersed to various Korean airfields, changing locations about once a month for the first six months of the war, and performed diverse support functions as necessary. For example, the 6401st Field Maintenance Unit first deployed to Pohang (K–3)[26] where it performed aircraft battle damage repair and salvage work for the 6131st Tactical Support Wing. It then returned to Japan, moved to Kimpo (K–14) after the Inchon landing, and then moved to Pusan (K–1). The 6408th Depot Support Unit activated in September 1950 and moved to Suwon Air Base (K–13) where its personnel operated an ammunition dump, built roads, drove ammunition trucks, and mixed napalm. In October, the unit moved to Kimpo, then to Pyongyang (K–24) in November; it evacuated to Seoul Municipal Airport (K–16) by early December and then moved to Chinhae (K–10) to support the 18th Fighter Bomber Wing. The 543d Ammunition Supply Squadron arrived in September 1950 at Pusan, where its personnel began construction of a pierced steel planking (PSP) reclamation facility, built revetments, provided guards, and constructed and operated an ammunition dump. The KAMU units deactivated after the battle lines stabilized, and their personnel returned to Japan. These units advanced and retreated with the fighter wings and fighter-bomber wings they supported. Their contributions filled an initial logistical support void in the Fifth Air Force tactical organization that would have otherwise severely limited the operational capability of the combat wings.[27]

The greatest obstacle to operations faced by tactical air units during the first two years of the war was the lack of adequate, secure air bases in Korea. Kimpo Airfield, just northwest of Seoul, was the only modern airfield in South Korea when the war began. Unfortunately, the North Koreans quickly captured Kimpo. In response, FEAF heavily damaged its two runways and support structures during air attacks. Only a few other airfields existed in South Korea. Most of these were built by the Japanese for light aircraft use during World War II and had subsequently fallen into disrepair. Although the Air Force had rushed all of its engineer aviation units to Korea, they proved too few and too poorly equipped. Also, the rapid movement that marked the first year of the war kept the heavy construction units and their equipment on the move and, therefore, able to accomplish only the minimum work necessary to sustain combat operations at the growing number of airfields.[28]

Responsibility for airfield construction and maintenance was divided among several military organizations. Although each type of unit was charged with specific responsibilities, civil engineering projects were completed by the organizations possessing the necessary personnel and equipment. The task of repairing and expanding existing airfields and building new ones fell to the engineer aviation units. These were Special Category Army Personnel with Air Force organizations. As with other military organizations rushed to service in Korea, these hybrid Army–Air Force units lacked sufficient trained personnel and equipment.

In the summer of 1950, the most pressing task involved rebuilding and upgrading the only three Korean airfields that had not yet fallen into enemy hands—Pusan, Taegu, and Pohang. At Pusan, the 802d Engineer Aviation Battalion (EAB) found the concrete runway crumbling under the weight of transport aircraft, but it was nonetheless serviceable. Therefore, the 802d EAB departed for Pohang, leaving behind a small detachment to repair the runway and keep it open. At Pohang, the 802d EAB added a 500-foot PSP extension to the existing concrete runway, built hardstands, added a PSP apron, and built a cross taxiway. The engineers evacuated on August 13, 1950, as North Korean forces entered the area. The 822d EAB and the 919th Engineer Aviation Maintenance Company (EAMC) arrived at Taegu in late July and immediately laid down a PSP runway while they resurfaced the existing hard clay runway. On August 16, 1950, enemy troops advanced close to Taegu, forcing engineers to evacuate. However, a small contingent of the 919th EAMC remained to support aircraft that continued to stage from the airstrip.

Beginning in September, after the UNC amphibious landing at Inchon and the subsequent rout of the North Korean Army, tactical fighter and bomber units moved into a string of airfields ranging as far north as Yonpo, North Korea (K–27). The advancing tactical air units brought along as much engineering, maintenance, and supply capability as time and transportation allowed, but competition with the Army for scarce transportation seriously limited the amount of heavy equipment that reached the advanced bases. When the Chinese counterattacked in December 1950, the forward-based tactical air units retreated south with the U.N. armies. Because they had neither enough time nor enough equipment to establish extensive support facilities, the amount of supplies and equipment they abandoned was relatively small. However, they lost a considerable amount of equipment in the overall confusion. Once the battle line stabilized near the 38th parallel, FEAF concentrated on improving existing runways, building new runways, and building support structures at air bases in South Korea to support jet aircraft and heavy transports. Until now, no effort had been made to accomplish anything more than temporary repairs and improvements to existing airfields or to carve out simple landing strips for use by liaison aircraft or to use as supply points for ground troops. Consequently, many major air base construction projects continued up to and beyond the cease-fire, and components of the three engineer aviation groups in Korea remained attached to each major base until the end of war.[29]

Runway and support structure construction followed a similar pattern at almost all airfields in South Korea. The one exception was at Osan-ni (K–55), which was built from the ground up following a master plan. Most often, engineer aviation units would arrive at an airfield, fill in bomb craters when necessary, then lay down PSP surfaces and extensions. Other support units or local laborers would concurrently erect temporary tent housing and crude maintenance shelters. As heavy construction equipment became available, the engineers enlisted local labor to help construct asphalt runways. This pattern held true from the initial deployment to South Korea through the advance to the Yalu River and subsequent retreat back to the 38th parallel. After the fighting front stabilized, engineer aviation groups and installations squadrons concentrated on expanding and improving the airfields. For example, units of the 931st Engineer Aviation Group, which arrived in Korea in April 1951, spent the spring and summer of 1951 constructing runways at Kimpo (K–14), Pyongtaek (K–6), and Kunsan (K–8) and building the basic infrastructure—roads, sewers, drainage, water, fuel tanks, hangars, and housing—required by the operational air base at Suwon (K–13).[30] The Fifth Air Force also maintained more than a dozen rough airstrips for Army resupply and liaison, with one strip restricted to F–51 operations. At these locations, sod, gravel, or sand runways sufficed. By July 1953, FEAF counted thirty operational airfields in Korea and dozens more in Japan, Guam, and Okinawa.[31] In addition to runways, the engineers also built roads, aircraft fuel facilities, revetments, water distribution systems, drainage systems, electrical systems, and ammunition storage facilities. Because almost all airfields in South Korea were constructed in areas with high water tables, maintaining adequate drainage was imperative to avoid flooding and runway foundation erosion.[32]

Once the engineering aviation units completed the initial heavy construction at a combat zone airfield, Air Force installations squadrons were to assume responsibility for runway upkeep, base engineering support, and facility improvements. However, engineering aviation units continued to be attached to the major air bases and remained involved in heavy construction and maintenance for the duration of the war. As a result, the installations squadrons very often worked with the engineering aviation units rather than replace them. Installations squadron support activities changed with the three phases of the war. FEAF first rushed small detachments of installations squadrons to the crude Korean airfields to support staging operations for tactical aircraft flying from Japan. After the engineer aviation units completed the necessary heavy construction and repair and moved on, some elements of the installations squadrons remained to continue to provide firefighting and base engineering support while other elements moved north to newly captured airfields to support staging operations. After the retreat from North Korea and stabilization of the fighting front, the installations squadrons concentrated on sustaining maximum operations at the airfields in South Korea. During the early months of the war, installations squadrons lacked the heavy equipment and personnel to accomplish necessary runway repairs and construction. They turned to local contract laborers who used simple hand tools to repair and extend runway surfaces, dig drainage networks, build sandbag revetments, and erect tents. At first, runways were lighted by portable lighting systems powered by small generators. As FEAF concentrated more air units in South Korea and as the necessary equipment and building materials became available, the installations squadrons turned to building support structures, establishing base-wide electrical systems, improving runway lighting, and constructing fuel storage and distribution facilities. For all of these tasks, installations squadrons relied heavily on local contractors to supply laborers, plumbers, carpenters, electricians, draftsmen, firefighters, and craftsmen. The installations squadrons were also pressed into service constructing off-base roads (normally an Army responsibility) to connect outlying sites housing SHORAN beacon units, aircraft control and warning squadrons, and radio relay detachments. Once the buildings, pipelines, electrical systems, and roads were built, the installations squadrons maintained them in working order.[33]

Keeping the forward-based units supplied involved filling a supply line that usually stretched back to the United States. The three items required in the greatest bulk quantities by FEAF flying units were aviation fuel, munitions, and PSP. Fuels and lubricants represented more than 60 percent of the tonnage of all materiel shipped to Korea. Fuel was transported in tanker ships from CONUS refineries as well as from the Middle East. By 1950, FEAF had established a relatively efficient fuel distribution system in Japan, but no such system existed in Korea. At first, the only means to transport fuel to forward operating bases was to offload fuel drums at Pusan, or later at Inchon, and deliver the product by truck. At an operational base, it had to be transferred from drums to aircraft refueling units. When absolutely necessary, fuel drums could be airlifted aboard cargo aircraft, but air transport proved inefficient. As more transportation and construction engineering personnel arrived in Korea, the Army began transporting fuel in bulk by rail car, and eventually the Eighth Army's 82d Engineer Petroleum Company began operating a fuel pipeline between Inchon and Seoul. By late 1952, the main air bases had adequate fuel storage and distribution facilities. The Air Force used four types of fuel: JP–1 or JP–4 for jet aircraft;[34] 100/130 octane aviation gasoline for piston-engine aircraft; 87 octane gasoline for engine vehicles and ground support equipment; and diesel fuel for some trucks, heaters, and heavy equipment. The bulk of fuel consumed by the Air Force was JP–4 and high-octane gasoline. Large quantities of gasoline were also used to make napalm, which was mixed onsite at the tactical air unit operational bases.[35]

FEAF expended a tremendous amount of munitions during the war, including 386,000 tons of bombs, 32,000 tons of napalm, 313,000 rockets, and 166 million rounds of .50-cal. ammunition.[36] Surplus World War II stocks provided a ready supply of bombs and .50-cal. ammunition; fortunately, substantial stores were still located on Guam and Okinawa. No large stock of napalm tanks existed, however. To meet the emergency requirement for napalm tanks, AMC modified the standard F–80 75-gal. external wingtip fuel tank to produce a 110-gal. napalm bomb. FEAMCOM arranged for Japanese firms to manufacture the tanks.[37] The Air Force relied on the Navy for its supply of five-inch high-velocity aerial rockets (HVARs). An adequate supply of HVARs existed in the United States to meet both initial FEAF and Navy needs, and American contractors soon increased production to meet the additional demand. During the early weeks of the war, MATS cargo aircraft flew emergency shipments of HVARs to Japan.[38] However, airlifting bombs and rockets, even in-theater, was avoided if possible. The Military Sea Transportation Service carried almost all munitions from the United States to Korea. Trucks and rail provided land transport to the munitions depots and operational bases. FEAMCOM operated two large munitions supply dumps in Japan. Additionally, the 546th Ammunition Supply Squadron maintained a facility on Okinawa and the 13th Ammunition Supply Squadron maintained one on Guam. In September 1950, the 543d Ammunition Supply Squadron moved to Pusan AB and established a receiving, storage, and distribution dump to support Korean-based air units.[39]

The rapid construction of airfields in Korea, and the expansion of those in Japan, could most easily be accomplished using PSP. However, PSP was heavy, bulky, and in short supply. FEAMCOM scoured the theater for all the PSP available and requisitioned more from the United States. Still, engineer and installation units in Korea could not get enough to meet their new construction needs.

In addition, the jet aircraft and heavy transports quickly bent and warped the PSP, forcing the installations squadrons to constantly replace damaged sections. To help meet the need, FEAMCOM established two PSP reconditioning plants, one in South Korea and one at its depot in Japan. The plants first repaired the 60,000 used sheets located in theater; then they continued operations to recondition damaged planks as they accumulated. Because it was located nearest to the bulk of the PSP runways, the Korean plant operated at a much higher capacity than the Japanese facility did.[40]

Both construction and aircraft support required large numbers of specialized vehicles and machines, including bulldozers, graders, fuel trucks, fire trucks, dump trucks, rock crushers, refrigeration units, water pumps, and electrical test equipment. Some medium-duty trucks were purchased in Japan, but everything else had to be shipped from existing stocks at FEAF air bases or from the United States. Initially, almost all vehicles and equipment were drawn from World War II surplus. However, as old equipment wore out and as the number of jet aircraft and new transports in theater increased, new support equipment and vehicles flowed into Korea. Some equipment and spares came directly from the assembly line to Korea.[41]

Fortunately for the United States, Japan proved to be a welcome source of local manufacture, repair, and skilled labor. During the occupation of Japan, responsibility for all FEAF local purchase rested with FEAMCOM. This system of centralized control worked well when the Air Force relied very little on the local economy. However, when the war began, both the U.S. sources of supply—some, 10,000 miles away—and transportation links to FEAF bases became overwhelmed. Accordingly, AMC urged FEAMCOM to procure locally as much as it could. In response, FEAF decentralized purchasing authority to the base level to enable local commanders to contract for base-level goods and services. This allowed the newly established FEAMCOM Procurement and Industrial Planning Directorate to concentrate on acquiring combat-critical materiel. The first major item procured in Japan was napalm tanks. With this production contract and with later contracts, Japanese manufacturers initially experienced problems maintaining both high quality and high rates of production. They eventually solved the problems, and FEAMCOM poured millions of dollars into the Japanese economy to purchase items such as jettisonable fuel tanks, radio transmitters and receivers, napalm bomb igniters, and tools. In addition to supplying items necessary to support the forces engaged in Korea, Japan soon became a source of offshore procurement for the Military Defense Assistance Program.

The Korean War served as an immediate catalyst for the expansion and modernization of the U.S. Air Force. After World War II, as the military rapidly demobilized, Army Air Forces skilled personnel, both military and civilian, returned en masse to private industry, as private industry reverted to a peacetime economy. What resulted was a huge surplus of war materiel at home and scattered about the Pacific, excessive infrastructure in the United States, dwindling budgets, and a lack of skilled personnel in all the services. When the Korean War broke out, the Air Force was able to draw on available resources to stem the tide of the enemy onslaught and then to support the FEAF units operating from established air bases and primitive Korean airfields. China's entry into the war forced the Air Force to build a string of permanent air bases in South Korea, commit large numbers of modern jet aircraft to combat, vastly improve Korea's transportation infrastructure, and establish the necessary logistics pipeline to support the air war. Concurrently, the war stoked fears in Washington and Europe that the Soviet Union might initiate a conflict in Europe. In response, the United States embarked on a major rearmament program for itself and its allies and established a string of air bases around the globe. Although the Korean War is now a distant memory and the Cold War is behind us, the United States still maintains a steady vigil in South Korea.[42]

Notes

1. A contemporary overview of U.S. Air Force logistics support during the Korean War is provided by Maj. Gen. Paul E. Ruestow, comdr FEAFLF, in "Air Force Logistics in the Theater of Operations," *Air University Quarterly Review* (summer 1953): 46–56. The most recent coverage of U.S. Air Force Korean War logistics is Beth F. Scott, et al., "The Logistics of War: A Historical Perspective" (Air Force Logistics Management Agency, Gunter Annex, Ala., Aug 1, 2000).
2. United States Air Force Statistical Digest 1947, Dir. of Stat. Svcs., Compt., HQ USAF, Washington, D.C., 1948, pp 15–16, 72, 132, 134. Air Force–produced studies are available at the Air Force Historical Research Agency (AFHRA) at Maxwell AFB, Ala.
3. Air Force surplus property disposal efforts between World War II and the Korean War are described by E. Clifford Snyder in "History of USAF Supply Programs and Problems (1945–1949)" (Hist. Office, HQ AMC (AMC/HO), W-PAFB, Ohio, Nov. 1950), pp 21–118; Sarah A. Zimmerman, "History of USAF Packaging and Deterioration Control 1942–1952" (AMC/HO, Apr. 1953), pp 53–82; and Dorothy Miller, "USAF Surplus Property Disposal 1 Jul 49–30 June 1950" (AMC/HO, Sep 1951).
4. The Five Year Aircraft Procurement Program is described by Mary R. Self in "History of the Five Year Aircraft Procurement Program (1 January 1948–1 July 1949)" (AMC/HO, Dec 1949); Ethel M. DeHaven, "History of the USAF Five Year Aircraft Procurement Program 1 July 1949–31 December 1949" (AMC/HO, Sep 1950); and Ethel M. DeHaven, "History of the USAF Five-Year Aircraft Procurement Program 1 January–30 June 1950" (AMC/HO, Aug 1952). Also see "Survival in the Air Age," Report by the President's Air Policy Commission (Washington, D.C.: Government Printing Office, Jan 1, 1948); and Report of the Board of Officers to the Chief of

Staff, USAF, Recommending General Policy and Air Force Action Regarding the President's Air Policy Commission Report and the Congressional Aviation Policy Board Report (HQ USAF, Mar 23, 1948). Excerpts relevant to USAF aircraft procurement from Sen. Rprt. 949, Report of the Congressional Aviation Policy Board, National Aviation Policy, 80th Cong., 2d sess are included as a supporting document in Self, "History of the Five Year Aircraft Procurement Program." In July 1950, the combat strength of the USAF consisted primarily of a little more than two thousand B–29s and B–50s, ninety-six jet-powered B–45s, seventy-nine B–36s, approximately two thousand first-line jet fighters (F–80s, F–84s, and F–86s), eighty-one F–82 piston-engine Twin Mustangs, thirty-five hundred second-line fighters (mostly propeller-driven F–47s and F–51s), and twelve hundred second-line medium bombers (B–25s and B–26s). Aircraft figures are from *United States Air Force Statistical Digest*, Nov 1952, pp 162–64.

5. "History of FEAMCOM January to June 1950," p 172. Very soon after the fighting began in Korea, AMC initiated Project HOLD-OFF, a crash effort to withdraw mothballed aircraft from storage and return them to operational condition. See Dorothy W. Trester, "History of the AF Storage and Withdrawal Program (1945–1952)" (AMC/HO, Apr 1954), pp 1–88.
6. Chidlaw was succeeded by Gen. Edwin W. Rawlings in Aug 1951.
7. The entire Aug 4, 1952, issue of *Aviation Week* is dedicated to a very detailed examination of AMC.
8. Doyle was succeeded by Maj. Gen. Paul E. Ruestow in June 1952.
9. For a description of AMC and FEAMCOM on the eve of the Korean War, see Frederick A. Alling, et al., AMC Historical Study Number 291, "History of the Air Materiel Command 1 January – 30 June 1950" (AMC/HO, Oct 1950); and Theodore A. Faulkner, et al., "History of FEAMCOM January to June 1950" (FEAMCOM/HO, Tachikawa, Japan, Sep 1 1950), microfilm copy AFHRA roll number A7367. AMC Korean War supply efforts are briefly described by Dorothy L. Miller in "History of Supply of Overseas Air Forces 1947–1954" (AMC/HO, Jun 1953), pp 9–21.
10. For a description of the Korean War activities of Combat Cargo, see Annis G. Thompson, *The Greatest Airlift: The Story of Combat Cargo* (Tokyo: Dai Nippon Printing Company, 1954).
11. Ruestow, "Air Force Logistics in the Theater of Operations," p 33.
12. U.S. Army Korean War logistics activities are described by John G. Westover in *Combat Support in Korea*, U.S. Army in Action Series (Washington, D.C.: GPO, 1987); and by James A. Huston in *The Sinews of War: 1775–1953*, Army Historical Series (Washington, D.C.: GPO, 1966), pp 615–52. Also see Roy E. Appleman, *South to the Naktong, North to the Yalu (June–November 1950)*, United States Army in the Korean War Series (Washington, D.C.: GPO, 1961), pp 260–61.
13. The initial response of AMC to the war is described in Frederick A. Alling,

et al., "History of Air Materiel Command Support of the Far East Air Force in the Korean Conflict" (AMC/HO, Dec 1950).

14. For a comprehensive account of AMC during the war, see Frederick A. Alling, et al., "History of Air Materiel Command 1 January–30 June 1951" (AMC/HO, Nov 1951); Helen B. Joiner, "History of Air Materiel Command 1 July–31 December 1951" (AMC/HO, Jul 1952); Ethel M. DeHaven, et al., "History of Air Materiel Command 1 January–30 June 1952" (AMC/HO; "History of the Air Materiel Command 1 July–31 December 1952" (AMC/HO); and Doris A. Baker, "History of Air Materiel Command 1 January–30 June 1953 (AMC/HO).
15. The early 1950s aircraft buildup and initial distribution of air materiel through the MDAP are described by E. Clifford Snyder in "History of Production Problems During the Air Force Build-Up 1950–1954" (AMC/HO); Mauer Mauer, "History of USAF Activities in Support of the Mutual Defense Assistance Program, Part I – to 1 July 1950" (AMC/HO, Apr 1951); Mauer Mauer, "History of USAF Activities in Support of the Mutual Defense Assistance Program, Part II – 1 July to 31 December 1950" (AMC/HO, Nov 1951); and Mauer Mauer, "History of USAF Activities in Support the Mutual Defense Assistance Program, Part III – 1 January to 30 June 1951" (AMC/HO, May 1952).
16. The mission and organization of FEAMCOM are described in "FEAMCOM Mission," HQ FEAMCOM, FEAMCOM AB, ca. 1952; "FEAMCOM," *Air University Quarterly Review* (summer 1951): 76–82; and Capt Calvin J. Romrell, USAF, "The Logistics Planning Process of the Far East Air Materiel Command During the Korean War," (M.A. thesis, Air Force Institute of Technology, 1988).
17. 13th Maintenance Group activities are described in "History of FEAMCOM 1 Jul–31 Dec 50" (FEAMCOM/HO, Tachikawa, Japan, ca. 1951), pp 199–247, AFHRA microfilm copy, roll K7413.
18. "History of FEAMCOM 1 January 1951–30 June 1951" (FEAMCOM/HO, Tachikawa, Japan, ca. 1951), pp 125, 142–167, AFHRA microfilm copy, roll K7415; and "History of FEAMCOM 1 July 1951–31 December 1951," (FEAMCOM/HO, Tachikawa, Japan, ca. 1952), pp 90–97 AFHRA microfilm copy, roll K7416. FEAMCOM depot activity is also described in "Historical Report for January 1952" to CG, FEAMC (HQ 6400th Air Depot Wing, APO 323, Jan 1952), AFHRA microfilm copy, roll PO 300; and "History, 6400th Air Depot Wing February–June 1952" (HQ 6400th Air Depot Wing, APO 323, Jun 1952), AFHRA microfilm copy, roll PO 300.
19. "FEALOGFOR and Japanese Labor," *Air University Quarterly Review* (summer 1953): 93–97. Also see "History, 6400th Air Depot Wing."
20. FEAF aircraft maintenance is discussed in detail by Capt James I. Forney, USAF, in "Logistics of Aircraft Maintenance During the Korean War" (M.A. thesis, Air Force Institute of Technology, 1988). Logistics difficulties

are examined in USAF Historical Study no 72, "United States Air Force Operations in the Korean Conflict: 1 November 1950–30 June 1952" (USAF Historical Division, Air University, 1953), pp 100–102, 118–25. Part of a three-volume monograph study of the Korean War written by Frank Futrell, this study served as the basis for Futrell's later book, *The United States Air Force in Korea 1950–1953* (New York: Duell, Sloan, & Pearce, 1961). The USAF monographs contain logistics-related information not included in the book.

21. The Air Service maintained a similar system in France during World War I with the use of air depots located a safe distance from the front lines. See *The U.S. Air Service in World War I*, vol I; and Mauer Mauer, ed, *The Final Report and a Tactical History* (Washington, D.C.: Office of Air Force History, 1978), pp 55, 117–27.
22. Production-line third-echelon maintenance was tried less successfully with transport aircraft in the China–Burma theater during World War II at the direction of then Brig. Gen. William H. Tunner. See *The Army Air Forces in World War II*, vol 7, *Services Around the World*, Wesley F. Craven and James L. Cate, eds (Chicago: University of Chicago Press, 1958; repr., Washington, D.C.: Office of Air Force History, 1983), pp 140–41.
23. Maj. Carl G. Nelson, USAF, "REMCO, A Korean War Development," *Air University Quarterly Review* (summer 1953): 78–85; "United States Air Force Operations in the Korean Conflict: 1 November 1950–30 June 1952," pp 100–104.
24. "United States Air Force Operations in the Korean Conflict 1 July 1952–27 July 1953," pp 272–75; and "History of the Air Materiel Command 1 July–31 December 1952," pp 413–15, 540–41.
25. Korean geography and transportation facilities, as of 1950, are described in USAF Historical Study no 71, "U.S. Air Force Operations in the Korean Conflict: 25 June–1 November 1950" (USAF Historical Division, Oct 1, 1952), pp x–xiii.
26. The FEAF assigned a K–number designator to each of its airfields in Korea.
27. KAMU organization and support activities are described in "History of FEAMCOM 1 Jul–31 Dec 50," pp 2–42.
28. The problems of airfield construction are described in USAF Historical Study no 127, "United States Air Force Operations in the Korean Conflict, 1 July 1952–27 July 1953" (USAF Historical Division, Air University, Jul. 1, 1956), pp 172–83.
29. "U.S. Air Force Operations in the Korean Conflict: 25 June–1 November 1950," pp 18–24; and "United States Air Force Operations in the Korean Conflict: 1 November 1950–30 June 1952," pp 10–16.
30. The activities of the 931st EAG for mid-1951 are described in "Monthly Historical Data Report", AF-DS-U3A, 931st Engineer Aviation Group, Mar 1951, and subsequent reports for Apr 1951, May 1951, Jun 1951, Jul 1951,

and Aug 1951 (AFHRA microfilm, Roll K0169).

31. "United States Air Force Statistical Digest, Fiscal Year 1953," pp 10–14.
32. The activities of the Engineer Aviation Units are described by Col R. I. Millberry in "Engineer Aviation Forces in Korea," *Air University Quarterly Review* (fall 1953): 114–19. FEAF runways, facilities, and the vehicles and machinery used in their construction are described in "Vehicles, Air Installations and Aviation Engineer Equipment and Facilities" (Air Research and Development Command, Task Group for Base Systems, Jul. 20, 1953); and "Aircraft Maintenance and Servicing Equipment and Facilities" (Air Research and Development Command, Task Group for Base Systems, Jul. 20, 1953).
33. Maj Leonard B. Reppert, "The Installation Squadron in Korea," *Air University Quarterly Review* (spring 1952): 89–97.
34. The FEAF switched to JP–4 in Mar 1952, prior to which JP–1 was used.
35. "U.S. Air Force Operations in the Korean Conflict: 25 June–1 November 1950," p 72; and "United States Air Force Operations in the Korean Conflict 1 July 1952–27 July 1953," pp 178–79. Fuels and equipment used by all services are discussed in "Service Performance of Fuels, Lubricants, and Petroleum Distribution Equipment in the Far East Theater" (Washington, D.C.: U.S. Research and Development Board, Committee on Fuels and Lubricants, Apr 1953).
36. "United States Air Force Statistical Digest, Fiscal Year 1953," pp 47–49.
37. Alling, et al., "History of Air Materiel Command Support of the Far East Force in the Korean Conflict," pp 37–38.
38. *Ibid.*, pp 36–37. The USAF also used a Navy 6.5-inch antitank aircraft rocket that was derived from the HVAR.
39. "History of FEAMCOM 1 Jul–31 Dec 50," pp 37–43; and "FEAMCOM Mission," p 5.
40. "Steel Planking," *Air University Quarterly Review* (summer 1953): 128–32.
41. "Vehicles, Air Installations and Aviation Engineer Equipment and Facilities"; "Aircraft Maintenance and Servicing Equipment and Facilities."
42. Col Hugh J. Mattia, "Air Force Procurement in Japan," *Air University Quarterly Review* (fall 1953): 123–27. Because the United States could not produce all of the goods needed for MDAP, it turned to foreign, offshore manufacturers.

Logistic Support for Conducting Sustained Air Operations at Sea: The U.S. Navy Experience in Korea

Thomas Wildenberg

The idea of using underway replenishment as a means of keeping a carrier's air group continuously supplied at sea—so that air operations could be conducted on a continuous basis for an extended period without the fleet having to return to port—first emerged in the closing months of 1944 as the Fifth Fleet began preparing for the invasion of Iwo Jima and Okinawa.[1] Strategists planning the first assault on Japanese territory realized that both islands were close enough to Japan to receive direct air support from the home islands. To counter this threat, they directed the commander of the Fifth Fleet, Adm. Raymond A. Spruance, to undertake intensive air strikes against air bases in Japan proper during the assault to forestall the massive kamikaze counterattacks expected to follow the landing. Spruance, who planned to conduct the raids with the fast carriers of Task Force 58, was well aware of the logistic problem involved in keeping twelve or more aircraft carriers on station almost 2,000 miles from Ulithi, the nearest advanced base. The experience gained during the recently completed invasion of Leyte had shown that carrier-borne aircraft conducting powerful attacks on ground targets were likely to deplete the carrier's stores of ordnance after three or four days of concentrated action. He understood that it would be highly advantageous to replenish the force at sea to avoid the ten- to twelve-day turnaround that would otherwise have been required to steam back to Ulithi, replenish ammunition, and then return to station for further air strikes. Although refueling at sea was now a routine matter, no effort had been made to develop a means of transferring ammunition, provisions, or stores on a major scale. The ability to transfer large amounts of cargo among ships at sea would allow the task force to replenish its depleted stocks of ammunition without having to return to port.

In December, while plans for the invasion were still being formulated, Spruance directed his staff to develop a method for replenishing a carrier's ammunition at sea so it could stay on station for as long as needed.[2] Within weeks, the logistic planning staff devised a method to transfer cargo or ammunition at sea using the standard winches, booms, and cargo nets normally carried by a typical supply ship. The system, known as the Burton method, was first used operationally on February 23, 1945, when the ammunition ship USS *Shasta* (AE–6) transferred ammunition to the aircraft carrier USS *Bennington* (CV–20) during operations in support of the invasion of Iwo Jima.[3] Reprovisioning was not provided until March 26, when the cargo ship USS *Mercury* (AK–42) passed fifty-four tons of fresh food and other provisions to the ships of Task Force 58.

During the remaining months of World War II, the task force was free to remain on station almost indefinitely, although individual task groups were rotated periodically to Ulithi for routine upkeep and repair. After striking at Japan for one or two days, Task Force 58 would sail all night to rendezvous with the replenishment group at first light. During some days, as many as one hundred ships would be lined up along a forty-mile front as they steamed through the line of supply ships, coming alongside oilers, breaking away, then coming alongside ammunition ships, breaking away, then coming alongside stores ships, and breaking away. The task force would then spend the following night steaming to its next objective. Two days of air strikes required two nights and a day out of combat to replenish, but this was far shorter to the ten or twelve days out of combat required if the task force had to return to the nearest port.

In the demobilization in the years immediately after World War II, the U.S. Navy had to decommission large numbers of combatants and disassemble the immense logistic organization it had established during the war. The financial and personnel cutbacks were so severe during this time that the service was temporarily forced to abandon the concept of mobile logistic support that had enabled the fast carriers of the Fifth Fleet to remain at sea for weeks at a time.

By 1950, demobilization had drastically reduced the size of the U.S. Pacific Fleet. When the North Koreans invaded the Republic of South Korea on June 25, 1950, the USS *Valley Forge*, then operating in the Subic Bay area of the Philippines, was the only U.S. aircraft carrier in the western Pacific. The ship was immediately ordered to Buckner Bay, Okinawa (the nearest naval base of any size to Korea), to take on fuel, ammunition, and supplies before heading for the Sea of Japan to support U.S. forces in South Korea. The *Valley Forge*, with Carrier Air Group 5 (CAG–5) embarked, departed Buckner Bay on July 1, 1950, in company with elements of the Seventh Fleet, and began steaming toward the fighting.[4]

As the ship steamed toward the Korean peninsula, her air group began preparations to conduct air strikes against the North Koreans. CAG–5 was well prepared for this task because it had received extensive training in close air support before deploying on the *Valley Forge*. It was also the first Navy group to operate extensively with jet aircraft and had embarked with two sixteen-plane squadrons of Grumman F9F–3 Panther jet fighters modified to burn aviation gasoline (avgas), the only aviation fuel then carried aboard ship. In addition to the jets, the air group included two twelve-plane squadrons of Vought F4U–4B piston-powered Corsair fighter-bombers, one sixteen-plane squadron of the new Douglas AD–1 Skyraider attack plane, also piston powered, plus three detachments of ten highly specialized piston-powered aircraft configured for night fighting, radar warning, and photoreconnaissance.[5] The jets had never flown in combat, and their addition to the air group would pose several operational problems for the carrier.

The air group went into action for the first time on July 3, when it struck two enemy airfields at Pyongyang.[6] Air operations continued throughout the next day until an AD–1 without a tail hook bounded over the crash barrier, causing major damage to several aircraft parked on the forward end of the flight deck.[7]

Because no underway replenishment forces were in the Far East when hostilities commenced, the *Valley Forge* had to return to Buckner Bay for fuel and ammunition. Of the ten oilers assigned to the Service Force Pacific Fleet when hostilities began, two were on shuttle duty serving the Seventh Fleet and eight were in West Coast ports. Only one ammunition ship, the USS *Mount Katmai*, was available for this duty, but it was tied up at a pier in Port Chicago (now Concord), California.

As soon as the fighting broke out, Rear Adm. Francis C. Denebrink, the commander of the Service Force, immediately began to redeploy his ships to the Far East. By July 10, seven auxiliaries were headed north from the south Pacific, another six were on their way from Pearl Harbor, and seven more had departed from ports on the U.S. West Coast.[8] Such activity required a coordinating authority, so the CNO on that date established Service Squadron 3 (Servron–3). Capt. Bernard L. Austin was transferred from Servron–1 to take command of the new force that was gathering at Buckner Bay. Servron–3 quickly became principal logistic agent for the supply of all naval forces at sea in the western Pacific.

The need to keep *Valley Forge*, the only U.S. carrier then operating in Korean waters, close to the source of action brought a rapid return to refueling at sea. Despite a shortage of oilers, underway replenishment was quickly begun. The first of these operations was initiated on July 23, 1950, when the fleet oiler USS *Navasota* refueled the *Valley Forge* at sea, south of Cheju-do, transferring 20,184 barrels of fuel oil and 147,000 gallons of avgas to the carrier.[9] From then on, at least one oiler was on station continuously near the carrier's operating area to meet the fuel requirements of the carrier and her escorts.[10]

The availability of a standby oiler proved to be a godsend for the *Valley Forge*, the first U.S. carrier to conduct combat operations with jet aircraft. The two F9F squadrons assigned to CAG–5 used prodigious amounts of fuel. The jets—Grumman Panthers—burned avgas at a rate four times that used by their propeller-driven cohorts. Their huge appetite for fuel would have quickly drained the ship's supply of avgas had it not been for the *Navasota*, which topped off the the carrier's fuel tanks twice during her next cruise. Between July 16 and 31, the ship's planes burned more avgas (252,135 gallons)[11] than the ship carried

(231,650 gallons).[12] Although the number of hours flown by the jets was less than 20 percent of that flown by the propeller-driven aircraft on board, the Panthers burned almost half the avgas consumed during the entire cruise.[13]

By September, as the tempo of *Valley Forge*'s air operations increased, her jets were averaging thirty-six sorties a day, and the consumption of aviation fuel increased accordingly, reaching approximately 30,000 gallons a day.[14] This necessitated taking on of some 100,000 gallons every three or four days from one of the three oilers assigned to the fueling group that was now dedicated to the task of keeping the *Valley Forge* and her escorts loaded with fuel. By the end of the carrier's third deployment on station, the need to take on avgas had become critical in determining when and how often it needed to come alongside an oiler to top off her fuel tanks. As underway replenishment operations progressed, it quickly became apparent that the time needed for refueling was limited by the maximum rate at which gasoline could be transferred.

Fleet oilers were still using the same four-inch-diameter hose that had been used in World War II to pump gasoline from a single pumping station. This allowed the oiler to transfer avgas at approximately 27,000 gallons per hour.[15] If 100,000 gallons were required, the carrier had to stay alongside the oiler for at least four hours. The aviation fuel problem was so acute during the first six months of the fighting that, on at least two occasions, the time needed to top off the *Valley Forge*'s avgas supply exceeded five hours.[16] Also, gasoline replenishment was so frequent that it limited the *Valley Forge*'s replenishment rate to one day out of three, reducing by one-third her availability to conduct air operations. This was considered excessive in view of the trend in close air support and interdiction operations that required aircraft on station around the clock.

The addition of a second four-inch hose line to the oiler's underway replenishment gear and converting a second pumping station for the delivery of avgas offered a temporary solution by doubling the rate of fuel transfer and reducing the replenishment time. However, it did not solve the basic problems of avgas distribution because safety considerations involving this highly volatile fuel imposed severe limitations on tank pressures and linear flow rates for high-octane gasoline. It also contributed to the subsequent adoption of HEAF (JP–5) jet fuel, a much less volatile fuel, similar to kerosene.

As noted earlier, the USS *Mount Katmai*, the only ammunition ship available to the Seventh Fleet, had been tied up on the West Coast and did not arrive in the Far East until mid-August. In the interim, *Valley Forge* had to retire to Sasebo every few days to rearm from the cargo ship USS *Grainger* that had ferried ammunition there from the extensive naval facilities at Guam. The need to suspend air operations for two days—the time needed to steam to Sasebo, rearm, and return to the carrier's operating area—was eliminated once the *Mount Katmai* arrived on station.

Instead of the single Burton rig used in World War II, rearming of the carriers was accomplished using two rigs simultaneously: one from the No. 2 hatch, and the other from the No. 3 hatch, both on the port side. During the next ten weeks, *Mount Katmai* participated in twenty-seven rearming operations, transferring 3,270 short tons of ammunition to the carriers.[17] Eventually, both the ammunition ships (AEs) and carriers were outfitted with three transfer rigs instead of two, increasing the average transfer rate to 125 tons of ammunition per hour. The hazards of breaking out ammunition at sea on the AEs—converted merchant hulls from World War II—had not diminished. *Mount Katmai*, like the other AEs that served in Korea, were originally laid down by the United States Maritime Commission as C2 cargo ships. To achieve the high rate of transfer during these operations, it was necessary to break out the ammunition well in advance of the actual replenishment operation and arrange it on deck so that it would be readily accessible for Burtoning. When the seas become too rough to continue replenishment operations, the AE would be left facing heavy weather with hundreds of tons of ammunition loosely stowed on the weather deck. One commanding officer likened it to "trying to carry an egg on a spoon." Another problem experienced by the AEs, as well as the types of replenishment ships, was the frequent failure of their booms when the transfer wires stretched too far as the two ships rolled apart.[18]

The AE was not able to supply all of the carriers' needs all the time. In most cases, the rearming operation amounted to topping off the carriers stocks. When certain ammunition components were not available from the AE, the carrier had to dip into its own reserves. These, in turn, would be replenished later when the stores became available.

Until the end of October, *Mount Katmai* was the only AE available for replenishment duties. By then, two additional carriers—the USS *Philippine Sea* and the USS *Boxer*—had joined the *Valley Forge* assigned to Task Force 77. As a stopgap measure, two attack cargo ships (AKAs)—USS *Chara* (AKA–58) and the USS *Leo* (AKA–60) —were temporarily pressed into service until the USS *Paricutin* (AE–18) arrived at the end of October. The ammunition stowage spaces and handling facilities of these ships were inferior to those of the AEs in some instances and thus required the overloading of cargo. Movement of heavy ammunition from one hatch to another proved difficult on the AKAs because their cargo winches where not as capable as those on the AEs. The biggest shortcomings of these ships were their cargo holds which lacked the air conditioning systems and insulation specifically installed on the AEs to maintain the temperature of the ammunition during operations in the tropics. Fortunately, this deficiency did not mitigate their use in the cooler climate of Korea.[19]

As the operations of Task Force 77 increased in the Sea of Japan off Korea, refrigerated provisions ships (AFs) and stores ships (AKs) were added to the line of replenishment ships standing by to resupply the combatants with their proverbial beans, bullets, and black oil. Throughout the rest of conflict, the carriers and escorting destroyers of Task Force 77 were continually sustained at sea with fuel, ammunition, and stores by underway replenishment. The task force, which was on station in the Sea of Japan not far from the 39th parallel, would rendezvous with the underway replenishment group, one hundred miles south in the lee of Ullun Island, every fourth day. Replenishing an aircraft carrier was a long and somewhat treacherous task that required the carrier to come alongside and then break away from three different ships: an oiler for fuel, an ammunition ship for provisioning, and either a reefer or other ship for provisions—an operation that took from ten to twelve hours to complete. This was followed by many more hours of hard work by the large working party from the ship's crew (as many as 150 men were required) that had to strike down the ordnance and clear the hangar deck once the ordnance was on board. The alternative for the carriers would have been a round trip of 1,000 miles to the refurbished naval base at Yokosuka, Japan.[20]

A typical underway replenishment day would begin at dawn with the carrier pulling alongside an oiler to take on fuel oil and avgas. Two six-inch fuel oil lines and one four-inch gasoline line would be rigged between the ships, and 300,000 gallons of Navy special fuel oil and 150,000 gallons of avgas would be transferred while the two ships steamed side by side for approximately three hours. After breaking away from the oiler, the carrier would move to the next replenishment ship, perhaps an AF, typically on a thirty-day schedule. Provisions would be transferred using two Burton stations forward, placed on wooden skids and hauled by flight-deck tractors on the hangar deck aft. Supplies that arrived from the AF were separated into meats, vegetables, fruits, and dry stores. Provisions were passed below through all available hatches. On average, it would take another three hours to pass the 145 tons of provisions transferred during a typical replenishment operation. Lastly, the carrier would come alongside an AE, and 250 tons of ordnance would be passed to the ship via two Burton stations and at a modified hosefall rig farther aft that had been added to increase the transfer rate.

By the end of 1950, the oilers of Servron–3 had conducted one hundred carrier refuelings at sea during seventy-two meetings with the ships of Task Force 77. The USS *Mount Katami*, aided by the reactivated USS *Paricutin* and the AKAs *Chara* and *Leo*, had rearmed the force on fifty-four separate occasions. In six months of operations at sea, the underway replenishment group supplied the ships of Task Force 77 with 1,750,000 barrels of fuel oil, 7,182,000 gallons of avgas, 7,665 short tons of ammunitions, and transferred numerous passengers and miscellaneous commodities by highline.[21]

With carriers now on station for weeks at a time, the need for a timely delivery of high-priority items like mail, newspapers, and spare parts became paramount. To achieve this, the Navy initiated a small air shuttle service between airfields in Japan and the carriers at sea. The plane selected for this task was a modified version of the Grumman Avenger torpedo-bomber reconfigured into small transports redesignated TBM–3R.

The Turkey Transports (as the TBM–3Rs were unofficially called) were standard TBMs that had been field-modified for carrier onboard delivery of passengers and cargo. All of the plane's armament and heavy armor were removed, side-by-side seating was added in the "greenhouse" where the bombardier/radioman and gunner had sat before, and the fuselage space around the tunnel gun emplacement was modified into a small passenger cabin.[22] Replacing the 2,000-pound torpedo or four 500-pound bombs in the bomb bay, the aircraft now carried a specially designed wire-mesh screen basket tailored for cargo. The wire basket simplified stowage of cargo and ensured that it would not be damaged during takeoffs and landings. Regular bomb hoists were used to raise and lower the cargo basket, which could be completely removed to expedite loading and unloading.

The shuttle service was inaugurated in January 1951 when the aircraft assigned to Fleet Service Squadron 11 began making two trips a day. In April, the task was transferred to a detachment of Transport Squadron 21 that began operating six TBM–3Rs from Haneda, Japan, on the 12th.[23]

By the end of the Korean War, techniques used at sea to transfer fuel, ammunition, and provisions had improved tremendously. Task Force 77, which now included several aircraft carriers rotated so that one was always on station, was being routinely serviced every fourth day in approximately nine hours. Nighttime replenishment, which had been considered so dangerous as to be impracticable at the start of hostilities, became a normal occurrence, making replenishment operations possible at any time. The ability of a carrier and its task force to rearm, refuel, and reprovision regularly for only a few hours' steaming time from their operational area proved to be such a force multiplier that it enabled the carriers to more than double the pace of air operations. The increased operational performance of the USS *Valley Forge* (CVA–45) demonstrates this fact. In 1950, the *Valley Forge* was at sea for 16 days, from July 16 to 31. Ten of those days were spent on station, while on seven, air operations were performed. In 1953, it spent 28 days at sea from April 20 to May 17, of which twenty-two were spent on station and seventeen were given to air operations.

As a result of its experience with underway replenishment in Korea, the Navy continued to develop new methods and ships to improve the transfer rate of supplies, fuel, and ammunition, especially to the carriers, while reducing the vulnerability of such operations to the uncertainties of inclement weather. From the research emerged a new generation of one-stop underway replenishment ships that could supply all of the needs of a carrier task force, which led to the commissioning of the Navy's first replenishment fleet tankers and fast combat support ships. Among other innovations adopted were the use of the helicopter to transport troops quickly to shore and the concept for the roll-on–roll-off ship that would play such an important part in the logistic buildup in the Gulf War some forty years later.

Notes

1. Marvin O. Miller, John W. Hammett, and Torence P. Murphy, "The Development of the U.S. Navy Underway Replenishment Fleet," (hereafter Development of UNREP), paper presented at the Annual Meeting of the Society of Naval Architects and Marine Engineers, New York, N.Y., November 11–14, 1987, p 4.
2. Marvin O. Miller, "Stand By for Shotline," *Underway Replenishment Journal* (winter 1988): 2.
3. Worral Reed Carter, *Beans, Bullets, and Black Oil* (Washington, D.C.: Department of the Navy, 1952), pp 357–58
4. "The Valley Forge Story," *Naval Aviation News* (July 1952): 17.
5. The air group makeup was reconstructed using loses from the first cruise of the Valley Forge as recorded in the ship's deck log (RG-24, National Archives, College Park, Md.) and the "Organization of Carrier Air Group Five," on p 15 of the after-action report for Valley Forge for the period 16 July to 31, 1950, Aviation History Branch, Naval Historical Center (hereafter NHC), Washington, D.C.
6. "The Valley Forge Story," p 17.
7. Valley Forge Log Book, entry for 5 July 1950, RG-24, National Archives, College Park, Md.
8. James A. Field, Jr., *History of United States Naval Operations Korea* (Washington, D.C.: Department of the Navy, Naval History Division 1962), pp 81, 378; and "Commander in Chief U.S. Pacific Fleet Interim Evaluation Report No. 1, Period 25 June to 15 November 1950," Supporting Operations Section, Logistics (hereafter Interim Report No. 1), p 1172.
9. Valley Forge Log Book, entry for 23 July 1950.
10. Field, *History of United States Naval Operations Korea*, p 378.
11. Commanding Officer [USS Valley Forge (CV-45)] to Commander Seventh Fleet, Report of Operations 16 July to 31 July 1950 , date stamped 9 August 1950 (hereafter Valley Forge After-Action Report 16 July to 31 July 1950), tabulated data, enclosure 3, Aviation History Branch, NHC.
12. Norman Friedman, *U.S. Aircraft Carriers: An Illustrated Design History* (Annapolis, Md.: Naval Institute Press, 1983), Essex Class carrier characteristics, Appendix E, p 394.
13. Valley Forge After-Action Report 16 July to 31 July 1950, tabulated data, enclosure 3.
14. Commanding Officer [USS Valley Forge] to Chief of Naval Operations, Action Report for Period 6 through 21 September 1950, 4 October, 1950, p 2, Naval Aviation Historical Branch, NHC.
15. *Ibid.*
16. Interim Report no 1, p 1249.
17. *Ibid.*, p 1266.

18. Miller, *Underway Replenishment of Naval Ships* (Port Hueneme, Calif.: Underway Replenishment Department, Port Hueneme Division, Naval Surface Warfare Center, 1992), p 317; Miller, Hammett, and Murphy, Development of UNREP, p 5.
19. Interim Report no 1, pp 1250–52, 1258.
20. Marvin O. Miller, "Mobile Logistic Support for Aircraft Carriers," *Naval Engineers Journal* (Aug 1977): 55.
21. Field, *History of United States Naval Operations Korea*, p 380.
22. "'Turkeys' Now Transports," *Naval Aviation News* (Jul 1951): 25.
23. "'Turkeys' Now Transports," p 25; and Commanding Officer Fleet Service Squadron 11 to CNO, Historical Report for the Period 1 Jan to 1 July 1951, Fleet Service Squadron 11, Squadron Histories, Aviation History Branch, NHC.

Testing Vertical Envelopment in the Skies over Korea

James A. Ginther

When the North Korean Army poured over the 38th parallel in June 1950, the Marine Corps was in the midst of a doctrinal changeover. Leaving behind the massed sea-based amphibious assaults of World War II, the Marine Corps was focusing on a new role in the nuclear era as the nation's force-in-readiness. The goal was to project American military might anywhere in the world on short notice and hang on until reinforcements arrived. To accomplish this mission, Marine Corps planners had developed a new tactical doctrine called vertical envelopment. This doctrine envisioned assaulting an enemy from the sea with a widely dispersed force that was invulnerable to counterattack and landed with pinpoint accuracy via helicopters. In this scenario, helicopter transport squadrons would be the key, providing logistical support for the assault waves. No one, in or out of the Marine Corps, knew if such a tactical employment of helicopters would work. In Korea, the marines would find out.[1]

When the Korean War broke out, the idea of using helicopters in amphibious assaults was advanced in the report of a special board convened by Marine Corps Commandant Gen. Alexander A. Vandegrift, in response to the dangers posed by atomic weapons to massed amphibious landings of the kind seen in World War II.[2] Shortly thereafter, officers attached to the Marine Corps schools, including Colonels Victor H. Krulak and Edward C. Dyer, began talking to helicopter manufacturers Igor Sikorsky and Frank Piasecki. Both believed that the concept was sound and that eventually the aircraft could be developed to meet the Marine Corps goals.[3]

However, the enthusiasm of helicopter manufacturers and senior marine officers was not shared by the corps's pilots. Early on, few believed that the helicopter could ever be used effectively in combat, and many of the corps's young pilots were unwilling to risk their careers in developing the idea. Nonetheless, in November 1947, General Vandegrift ordered the formation of the corps's first helicopter squadron, HMX–1, under the command of Colonel Dyer. Dyer

First helicopter lift demonstration, Quantico (1948)

assembled men and aircraft, and by May 1948, HMX–1 had twelve officers and thirty-two enlisted men and was equipped with five Sikorsky HO3S helicopters. Despite these limited resources, that month the squadron participated in the first Marine Corps landing exercise to use helicopters, Operation Packard II.[4]

Packard II was an amphibious landing simulation designed to give students at the Marine Corps schools hands-on experience in command and employment of new tactics and techniques for amphibious attacks. With that in mind, shortly after HMX–1 was formed, conferences began to determine how the squadron might be used in the exercise. Four basic objectives were outlined: gather information on the practical problems involved in employing helicopters for ship-to-shore movement; develop planning procedures for employing helicopters in an amphibious landing; determine the details of coordinating a ship-to-shore movement by helicopter; and learn how the use of helicopters might affect recognized concepts of organization, command, and control in amphibious operations. The operation was complicated by a failure to appreciate the level of coordination required between marine helicopter units and ground and naval forces and by a lack of understanding of the very limited capabilities of the HO3S. Nonetheless, during the exercise, HMX–1 landed a regimental combat team (RCT) command post and simulated the delivery of follow-on waves of men and equipment. Although using only one helicopter to suggest the transport of successive series of troops and supplies, umpires declared the exercise a success, ruling that the helicopters had successfully landed and supplied an RCT.[5]

The information gathered from Packard II became the basis of the corps's first doctrinal publication on helicopter operations. In November 1948, the

Victor H. Krulak (left) and Edward C. Dyer (right)

Marine Corps schools distributed a manual, *Amphibious Operations: Employment of Helicopters*, more commonly known as PHIB–31. Written by Colonels Krulak and Dyer, its purpose was to guide what could be expected from helicopter squadrons in providing logistical support to an amphibious assault.[6]

Drawing on the lessons learned during Packard II, PHIB–31 outlined a planning process for helicopter operations, provided technical data on aircraft capabilities, and set forth command relationships and primary missions for helicopter units. PHIB–31 explained that helicopters would be used tactically "in a fashion quite similar to that now discharged by amphibian tractor units." Helicopter squadrons would be charged with four basically logistical missions: ship-to-shore movement of ground forces; command, control, reconnaissance, and observation flights; aerial resupply of ground forces; and evacuation of wounded.[7]

Shortly thereafter, the Marine Corps helicopter program bogged down due to technological limitations. HMX–1 continued to experiment and participate in Packard series exercises, but the helicopter transport squadrons envisioned by PHIB–31 failed to materialize. The outbreak of hostilities in Korea provided focus, a sense of urgency, and the opportunity to more effectively expedite this development. In July 1950, the same day the 1st Provisional Marine Brigade was activated for duty in Korea, HMX–1 detailed eight officers, thirty men, and four helicopters to the Marine Corps Air Station, El Toro, California. This contingent became part of the first composite aviation squadron in the Marine Corps, Marine Observation Squadron 6 (VMO–6) under the command of Maj. Victor J. Gottschalk. Shortly thereafter, the unit was deployed to Korea with the brigade. Its assignment was to reinforce U.S. Army, Republic of Korea (ROK), and U.N.

VMO–6 helicopters aboard the USS *Badoeng Strait*

troops holding the Pusan perimeter.[8]

The helicopters of VMO–6 saw immediate duty as logistical workhorses along the lines envisioned by PHIB–31. On the trip over, flying from the USS *Badoeng Strait,* the squadron's HO3S helicopters served the fleet by delivering guard mail and shuffling personnel ship-to-ship.[9] On arrival in Korea, the aircraft were instantly employed in a number of tasks, which made an immediate impression on brigade officers. The brigade commander, Brig. Gen. Edward A. Craig, recalled:

> One of the first [missions]…was on our right flank…. The reconnaissance platoon was…on a high mountain. They'd run into scattered Korean resistance up there. It must have been some kind of an outpost or lookout. The heat was very intense at this time of year in the perimeter there. They wanted these men evacuated, and they wanted a mortar together with other supplies. We put two helicopters on this job, and they had the supplies up to the top of the mountain in no time, and the heat cases back in the sick bay. And from that time on we really used these machines to the limit.[10]

Helicopters also made it possible for unit commanders to quickly and easily move among their scattered units and personally direct a rapidly developing combat situation, which otherwise would have been impossible with normal modes of overland and aerial transport. Gottschalk recalled:

> The Brigade commander in one instance was able to stop the Brigade at another front due to the changing situation. General Craig was able to move out, to stop the column, pick up the Battalion Commander, make a reconnaissance of the area to which the Brigade was assigned, pick out areas in which the troops would be deployed and pick out the command posts for the units involved. This job was accomplished in a period of less than two hours. Without the helicopter it is considered that these tasks would probably take at least two or three days.[11]

The report made by the 1st Provisional Marine Brigade on their first month of operations in Korea stated:

> All units praise the helicopter. Brigade states that it "has utilized helicopters for liaison, reconnaissance, evacuation of wounded, rescue of Marine flyers downed in enemy territory, observation, messenger service, [to] guard mail at sea, posting and supplying of outguards on dominant terrain features, and re-supplying of small units by air." Brigade recommends that "at least (8) liaison and (2) transport type helicopters be added to the observation squadron for employment by Marine divisions."...The present importance of the machine indicates, at least, that the possibilities of use may outrun its technical development.[12]

At Inchon, helicopters of VMO–6 were pivotal in evacuating the wounded and in moving men, supplies, and commanders, the first of these being perhaps the most important. Gottschalk recalled:

> The fighting being heavy many casualties were suffered. If the wounded had been carried several miles by jeep, then across the [Han] river by boat and again by jeep to Kimpo for air evacuation or to the Division hospital, it would have been too great an ordeal for many of the critically wounded suffering from loss of blood, shock or concussion. By the use of the helicopter, the total time elapsed from the request of a Battalion or Regimental forward air controller for a helicopter until the patient reached the hospital was only ten or fifteen minutes. These evacuations in almost unbelievably short time were credited directly by the Division Surgeon with saving the lives of scores of wounded.[13]

VMO–6 helicopter performing a medical evacuation.

Casualty transport was not limited to 1st Division troops. On many occasions, the squadron's helicopters evacuated the wounded from the 1st Cavalry Division and other elements of the Eighth Army which had advanced so rapidly that they had outdistanced their medical facilities.[14]

Liaison flights also continued to be important assignments. The first allied aircraft that landed at the Kimpo airfield was an HO3S flown by Capt. Victor Armstrong and bearing Assistant Commandant of the Marine Corps Lt. Gen. Lemuel C. Shepherd and 1st Marine Division Operations Officer Col. Victor H. Krulak. General Almond, in command of the U.S. Army X Corps, also used the marine helicopters to make personal visits to division, regimental, and battalion commanders to evaluate the current situation and give directions. After observing the squadron's operations at Inchon, Shepherd reported:

> There are no superlatives adequate to describe the general reaction to the helicopter. Almost any individual questioned could offer some personal story to emphasize the valuable part played by the five HO3S planes available. Reconnaissance, liaison, visual flank security, movement of security patrols from one key locality to the next, posting and supply of security detachments, and many more. There is no doubt that the enthusiasm voiced by the brigade is entirely warranted. Moreover, the usefulness of the helicopter is not by any means confined to a situation such [as] encountered in Korea. No effort should be spared to get helicopters 'larger than the HO3S if possible' but helicopters in any form, to the theater at once and on a priority higher than any other weapon…helicopters, more helicopters, and more helicopters in the Korean area![15]

Enthusiasm for the new aircraft could go too far, however. After the landing at Wonsan, due to the force's rapid advance and dispersion, the helicopters of VMO–6 were distributed among the regiments either through assignment or loan. Local commanders began using the asset frivolously to evacuate men who needed minor medical attention, to recover the dead, and as personal jeeps.[16]

To remedy this, 1st Division commander, Maj. Gen. O. P. Smith, recalled the helicopters. He returned direct divisional control to the squadron and created a staff position for an air officer who would monitor requests for helicopter support submitted through the tactical air request net and then prioritize them according to aircraft availability. From this time forward, it was made clear that marine helicopters were to be used as tactical tools in tasks specifically germane to the vertical envelopment concept, not simply as a sort of flying truck.[17]

During the Chosin Reservoir campaign, VMO–6 aircraft provided the only reliable means of contact between the five scattered pockets of marines around the reservoir. They flew seriously wounded marines from Yudam-ni to Hagaru-ri for evacuation to hospitals, saving many lives that would have otherwise been lost. During the breakout and withdrawal, the squadron evacuated the seriously wounded from the column, freeing troops to fight. Gottschalk believed this lib-

VMO–6 helicopter at Chosin

eration of manpower reduced the vulnerability of the column to enemy attack and contributed directly to the movement's success.[18]

VMO–6 operations during the first year of the war proved that helicopters could be used in moving and supplying troops, evacuating the wounded, and supplementing the ability of commanders to control field operations. However, the squadron was limited in its effectiveness by its aircraft. The HO3S–1 could carry only one wounded man or three passengers per flight, or a very small payload of supplies or equipment. Moreover, it was slow and unable to fly safely at night. If the Marine Corps were to realize its vision of amphibious assaults by vertical envelopment, specifically organized and equipped helicopter transport squadrons would have to prove their ability to accomplish these logistical missions on a much larger scale.[19]

In July 1951, anticipating the arrival of a fully equipped helicopter transport squadron, 1st Marine Division and VMO–6 personnel met and formulated a tentative operating procedure for the use of a transport squadron in Korea.[20] On August 15, 1951, the Marine Corps's first helicopter transport squadron, HMR–161, sailed from San Diego for duty in Korea. It landed on September 10 and immediately went into operation from the same field as that used by VMO–6. On the 13th, it performed the first major helicopter resupply operation in history, Operation Windmill.[21] The operation reports states:

> the Division was heavily engaged with enemy forces in a relatively inaccessible mountain area. Supply was extremely difficult because of unde-

Operation Windmill (1950)

> veloped communication routes, enemy interdiction of existing roads and extraordinarily rugged terrain. Casualties had been heavy and evacuation was serious problem. During the night of 12–13 September, it became apparent that supplementary logistical effort was required to support the 1st Marine Regiment. Under other circumstances it would be necessary either to call for a parachute drop or to increase greatly the native bearer compliment assigned to the regiment. The situation represented a clear opportunity to exploit the mobility of the helicopter.[22]

A planning conference held on the morning of September 13—which was attended by Division Chief of Staff Colonel Krulak, operations officer Col. Bruce T. Hemphill, logistics officer Col. Frank P. Hager, Division air officer Maj. Edward V. Finn, shore party commander Lt. Col. George G. Pafford, and HMR–161 skipper Lt. Col. George W. Herring—established the parameters of the mission.[23] HMR–161 would airlift a day's supplies for a reinforced battalion, Lt. Col. John E. Gorman's 1st Battalion, 1st Marines. The distance to be covered was seven miles. Herring's helicopters were to deliver supplies on the outbound leg and evacuate casualties on the return trip. The 1st Marines were to select a drop site, and Pafford's shore party would use its recently formed helicopter support team—composed of sections for the embarkation point and the landing point—to assemble, organize, and load supplies and casualties and keep the flow moving on each end of the operation.[24]

Keith McCutcheon, Korea, Commanding HMR–161

On the morning of September 13, the Embarkation Point Section began to segregate a day's rations, water, ammunition, signal supplies, field fortification materials, and medical supplies for a reinforced company into balanced helicopter loads for delivery. Loading commenced at 1520, and within a half hour four helicopters loaded with the Landing Point Section and seven additional supply bearers were ready to lift off. Remaining provisions were loaded into cargo nets beneath the helicopters in "flying crane lifts" for delivery on succeeding trips.[25]

At 1610, the first helicopters began arriving at the landing point, a spot on the reverse slope of a hill 600 feet above the valley floor, behind the perimeter of the 1st Marines. The landing site previously scouted was unsatisfactory, and the squadron had to disembark the Landing Point Section by hovering with two wheels touching on the slope until the party could clear the landing area. It took approximately thirty minutes to clear a twenty- by forty-foot area and mark the helicopter landing zone and the cargo drop point with fluorescent "Y" and "T" panels. The team then quickly set up a dump area for supplies and an assembly area for sorting casualties for transport. Shortly thereafter, helicopters began landing at two-minute intervals. Within one minute, each aircraft discharged its cargo and reloaded with an average of two stretcher cases and five ambulatory patients. Supplies were sorted and immediately issued to waiting troops. During the course of the operation, which required just over three hours, the eleven helicopters of HMR–161 delivered 18,848 pounds of supplies (including the shore party) and evacuated seventy-four casualties.[26] Krulak recalled, "HMR–161 bailed out the 1st Marines, delivered the essential supplies necessary to maintain the momentum of the attack, hauled out its casualties and, for our money, the helicopters were in business."[27]

One week later, the same team conducted an identical operation, Windmill II. The operation concluded successfully, and division planners began preparing the squadron's next test: transporting troops.[28]

Operation Summit focused on moving a reinforced company. A period of heavy action resulted in the 1st Marine Division taking responsibility for a zone previously under the control of the 8th and 11th ROK Divisions. Terrain was mountainous and subject to observation and fire as well as to incursion by small units. A reconnaissance was necessary to determine the ground's tactical potential and to effect a linkup with the ROK units being relieved. Nine hours would be required for the division's reconnaissance company to reach the area on foot, so HMR–161 was tasked with moving the men and initial supplies to the division's right flank, near Hill 884.

Aerial reconnaissance flights found the only possible landing site, located 584 feet above the valley floor, but it would have to be cleared and would then accommodate only one helicopter at a time. The decision was made to land a squad from the reconnaissance company to secure the area and then insert the Helicopter Landing Point Team, dropping them down by knotted ropes from the lead helicopters. An orbiting helicopter managed inbound and outbound air traffic control, and follow-on waves landed the rest of the reconnaissance company. Each helicopter carried five fully equipped combat troops. In four hours, the squadron lifted 224 troops and 17,772 pounds of cargo into the landing site and evacuated one casualty. The success of the operation converted many of the remaining helicopter skeptics in the division.[29]

Krulak would tell an audience at the Marine Corps schools four months later, "The 'Doubting Thomases' who had said, 'Everybody knows that you can carry boxes and bails in a helicopter,' then had to admit you could carry Marines and BARs [Browning automatic rifles]."[30] These fundamental tests of the capabilities of the marine helicopter transport squadron drew high praise. As 1st Division reported:

> These initial efforts have demonstrated strikingly the great contribution to tactical and logistical flexibility that the assault helicopter offers. The three operations…resulted in a measure of enthusiasm on all sides which leaves little doubt but that the helicopter functions will be progressively enlarged as time passes and that the aircraft type must be recognized as a requisite component of a balanced military force. Comments by using personnel emphasize their usefulness as an element of the amphibious task force, and it is on developments in that field that the greatest possible emphasis should be placed.[31]

Over the next few months, HMR–161 gradually expanded the scope of its operations, adding new elements to these two basic mission types. Operation Blackbird was similar to Summit but with the added the dimension of darkness. In Operation Bumblebee, information was gathered on the time and planning necessary to move an entire battalion into an operational area. Operation Houseburner tested the ability to deliver troops for the destruction of specific targets, in this case abandoned houses being used by guerrillas for shelter. Operation Bushbeater targeted the guerrillas themselves, using helicopters to deliver and recover infantry companies sweeping areas for enemy activity. The operation used the tactic of dropping one squad on the ground to search for the guerrillas while covering it with machine guns in a second airborne helicopter. It convinced division planners that helicopter-borne troops could be used to perform rear area mop-up

Operation Houseburner (1951)

and security patrol missions.[32] However, this series of antiguerrilla operations hit a sour note with at least one military unit, the I ROK Corps. Krulak remembered that the commander of the I ROK Corps told him that he resented these operations for two reasons. "First we chased all the guerrillas into his area, and second we refused to lend him the 'copters to chase them back."[33]

Slowly and methodically, marine helicopter pilots were convincing ground commanders of the value of helicopter transport squadrons, or assault helicopter squadrons as referred to frequently in reports. Herring wrote HMX–1 commander Col. Keith McCutcheon, "[1st Marine Division Commander] General [Gerald C.] Thomas and Col. Krulak are solidly behind us as regards our theories and ideas for employing HMR's. They authorize our use only for tactical operations and emergency supply missions for attacking units. Krulak frequently refers to us as the Division's strategic reserve."[34]

HMR–161 scored its greatest logistical success, however, during November in Operation Switch. Capitalizing on the lessons of Operation Bumblebee, HMR–161 was tasked to relieve the 2d Battalion, 5th Marines by replacing it with the 2d Battalion, 1st Marines. All movement of troops in and out of the combat zone was to be by helicopter. Beginning in the early morning hours of November 11, the twelve helicopters of HMR–161 transported 950 combat-equipped men to Hill 884 and returned 952 to landing strip X–83 in ten hours.[35]

Colonel McCutcheon arrived at HMR–161 headquarters in early December 1951, replacing Herring and just in time to participate in Operation Farewell.[36] For this mission, HMR–161 again operated in the area of Hill 884 and transported the 1st Battalion, 5th Marines to the front in relief of the 2d Battalion, 5th

Marines. The next month proved a busy one for the squadron. Operation Muletrain was conducted to resupply the 1st Battalion, 5th Marines on Hill 884. It revealed that, in some cases, things could go only too well. Delivering cargo in nets, the helicopters moved the 159,730 pounds of provisions so quickly that the 580 Korean laborers who had been accustomed to the previous pace found it difficult to sort and efficiently distribute the supplies.[37]

McCutcheon's first month of command concluded with two more operations of significance. Operation Changie-Changie expanded on the battalion relief experiment conducted during Operation Farewell. However, multiple company pick-up and drop-off sites were used to relieve the battalion, rather than having the battalion assemble at a single designated area. The second operation, Mousetrap, built on Houseburner and Bushbeater. This time, HMR–161 provided helilift on an on-call basis with minimal prior planning to troops engaged in antiguerrilla operations in the Korean countryside.[38]

By February 1952, the operations of HMR–161 had become routine. On February 24, the squadron carried the 1st Battalion, 7th Marines to the now familiar landing sites on Hill 884 during Operation Rotate. The operation ran so smoothly that historian Lynn Montross commented that little of significance was gained from it in terms of learning anything new about helicopter operations.[39]

Operation Rotate marked the end of HMR–161 operations in Korea's Punchbowl area. During its initial six months of operation, the squadron lifted 14,072 marines, delivered 1,659,239 pounds of supplies, and evacuated 293 wounded personnel. In mid-March, HMR–161, along with the rest of the 1st Marine Divi-

Operation Rotate (1951)

sion, moved 180 miles west into the I Corps area, where the division would anchor the western end of the line held by the Eighth Army. The forward operational echelon of HMR–161 relocated to a site near Field A–17. Its headquarters and support facilities settled in at Field A–33 near Ascom City. Shortly thereafter, the squadron embarked on a series of successful operations that would have far-reaching effects on the evolution of the concept of Marine Corps vertical envelopment.[40]

During April, HMR–161 executed Operations Pronto, Leapfrog, and Circus, each yielding valuable data regarding helicopter transport under combat conditions. Operation Pronto was designed to test the squadron's ability to provide large-scale troop transport into a combat zone on an on-call basis. In this maneuver, HMR–161 lifted 622 fully equipped troops of the 2d Battalion, 7th Marines to an area six miles from its initial location with little previous notice and no coordinated planning between air and ground forces. In fact, McCutcheon noted in the report on Pronto that the squadron had only three hours notice of the lift and "not so much as a phone call between the units involved." He concluded, "This airlift more than any other in which HMR–161 has participated, proved that a Marine Transport Helicopter squadron can successfully operate intact as an 'on call' tactical tool."[41] It also demonstrated the comfort level now attained between the squadron and division infantry units working together in such movements. In all previous operations, detailed planning and significant advanced notice had been customary in arranging the squadron's large troop transports. The Pronto lift set a new standard for helicopter transport operations.[42]

Operation Leapfrog added two new dimensions to the problem of troop transport: water and the language barrier presented by the participation of marines from two different nations. HMR–161's task this time was to lift the 5th Battalion, ROK Marines over the Han River to the Kimpo peninsula to relieve the rad Battalion, ROK Marines. The lift covered a distance of only six miles or so, but it was the first attempt at using helicopters to carry troops over water. During the operation, all passengers and crew wore life jackets, the cargo doors of the aircraft remained open to facilitate escape, and marine amphibious trucks stood by in the river to conduct rescue operations. HMR–161 accomplished the mission in just under three and a half hours. In his report, McCutcheon wrote that the exercise proved the feasibility of using helicopters for short-distance transport over water. He also noted that the language barrier proved to be no problem when conducting transport operations. Moreover, the smaller stature and lighter weight of the Koreans made it possible to move more Korean marines than U.S. marines per flight.[43] Circus was essentially a rerun of Leapfrog, only this time it was American troops of the 1st Battalion, 7th Marines who were involved in the move.[44]

By summer 1952, operations along the main line of resistance became static. The ultimate goal of the marines' helicopter experiments in Korea was to test the

Marlex I (1952)

ability of a helicopter squadron to provide logistical support for a vertical envelopment–type amphibious assault. Because no operational need existed to conduct such an assault, an exercise was developed to simulate one. On June 10 and 11, the squadron participated in Marlex I. Its purpose was to test the possibility of delivering troops by helicopter in conjunction with an amphibious assault. In this instance, HMR–161 lifted I Company, 3d Battalion, 5th Marines onto a target beach as other elements of the 1st Marine Division made a simultaneous amphibious landing. Because the Navy could not spare a carrier for the operation, the island of Sung Bong-do substituted as a loading zone for the helicopters, and the vertical and amphibious assaults were made on nearby Tokchok-do.[45]

Over the course of two days, the squadron landed 475 troops in just a little over nine hours of operational time. After the original event, a series of Marlex exercises was conducted, each reinforcing the Marine Corps belief in the future of vertical envelopment as a technique for amphibious assault. Three months later, in the most successful of these, Marlex VII, HMR–161 would double the numbers it generated in the first Marlex exercise. In a little over four and a half hours of operational time, half the time of the original, over a two-day period, the squadron landed 912 troops and 52 weapons.[46]

In spring of 1953, HMR–161 conducted the most ambitious marine helicopter supply operation during the war. Operation Haylift II was designed to test the ability of the squadron to simultaneously supply two marine regiments by helicopter alone for a period of five days. During the course of the exercise, HMR–161 helicopters lifted more than 800 tons (1,612,306 pounds) of supplies to the regiments, delivering 200 tons of that total in a single day.[47]

In operation after operation, experiments conducted by the Marine Corps helicopter squadrons in Korea proved the combat utility of the helicopter. Whether moving commanders to trouble spots, lifting men and supplies, or evacuating the wounded, the marines proved that helicopters could operate safely, effectively, and efficiently in a sustained combat environment. Refuting doubts of ground and air officers alike, the capabilities of Marine Corps helicopter squadrons expanded during the period, taking them from being little more than experimental demonstration teams to providing the sole logistical support for two engaged marine regiments on the main line of resistance. In doing so, helicopter squadrons won a place in the Marine Corps arsenal. The marines converted not only their own cadre but Eighth Army and U.N. observers as well.[48] In the future, no balanced combat force would be considered complete without helicopter squadrons.

Marine helicopter operations proved so successful from a logistical standpoint that the danger was that these new aircraft would become essentially flying trucks. However, the corps wanted something more. In Korea, Marine Corps helicopter operations were conducted more or less as a series of experiments aimed at determining the validity of a new Marine Corps warfighting doctrine, vertical envelopment. Pointedly, in the reports on helicopter operations, despite their naval designation as transport squadrons, Marine Corps commanders referred to these units as "assault helicopter squadrons." Although at the heart of the vertical envelopment doctrine lay a requirement for helicopter squadrons that could land and logistically sustain amphibious assault forces in a hostile environment until help arrived, the purpose of the squadrons was the tactical on-call projection of combat force, not the routine movement of men and supplies. Senior marine air and ground officers alike worked hard to maintain this focus in their choice of operations. The success of these experiments set the tone for future Marine Corps planning and helicopter operations. Moreover, they proved the validity of the concept behind the vertical envelopment doctrine, suggesting that amphibious assaults could play a key role in projecting American military power in the Cold War era.

For the Marine Corps, this could not have been better news. Proof of the success of vertical envelopments suggested that amphibious warfare and amphibious forces could survive a World War III. Amphibious assault could now be viewed as a timely and effective means of projecting American military might into the world's trouble spots. The Marine Corps, on the verge of extinction at war's end, thus received a new lease on life as the nation's premier force-in-readiness.

Notes

1. For a good explanation of the Marine Corps view of itself as a force-in-readiness during the Korean War, see Clifton B. Cates, "The Role of the Marine Corps in Global War," folder 1, box 16, Lecture Collection, Research Collection, Marine Corps University Research Archives, Gray Research Center, Quantico (hereafter MCU Research Archives). For detailed descriptions of the early days of the Marine Corps helicopter programs, see Victor H. Krulak, interview by Benis M. Frank, Jun 12, 1970, transcript, Washington, D.C.: History and Museums Division, hqs, U.S. Marine Corps, 1973, and Edward C. Dyer, interview by Benis M. Frank, Aug 7, 1973, transcript, Washington, D.C.: History and Museums Division, hqs, U.S. Marine Corps, 1973.
2. The board was composed of Maj Gens Lemuel C. Shepherd, Field Harris, and Oliver P. Smith, and a secretariat that included Cols Merrill B. Twining, Edward C. Dyer, and Lt Col Clair W. Shisler. See Eugene W. Rawlins and William J. Sambito, *Marines and Helicopters 1946–1962*, (Washington, D.C. History and Museums Division, hqs, U.S. Marine Corps, 1976), pp 11–13. For a full discussion of the perceived threats of atomic weapons to amphibious assaults, see Roy S. Geiger, "Report on Able and Baker Atomic Bomb Tests Held at BIKKINI, July 1946" in folder 2, box 18, Oliver P. Smith Papers, Personal Papers Collection, MCU.
3. Benis M. Frank, interview of Edward C. Dyer, Aug 7, 1973, transcript, (Washington, D.C.: Historical Division, Headquarters, U.S. Marine Corps, 1973), p 199; and Benis M. Frank interview of Victor H. Krulak, Jun 12, 1970, transcript (Washington, D.C.: Historical Division, hqs, U.S. Marine Corps, 1973), pp 115–16.
4. Dyer interview, pp 209–10, 216; Krulak interview, pp 116–17; and Rawlins and Sambito, *Marines and Helicopters*, p 24.
5. Report on Operation Packard II, folder 14, box 35, Exercise Collection, Research Collection, MCU Archives.
6. Krulak interview, p 116.
7. *Amphibious Operations: Employment of Helicopters*, (Quantico, Va.: Marine Corps Schools, 1948), p 3.
8. Rawlins and Sambito, *Marines and Helicopters*, pp 30–39; and Montross, *Cavalry of the Sky: The Story of U.S. Marine Combat Helicopters*, (New York: Harper & Brothers, Publishers, 1954), pp 101–105, 107.
9. Vincent J. Gottschalk, "Transcript of Informal Remarks of Major Victor J. Gottsschalk, USMC, Former CO of VMO-6, 1st MAW at HQMC, May 17, 1951" in folder 8, box 12, Korean War Collection, Research Collection, MCU Research Archives, Gray Research Center, Quantico, p 2.
10. L. E. Tatem, interview with Edward A. Craig, May 16, 1968, transcript (Washington, D.C.: Historical Division, hqs, U.S. Marine Corps), p 168.

11. Gottschalk, p 4.
12. Consolidation of Comments and Recommendations Made in Special Action Report 1st Provisional Marine Brigade, FMF 2 August–6 September 1950, Operations with Eighth U.S. Army, Korea," folder 23, box 1, Korean War Collection, Research Collection, MCU Archives.
13. Gottschalk, pp 8–9.
14. *Ibid.*, p 9.
15. Shepherd report quoted in Montross, *Cavalry of the Sky*, pp 135–36.
16. *Ibid.*, p 133-42.
17. *Ibid.*, p 13.
18. Montross, *Cavalry of the Sky*, p 142; and Gottschalk, p 15.
19. Gary W. Parker and Frank M. Batha, *A History of Marine Observation Squadron Six* (Washington, D.C. History and Museums Division, hqs, U.S. Marine Corps, 1982), p 14.
20. "Type 'C' Special Report: Employment of Helicopters," Oct 4, 1951, folder 4, box 14, Korean War Collection, Research Collection, MCU Archives, Appendix 1, p 1 (hereafter Type C Report, Oct 4, 1951).
21. Montross, *Cavalry of the Sky*, pp 157–59; and Type C Report.
22. Type C Report, pp 1–2.
23. Lynn Montross, Hubbard D. Kuokka, and Norman Hicks, *U.S. Marine Operations in Korea, 1950–1953*, vol 4, *The East-Central Front* (Washington, D.C.: Historical Branch, G-3, hqs, U. S. Marine Corps, 1962), pp 269–70, 305.
24. Type C Report, pp 2–3.
25. *Ibid.*
26. Type C Report, pp 3–5; and Montross, *Cavalry of the Sky*, pp 159–62.
27. Victor H. Krulak, "Text of lecture given by Colonel V. H. Krulak, USMC to Senior School, 15 February 1952," folder 2, box 16, Lecture Collection, Research Collection, Marine Corps University Research Archives, Gray Research Center, Quantico, p 9.
28. Type C Report, pp 5–6.
29. *Ibid.*, pp 7–14
30. Krulak lecture, p 10.
31. *Ibid.*, p 13.
32. Type C Report Enclosure I, pp 1–17.
33. Krulak, p 12
34. George W. Herring to Keith Barr McCutcheon, Sep 27, 1951, folder 4, box 6, McCutcheon Papers.
35. Montross, *Cavalry of the Sky*, pp 174–75.
36. Operation Farewell was so named because it was the squadron's last operation under the command of Lt Col George Herring. Keith B. McCutcheon to Lynn Montross, Jul 20, 1953, McCutcheon Papers.
37. Montross, *Cavalry of the Sky*, p 177.

38. *Ibid.*, p 178.
39. *Ibid.*, pp 178–79.
40. *Ibid.*, pp 180–81.
41. Keith Barr McCutcheon to John T. Selden, "Operation Pronto, report on," Apr 22, 1953, folder 9, box 31, McCutcheon Papers.
42. Montross, *Cavalry of the Sky*, p 184.
43. Keith Barr McCutheon to John T. Selden, "Operation Leapfrog, report on," Apr 28, 1953, folder 9, box 31, McCutcheon Papers; and Montross, *Cavalry of the Sky*, pp 184–85.
44. Montross, *Cavalry of the Sky*, p 185.
45. *Ibid.*, p 187.
46. *Ibid.*, pp 187–89; and HMR-161 Report on Marlex VII, Sep 12, 1952, Korean War Command Chronologies, digitized copy, MCU Archives.
47. Edwin A. Pollock, "Logistics Support to Two MLR Infantry Regiments by Helicopter," folder 13, box 19, Korean War Collection, Research Collection, MCU Archives; and Pat Meid and James M. Young, *U.S. Marine Corps Operations in Korea, 1950–1953*, vol. 5, *Operations in West Korea* (Washington, D.C.: Historical Division, hqs, U.S. Marine Corps, 1972), p 497.
48. Meid and Young, *Operations in West Korea*, p 496; and Robert F. Futrell, *The United States Air Force in Korea, 1950–1953* (Washington, D.C.: Office of Air Force History, 1983), pp 569–72.

Transportation in the Korean War

Benjamin D. King

The North Korean invasion of South Korea on the morning of June 25, 1950, caught both South Korea and the United States completely by surprise. Well trained, well equipped, and well motivated, the North Korean Army quickly overran major portions of South Korea. At the outset, U.S. planners naively believed that a show of force would dissuade the North Koreans from continuing their invasion and, on June 30, flew a battalion-size task force under the command of Lt. Col. Charles B. Smith to Korea. Only six C–54 aircraft were available, and these planes had to make ten trips to move Smith's command. A few days later, Task Force Smith took up position at Osan Air Base. There, on July 5, it was routed by a division-size North Korean force that was better trained and better equipped. Thus, in a few short days, the United States was stripped of its illusions concerning the situation in Korea and the condition of the U.S. Army as a whole. In the following weeks, additional U.S. forces were committed piecemeal and suffered a similar fate. Like Task Force Smith, most of the units in the U.S. Army committed to Korea were undermanned and short of equipment. Much of the existing equipment was left over from World War II and worn out. To make matters worse, the available troops were trained for occupation duty rather than for combat. When President Harry Truman decided to aid the South Koreans, the four divisions occupying Japan—the 7th, 24th, and 25th Infantry Divisions and the 1st Cavalry Division—were the nearest U.S. forces to Korea and were the ones first selected to respond to the crisis.

The 24th Division was the first to deploy to the war zone, and its condition was typical of all the units stationed in Japan. It was organized on triangular lines, and, although it had all three of its authorized infantry regiments, each regiment had only two of three authorized battalions. The division artillery was similarly below strength, with four battalions, but each had only two batteries instead of three. The division armored battalion was in the worst shape. It had only one company of tanks instead of three, and it was equipped with the M–24 light tank, instead of the more modern M–26 medium version. The division antiaircraft artillery battalion was also short of guns. In some cases, modern equipment in the pipeline had not yet reached the division. For antitank defense, the infantry of the 24th Division was equipped with the 2.36-inch rocket launcher instead of the new 3.5-inch rocket launcher. Both the M–24 light tank and the 2.36-inch rocket launcher were World War II–era weapons, considered only marginally effective by the end of that war. The divisions also experienced shortages of 4.2-inch mortar ammunition and trucks.[1] In all, most units had, at best, 60 percent of their combat strength.

The shortages of troops and equipment and the distance of Korea from the continental United States meant that transportation was a critical issue from the beginning of the conflict. Except for the four understrength divisions in Japan, nearly all of the equipment and manpower had to come from the United States. Fortunately, transportation was the one resource in which the United States from the beginning held an advantage over North Korea. While the North Koreans were closer to the combat theater and had at their disposal a large stockpile of weapons, they lacked the ability to support a major war without outside assistance and resources. Recovering from a long civil war, communist China was not able to produce enough steel and other military commodities for its own uses, let alone enough to assist North Korea. Consequently, most of the resources supporting the North Korean effort had to come from the Soviet Union. The distances from major Soviet industrial areas ranged from 4,000 to 5,000 miles, which required a ten- to twelve-day trip by railroad. This meant that approximately 14,000 tons could be carried daily over the rail network.[2]

Once cargo was delivered to a rail head, the North Koreans lacked the capability to clear it in a timely manner. Supply by sea, from the Soviet port of Vladivostok, was not a viable alternative. Neither Hungnam nor Wonsan, on North Korea's eastern coast, could support a major supply effort, and the United States and its allies controlled the seas.

In addition to controlling the seas, the United States had several other advantages. It had in Japan an excellent staging area with a good transportation system that featured railroad centers away from the combat area and an industrial base that could support the repair of major end items and provide hospital care. In Korea the United States enjoyed the use of Pusan, the largest port in the country and one capable of handling the cargo necessary to support an army in the field. Unlike during World Wars I and II, the U.S. Army had an established transportation corps and school. The importance of an existing transportation corps cannot be underestimated because it meant that the equipment, doctrine, and skilled personnel necessary to support the effort in Korea were already in place. It also meant that a school and training infrastructure could expand the corps when necessary. The advantages of having such an organization were not lost on the Truman administration. On June 28, the Transportation Corps became a permanent branch of the U.S. Army.

Unfortunately, Far East Command failed to capitalize on the expertise of the Transportation Corps during the early stages of the commitment to Korea. While theater commanders were consistently faced with the conundrum of how much combat power and how much support to bring ashore in the early stages of the deployment, major transportation units did not arrive in theater until a month after the opening of hostilities. Likewise, the 2d Logistics Command was not established until two months after the start of hostilities. The seriousness of not having established combat service support units on the ground was aptly demonstrated by the move of 25th Division to the southern end of the Pusan perimeter, as discussed later.

Shipping and Terminal Operations

The primary mode of transportation to Japan and Korea was by sea. The port that provided the most support was the San Francisco port of embarkation (SFPOE), which was subordinate to the chief of transportation. Located at the SFPOE was the Overseas Supply Division (OSD) of the Department of the Army's Deputy Chief of Staff, Logistics. The OSD was staffed by representatives of the Quartermaster, Ordnance, and Chemical branches to oversee the movement and requisition of their classes of supply. During the war, the OSD processed more than 98,000 requisitions a month from Korea.[3] The bulk of the 31.5 million tons of supplies and approximately 70 percent of the troops went to the combat theater by sea, most of it via Liberty and Victory ships. The Liberty and Victory ships had a capacity of 6,000 to 7,000 tons each and took 16 to 20 days to reach Korea. In the deployment phase of the Korean War, SFPOE saw its monthly tonnage shipped jump from 94,000 tons in June to 501,823 in August 1950. In that month, SFPOE also shipped 10,238 tanks, trucks, and other vehicles.[4] This was almost triple the peak monthly outload during World War II, and it was achieved with very little increase in manpower, a tribute to having a military transportation infrastructure in place.

As with all other ports that the U.S. Army operated in the twentieth century, Pusan and the other Korean ports posed three major problems never completely solved during hostilities. Port congestion, the most serious among them, was due to an inexperienced work force, large storage depots located too close to the discharge areas, and, most importantly, too few transportation assets dedicated to port clearance. In the initial stages of the war, lack of an experienced work force led to very low discharge rates. By U.S. Army standards, a crew of eighteen men needed fourteen days to unload a Victory or Liberty ship. In the early stages of the Korean War, discharge rates were far slower. At one time, the Port of Inchon recorded thirty-six ships that averaged twenty-two days to unload.[5]

In July, the 8057th Provisional Port Company discharged 309,000 tons of cargo. This daily average of less than 10,000 tons a day was at a port with the capability of discharging 45,000 tons a day. Another factor contributing to the reduced discharge rate was the shortage of watercraft and lighterage. Gen. Omar Bradley, the first chairman of the Joint Chiefs of Staff to be named after World War II, was convinced that the U.S. armed forces would never again have to make a large amphibious invasion. As a result, both the Army and the Navy were short of light craft. Slow unloading also led to increased demurrage charges for ships unable to berth on a timely basis. Additional cost came from the need for contract lighterage and tugs. In the brief time available to respond to the shortage of watercraft, lighters, tugs, and coastal vessels, the Transportation Corps was compelled to resort to contractors from all parts of the Pacific. One problem that affected Pusan especially was the location of major depots inside the port. As the North Korean Army closed in on Pusan in the late summer of 1950, no other safe place was available to station the depots. This stockpiling of thousands of tons of supplies and equipment close to the piers added to the congestion. A shortage of skilled personnel and a lack of necessary documentation slowed reception of every type of cargo even further. In many instances, supplies merely sat, consuming valuable space until the end of hostilities. The other problems of pilferage and breakage were related to port congestion. Pilferage at the ports and throughout the country was an exceptional problem. For many Koreans condemned to poverty by decades of Japanese occupation, theft had long been a means of simple survival. Thus, the materiel entering the country through the ports was considered fair game. But pilferage occurred in retrograde cargo; axles of wrecked vehicles were especially sought after and often pilfered.[6] In many cases, breakage was directly related to the problem of pilferage, as when stevedores intentionally dropped crated cargo to gain access to the contents.

Although solutions to the various problems in the ports were self-evident, time was required to implement them. Initially, sufficient infrastructure had to be present to handle the job of port operations as well as the onward movement of cargo within the theater. By the end of 1950, the 7th Transportation Major Port replaced the 8057th Provisional Port Company as the port operator. Initially, the Japan Logistical Command established the Pusan Base Command to receive, store, and forward supplies to Eighth Army units. The rapid escalation of the theater led to the creation two months later of 2d Logistics Command, a headquarters specifically designed under a table of organization and equipment for theater support. It was commanded by Brig. Gen. Paul F. Yount, who later became chief of transportation in 1953. Security of the port and the cargo was a full-time job filled by military police units assigned to 2d Logistics Command.

The combined problems of port congestion, pilferage, and breakage led to the development of a reusable steel container that resembled a bank vault. Initially called the transporter, it was designed to be easily carried by all modes of surface transportation. In late 1952, the Transportation Corps used the transporter and began an express service from the United States to the Far East. The containers left San Francisco by Marine Express to Yokohama, Japan; from there they were shipped to allied ports in Korea. Military vehicles delivered the containers to the consignees, who returned the empty containers. The savings in time and money were significant. The average round trip was approximately fifty-five days with almost no breakage or pilferage. This meant an average saving of twenty-five to thirty days of transit time. The service became known as the Container Express and from that time on the container has been widely known as the CONEX.

Truck Operations

The terrain of the Korean peninsula presented U.S. Army transporters with a formidable challenge. The peninsula was mountainous, and the road system, primitive. The only suitable road by American standards was the Seoul-Inchon Highway, a two-lane paved road. The other roads in the country were barely wide enough for one-way traffic and surfaced with crushed stone. The numerous bridges in the country were also narrow and had low weight limits. Adverse weather severely affected the roads: during the rainy season they became quagmires, and in the winter they were covered with ice. When it was dry, even small convoys created clouds of dust, revealing their location to enemies miles away. More than 70 percent of the country featured slopes with greater than 30 percent grades. The mountainous nature of the country, along with the poor roads, also restricted the size of the vehicles that could be used to haul cargo. Ten-ton line-haul trucks could only be used in a limited area. Even the ubiquitous 2½-ton truck could not go everywhere. In many cases, Jeeps and even human bearers were the only forms of transport that could make it to the front lines in mountainous areas. U.S. and Korean engineers began a massive road-building program that, by the end of hostilities, resulted in the construction of 2,700 miles of new roads that were reserved strictly for military use.

The shortage of trucks in the early stages of the war was particularly serious and had an adverse effect on both supply and tactical operations. In one instance, Gen. John H. Church, commander of the 24th Division, planned a counterattack along the Naktong River that was scheduled to jump off at 0800 on August 17. One of the units involved in the counterattack was the 1st Provisional Marine Brigade commanded by Brig. Gen. Edward Craig, USMC, who had just arrived from the southern part of the Pusan perimeter. General Craig requested 144 trucks to get his units into position on time. Departure was scheduled for 1600 on August 16. The 53d Transportation Company, with only 43 trucks, arrived at 1900, three hours late. The division managed to scrounge another 29 trucks, but the total was only half of what General Craig needed. Despite the use of a shuttle system, only one of the marine brigade's battalions was in place on time. One arrived on time but was tired because it had to move on foot; another did not arrive until midday on August 17.[7]

By World War II standards, a theater the size of Korea required 48 truck companies, but by mid-1951 the theater had only 36, with a total inventory of 1,491 light (2½ tons) trucks and 181 10-ton tractor-trailers. Thus, the line-haul capability made up only 11 percent of the entire truck fleet.[8] To make matters worse, the amount of ammunition used in Korean War battles was sometimes astronomical by World War II standards. This was partially due to the positional nature of some of the battles that reduced combat to World War I conditions, with both sides heavily entrenched. Another factor was the willingness to use massive firepower to limit U.S. casualties. During the Battle of Soyang, May 17–23, 1952, the twenty-one artillery battalions supporting X Corps fired 309,000 rounds, more than 8,730 tons, of ammunition. All of it had to be carried by truck, and, even at five tons per vehicle, at the road cargo rate for the deuce-and-a-half truck, this required more than 1,700 truckloads.[9]

The expenditure of ammunition was so high that the corps organized a truck bank to maximize its lift capacity. The corps gathered trucks from every possible unit, and the military police set up checkpoints on routes leading into the corps area. Any empty truck was compelled to carry ammunition. On numerous occasions, the 52d Transportation Battalion commandeered trucks to haul Class V to forward ammunition points. The methods that X Corps resorted to helped the corps launch a counteroffensive against the communist Chinese. Although somewhat unconventional, these methods are very similar to the Red Ball Express that operated in France from August to November of 1944.

Despite the shortage of vehicles, Army truckers in the Korean theater chalked up some remarkable records. The average readiness rate was 80.5 percent for 2½-ton trucks and 74 percent for 10-ton trucks. The 73d Transportation Company held the record, driving more than a million truck miles without having one of its forty-eight trucks lose a day of service. With the proviso that the Korean rail system was functioning well, the number of trucks in the theater was barely adequate.

Rail Operations

Before the outbreak of hostilities, the South Korean rail system was the main mode of transport for passengers and cargo. As a result, it was in far better condition to support military operations than the road system was. When the 3d Transportation Military Railway Service (Provisional) (TMRS-P) assumed control of all railway operations in August 1950, the rail system comprised 270 miles of track, 280 locomotives, 4,300 freight cars, and 450 passenger cars, all in varying states of disrepair.[10] The 3d TMRS-P had two railway operating battalions and one shop battalion. One of the first rail operations of the war was a critical tactical move. On August 1, the enemy threat along the Pusan perimeter was grave, and Eighth Army had to move the 25th Division 150 miles to the southernmost part of the perimeter. Resources to move the division were not readily available and the Korean rail system was in complete disarray. Southern tracks were cluttered with the rolling stock used by the 1st Cavalry Division in its move to the perimeter. Korean refugees, desperately trying to escape the North Koreans, cluttered the rail yards and crowded the roads. The Transportation Section of the Eighth Army cleared the rolling stock from the tracks while the U.S. military police and Korean national police cleared some 7,500 refugees from the staging areas. Once the lines were cleared, the Transportation Section marshaled seventy-five railcars and locomotives to begin moving the division. In coordination with the 73d Truck Company and road marches, the 25th Division moved into its assigned position in thirty-six hours. Gen. Walton H. Walker, commanding general of Eighth Army, called it a "history making maneuver."[11]

During the succeeding year, U.S. transporters and engineers worked tirelessly to improve track beds and rolling stock. By July 1951, the rail system was moving twenty-five trains with a total of 42,000 short tons of cargo per day. Three trains carried troops, while an additional two trains moved casualties to the rear. An aggressive locomotive rebuilding program in Japan increased the rail capability even further. By 1952, the 3d TMRS-P was moving 153,000 tons of cargo and 19,500 passengers each week. When hostilities ended, the Korean rail system, under U.S. transporters, was moving 1.25 million tons of cargo and 300,000 passengers a month.

Air Transportation

The tonnage moved by air during the Korean War amounted to approximately 1 percent of the total tonnage moved, and this small percentage was primarily due to expense. Regardless that sea cargo cost $38 per ton to move and air cargo cost $5,000 per ton,[12] air transportation in the theater was vital. The doctrine developed for its use specified that the first use of air transportation was for emergency evacuation of U.S. civilians from the theater, delivery of the first U.S. combat troops to the theater, and delivery of high-priority cargo such as whole blood and the new 3.5-inch rocket launchers along with their rockets.

The first organization responsible for air transport was the Far East Air Forces Combat Cargo Command (Provisional) established on August 26, 1950, under the command of Gen. William H. Tunner, who had played a significant role in the Berlin Airlift. On February 25, 1951, the 315th Air Division (Combat Cargo) replaced it and performed air transportation duties for the remainder of the war. Coordination in Japan was the responsibility of the Far East Command Joint Air Priorities Board that allocated airlift capacity in tonnage to individual commands. In the theater, the Joint Air Lift Control Organization made known the priorities of air movements.

Initially, control of the aerial ports of debarkation (APOD) rested with the Transportation Corps, but this responsibility passed to the Air Force with the establishment of the 315th Air Division (Combat Cargo). Thereafter, the Transportation Corps was responsible only for Army cargo at the APOD. Forwarding Army cargo was the responsibility of the Transportation Air Forwarding Division (later the Air Movement Control Division), which provided liaison teams to the APODs. Some confusion existed throughout the war about who ran what, so in 1953 the Army and Air Force resolved the issue in a memorandum of understanding by awarding the responsibility of operating all aerial ports to the USAF.

Intratheater airlift was one of the most important aspects of air transport during the Korean War. During the pursuit of the retreating North Korean Army in October and November of 1950, air resupply was used frequently to support forces that had outrun their supplies because the roads and bridges had been destroyed by U.N. air forces. During the retreat from the Yalu River, air resupply was used to drop fuel and, in one case, a temporary bridge. On occasion, airlift was used to transfer troops to critical areas. One example was the transfer of the 187th Regimental Combat Team to help quell the prisoner riots at Koje-do in the summer of 1952.

Other air responsibilities included the transport of troops into the theater and the evacuation of serious frontline casualties to hospitals in Japan. Unfortunately, no doctrine governed intratheater airlift so some effort was wasted when valuable aircraft were used for tasks not essential to the mission or when varying tasks conflicted. In some cases, shortages of aircraft occurred when the 315th Air Division (Combat Cargo) was needed for both Air Force and Army supply missions simultaneously. The effort in Korea demonstrated the need for a single reliable intratheater aircraft. In Korea, the Air Force operated several aircraft, but all had limitations. The Curtiss C–46 Commando and the Douglas C–54 Skymaster were both developed in World War II and their carrying capacity was limited. Unfortunately, two new cargo aircraft—the Fairchild C–119 Flying Boxcar, a roomy aircraft suitable for dropping cargo and paratroopers, and the Douglas C–124 Globemaster II, a modern four-engine cargo plane capable of carrying thirty tons of cargo—had severe mechanical problems that limited their benefit in the early stages of their deployment. One particularly tragic accident involving a C–124 cost the lives of all 129 passengers and crew.

Helicopter Operations

The Army recognized the utility of the helicopter in World War II when small helicopters were used to evacuate the wounded in the Far East. After World War II, the helicopter became recognized as a useful tool for many of the Army's aviation requirements, and Far East Command requested helicopters immediately. However, they were not forthcoming. Very few helicopters were available, and the aircraft industry did not have the floor space, machines, or personnel to expand its facilities rapidly. Doctrinally, because the U.S. Air Force was responsible for delivering both troops and cargo by air to the combat area, it did not see the need for Army helicopters to assume part of that mission. Consequently, the few helicopters that reached the theater early in the war were the small, two-seat types used to evacuate battle casualties to hospitals, where they could receive quick treatment and significantly increase their chances for survival. The Army activated the 1st Transportation Helicopter Company at Fort Sill, Oklahoma, on December 1, 1950. It was equipped with Bell H–13 and Hiller H–23 light helicopters. On August 1, 1951, it was redesignated the 6th Transportation Helicopter Company and, in December 1951, received its first Sikorsky H–19, a viable cargo helicopter capable of carrying ten troops, eight litter cases, or approximately 2,000 pounds of cargo. After the 6th participated in a number of exercises, the Army activated two additional transportation helicopter companies, the 13th and 506th.

The 6th Transportation Helicopter Company sailed for Korea on December 16, 1952. Its baptism of fire came on March 20, 1953, when it flew missions to a platoon of the 3d Infantry Division after floodwater had cut off the platoon's normal supply route. Three days later, it evacuated casualties from Old Baldy, and from April 20 to 26 it participated in the first mass evacuation of casualties in Operation Little Switch. While the 6th continued with evacuation and resupply operations, the 13th arrived in country on May 1, 1953. In June 1953, both companies participated in a U.N. operation that delivered 700 South Korean troops into a blocking position to hold critical terrain during the truce negotiations. This was something the Marine Corps had already done.

Although very few helicopters were in the Korean theater, their contributions were significant in saving lives and demonstrating the military potential of rotary-wing aircraft in military operations. That these early operations pointed clearly to the future is evident by the fact that, twelve years later, an airmobile division was engaged in combat operations in Vietnam, and helicopters routinely performed a good deal of resupply in that theater. Of course, the competence of helicopter units flying medevac missions was almost legendary.

Conclusions

In many ways, transportation operations in the Korean War were a necessary reprise of the same types of operations in World War II. Technology and doctrine were nearly the same as they had been in World War II, and most of the general officers and colonels in Korea were veterans of World War II. Combat commanders are always faced with the conundrum between choosing how much combat power and how much combat service support to put on the ground in the initial stages of a deployment. In Korea, in the initial stages of the campaign, the failure to bring sufficient transportation equipment and personnel to the theater was clear. Thus, troops were committed piecemeal, offensives were delayed, and critical supplies languished in congested ports.

The problem of congestion that occurred in the ports at Pusan, Inchon, and other places was a function of personnel, equipment, and space. It was not solved in Korea, and it was not solved in Vietnam or in the Gulf War. Nevertheless, the Korean War saw the birth of the age of containerization with the development of the CONEX, which significantly reduced the problems of breakage and pilferage. Although containers have increased the speed of loading and discharging vessels, larger containers have caused their own congestion problem when they need to be unpacked and the cargo in them needs to be rerouted. Once again, the determinants are personnel, equipment, and space.

Truck and rail operations saw little new in the Korean War. Just as in the first three months after the Normandy invasion, too few trucks were in the theater, and very few were line-haul vehicles. Theater-level movement control was nearly nonexistent, as evidenced by the truck bank of the X Corps and the need to commandeer trucks. Lack of effective movement control remains a weak point in transportation operations. During Operation Desert Shield in the Persian Gulf War, the 22d Supply Command lost control of 78 percent of its trailers before hostilities began. Better control of rail cargo did not occur until 1997 when the doctrine changed.

Air logistical support also showed little that was innovative when compared to_ World War II for the same reason that truck operations were similar. Undoubtedly, the most important innovation was the use of the helicopter in tactical, logistical, and medical operations. Although transportation in the Korean War was a reprise of operations in World War II, CONEX and the helicopter were harbingers.

Notes

1. William Glenn Robertson, *Leavenworth Papers No. 13, Counterattack on the Naktong, 1950* (Fort Leavenworth, Kans.: Combat Studies Institute, U.S. Army Command and General Staff College, 1985), p 6.
2. James A. Huston, *The Sinews of War: U.S. Army Logistics 1775–1953* (Washington, D.C.:, Office of the Chief of Military History, United States Army, 1966), p 617.
3. Benjamin King, Richard C. Biggs, and Eric R. Criner, *Spearhead of Logistics: A History of the United States Army Transportation Corps* (Fort Eustis, Va.: U.S. Army Transportation Center, 1994), p 304.
4. *Ibid.*, p 305.
5. *Ibid.*, p 308.
6. Lt Gen Jack C. Fuson, USA (Ret), *Transportation and Logistics: One Man's Story* (Washington, D.C.: Center of Military History United States Army, 1994), p 64.
7. Robertson, *Counterattack*, p 87.
8. In the 1990–1991 Gulf War, in a far more lavishly equipped theater and more suitable terrain, the vehicle mix in echelons above division was nearly reversed.
9. King, Biggs, and Criner, *Spearhead*, p 310.
10. *Ibid.*, p 312.
11. Roy E. Appleman, *South to the Naktong, North to the Yalu (June–November 1950)* from the *United States Army in the Korean War* series (Washington, D.C.: Office of the Chief of Military History, Department of the Army, 1961), p 249.
12. James A. Huston, *Guns and Butter, Powder and Rice* (Selsingrove, Pa.: Susquehanna University Press, 1989), p. 218.

Reprise

Korea, Fifty Years Later

Brig. Gen. David E. Clary, USAF

Good morning, I am Brigadier General Dave Clary and I am the Director of Homeland Security on the Air Staff in Washington, D.C., at the Pentagon. Probably more germane to all of you, as far as my credentials are concerned, is that I have recently returned from an assignment in Osan, Korea, after serving two years as the commander of the 51st Fighter Wing. I have been asked to provide you with an update on the situation in Korea. I will present the briefing on the mission of the Seventh Air Force Air Component Command that my former boss, Lt. Gen. Lance L. Smith, prepared.

Seventh Air Force was originally organized in 1940 as the Hawaiian Air Force. It was primarily an administrative command that dealt with maintaining the air bases in the Pacific and defending Hawaii. It was twice renamed, becoming Seventh Air Force in 1942 and the Pacific Air Command in 1947. It was deactivated in 1949.

In 1966, the command was activated as a combat command and made responsible for all air operations providing military assistance to Vietnam. Headquarters was set up at Tan Son Nhut Air Base near Saigon. Seventh Air Force served as the Air Component Command to Military Assistance Command, Vietnam, throughout the Vietnam conflict. Seventh Air Force was inactivated at the end of the Vietnam War.

In 1986, the Seventh Air Force was once again reactivated at Osan Air Base in the Republic of Korea (ROK), replacing the 314th Air Division. Seventh Air Force is one of the four numbered Air Forces under the Pacific Air Force, now commanded by Gen. William J. Begert. Assets from each numbered Air Force would augment the Korean theater if war should erupt on the peninsula. Additional personnel to manage the collocated operating bases and other facilities that support the overall Air Component Command and Seventh Air Force mission would receive augmenting forces in the case of war.

Seventh Air Force works closely with its ROK Air Force counterparts at every level to defend the integrity of the South Korean government. As part of Air Component Command, the ROK Air Force, as I will refer to them, has more than 60,000 personnel who fly and maintain twenty-nine fighter squadrons. Among their planes are the KF–16 (a Korean-produced version of the American fighter), F–16, F–4, F–5, and A–37 aircraft. The USAF structure in Korea includes four assigned fighter squadrons. Two squadrons are at Osan and include twenty-four F–16s and twenty-four A–10s and OA–10s; the other two squadrons are at Kunsan Air Base and have thirty-six F–16Cs.

At present, Army Gen. Leon J. Laporte is the overall commander in charge of Combined Forces Command, United Nations Command, and U.S. Forces Command. He is triple-hated, commanding three different organizations. He commands any coalition forces arrayed against North Korea. The commander of Combined Forces Command is his wartime hat, which combines the ROK and U.S. war effort against North Korea. The reason United Nations Command differs from the Combined Forces Command is because South Korea never signed the armistice agreement after the Korean War. Therefore, the South Koreans do not fall under the United Nations Command umbrella.

General Smith commands the Air Component Command and would be in charge of U.S. and ROK Air Forces. The Air Force Operations Center, the Korean fighter command, is headquartered at Osan Air Base. Other component commanders currently include the ground component commander under ROK Gen. Nam Jae Joon; the Naval Component Command in Japan under U.S. Adm. James Metzger; the Combined Marine Forces Command in Hawaii headed by U.S. Lt. Gen. Earl B. Hailston; the Combined Unconventional Warfare Task Force commanded by ROK Lt. Gen. Kim Yun Seok; and the Combined Psychological Operations Task Force commanded by ROK Brig. Gen. Ahn.

General Smith's deputy is ROK Air Force Lt. Gen. Lee, who commands the Air Force Operations Command. The Air Component Command Chief of Staff and vice commander of Seventh Air Force is Maj. Gen. Dennis R. Larsen. General Larsen's deputy is Brig. Gen. (select) Lee, who also serves as the Chief of Staff of the Air Force Operations Command. Directly under their command are the air staffs. The ROK and the U.S. assistant chiefs of staff both share air staff management. A counterpart from the alternate nation acts as the air staff deputy.

As the Combined Air Component commander, General Smith would have four defined wartime responsibilities: Combined Force Air Component Commander; command of all air forces in the theater; all air defense assets and theater missile operations; and control over all airspace, except that which is in the immediate battle area and where operations are coordinated with the Ground Component commander. General Smith is also the coordinating authority for space, in which he is the focal point for space requirements with Combined Forces Command. He ensures unity of command and enables the commander to focus on strategic-level decision making. He integrates space with air and information operations and is the supported commander for Joint Space Operations assigned by Combined Force Commander.

Northeast Asia: A History of Conflict

Instability has characterized northeast Asia for the 125 years predating the United States' permanent presence in the region. Regional powers used the Korean peninsula as a battleground for interregional wars in every decade from the 1830s to the end of the Korean War. There was the Opium War in China during the 1830s and 1840s, the Taiping Revolution in China during the 1850s and 1860s, and the Meji Revolution in Japan in the 1860s. Japanese and Chinese forces fought in Korea during the 1870s, while Russia occupied northwest China and the Manchurian border areas. During the 1890s, China and Japan fought frequently, with most of the fighting occurring in Korea and Manchuria. During the 1900s, as the Boxer Rebellion erupted in China, Japan stationed troops in Korea and took control of Korean foreign affairs. This was also the era of the Russo-Japanese War. The next decade saw Japan officially colonizing Korea; Sun Yat-sen leading a revolution in China; Mongolia gaining independence from China; and the Czarist regime in Russia being overthrown by a new Bolshevik (communist) movement. The 1920s witnessed a communist insurgency in China and Manchuria. During the 1930s, Japan invaded both Manchuria and China. In World War II, Japan took over Korea and dominated the Asia and Pacific area. In June 1950 came the Korean War.

Northeast Asia Today: Its Importance to the United States

Northeast Asia is the second largest trade region of the United States. It is exceeded only by the North American Free Trade Agreement, which allows us to conduct free trade with Mexico and Canada. Northeast Asia is vital to American economic and security interests. Korea is the hub of northeast Asia's economy; it has an enormous impact on the U.S. economy. Indeed, if the United States is included, the world's third largest gross domestic product has its roots in the economy of northeast Asia. Consequently, a conflict in northeast Asia would produce an economic disaster for the American economy. Northeast Asia has four of the world's six largest military establishments; five of the six largest if the United States is included. Numerous nuclear powers are present in the region, and the United States provides nuclear umbrellas for bilateral alliances as well as a nuclear balance in the region. Hopefully, we will be able to keep Japan and Korea from acquiring nuclear weapons. The American presence helps mitigate historical animosities from becoming military problems. Although Korea is the geographic hub of northeast Asia, Seoul actually has closer ties to Beijing than to Tokyo.

Suffice it to say that U.S. presence in Korea today and tomorrow is critical to American and allied interests. Our presence in Korea prevents war, not only between the two Koreas but also between regional rivals who have historically used the peninsula as a battlefield. Our presence in Korea also provides peninsular and regional stability. The ROK-U.S. alliance serves as a deterrent to the greatest threat to regional stability. Furthermore, U.S. presence and the alliance deter the flare-up of animosities within the region by serving as a buffer between historical rivals. And U.S. presence may enhance the possibility of reconciliation between North and South Korea. The U.S. presence in Korea also promotes peace and prosperity for the peninsula, the region, and the world because everyone benefits from the region's trade and economic growth. Before the 1950 entry of the United States into Korea, there was never a time in northeast Asian history during which the region has enjoyed fifty years of uninterrupted prosperity.

But we are not at peace; we are still at war on the Korean peninsula. Signed on July 27, 1953, the armistice agreement remains in place nearly fifty years later, due in large part to the North Korean intentions to dominate the peninsula and the effective deterrence and determination solidified by the of the ROK-U.S. alliance. Throughout this period, the Korean peninsula has remained a very dangerous place, as evidenced by the number of major armistice violations and the number of personnel killed in action on both sides.

Beyond these armistice violations, many of North Korea's actions have significant military impact on the peninsula and the region. The continuous string of provocative incidents over the decades has occasionally been interrupted by gestures of peace and reconciliation. The most recent is the unprecedented North Korean–South Korean summit that occurred in June 2000. However, besides the emotional boost provided to all Koreans by the summit, very little evidence exists, beyond family reunions, of true reconciliation between the two Koreas. The bottom line is that the peninsula remains the most heavily militarized area in the world and presents a very real threat to U.S. and allied interests.

Space shuttle photography shows a dramatic difference in energy use between the two Koreas. U.S. presence there has enabled the night skyline of South Korea to shine brightly on a world map of nighttime illumination, constituting one of the world's most impressive economic miracles. The same map shows a black hole north of South Korea's vibrant economy, a void that is North Korea. Inside the black hole, North Korea has a collapsed economy as well as a collapsed infrastructure. However, Kim Chong Il takes care of his military, for that is what supports his interests and intent. It is the North Korean military that is the glue holding his regime together. Although Kim Chong Il has a firm grasp of power, he faces a dilemma. All of his options must be supported by the military. His military is his first policy; it provides him with internal security, and it is the only element of national power.

With a size approaching that of the state of Indiana, North Korea possesses the world's fifth-largest military, third-largest army, and the largest special operation forces, artillery, and submarine force in the world. Over the last twenty years, North Korea has methodically moved 70 percent of its military south of Pyongyang, along the demilitarized zone. North Korea is positioned to attack with minimal preparations. Its large, forward-deployed conventional forces are complemented by world-class asymmetric capabilities. Some of North Korea's asymmetric capabilities include nuclear, biological, and chemical stockpiles—the world's third-largest stockpile—and a robust ballistic missile program. Until 1995, its possession of Scud missiles made North Korea a threat to the peninsula. Since 1995, it has acquired No Dong missiles. Their range of 2,500 kilometers gives them the ability to impact the region. Today, North Korea is in the process of developing a longer range Taepo Dong missile whose 8,500-kilometer range will enable it to impact other regions, including the United States.

The United Nations Command has the mission of maintaining the armistice and deterring attack. North Korea, not Washington, will determine if we go to war. We project three scenarios for what might direct future North Korean actions: implosion, explosion, or a soft landing. A succession crisis, by either coup d'état or revolution, could cause North Korea to implode. The same effect might also occur if North Korea's economy should collapse or if its government should experience a popular loss of confidence and a popular uprising occur. Explosion as a result of isolation, provocative actions, or war is also seen as a possibility. War, whether with ambiguous warning, unambiguous warning, or accidental, would produce an explosive result. The third scenario, a soft landing, would be a peaceful reunification. A North Korean attack on the Republic of Korea is obviously the most dangerous of the three scenarios. As I noted earlier, 70 percent of North Korean forces are forward-deployed. Two thousand artillery pieces are stationed along the demilitarized zone, many in underground facilities. Seoul, which is only eight to ten miles from the border, is at risk from those artillery pieces. Thirty-five million noncombatants live in the combat zone, and more than a million casualties could be expected. We would hope to stop a North Korean attack north of Seoul. The ROK army is the primary defense force, and U.S. forces are required to counterattack to defeat the North Korean People's Liberation Army. With the North Korean forces positioned in hardened underground facilities, we will win the fight, but at the cost of many casualties.

Let me talk about deterrent options and deterrent actions. If North Korea were to plan an attack, we would face an ambiguous warning situation, unsure of the north's intentions. To help us cope with this, we've established flexible deterrent options (FDOs) and force enhancements (FEs) that would be used to deter such an attack. FDOs are political and diplomatic efforts used to either calm tensions or threaten escalation. FEs are more militarily oriented, such as adding forces to those already on the peninsula. Should the transition to war become necessary, we have procedures in place that minimize the time required to prepare. We would start by activating our crisis action team and initiating checklists that help us prepare our base defenses and evacuate U.S. and other registered noncombatants.

Two hardened facilities are located at Osan, the Hardened Theater Air Control Center and, directly across from it, the Korean Combat Operations Intelligence Center. Inside these hardened facilities the Air Component Commander manages the air war, which includes building the integrated air tasking order.

This is the Combined Forces Command air plan of attack. It includes targets, aircraft assigned to them, and the time designated for attack, and it essentially spells out how we will fight the air war each day. The Combined Targeting Board (CTB) carries out this process. The CTB synchronizes theater air operations with the ground and maritime operations of the other component commanders via the Integrated Tasking Order. The CTB is the commander's component for coordinating, deconflicting, and synchronizing operations deep in Korea. The CTB process begins with guidance passed down through the commander. We will begin flying about fifteen hundred sorties a day, and by day 5 or 6 of the war we will be up to approximately twenty-five hundred sorties daily. At a rate of twenty-five hundred sorties a day, we will have an ops tempo comparable to that of Desert Storm with only one-fifth of the airspace.

One of our early actions would be to forward-deploy fighter aircraft. Other actions may increase the ground and airborne alert status of ROK Air Force fighter forces, or we might request that additional ROK Air Force and U.S. aircraft be added to the airborne alert. If we anticipate a massive first wave of North Korean aircraft coming south, Airborne Warning and Control Systems could be stationed to aid in the early detection of an air attack. Our first priority will be to gain battlefield air superiority. We will have airborne alert combat air patrols in the defensive counterair role, and they will move north as we gain control of airspace. Our initial attacks will be on the surface-to-air missile sites to achieve air superiority over the main battle area. We will also support the ground component commander by attacking bridges along major routes to slow the advance of second-echelon forces moving south. Our highest priority in supporting the Army will be the counterfire fight. The North Korean 240-mm and 170-mm batteries have a tremendous capability to rain massive firepower against our frontal defenses. We will use air power orbiting above the hardened facilities to wait for the guns to emerge, and then fire so we can attack and destroy them in the open.

Due to the demand to provide varied missions, we train and participate in several regularly scheduled exercises to hone our war-fighting skills. Cope Jade, Foal Eagle, Rapid Thunder, Ulchi-Focus Lens, and Reception, Staging, Onward Movement and Integration are the more important exercises that we participate in. These events represent more than sixty days per year devoted to increased levels of training.

Air Component Command's involvement in these joint, combined, and national exercises heightens Combined Forces Command and component readiness and provides an excellent means to assess capabilities, identify problems, and make corrections. It also highlights our dedication to protecting the integrity of the Republic of Korea.

Although the Air Component Command motto is Ready to Fight Tonight, we continue to prepare more fully to carry out our mission. Among the challenges we face are the need for early political decisions; precision all-weather weapons; sensor-to-shooter improvements; battlefield management; operations in a chemical environment; and base infrastructure improvements. Personnel issues, such as remote assignments, are also acknowledged.

In summary, Air Component Command supports Combined Forces Command in providing regional stability. Our primary mission is to maintain the Armistice by deterring a North Korean attack, and fight and win should deterrence fail. We do this by maintaining a forward presence in Korea, contributing to stability both on and off the peninsula through the application of air power.

Glossary

Glossary

AAF	Army Air Forces
AAU	Army Administrative Unit
AB	Air Base
AE	ammunition ship
AF	refrigerated provisions ship
AFB	Air Force Base
AFM	Air Force Manual
AFSA	Armed Forces Security Agency
AK	stores ship
AKA	attack cargo ship
AMA	air materiel area
AMC	Air Materiel Command
APOD	aerial ports of debarkation
ASA	Army Security Agency
ASA Pacific	Army Security Agency theater headquarters in Tokyo
ATO	air tasking order
avgas	aviation gasoline
BDA	battle damage assessment
CAFMS	computer-assisted force management system
CAG	Carrier Air Group
CAS	close air support
CCF	Chinese Communist Forces
CCRAK	Combined Command for Reconnaissance Activities, Korea
CENTCOM	Central Command
CFE	Central Fighter Establishment
CIA	Central Intelligence Agency
CIC	Counter Intelligence Corps
CINCFE	Commander-in-Chief Far East
CINCPAC	Commander-in-Chief of Pacific forces
CNO	Chief of Naval Operations
COMNAVFE	Commander, U.S. Naval Forces Far East
CONUS	continental United States
CTB	Combined Targeting Board
CVE	escort carrier
EAB	Engineer Aviation Battalion
EAMC	Engineer Aviation Maintenance Company

FAC	forward air controller
FDO	flexible deterrent option
FE	force enhancement
FEAF	Far East Air Forces
FEAMCOM	Far East Air Materiel Command
FEC	Far East Command
FECOM	Far East Command
FM	Field Manual
FO2 FEF	Flag Officer Second-in-Command Far East Fleet
GAT	guidance, apportionment, and targeting
GWAPS	Gulf War Air Power Survey
HARM	high-speed antiradiation missile
HMR	Marine Helicopter Transport Squadron
HMX–1	Marine Helicopter Squadron 1
HUMINT	human intelligence
HVAR	high-velocity aerial rocket
JAAF	Joint Action Armed Forces
JCS	Joint Chiefs of Staff
JFACC	Joint Force Air Component commander
JOC	Joint Operations Center
JP–5	jet fuel, similar to kerosene
JTD	joint training directive
KAMU	Korea Air Materiel Unit
KLO	Korea Liaison Office
KMAG	Korean Military Advisory Group
KTO	Kuwaiti theater of operations
MAG	Marine Air Group
MATS	Military Air Transport Service
MAW	Marine Air Wing
MDAP	Mutual Defense Assistance Program
MG	Maintenance Group
MIS	Military Intelligence Service
MLR	main line of resistance
NCAP	night combat air patrol
NCAS	night close air support
NKPA	North Korean People's Army
NSA	National Security Agency

OB	order of battle
OPCON	operational control
OSD	Overseas Supply Division
OSI	Office of Special Investigations
PHOTINT	photo intelligence
PLA	People's Liberation Army
PSP	pierced steel planking
RAAF	Royal Australian Air Force
RAF	Royal Air Force
RCT	regimental combat team
REMCO	Rear Echelon Maintenance Combined Operation
RN	Royal Navy
RO	radar officer
RO	radio observer
ROK	Republic of Korea
RTS	Reconnaissance Technical Squadron
SAC	Strategic Air Command
SAR	search and rescue
Servron–3	Service Squadron 3
SFPOE	San Francisco port of embarkation
SIGROD	electromechanical cipher machine
SHORAN	short-range navigation
SIGINT	signals intelligence
TAC	Tactical Air Command
TACP	tactical air control party
TCW	troop carrier wing
TLO	tactical liaison office
TMRS-P	Transportation Military Railway Service Provisional
TRS	Tactical Reconnaissance Squadron
TRW	Tactical Reconnaissance Wing
U.N.	United Nations
UNC	United Nations Command
USA	United States Army
USAF	United States Air Force
USMC	United States Marine Corps
USN	U.S. Navy

VMF	Marine Fighter Squadron
VMF(N)	Marine Night Fighter Squadron
VMO	Marine Observation Squadron

Author Biographies

Author Biographies

Fred H. Allison is a retired Marine Corps officer and an oral historian with the U.S. Marine Corps. He holds a master's degree in U.S. history from Texas A&M University and is ABD in U.S. military history at Texas Tech University. His writings include various journal publications and reviews. Mr. Allison also has extensive teaching experience.

Dr. Jeffrey G. Barlow has been a historian with the Naval Historical Center's Contemporary History Branch since 1987. A graduate of Westminster College in Pennsylvania, he received his M.A. and Ph.D. degrees in international studies from the University of South Carolina. An expert on the Joint Chiefs of Staff and on twentieth century American military policy and strategy, Dr. Barlow has written chapters for more than a dozen books dealing with the events of World War II and the postwar period. He is the author of *Revolt of the Admirals: The Fight for Naval Aviation, 1945–1950* (Washington, D.C.: Naval Historical Center, 1994). Awarded the 1995 John Lyman Prize for U.S. naval history, this book was republished by Brassey's in 1998 and by Ross & Perry in 2001.

Col. Richard J. Blanchfield, USMC (Ret.), is Senior Analyst and Assistant Director of the Strategic Assessment Center at SAIC in Washington, D.C. A CH–46 pilot in Vietnam, he later served with the Presidential Helicopter Squadron and at Marine Corps headquarters. A distinguished graduate of the Naval War College, he has participated in many study groups including the weapons, tactics, and training task force of the Gulf War Air Power Survey.

Brig. Gen. Philip L. Bolté, USA (Ret.), is a 1950 graduate of the U.S. Military Academy. He is also a graduate of the Canadian Army Staff College and the U.S. Army War College and holds an M.S. degree in mechanical engineering from the Georgia Institute of Technology. During his thirty years of Army service, he commanded armor units from platoon to brigade levels. He served in combat and was wounded in both the Korean War and the Vietnam War. His other assignments included service on the Army staff and secretariat as assistant program manager for tank main armament in the Abrams tank program and as program manager Bradley Fighting Vehicle Systems. General Bolté has published in *Armor* magazine. He is president of the U.S. Cavalry Association and serves on the board of the Patton Museum Foundation.

Colonel Donald W. Boose, Jr., USA (Ret.), is an adjunct professor at the U.S. Army War College. He has anthropology and Asian studies degrees from Cornell University and the University of Hawaii. He served as an Army officer for more than fourteen years in East Asia, including six years with the United Nations Command Component of the Military Armistice Commission in Korea. His writings include *Great Battles of Antiquity,* twenty-two articles on politico-military aspects of the Korean War for Spencer Tucker's *Encyclopedia of the Korean War,* and numerous other articles and reviews.

Brig. Gen. David E. Clary is the Director, Homeland Security, Deputy Chief of Staff for Air and Space Operations, Headquarters U.S. Air Force, Washington, D.C. Most recently he commanded the 51st Fighter Wing, Osan Air Base, South Korea. The general entered the Air Force in 1976 after graduating from the U.S. Air Force Academy. He has commanded at the squadron, group, and wing levels and has served in a staff assignment at U.S. Strategic Command. He is a command pilot with more than 4,500 flying hours, primarily in attack and fighter aircraft. General Clary completed Squadron Officer School, Air Command and Staff College, and Air War College, and he earned an M.S. degree in management from Troy State University in Alabama. His assignments include T–37 instructor pilot, 96th Flying Training Squadron, Williams AFB, Ariz.; A–10 instructor pilot, safety officer, flight commander, 511th Tactical Fighter Squadron, RAF Bentwaters, England; exchange officer and A–7E instructor pilot, Attack Squadron 122, Naval Air Station Lemoore, Calif.; A–7E pilot, Attack Squadron 27, USS *Carl Vinson*; joint warfare faculty instructor, Air Command and Staff College, Maxwell AFB; assistant operations officer, 78th Tactical Fighter Squadron; operations officer, 92d Tactical Fighter Squadron; commander, 91st Tactical Fighter Squadron; assistant deputy commander for operations, 81st Tactical Fighter Wing; and commander, 81st Communications Squadron, RAF Bentwaters and RAF Woodbridge, England; deputy commander, and later commander, 355th Operations Group, Davis-Monthan AFB, Ariz.; commander, 27th Fighter Wing, Cannon AFB, Ariz.; and chief of staff, U.S. Strategic Command, Offutt AFB, Neb.

Dr. Conrad Crane holds the General Douglas MacArthur Chair of Research in the Strategic Studies Institute of the Army War College. Before retiring from the Army after a twenty-six-year career that included two years' service in Korea, he spent nine years as a professor of history at the U.S. Military Academy. He is a graduate of USMA and the Army War College, and earned his Ph.D. from Stanford in 1990. He has written and lectured widely on military and air power topics, and is the author of *Bombs, Cities, and Civilians: American Airpower Strategy in World War II* and *American Airpower Strategy in Korea, 1950–1953*, both published by the University Press of Kansas.

Brig. Gen. Michael E. De Armond, USAF (Ret.), graduated from West Point in 1950 and was commissioned in the USAF. After winning his pilot's wings in 1951 and completing combat crew training, he was assigned to the 335th Fighter Interceptor Squadron, 4th Fighter Group in Korea. On his 47th combat mission he was shot down by a MiG–15 and spent seventeen months in a Chinese prisoner of war camp. Upon his return to the United States, he was assigned to the 95th FIS (Air Defense Command), where he served from December 1953 until February 1956. He was then assigned to the athletics department at the U.S. Air Force Academy. In October 1957, De Armond became a T–33 instructor pilot at Vance AFB, Oklahoma, followed by an assignment to the 66th Tactical Reconnaissance Wing at Laon AB, France. In November 1964, he served with the Deputy Chief of Staff for Operations at USAF headquarters. He served a combat tour in Vietnam as commander of the 355th Tactical Fighter Squadron. He then served as deputy commander for operations in the 36th TFW at Bitburg AB. He ended this tour in Europe as Director of Safety at USAFE before returning in January 1973 to command the 50th TFW at Hahn AB. Returning to the United States in August 1974, General De Armond served as commander of the Defense Contract Administration in Los Angeles. A command pilot with 4,500 hours flying time and 268 combat missions in Korea and Vietnam, his decorations include the Legion of Merit, Distinguished Flying Cross, and Air Medal with 13 oak leaf clusters. He holds graduate degrees from George Washington University, Air Command and Staff College, and the Industrial College of the Armed Forces.

Col. Samuel T. Dickens, USAF (Ret.), was commissioned in the Air Force following graduation from West Point in 1951. He flew twelve RF–80 missions with the 15th Tactical Reconnaissance Squadron during the Korean War. After the war, he served as an assistant operations and flight commander, developing plans for the RF–86F. Subsequently, he made a photographic overflight of the USSR. His later assignments included flight commander of RAF squadron No. 263; assistant air attaché, Spain; operations officer and commander 615th TFS, South Vietnam (226 combat missions); Air Staff action officer; base commander, Torrejon AB, Spain; director of operations, 401st TFW, Spain; and chief, Western Hemisphere Division, Plans and Policy, USAF. After retiring in 1979, he served with the American Legion and American Security Council Foundation. He has testified before Congress, appeared on CNN's "Crossfire" and "Larry King Live." He holds graduate degrees from George Washington University, Air Command and Staff College, and the Industrial College of the Armed Forces.

Dr. John Patrick Finnegan graduated magna cum laude from Boston College in 1957 with an A.B. in English literature. After a period of civilian employment with the National Security Agency and military service as a member of the U.S.

Army Counter Intelligence Corps, he went on to receive M.A. and Ph.D. degrees in American history from the University of Wisconsin-Madison. Between 1964 and 1979 Finnegan taught courses in American history at Ohio University, the Far East and Atlantic divisions of the University of Maryland, Chicago State University, and Texas Tech University. From 1974 to 1977 he served as a Principal Education Officer with the Nigerian Federal Ministry of Education, and as Senior Lecturer in History at the University of Ibadan, Nigeria. Joining the Federal Civil Service in 1979, Finnegan served as a historian with the U.S. Army Center of Military History before becoming a historian with the U.S. Army Intelligence and Security Command in 1982. He is the author of *Against the Specter of a Dragon: The Campaign for American Military Preparedness, 1914–1917; Military Intelligence: A Picture History; The Military Intelligence Story: A Photo History;* and *Military Intelligence,* a volume in the U.S. Army Center of Military History's Army Lineage Series. He also coedited *U.S. Army Signals Intelligence in World War II: A Documentary History*. His most recent publication is *The U.S. Army in the Korean War, 1950–1953: Operations and Intelligence Report.*

Dr. James A. Ginther serves as Personal Papers Archivist for the Marine Corps University Research Archives aboard Marine Corps Base Quantico, Virginia. He holds a Ph.D. in military history from Texas Tech University, an M.A. in history from Abilene Christian University, and a B.S. in business administration from the University of Missouri-St. Louis. His professional experience includes serving as an instructor of American history at Abilene Christian University and as the archivist for the Southwest Collection and Vietnam Archive at Texas Tech. His dissertation and master's thesis focused on Marine Corps aviation topics. The former is a biography of Gen. Keith Barr McCutcheon; the latter, a biographical work on the Corps' first pilot, Lt. Col. Alfred Austell Cunningham. Dr. Ginther is revising his McCutcheon manuscript with a view toward publication.

R. Cargill Hall is Chief Historian, National Reconnaissance Office, an agency of the Department of Defense. He previously held a variety of posts in the U.S. Air Force History Program, among them, Contract Histories Manager at the Air Force History Support Office (1989–1998) and Chief of the Research Division and (concurrently) Deputy Director of the USAF Historical Research Agency (1981–1989). Previously, he served as a National Aeronautics and Space Administration historian at Caltech's Jet Propulsion Laboratory. Hall is the author of *Lunar Impact: A History of Project Ranger* and the editor of *Case Studies in Strategic Bombardment, The U.S. Air Force in Space,* and *Lightning Over Bougainville: The Yamamoto Mission Reconsidered.* A contributing editor to *Air & Space Smithsonian*, he also is a member of the International Institute of Space Law, the International Academy of Astronautics, and the board of directors of the Cold War Museum. Hall has contributed articles and chapters on the history of aeronautics and astronautics to numerous journals, anthologies, and encyclopedias. His most recent work in the open literature on the genesis of American overhead strategic reconnaissance appears in *Eye in the Sky: The Story of the CORONA Satellites*, published by the Smithsonian Institution Press in 1998.

Ronald W. Harbison served as an aviation ordnance man in the U.S. Marine Corps in 1946–1947. He reenlisted in 1950 as a basic electronics specialist. After training he was assigned as an airborne interceptor operator. He served in the Korean War with the VMF (N)–513 at Kunson Air Base (K–8). Harbison flew 50 missions aboard the F7F until the plane was phased out in May 1953. In May and June 1953, he flew six missions aboard the F3D; he left the Marine Corps in September.

Air Vice Marshal William "Paddy" Harbison joined the Royal Air Force in 1941. After flying training in Canada, he graduated pilot training and then joined the No. 118 Squadron, with which he remained until the end of World War II, flying Spitfires and Mustangs in the European theater. After the war, he served in various squadrons, flying Mustangs, Hornets, and Meteors. In 1948 he was posted to March AFB, California, as an exchange pilot with the 1st Fighter Group, where he flew F–80s and F–86s. Returning to England in 1950, he completed a tour with the All Weather Development Squadron at the Central Fighter Establishment. During this time, he was assigned to active flying duty with the U.S. Air Force's 4th Fighter Group to observe and report on the Korean War. In late 1952, he was posted to the 2d Allied Tactical Air Force in West Germany as commander of the No. 67 Fighter Squadron, equipped with Sabres. In 1956 he was awarded the Air Force Cross and returned from Germany to attend the Army Staff College at Camberly.

From 1957 to 1962, AVM Harbison served in air defense operations in the Ministry of Defence and, on return, attended the Joint Services Staff College. After graduation, he was named commander of RAF Leuchars, a major fighter base in Scotland. He was then selected to attend the Canadian National Defence College. During this period, he became a commander of the Order of the British Empire.

After completion of the Canadian National Defence College came a tour as group captain for operations at Fighter Command headquarters. In 1969 he was promoted to air commodore and became director of operations of the National Air Traffic Services in London. In August 1972 he became air attaché and commander, RAF staff in Washington, D.C.

After promotion to air vice marshal in 1975, he was appointed air officer commanding No. 11 Group RAF Strike Command. No. 11 Group succeeded RAF Fighter Command and was responsible for air defense of the United Kingdom and controlled fighter interceptors, ground radars, surface-to-air missiles, and airborne early warning aircraft. In January 1977, AVM Harbison became a Companion of the Order of the Bath.

At the end of his tour, he retired from the RAF and returned to the United States, where he has since represented British Aerospace interests, first as a vice president and then as a consultant to the company.

Commander David Hobbs joined the Royal Navy in 1964 and, since qualification as a pilot, has flown both fixed and rotary wing aircraft "to the deck," including Gannet airborne early warning aircraft, Wessex Commando helicopters, and Canberra electronic counter-countermeasure aircraft. He has served on the aircraft carriers *Victorious, Centaur, Hermes, Bulwark, Albion,* and two *Ark Royals* (the 1955 and 1985 ships) with Nos. 849, 845, 846 Naval Air Squadrons and the No. 360 RN/RAF Joint Squadron. While serving in the Director General Aircraft (Naval) Department, he was responsible for developing the visual and electronic recovery aids for the Sea Harrier. He also organized the flying trials that cleared the Invincible class and Hermes to operate the modern generation of aircraft at sea. After a lifetime interest in naval history, he is the author of numerous books, contributes regularly to a variety of international publications, and has presented papers at naval historical symposia in Australia, France, New Zealand, the United States, and Great Britain. He is an adviser to the Naval Staff on a range of aircraft carrier matters.

Admiral J. L. Holloway III, USN (Ret.), graduated from the U.S. Naval Academy in June 1942. During World War II, he served aboard destroyers on North Atlantic convoy duty, on North African waters, and in the Pacific where he participated in the Saipan, Tinian, Palau, Peleliu campaigns and the Battle of Leyte Gulf. He was a gunnery officer aboard the USS *Bennion*, which was credited with torpedoing a Japanese battleship and sinking an enemy destroyer at the Battle of Surigao Straits. He made two carrier tours to Korea, flying Grumman F9F–2 Panther jets on combat missions against the Chinese Communists and took command of Fighting Squadron 52 when his commanding officer was shot down. He commanded the USS *Enterprise*, the Navy's first, and at the time its only, nuclear powered aircraft carrier for two combat cruises in the Gulf of Tonkin against the North Vietnamese. On this deployment, the *Enterprise* established a record for the number of combat sorties flown, won the "E" award for the best carrier in the fleet, and received the Navy Unit Commendation award.

Returning to the Pentagon, in 1968 Holloway established the Navy's Nuclear Powered Carrier Program, building the USS *Nimitz* and paving the way for nine more supercarriers of this class. In 1970, he was Commander of the Carrier Striking Force of the Sixth Fleet and deployed to the Eastern Mediterranean to conduct carrier air operations in reaction to the Syria's invasion of Jordan. After the strong U.S. military response resulted in a withdrawal of the Syrian armored column, his task force covered the evacuation of an Army MASH unit from Amman, Jordan, by a Marine Expeditionary Group. He took command of the U.S. Seventh Fleet in 1972 during the Vietnam War and directed the massive carrier strikes against Hanoi that led to the Vietnam cease-fire in 1973. Subsequently, the Seventh Fleet, under his command, performed the airborne mine-clearing operations in the North Vietnam ports, which were a condition of the negotiated terms of the armistice. As Chief of Naval Operations from 1974 to 1978, he was a member of the Joint Chiefs of Staff, and during this time served as its Chairman during the evacuation of Cyprus; the rescue of the SS *Mayaguez* and the punitive strike operations against the Cambodian forces involved in its seizure; the evacuation of U.S. nationals from Lebanon; and the Korean DMZ incident in August 1976.

After retiring from the Navy in 1978, he chaired the Department of Defense Special Operations Review Group that investigated the aborted Iranian hostage rescue attempt. In 1985 he served as Executive Director of the President's Task Force on Combating Terrorism. In 1986 he was appointed by Vice President George Bush as Special Envoy to the Middle East to resolve a territorial dispute between Bahrain and Qatar. In 1985 he was Technical Advisor to the movie *Top Gun.* In 1999 he was elected to the National Wrestling Hall of Fame. Most recently he was selected for the U.S. Naval Academy's Distinguished Graduate Award for 2000, the second year of its institution. Among his more than forty military decorations and medals are two Defense Distinguished Service Medals, four Navy DSMs, two Legions of Merit, the Distinguished Flying Cross, three Air Medals, the French Legion of Honor with the rank of Commandeur, the Grand Cross of Germany, and the Order of the Rising Sun from Japan.

Dr. Thomas A. Keaney is executive director of the Foreign Policy Institute and senior adjunct professor of strategic studies at the Paul H. Nitze School of Advanced International Studies, Johns Hopkins University, Washington, D.C. During his U.S. Air Force career, he was a forward air controller in Vietnam and a B–52 squadron commander. After retirement as a colonel, he coauthored the effectiveness report and the summary report of the Gulf War Air Power Survey. He and Eliot Cohen published a revised version of the survey, titling it *Revolution in Warfare?: Air Power in the Persian Gulf* (Naval Institute Press, 1995).

Lt. Gen. Robert P. Keller, a naval aviator and holder of the Silver Star Medal, three Distinguished Flying Crosses, and three awards of the Legion of Merit, retired from active duty on September 1, 1974. He was born in Oakland, California, on February 9, 1920. He earned a B.S. degree from the University of Maryland and an M.A. degree from George Washington University. During World War II, he served with Marine Fighter Squadron 212 in California and deployed to Midway Island, where he was transferred to Marine Fighter Squadron 223, serving as squadron executive officer and, later, as commanding officer. He destroyed one enemy aircraft and damaged two others in aerial combat. He returned to the United States in 1944 and completed night-fighter training before deploying to Okinawa in 1945 as commanding officer of Marine

Night Fighter Squadron 533. When the war ended, Major Keller and his squadron flew to Peiping, China, to assist in the repatriation of Japanese forces to their home islands.

During postwar assignments, Major Keller attended the Amphibious Warfare School; served as Aviation Safety Officer on the Staff of the Chief of Naval Air Training in Pensacola; attended the Air Command and Staff College at Maxwell AFB, Alabama; and was executive officer and, later, commander of Marine Fighter Squadron 214 at El Toro, California. He deployed with the initial Marine Corps forces to reach Korea in 1950. Operating from an aircraft carrier initially, his squadron moved to a shore base. In November, Major Keller was detached to become Liaison Officer for the 1st Marine Aircraft Wing to the Eighth Army–Fifth Air Force Joint Operations Center in Seoul. After his return to the United States in 1951, he saw duty at the Marine Corps Development Center, Quantico, Virginia; at the Marine Corps Base, Camp Lejeune, N.C.; and as head, Operational Planning Section, Plans and Readiness Branch, Division of Aviation at Headquarters Marine Corps. Completing the latter duty in January 1956, Lt. Col. Keller became a student at the Armed Forces Staff College, Norfolk, Virginia. That summer, he was assigned as Maneuver and Exercise Officer of the Staff of the Commander-in-Chief, Allied Forces, Southern Europe in Naples, Italy.

Lt. Col. Keller returned to the United States in August 1958 to undergo helicopter training at Pensacola. In November he became executive officer of Marine Aircraft Group 16 in Japan. Promoted in October 1959, he served until February 1960 as Assistant Chief of Staff, G–3, 1st Marine Aircraft Wing, at Iwakuni. Returning to the United States, Col. Keller reported to the Armed Forces Staff College as a member of the faculty. He served there until June 1963 when he was ordered to El Toro to become Assistant Chief of Staff, G–5 (Plans and Programs), Aircraft, Fleet Marine Force, Pacific. Assigned to the 3d Marine Aircraft Wing in June 1964, he became Commanding Officer of Marine Aircraft Group 15 the next month. Relinquishing command of that unit in June 1965, Keller returned to Headquarters Marine Corps where he was assigned to the Office of the Deputy Chief of Staff (Plans and Programs) and served as head of the Joint and Special Plans Team, Assistant Director, and, later, as Director, Joint Planning Group. On August 4, 1966, he was promoted to brigadier general and received orders to duty in South Vietnam.

For exceptionally meritorious performance of duty as Assistant Wing Commander, 1st Marine Aircraft Wing from April 1967 to April 1968, he earned the Legion of Merit with Combat "V." In June 1968, he reported to Glenview, Illinois, for duty as Commanding General, 4th Marine Aircraft Wing/Marine Air Reserve Training Command, where he received a second award of the Legion of Merit during this assignment. While stationed at Glenview, he was promoted to major general, August 4, 1969. In March 1971, he assumed duty as Assistant Chief of Staff, J–3, Pacific Command, and earned a third award of the Legion of Merit. He was advanced to the rank of lieutenant general, July 1, 1972, and undertook the duties of Commanding General, Marine Corps Development and Education Command, Quantico. He was awarded the Distinguished Service Medal upon his retirement on September 1, 1974.

Benjamin King graduated from the University Connecticut in 1965 with a degree in history. He then served in the U.S. Army in Germany and Vietnam, where he was awarded the Bronze Star with "V," the Purple Heart, and the Air Medal. After his active duty, he served as a contract historian to the Casemate Museum from 1978 to 1979. In 1984 he became Chief of Simulations at the U.S. Army Transportation School, a position he held until 1992 when he became the Command Historian of the U.S. Army Transportation Corps. From 1992 to 1995 he headed the team that wrote *Spearhead of Logistics, A History of the U.S. Army Transportation Corps*. In 2000 he accepted his current position as Research Historian in the U.S. Army Training and Doctrine Command's Military History Office. Mr. King is also the chief author of *Impact: The History of Germany's V-Weapons in World War II*, published in 1998, and articles in *The Field Artillery Journal*, *The Transportation Professional Bulletin*, and *Vietnam* magazine.

Capt. Keith F. Kopets, USMC, is a student at the Marine Corps's Amphibious Warfare School in Quantico, Virginia. He holds a bachelor's degree in mathematics from the State University of New York at Albany and is near completion of a master's degree in military studies. His articles and reviews have appeared in the *Marine Corps Gazette* and the *Journal of Military History*. Captain Kopets has four articles covering Marine air operations in Korea to his credit.

Dr. Mark D. Mandeles formed The J. de Bloch Group in 1993 to examine a wide range of national security and foreign policy issues for government agencies and private firms. Currently, he is writing a monograph on national security transformation strategy for the Office of Secretary of Defense/Net Assessment. Formerly, he was chairman of the Air Warfare track of the American Military University. He has published articles and book chapters on command and control, naval weapons acquisition, professional military education, military doctrine, nuclear strategy, military innovation, the revolution in military affairs, and ballistic missile and nuclear weapons proliferation. Dr. Mandeles is author of *The Future of War: Organizational Structures for the Revolution in Military Affairs; The Development of the B–52 and Jet Propulsion;* coauthor of *Managing "Command and Control" in the Persian Gulf War*; and *American & British Aircraft Carrier Development.*

Dr. Edward J. Marolda is Senior Historian at the Naval Historical Center, Washington, D.C. He earned the B.A. and M.A. degrees in history from Pennsylvania Military College and Georgetown University and a Ph.D. at George Washington University. Dr. Marolda served as an officer in the U.S. Army's 4th

Transportation Command in the Republic of Vietnam during 1969 and 1970. He has authored and coauthored several official histories of the U.S. Navy, including *By Sea, Air, and Land: An Illustrated History of the United States Navy and the War in Southeast Asia* and *Shield and Sword: The United States Navy and the Persian Gulf War*. His latest book is *Theodore Roosevelt, the U.S. Navy, and the Spanish-American War* (New York: St. Martin's Press, 2001), which he edited.

Maj. Charles D. Melson, USMC (Ret.), is Chief Historian, Headquarters U.S. Marine Corps. He has history degrees from Sonoma State University and St. John's College. His writings include *U.S. Marines in Vietnam: The War That Would Not End, U.S. Marines in the Persian Gulf: Anthology and Annotated Bibliography*, and numerous published articles and reviews. He is a career Marine Corps officer and airborne forward air controller.

Vice Admiral Jerry Miller, USN (Ret.), enlisted in the U.S. Navy on his seventeenth birthday. During the next thirty-eight years, he served in the Pentagon and aboard battleships, cruisers, and aircraft carriers, participating in combat in three wars. As a naval aviator for more than thirty years, he flew some sixty different types of aircraft, including helicopters, the Air Force's B–52 bomber, and the Russian MiG–15. He had a recurring relationship with nuclear weapons. The Smithsonian Institution Press has recently published his first book, *Nuclear Weapons and Aircraft Carriers: How the Bomb Saved Naval Aviation*. A second book under preparation is tentatively titled "The Story behind 10,000 Strategic Nuclear Weapons." Admiral Miller was intimately involved in the Korean War from the first to the last day.

Patrick C. Roe enlisted in the Marine Corps in March 1945 and was commissioned in August 1948. During a twenty-year Marine Corps career, he served in intelligence billets at the battalion, regimental, brigade, and division levels, in addition to serving as a tactics instructor at the Marine Corps Amphibious Warfare School, among other routine assignments. He attended the University of South Carolina and is a graduate of the U. S. Navy Electronics Material School, the Marine Corps Amphibious Warfare School, and the U. S. Army Intelligence School. In Korea he served as intelligence officer of the 3d Battalion, 7th Marines, during the Chosin campaign. Since retiring from the real estate business in 1992, he has pursued the study of military history, particularly that of the Korean War.

Dr. William Suit is a historian at Headquarters Air Force Materiel Command, Wright-Patterson AFB, Ohio. He is a regular contributor to *Air Power History* and has had several papers included in the published proceedings of various military aviation and technology symposia. He also contributed essays on USAF logistics to *The Eagle in the Desert: Looking Back on U.S. Involvement in the*

Persian Gulf War and ABC-CLIO's forthcoming *Encyclopedia of Military Aviation.*

Dr. Wayne Thompson is chief of analysis at the Air Force History Support Office in Washington. He was Senior Historical Advisor for the Gulf War Air Power Survey. His *To Hanoi and Back: The U.S. Air Force and North Vietnam, 1966–1973,* was published by the Air Force and the Smithsonian Institution Press in 2000. He and Bernard Nalty wrote a brief account of the Air Force in the Korean War entitled *Within Limits* (Air Force History and Museums Program, 1996).

Dr. Kenneth P. Werrell is an aviation historian and professor emeritus at Radford University, Virginia. He earned a B.S. degree from the U.S. Air Force Academy and the M.A. and Ph.D. degrees in history at Duke University. He served in the USAF from 1960 to 1965, flying WB–50s from Japan. Among his many publications are *Blankets of Fire: US Bombers over Japan during World War II*; *The Evolution of the Cruise Missile; Archie Flak, AAA, and SAMs*; and *Who Fears?: The 301st in War and Peace, 1942–1979.* He recently completed a history of the development of USAF technology since 1965.

Thomas Wildenberg is an independent historian who has written extensively about the U.S. Navy during the interwar period, the development of naval aviation, and logistics at sea. He is the author of *Gray Steel & Black Oil: Fast Tankers and Replenishment at Sea in the USN, 1912–1992; Destined for Glory: Dive Bombing, Midway, and Carrier Air Power;* and *All the Factors of Victory: Admiral Joseph Mason Reeves and the Origins of Carrier Airpower.* Mr. Wildenberg has served successive terms as Ramsey Fellow and Adjunct Ramsey Fellow for Naval Aviation History at the Smithsonian Institution. In 1998 he was the first recipient of the Edward S. Miller Naval War College Research Fellowship and received an honorable mention in the Ernest J. Eller Prize in Naval History in 1994.

William T. Y'Blood, after graduating from the University of Oregon in 1959, joined the USAF and flew B–, EB–, and RB–47s from 1960 to 1966. He then became an airline pilot from 1966 to 1985 and has accumulated over 11,000 hours of flying time. In 1986, he joined the Office of Air Force History (now the Air Force History Support Office). He wrote two volumes on USAF operations during Desert Shield, *The Eagle and the Scorpion* and *Sharpening the Eagle's Talons*, as well as the concluding chapters of the History Support Office's 50th anniversary history of the Air Force. Y'Blood edited the Lt. Gen. George E. Stratemeyer Korean War diaries, published in 1999. Additionally, he wrote several monographs on the USAF in the Korean War for that conflict's 50th anniversary commemoration. Commercially, he has written numerous articles and book reviews for various newspapers and magazines. He is the author or coauthor of six books on military and naval history, including *Red Sun Setting: The Battle of the Philippine Sea*, and *The Little Giants: U.S. Escort Carriers Against Japan*, both published by the Naval Institute Press, and he was a contributor to the *Oxford Companion to American Military History* that was published in 1999. He is currently working on a history of the three World War II Air Commando groups.

Index

Index

Lightning Source UK Ltd.
Milton Keynes UK
172230UK00001B/2/P

9 781780 392783